THE RASIKAPRIYĀ OF KESHAVADĀSA

Translated into English verse
by
K. P. BAHADUR

MOTILAL BANARSIDASS
DELHI :: PATNA :: VARANASI

Head Office : BUNGALOW ROAD, JAWAHAR NAGAR, DELHI-7
Branches : (1) CHOWK, VARANASI-1 (U.P.)
(2) ASHOK RAJPATH, PATNA-4 (BIHAR)

UNESCO COLLECTION OF REPRESENTATIVE WORKS—INDIAN SERIES

This book has been accepted in Indian Translation Series of the UNESCO collection of the Representative Works, jointly sponsored by the United Nations Educational, Scientific and Cultural Organization (UNESCO) and the Government of India.

First Edition
1972,1990

Printed in India
BY SHANTILAL JAIN AT SHRI JAINENDRA PRESS, BUNGALOW ROAD, JAWAHAR NAGAR, DELHI-7 AND PUBLISHED BY SUNDARLAL JAIN, MOTILAL BANARSIDASS, BUNGALOW ROAD, JAWAHAR NAGAR, DELHI-7.

What the Book is About

Keshavadāsa wrote *Rasikapriyā* to provide entertainment to such readers as were interested in the poetry of love. Love was considered to be the primary emotion, not only by the poets of Keshava's time but also by those who had preceded him. *Rasikapriyā* deals with love in all its varied aspects. The lover, portrayed in Keshava's book is Kṛiṣṇa and the beloved is Rādhā. In poetical language they are often called *nāyaka* and *nāyikā*.

The book describes the different kinds of *nāyakas* and *nāyikās*—their lovemaking, their moods, sentiments, and emotions, and illustrates these by vivid accounts of the lovers in various situations. These are classified all through the book under two heads 'hidden' and 'manifest'—the former showing the secret desires of the lovers and the latter their outward manifestation.

In the beginning the Poet describes the youthful charm of the growing maiden, the tips of whose breasts grow with each day, whose eyebrows dance with pleasure, whose rump grows heavy, and whose eyes begin to be troubled by shyness. Such an inexperienced girl resists the advances of her beloved. She wants to remove even the animals and birds from her bed-chamber lest they witness her lovemaking, and wants to turn low the flame of the lamp. She cannot gaze into the eyes of her lover even when he forces up her chin with his thumb. Such a girl exhausts the *nāyaka's* patience, and he goes to the extent of drugging her and then making her sleep with him. Gradually age and experience make the *nāyikā* change her bashful attitude. She has learnt the different ways of love-making, and shame has abandoned her. Her lustful cries awaken even the birds. With her mounting experience the *nāyikā* can now detect the *nāyaka's* infidelity from his drowsy eyes, and his distraught condition.

The meeting of lovers is described with all its rapture and fulfilment. The *nāyikā* tries to steal a glance at her lover but her bashfulness will not let her look, and she peers at him with fond eyes from beneath her end-cloth. She sees him in her dreams, and on waking rushes to clasp him, but alas ! he is not there ! Burning with desire to meet the *nāyaka* she stretches her limbs, yawns, and laughs, and leaving her breasts unclothed nestles against her woman friend to show her desire. The lovers devise many tricks to accomplish their end. The *nāyaka* entices his beloved into the forest to share his loneliness and to make love to her. When fire suddenly breaks out in the house of Rādhā's father, the lover Kṛiṣṇa, taking advantage of the general confusion, goes upto sleeping Rādhā and wakes her up by kissing her eyes, chin, and breasts, and clasping her to his bosom. On another occasion there is a large gathering at the house of Kṛiṣṇa's father on the occasion of the birthday of Balarāma, his brother. Every corner of the house is full of people. The sleepy Rādhā can't find a bed, and seeing that of Kṛiṣṇa empty, she flings herself on it and is soon fast asleep. When Kṛiṣṇa comes back, the temptation of sharing a bed with Rādhā is too much for him, and he lays himself by her side without further ado. Nanda's house is the scene of yet another meeting of the lovers. This time Rādhā has been invited for a feast. After meals are over she goes on the roof for a breath of air, when she sees her lover, Kṛiṣṇa, come towards her. Filled with confusion she takes to flight, but Kṛiṣṇa will not be put off. He catches her by her dangling braid, and clasps her to his breast. The various places where lovers meet for the first time according to Keshavadāsa, are the house of a maidservant, of a bosom companion, a nurse, a lonely house, a forest dwelling, or at an entertainment or function, under pretence of illness, or when the *nāyikā* is frightened.

A section of the *Rasikapriyā* is devoted to a description of various other kinds of emotions, amongst them that of amusement in which the lover and beloved disguise themselves as each other and have much fun. Then there is the emotion of ecstasy which is delicately portrayed. Kṛiṣṇa is trying to woo Rādhā, and even falls on her feet, but she is not appeased. At that very moment dark clouds arise all of a sudden, and lightning strikes. What could not be accomplished by persuasion is done by fear, and the trembling girl leaps upon her lover and weaves her limbs round him.

On another occasion, the Poet is illustrating the emotion of slight. Kṛiṣṇa approaches Rādhā, but she feigns sleep and keeps lying on the bed. The audacious lover places his hand on her breasts, and finding no opposition begins to untie the knot of her waist-garment. Rādhā suddenly gets up and exclaims: 'Oh! ill-bred boor! you tend cows all day, and at night return and force yourself into another woman's bed!'

Giving an example of the *nāyaka's* emotion of quarrelsomeness Keshava describes the stubborn *nāyikā* who does not bestow her favour on the *nāyaka* even after he has tried all ways. When he speaks to her she answers harshly, and when he falls on her feet she kicks him. Yet after all this he is able to win her over, and holds her face on his lap.

Eight kinds of *nāyikās*, along with their various subsidiary divisions, have been enumerated by Keshavadāsa, and he has given copious examples of each kind. The *Khaṇḍitā nāyikā* upbraids her lover for passing the night with a slut and then entering her room stealthily, 'like a shy owl, unseen.' The *kāmābhisārikā*, a passionate type of woman, is so eager to meet her lover that she cares not for the snakes which are entangled in her legs, nor for her ornaments falling off on the way as she hastens to keep tryst with him.

Having described the different kinds of *nāyikās*, Keshavadāsa goes on to define lover at first sight, which he says is that which comes about as soon as newly married couples behold each other's splendour, and which causes sorrow in their mutual absence. Then he enumerates the ten states or conditions which are produced when one is made restless by the beloved's sight or by hearing her bewitching song. These states are—yearning, anxiety, narration of merits, remembrance, fury, raving, intoxication, disease, stupor, and death. The last state, death, comes to the lover all of a sudden, when all devices to meet his beloved, even force and deceit, are of no avail. The many suicides which occur because of being thwarted in love seem to prove the truth of Keshava's contention.

The arrogance of woman, and the ways of removing it, has been a favourite subject of Hindi poetry, and following the tradition, Keshavadāsa devotes a portion of his book to this. According to him, arrogance in a woman means 'that excitement of loveliness which is caused by the power of perfect love'. Illustrating arrogance in the *nāyikā*, the Poet relates the occasion on which having met Rādhā after a long time, Kṛiṣṇa makes love to her with gusto, driving away her sullenness by laughter and joy. All goes well till by chance her gaze alights beneath his doublet, and she observes tell-tale nail-marks on his bosom which leave her shocked and dumbfounded.

On another occasion the *nāyikā* is suspicious, and asks her lover where he has passed the night, and why there are nail-marks on his body and redness in his eyes. Her lover, Kṛiṣṇa, gives a satisfactory excuse for all of these, and it is only after her doubts are thus removed that she allows him reluctantly to clasp her to his bosom.

So arrogant has the *nāyikā* turned that she cannot even bear to hear her lover utter another woman's name. A cowherd maiden is laughing and conversing with Kṛiṣṇa, when by accident he takes the name of some girl whom he calls his bosom friend. This so astounds her that the betel which she is about to put into her mouth remains in her hand, and tears fill her eyes.

Keshavadāsa however cautions the *nāyikā* not to overdo herself in showing arrogance. She should not fret so much as to make her lover dejected and fed up of her. Arrogance should be shown once only, not again and again. By doing so mutual respect between lovers increases.

The ways of removing a woman's arrogance are described by Keshavadāsa, as gentleness, the giving of gifts, the creation of difference or diversion, humility, and delusion. Illustrations again are given of the use of each of these devices. Chastisement, the Poet says, has not been included, as it leads to loss of pleasure.

Most Hindi poets harped much on the grief of the *nāyikā* separated from her lover. Some like Ghanānanda devoted most of their verses to it. Keshavadāsa loved pleasure too much to make the theme of separation, which involved sorrow, a central one in his poetry. But he could not ignore it altogether, for it was usual for poets of his time to write about separation, and Keshavadāsa was a stickler for convention. 'Although it is not proper', he says, 'that mention of sorrow should be made while describing the ways of pleasure, yet since convention makes it necessary it must be done'. In writing about separation, Keshavadāsa also describes the state of the maiden when her lover goes away to a foreign land. In those days, when trains and jets were unknown, and travelling was by foot or on horseback, the separation of lovers was long and painful. Keshavadāsa's accounts of separation lack the pathos and the poignancy of poets like Bihārī and Ghanānanda.

After having described the state of the *nāyikā* in separation, Keshavadāsa goes on to relate the part played by go-betweens and bosom friends of the *nāyikā* in uniting her with her lover. The types of women who can be of assistance to the *nāyikā* in her love-affairs are a maid-servant, a nurse, the wife of a barber, gardener or goldsmith, a dancer, a woman neighbour, a female bangle or betel seller, a woman of mixed caste, a female recluse, and a woman who works on ornaments with silk and gold threads. As regards bosom companions, (female friends who were intimate with a *nāyikā*), their assistance consisted of entreating the *nāyikā* to pay heed to her lover, uniting her with him, and at times even chiding her for her indifference. Hindu women in Keshavadāsa's time did not intermingle with men, and kept to the inner quarters. Love-affairs were carried on in secret, and a go-between or a near friend of the *nāyikā* who could have access to the *nāyaka* without arousing suspicion, was of great help. The ways in which such women bring about the meeting of the lovers are vividly described by Keshavadāsa.

A close and interesting study is made of laughter, which is described as being of four kinds—feeble, sweet, violent, and loud. Illustrations are given of the various kinds by describing the situations of *nāyakas* and *nāyikās* indulging in it. Someone tells Rādhā that a very pretty girl has come from the Province Mahāvana. She sends for the 'girl' who is really the amorous lover, Kṛiṣṇa, disguised as a woman. Rādhā is delighted with the girl's beauty and clasps her to her bosom, realising the deception too late, while the mischievous cowherd girls around her hold their sides and laugh. On another occasion Kṛiṣṇa bars the path of a cowherd girl who is carrying a jar spattered with milk and curd, on her head. Kṛiṣṇa, who likes nothing better than milk and curd, is minded to steal some from the maiden's jar, but when he drags it down and peers inside, lo ! it is empty and he finds himself to be the victim of a hoax. The watching cowherd girls break into unrestrained laughter from beneath their veils.

Apart from laughter, the Poet describes other kinds of sentiments also, giving illustrations from the loves of the *nāyaka* and the *nāyikā*. The sentiments described by him are—tenderness, violence, valour, dread, loathsomeness, wonder, and calm.

Hindi poetry is classified by Keshava into four types—the *Kaushikī*, *Bhāratī*, *Ārabhaṭī* and *Sāttvikī*. Examples of each kind are given, along with the characteristics of each. Finally the defects which arise in poetry, and which should be avoided by all good poets, are mentioned. These are, conflict, dryness nauseousness, contrariness, and lack of wisdom.

The book ends with a little self-praise. By reading *Rasikapriyā*, the Poet says : 'Understanding of love increases, knowledge is gained of all sentiments and practices, and both pleasure and salvation are achieved'.

'As lovers appear to be unhappy day after day without their beloveds, so the poets of the spoken language appear inferior without *Rasikapriyā*.'

Keshava was a courtier and moved in the company of rulers and kings. He could afford to be proud. Besides, in an age in which reviewers were unknown, it was left to the author to point out the merits of his own work. The *Rasikapriyā* is a panegyric on love, and a mine of entertainment. Above all, it is a book of pleasure.

CONTENTS

CHAPTER I

INVOCATION AND BLESSING

Page

CHAPTER II

THE NĀYAKA

CHAPTER III

THE NĀYIKĀ

Chapter IV

THE MEETING OF LOVERS

Chapter V

WHERE LOVERS MEET, AND HOW ?

Chapter VI

THE EMOTIONS

CHAPTER VII

MORE NĀYIKĀS

Chapter VIII

LOVE AND THE TEN STATES

CHAPTER IX

ARROGANCE

CHAPTER X

WAYS TO REMOVE ARROGANCE

Chapter XI

THE SEPARATION OF LOVERS

Chapter XII

LOVE'S MESSENGER

CHAPTER XIV

LAUGHTER, AND OTHER SENTIMENTS

CHAPTER XV

THE KINDS OF POETRY

CHAPTER XVI

THE DEFECTS OF POETRY

INTRODUCTION

(A) Influences

1. *Political and Social*

Like every writer, Poet Keshavadāsa was a product of his age. He was born in the year 1555 and died in 1617, hence he lived in the reigns of Akbar (1542-1605) and Jahāngīr (1569-1627). This period was one of the most brilliant ones in Indian history. The firmness, security, and benevolence, of both of these Mughal Emperors were beneficial to the development of art and literature. Akbar was, in the words of Lane-Poole, 'the noblest king that ever ruled India.' He tried to achieve Hindu-Muslim unity by employing Hindus, calling them to his court, marrying Hindu wives, adopting Hindu dress, manners, customs, and religious symbolism, and abolishing the hated *jiziyā* tax. Blochmann has left us a fascinating account of the Emperor's catholicity. He says, 'The killing of animals on certain days was forbidden, as on Sundays, because this day is sacred to the sun. To please the Hindus His Majesty abstained altogether from meat, as a religious penance, gradually extending the several fasts during a year over six months and even more, with the view of eventually discontinuing the use of meat altogether...His Majesty had also one thousand and one Sanskrit names of the sun collected and read them daily, devoutly turning to the sun (like the Hindus worship the Gāyatrī). He also adopted several other practices connected with the sun-worship. He used to wear the Hindu (*ṭīkā*) mark on the forehead, and ordered the band to play at midnight and at break of day. Once a year also during a night, called Shivarāt, a great meeting was held of all the *Jogīs* of the Empire.'

Akbar called outstanding Hindu poets like Sūradāsa and Rāmadāsa, and Hindu musicians like Tānsena to his court, and showed such an active interest in the translation of Sanskrit books that he forced their hater Badaunī to do the *Mahābhārata* and *Rāmāyaṇa* to his utter disgust, which made him to exclaim: 'But such is my fate, to be employed on such works. Nevertheless, I console myself with the reflection, that what is predestined must come to pass.'

All this was bound to have a salutary effect on Hindi and Sanskrit literature of the period, particularly on Hindi poetry. As Vincent Smith says, 'The brilliant development of original Hindi poetry in the time of Akbar may be ascribed partly, like the contemporary development of literature in England, to the undefinable influence exercised by a glorious and victorious reign, which necessarily produces a stimulating effect on all the activities of the human mind. The Emperor's known and avowed partiality for Hindu practices and modes of thought, and the active interest which he showed in acquiring a knowledge of the ancient literature of India, contributed to the satisfactory result, as did the comparative peace secured by a government stronger than its predecessors. Almost all Hindi poetry of merit is closely associated with the unrestricted practice of the Hindu religion, which was absolutely assured by the government of Akbar. The impetus given to Hindi literature by the policy of Akbar lasted long after his death, throughout the reign of Jahāngīr, who ordinarily continued his father's system of government, and even into the reigns of Shāhjahān and Aurangzeb, the temple breakers.'

Akbar had an interest in all religions and he erected a House of Worship or *Ibādat-Khānā* in which religious discussions were held, thereby showing his unquenchable thirst for knowledge. About Akbar's *Ibādat-Khānā*, Abul Fazal wrote in his *Akbar-nāmā*:

'When the capital was illumined by the return of the Imperial presence, the old regulations came again into operation, and the house of wisdom shone resplendent on Friday nights with the light of holy minds. On the 20th *Mīr*, in that place of meeting, the lamp was kindled to brighten the solitude of seclusion in the banquet of society, and the merits of the philosophers of the colleges and monasteries were put to the test of the touchstone. Sūfīs, doctors, preachers, lawyers, Sunnis, Shias, Brahmans, Jains, Buddhists, Chārvākas, Christians, Jews, Zoroastrians, and learned men of every belief, were gathered together in the royal assembly, and were filled with delight. Each one fearlessly brought forward his assertions and arguments and the disputations and contentions were long and heated.'

Doubtless this was the right atmosphere for freedom of expression, a freedom which is rare in the rule of mighty potentates. Akbar himself was somewhat of a mystic, and had, it seems, flights of spiritual insight. An incident of this sort is mentioned both by Abul Fazal and Badaunī. The former says:

'When the Emperor was only thirty-six years old, while returning from a great hunt by the Jhelum river for which elaborate arrangements had been made, a sublime joy took possession of his bodily frame, the attraction of the cognition god cast its ray.' This experience is confirmed by Badaunī : 'Suddenly all at once, a strange state and strong frenzy came upon the Emperor, and an extraordinary change was manifest in his manner to such an extent as cannot be accounted for. And everyone attributed it to some cause or the other; but god alone knoweth secrets. And at that time he ordered the hunting to be abandoned. "Take care: for the grace of god comes suddenly. It comes suddenly; it comes to the mind of the wise".

On the occasion of the *Ilāhī* era, the Islamic millenium, when Akbar issued a new coinage, he also made certain innovations and issued orders for their coming into force. Amongst these Badaunī mentions the following:

Regarding wine.

'Wine was allowed if used for strengthening the body as recommended by doctors; but no mischief or impropriety was to result from the use of it, and strict punishments were laid down for drunkenness, or gatherings, and uproars. For the sake of keeping everything within proper limits, His Majesty established a wine shop near the palace, and put the wife of the porter in charge of it, as she belonged to the caste of wine-sellers. The price of wine was fixed by regulations, and any sick person could obtain wine on sending his own name and the names of his father and grandfather to the clerk of the shop.'

Regarding prostitutes.

'Similarly the prostitutes of the realm (who had collected at the capital, and could scarcely be counted, so large was their number) had a separate quarter of the town assigned to them, which was called the *Shaitānpura*, or Devil's village. *Darogah* and a clerk were also appointed for it, who registered the names of such as went to prostitutes, or wanted to take some of them to their houses. People might indulge in such connexions, provided the toll-collectors knew of it.'

Taboo on beef.

'Beef was interdicted, and to touch beef was considered defiling. The reason of this was that from his youth His Majesty had been in company with Hindu libertines, and had thus learnt to look upon a cow which in their opinion is one of the reasons why the world still exists—as something holy. Besides, the Emperor was subject to the influence of the numerous Hindu princesses of the harem who had gained so great an ascendancy over him, as to make him forswear beef, garlic, onions, and the wearing of a beard, which things His Majesty still avoids.'

Introduction of Hindu customs

'He had also introduced, though modified by his peculiar views, Hindu customs and heresies into the court assemblies, and introduces them still. In order to please and win the Hindus and their castes, he abstains from everything which they think is repugnant to their nature, and looks upon shaving the beard as the highest sign of friendship and affection for him. Hence this custom has become very general.'

Marriage

'It was also forbidden to marry one's cousins or near relations, because such marriages are destructive of mutual love. Boys were not to marry before the age of sixteen, nor girls before fourteen because the offspring of early marriages were weak. No one was to marry more than one wife, except in cases of barrenness; but in all other cases the rule was "One man, and one wife." If widows liked to marry they may do so".

Satī

'A Hindu girl, whose husband died before the marriage was consummated, should not be burnt. If a Hindu woman wished to be burnt with her husband, they should not prevent her but she should not be forced.'

It is of interest to note that on one occasion when information of such forced burning came to Akbar he mounted his horse, and himself rode with all speed to the place to stop it.

Freedom of worship and religion

'Hindus who , when young, had from pressure become Musalmans, were allowed to go back to the faith of their fathers. No man should be interfered with on account of his religion, and every one should be allowed to change his religion, if he liked. If a Hindu woman falls in love with a Muhammedan, and changes her religion, she should be taken from him by force, and be given back to her family. (Similarly for a Muhammedan woman marrying a Hindu). People should not be molested, if they wished to build churches and prayer-rooms, or idol temples, or fire temples.'

Akbar was tolerant of all religions, customs, beliefs, and faiths. Not only was he a great Emperor, but also a philosopher, and a unifying force. Lord Tennyson makes him say:

'I hate the rancour of their castes and creeds,
I let them worship as they will, I reap
No revenue from the field of unbelief,
I cull from every faith and race the best,
And bravest soul for counsellor and friend.'

In his abstinence of meat Akbar was remarkable. In the later years of his life he gave up meat almost entirely. Some of his sayings show how much he disliked meat-eating.

'Would that my body were so vigorous as to be of service to the eaters of meat, who would thus forgo other animal life, or that, as I cut off a piece for their nourishment, it might be replaced by another.'

'Men should annually refrain from eating meat on the anniversary of the month of my accession as a thanksgiving to the Almighty, in order that the year may pass in prosperity.'

'Butchers, fishermen, and the like, who have no other occupation but taking life, should have a separate quarter, and their association with others should be prohibited by fine.'

'It is not right that a man should make his stomach the grave of animals.'

Thus in his attitude towards *ahiṁsā*, or non-injury, Akbar was one with the staunchest Buddhist or Jain. About drink however he was minded differently, and though as the years went past, his consumption of alcohol became less, he took strong drinks and opium in his young age. This habit of his was conducive to merriment, and so gaiety persisted in the court, and poems, anecdotes, song, and music, were encouraged.

Jahāngīr also patronised art and literature, like his father Akbar. Hindi poets flocked to the court under his rule. According to popular tradition Jahāngīr ordered a collection to be made of Sūradāsa's poems, and contributed one gold *mohur* for every hymn. He also took keen interest in painting, calligraphy and music. On the occasion of *Naūroz*, and the weighing of the Emperor on his lunar and solar birthdays, merrymaking, and festivity ruled the court. Speaking of the *Naūroz* celebration Dr. Beni Prasad says, 'The vernal new year's feast called *Naūroz*, adopted from Persia by Akbar, was celebrated by Jahāngīr every year for nineteen days. In the *Dīwān-i-ām* was erected a tent some sixty paces long and forty-five paces broad, covered all around withc anopies of the richest and the most finely embroidered velvet, silk and cloth of gold, hung over with fringes of gold and pearls, jewels and diamonds, fruits of gold, silver pictures and paintings; and laid underneath with carpets of silk and cloth of gold. Besides the royal throne, square in form, borne up with four pillars, inlaid with mother-of-pearl and covered with cloth of gold, there were placed a few chairs of state with soft cushions. The Emperor appeared decked in pearls and jewels. Private rooms were provided for the ladies of the Imperial seraglio. Round the Emperor's tent, the nobles laid out theirs within the compass of some five acres, contending with each other for superiority of pomp and splendour. Houses of silver might be seen among the curiosities. The Emperor visited every apartment, and generally condescended to accept some gift. In return he bestowed titles and dignities, *jāgīrs* and promotions. Wine flowed in rivulets; verses and odes flew in hundreds. Gaiety and merriment ruled everything during the nineteen pleasant days of the spring festival. A fancy bazar was held where the ladies of the noble houses kept stalls. The Emperor and his ladies haggled with the fair shopkeepers with humour and pleasantry. Music and dance charmed the festive parties that were held by day and by night.'

Jahāngīr also continued the spirit of religious toleration which his father had shown. The Hindu festivals of *Dussherā*, *Rakshābandhan*, *Dewālī* and *Shivarātri* were celebrated in the the court along with Muslim ones. On *Dussherā* the Imperial horses and elephants were lined up for inspection, on *Rakshābandhan* Hindus tied *rākhī* on the Emperor's hands, and in *Dewālī* gambling took place in the palace in the traditional manner.

Jahāngīr was also greatly interested in *sādhus* and *fakirs*, and delighted in their company. One of these ascetics called Jadrūp made an unusual impression on him, and about him Jahāngīr himself has given us an account. 'On Saturday for the second time, my desire for the company of Jadrūp increased. After performing the midday devotions I ran and enjoyed his society in the retirement of his cell. I heard many sublime words of religious duty and knowledge of divine things. Without exaggeration he sets forth clearly the doctrines of wholesome Sūfism, and one can find delight in his society. On Wednesday I again went and bade him good-bye. Undoubtedly parting from him weighed upon my mind which desires the truth.'

Sir Thomas Roe describes vividly the meeting of the Emperor with a fakīr:

'This miserable wretch, clothed in rags, crowned with feathers, covered with ashes, His Majesty talked with for about an hour, with such familiarity and show of kindness that it must needs argue a humility not easily found among kings. The beggar sat where his (Jahāngīr's) son dare not do..and after many strange humiliations and charities, rising, the old wretch, not being nimble, he took him up in his arms, which no cleanly body durst have touched, embracing him; and three times laying his hand on his heart, calling him "father", he left him and all of us, and me, in admiration of such virtue in a heathen prince.' Regarding wine Jahāngīr followed the example of his father. Of this Hawkins says :

'His prayer being ended, four or five sorts of very well dressed and roasted meats are brought him, of which as he pleaseth eateth a bit to stay his stomach, drinking once of his strong drink. Then cometh forth into a private room, where none can come but such as himself nominateth. In this place he drinketh other three cupfuls, which is the portion which the physicians allot him. This done he eateth opium, and then he ariseth and being at the height of his drink, he layeth him down to sleep, everyman departing to his own home.'

Thus although Jahāngīr discouraged the use of wine amongst his subjects, he took it himself and believed that 'a little wine is a prudent friend.' One of his institutes was, 'No person is permitted to make or sell wine or any other prohibited liquor which occasions inebriety, though I myself am addicted to wine bibbing.'

The age in which Keshavadāsa lived was one of religious toleration, culture, and stability. In such an atmosphere art and literature could flourish without impediment. The patronage of the court, too, was a great incentive, and both Akbar and Jahāngīr added dignity to accomplished poets by their personal interest. Keshavadāsa was considered one of the nine jewels of Hindi literature flourishing during Jahāngīr's reign. Apart from writing literary works like *Rasikapriyā* and

Rāmachandrikā he wrote a poem, *Vīrsinghdeva Charita* on the life of Vīrsingh, the Bundela chieftain who murdered Sheikh Abdul Fazal. He also wrote a long eulogy on the life of the Emperor Jahāngīr who patronised his own patron. This poem is called *Jahāngīr Jas Chandrikā*.

Keshavadāsa remained mostly in the town of Orchhā and frequented the Orchhā durbar. Orchhā was bounded on the north by the river Yamunā, and in the south by the Nerbuddā river. The western boundary was from the river Chambal to the Tons. It was Rudra Pratāp Singh, the eldest son of Malkhān Singh, who founded Orchhā in the year 1531. His son Madhukar Shāh succeeded to the throne when Akbar was Emperor. The Mughal Emperor did not at all relish the independence of Madhukar Shāh and sent his armies thrice to overcome him. In 1588 Akbar sent (for the third time) his armies under Rājā Āsakaraṇa and Abdullāh Khan. The Mughal armies conquered almost all the principalities between Orchhā and Gwalior but, later on, the stubborn Madhukar Shāh took back some of them. Thereafter in 1591 another army under the command of Murād was despatched which defeated the Rājā who fled to the hills round Narwār where he died the next year. In the reign of Madhukar Shāh, who was a benevolent and just ruler, Orchhā Rāj made great progress. After him his eldest son Rāma-Shāh came to the throne and he was a contemporary of the Mughal Emperor Jahāngīr. All the work of the kingdom was done by his younger brother, Indrajīt Singh, and Rāma Shāh himself used to frequent Akbar's court where he was always given a seat of honour. The continued absence of Rāma Shāh from the kingdom led to the breaking up of the Orchhā into eight *jāgīrs* under various rulers. Rāma Shāh did not prove strong enough to subdue these *jāgīrdārs* who began to assert their own independence. As time passed, matters went from bad to worse, until the entire state of Orchhā became prey to civil wars and dissensions. Further divisions took place, and the number of *jāgīrdārs* increased from eight to twenty-two, eight being held by Madhukar Shāh's sons, and fourteen by others. Of these Vīrsingh was the most powerful and audacious ruler. His chief *jāgīr* was Baraunī to which he added by conquest some districts in the Mughal *sultanate*. Vīrsingh remained undaunted although Akbar tried his best to crush him. He sent Rājā Āsakaraṇa and Rāma Shāh for this purpose, and later Abdul Rahīm Khānkhānā and Daulat Khān but to no avail. Vīrsingh allied himself with the disgruntled Salīm, much to the chagrin of Akbar. Ultimately Akbar died without succeeding in his attempt to subdue Vīrsingh and Jahāngīr ascended the throne as Emperor. This changed the course of events, as Jahāngīr was Vīrsingh's supporter and soon he deposed Rāma Shāh and made Vīrsingh sole ruler of Orchhā, and also assisted him in maintaining his suzerainty despite some opposition by the displaced Rāma Shāh.

Pleasure and merriment dominated the Mughal durbar, and both Akbar and Jahāngīr patronised song, dance, music, and drinking. The Orchhā durbar was a reflection of its Mughal counterpart, and to some extent this was its condition in the time of Indrajīt Singh under whose patronage Poet Keshvadāsa lived. Indrajīt himself was a great lover of poetry, dance, and song, which he greatly encouraged. A number of lovely and accomplished damsels used to grace his apartments, of whom there were six whose names we prominently come across. These were Pravīṇrāye, Navrangrāye, Vichitranainā, Tantaranga, Rangarāye and Rangamūrti. Of these Praviṇrāye was the most prominent, as apart from song and dance, she was also skilled in composing poetry.

Thus not only the Mughal durbar, but the durbars of the Hindu *Jāgīrdārs* and rulers as well, were imbued with an atmosphere of gaiety and merriment. Song, dance, drinking love, and poetry—these received royal support and encouragement. The poets wrote of beauty, adornment, lovemaking, and pleasures. It was these influences which moulded Keshavadāsa's poetry and made him write about women and their amours in the *Rasikapriyā*.

2 *Literary*

The main schools of poetry existing when Keshavadāsa wrote, were six in number. These were (a) heroic poetry (b) poetry of devotion (c) *Sūfī* poetry (d) poetry about Rāma (e) poetry about Kṛiṣṇa, and (f) poetry of mannerism.

(i) Heroic Poetry—The foundation of heroic poetry was laid by Chandavardai and Jagnik and others. These writers have mentioned a metrical composition ascribed to a poet called Puṣpa, but this work is not traceable. Although stray works of heroic poetry were in existence from before, its real and continuous development began only from the period of the first Muslim invasions.

Heroic poems were written either in the form of connected series of verses, or individual separate stanzas. Of the first kind, the earliest example in Hindi poetry is *Khumanrāso* of Dalpati Vijaya which is a chronicle of the deeds of the ruler of Chittor—Khuman the second; but of this only an incomplete portion is in existence. After this comes a heroic narrative poem called *Pṛithvīrāja Rāso* of *Chandabardai*. Other notable works of heroic poetry are '*Jayachandra-Prakāsha*' of Bhaṭṭ Kedāra '*Jayamayanka-Jas-Chandrikā*' of Madhukar, Hammirhath of Sharangdhar, and Vijayapāla Rāso of Nalla Singh.

Amongst short poems of the heroic kind, the most outstanding of this period is the *Vīsaldeva* Rāso of Narpati and the other prominent one is *Ālhākhaṇḍa* of Jagnik, but at the moment this work is not available in its complete form.

The subject matter of Hindi heroic poetry was the exploits of warriors and kings, the exultation of victory, and the the narration of deeds of valour. Wars and combats, the comings and goings of kings and chieftains, the moving about of royal camps and equipage—all these were described in glowing and vivid heroic language. Often the abduction of beautiful women was the *raison d'etre* of these wars, and so a subsidiary love interest is also found in the poems which indeed adds to their charm. The heroic poems were written in the literary language of old Rājasthān, though there are words of Sanskrit, Arabic, and Persian here and there.

Both the language and the emotional content of heroic poetry had its effect on Keshavadāsa. Some of his works, like *Ratanbāvanī*, *Vīrsinghdeva Charit* and *Jahāngīr Jas Chandrikā* fall under this category, and show the same qualities as are found in the heroic verse of this period.

(ii) Devotional Poetry—Although the language of the devotional poetry of the period did not have much influence on

Keshava, the thought and emotion contained in it did much to shape his verse. Devotional poetry started with Guru Gorakhnāth and continued in Keshava's time till Dādū (1544-1603). In between there were a number of saints like Rāidās, Kabīr, Nānak, Nāmdeva etc., who started their own religious creeds. Gorakhnāth kept himself aloof from politics and evolved his own system of spiritual discipline called *hatha yoga*, which has in later years become famous and extremely popular even in the western world. His doctrine came to be known in religious literature as *Nāthpanth*. Guru Gorakhnāth wrote a number of books in Hindi—*Gorakh-Ganesh-Gosthi*, *Mahādeva-Gorakh-Saṁvāda*, *Jñāna-Siddhānta*, *Yoga*, *Gorakhnāth ke Pada* etc.

Amongst devotional poets the ones who had the greatest influence on Keshavadāsa were Nānak and Kabīr. This was because they wrote about Hindu-Muslim unity, and made no distinction at all between high and low, rich and poor.

Devotional poetry has great importance from the point of view of spiritual and religious thought. It exalts the practice of *yoga*, renunciation, the evanscence of the world, the power of prayer, the immortality of the soul, and the elusive potency of *māyā*. In the *Vijñāna Gītā* we find the praise of the Absolute—the supreme power without attributes knowing which the soul loses its identity and becomes one with the the eternal *Brahman*. Keshavadāsa, too, extolled the *nirguṇa Brahman*, the one without the second, and praised *hatha yoga*, and its practices of *āsana*, and the control of breath. Bundelkhand, which was the Poet's native state, was the centre of the creed of Kabīr. This creed exercised great influence on him. Devotional poetry was born in the days in which the Hindu religion was being suppressed by the Muslim invaders, when temples were being desecrated, idols broken, and forcible conversions made. Kabīr, and other saints, harped upon the one god who was acceptable to both races, who was Rāma for the Hindus, and Rahīm for Muslims. They decried blind faith amongst both—the idol worship, vows, and pilgrimages of the Hindus, and the fasts, sacrifices, and prescribed prayers of the Muslims. They disclosed the emptiness and the hollow-

Not to be confused with *Brahmin* (or *Brāhmaṇa*) which means the priestly caste.

ness of such penances, and focussed the minds of men on the truth which is one for all, irrespective of caste and creed. Kabīr, and his precursor Nāmadeva, opened the doors of religion to all men, whether high or low, to all women, and to all those who were till then considered to be of inferior caste or untouchables. The language of these poets was Avadhī, Bhojpurī, Hindī, Braj, Punjābī and Rājasthānī.

(iii) The Sūfī Poets—Although the Muslim rule created some bitterness in the beginning, it gradually led to amity between the Hindus and the Muslims, and brought them closer to each other. Some of the Muslim monarchs, like Sher Shāh Sūri, even took a sympathetic attitude towards the Hindu religion. In the same way Sūfīs, while remaining Muhammedans, did not look down upon the Hindu faith.

Sūfī love-poetry began with the work entitled *Narak Chanda kī Kahānī* of Mulla Dāud. Thereafter there were some minor poets, precursors of the famous poet Jāisī, of whom he had made mention in his book *Padmāvatī*. According to him the books which these poets wrote were—*Madhumālatī*, *Svapnavatī*, *Mugdhavatī*, *Mṛigavatī*, *Khandravatī* and *Premavatī*. Of these, only *Madhumālatī* and *Mṛigavatī* are extant. The writer of *Madhumālatī* was Manjhan, and of *Mṛigavatī*, Kutban, the pupil of Sheikh Burhan. Apart from this Dr. Rāma Kumār has mentioned a work of the writer Dāmo called *Lakshmaṇa Sen Padmāvatī*, which however is essentially a heroic poem. Thereafter comes the period of Jāisī whose principal works are *Padmāvatī* and *Akhrāvat*. The former is an outstanding Poem about love and beauty and the subject matter of the latter is the soul, god, and creation. The Sūfī poets, following Jāisī who were contemporaneous with Keshavadāsa, were Usmān, Sheikh Nabī, Nūr Mohammed etc. Apart from the Muslim Sūfī poets, the name of a prominent Hindu love poet, who wrote in the same strain, is also worth mention, viz, Harrāj, whose work is called *Ḍhola Mārvani Chaupāhi*.

The Sūfī poets generally wrote their poems round some imaginative love-tale dealing with Hindu life and society, some like Jāisī interwearing their narrative with historical incidents. They wrote about the pleasures of love and the pangs of separation. Some used love stories to illustrate the love of the soul for god. The work usually began with a salutation to god and an eulogy about the reigning monarch. The poems were written in the Avadhī language, as most of such love poetry originated from Avadh. Though the subject matter of Sūfī poetry did not have any notable effect on Keshavadāsa's works, its style did influence them and his *Vīrsinghdeva Charita* is in the same manner.

(iv) Poetry of Rāma, Kabīr, Gorakhnāth, and other saints, tried to unify different races and sects by singing the praises of an attributeless *Brahman*. Such a concept, however, was beyond the understanding of the common man to whom a personal god having a shape and form was more appealing, a god whom he could serve and love, and before whom he could bow and pray, a god who could protect his devotees, and punish the evil doers. The *Gītā* had also visualised such a god, who took a human form when necessary to free mankind from trials and tribulations:

'Yadā yadā hi dharmasya glānir bhavati bhārata
Abhyutthānamadharmasya tadā 'tmānaṁ sṛjāmyaham
Paritrāṇāya sādhūnām vināshāya cha duṣkṛitām
Dharmasaṁsthāpanārthāya sambhavāmi yuge yuge.'

(Arjuna, wherever righteousness declines, and unrighteousness becomes uppermost, it is then that I myself body forth. For protecting the virtuous and destroying the evil-doers, for establishing firm righteousness, am I born from age to age.) Such a personal form of god was conceived of by the poets who wrote of the deeds of Rāma and Kṛiṣṇa. The story of Rāma was narrated for the first time in the Vālmīki Rāmāyaṇa which was written in Sanskrit. The viewpoint of this Rāmāyaṇa was worldly, and Rāma is depicted therein as a great personage. The other outstanding poet who wrote of the deeds of Rāma, was Keshava's contemporary Tulasīdāsa. Another was Munītal who was the Author of *Rāma Prakāsh*, but he came after Tulsīdāsa. Tulasīdāsa was in fact the greatest figure of his age. Vincent Smith calls him 'the tallest tree in the magic garden of medieval Hindu Poesy.' He goes on to praise the poet in glowing terms, 'Tulasīdāsa was the greatest man of his age in India—greater even than Akbar himself, inasmuch as the conquest of the hearts and minds of millions of men and women effected by the poet was an achievement infinitely more lasting and important than any or all of the victories made by the Mughal ruler. Tulasīdāsa upheld the honour of his race and re-established the dignity of four castes and their duties. He laid down in clear terms the ideals and duties of men and women in their relationship to each other, and pointed out the path which should be taken so that they could give to their subjects a faultless regime called Rāma Rājya. He extolled the virtue of right action, devotional worship, and of knowledge, and also laid down the precepts of individual self-restraint and meditation. In simple language and striking similes taken from every day life he showed how men and women could serve god and mankind best in their respective spheres, how brother should behave with brother, husband with wife, son with father, and friend with friend. His entire narrative breathes devotion to god and good-will to men. Hindus who read his *Rāmāyaṇa* become drunk with the love of Rāma, and the intoxication persists even after the lapse of centuries. The *Rāmāyaṇa* of Tulsīdāsa is today read and recited daily in almost every Hindu home.

Tulsīdāsa depicted almost all kinds of emotions in his *Rāmāyaṇa*, and his characterisation is marvellous. He used the language of Braja and that of Avadh (Brajabhāṣā and Avadhī) with equal skill, and the works composed by him *Rāmāyaṇa*, *Gītāvalī*, *Kṛiṣṇa Gītāvalī*, *Jānakī Mañgala*, *Pārvatī Mañgala*, and *Vinaya Patrikā*—are outstanding specimens of Hindi poetry.

The *Rāmāyaṇa* of Tulsīdāsa had been produced in Keshavadāsa's life-time, and so had a profound effect on the poet, so much so that he too wrote a series of poems, *Rāmachandrikā*, on the same theme.

(v) Poetry of Kṛiṣṇa—The first name in poetry written about Kṛiṣṇa is that of Jayadeva, who wrote in Sanskrit. His book *Gīta Govinda* is a description of the loves of Rādhā and Kṛiṣṇa and a masterpiece, which in the words of Keith, 'surpasses in its completeness of effect any other Indian poem.'

Although Jayadeva's contribution to Hindi was negligible, his *Gīta Govinda* even though in Sanskrit, had great influence on the poets who wrote about Kṛiṣṇa. The greatest effect was on another outstanding poet of the Kṛiṣṇa tradition who wrote in Maithilī, namely Vidyāpati, in whose love-poems we find the same portrayal of desire and longing as in the *Gīta Govinda* of Jayadeva. Vidyāpati, too, wrote charmingly of longing and passion of Rādhā and Kṛiṣṇa, of their meeting and separation, of their wistful yearning, and restless ardour.

The third poet who wrote on this theme with greater seriousness and religious fervour is Nāmadeva who wrote his poems about Kṛiṣṇa in Brajabhāṣā—the language of the Braja country. Following him came Sūradāsa, who is another great name in the history of Hindi poetry. His *Sūrasāgara*, also written in Brajabhāṣā, is an immortal work and a priceless contribution to Hindi literature. It is a happy combination of poetry, adoration, and song, and his descriptions of childhood's innocence and the heartfelt sorrows of separated lovers finds no parallel. Apart from Sūradāsa, there were some other poets also living in this period who wrote about the amorous sports of Kṛiṣṇa. Biṭṭhalnāth, the son of Vallabhāchārya, has collected the poems of the chief of these, in his *Aṣṭachhāpa*. Besides Sūradāsa the other poets mentioned by him are, Nandadāsa, Kṛiṣṇadāsa, Parmānandadāsa, Kumbhānandadāsa, Chaturbhujadāsa, Chitasvāmī, and Govindasvāmī.

Prior to Keshava, too, some poets wrote subjectively about Rādhā and Kṛiṣṇa. The chief amongst these was Mīrā, who instead of narrating the amours of Kṛiṣṇa, bound herself to him with overpowering and all-encompassing love and adoration. Her songs about Kṛiṣṇa are the very outpourings of her soul, and show a love at once chaste and consuming. As Mīrā sang rapturously of Kṛiṣṇa, Hithārīvansha the founder of Rādhāvallabhi school of Bhakti wrote about Rādhā, describing her beauty and her devotion. Other poets in a similar vein were Godādhar Bhaṭṭ, Madanmohan, Govindadāsa, and Svāmī Haridāsa.

These poets did not depict Kṛiṣṇa as the lord and saviour, as in the *Gītā*; rather they portrayed him as a human being, a youth who loved the cowherd maidens though it must not be forgotten that this lover of which the poets wrote was free of desire and of the purest and noblest kind. The language used in Kṛiṣṇa poetry was Brajabhāṣā, which indeed was most suited to such a subject because of its simplicity, melodiousness and richness of sound. These poets wrote in short stanzas, and it was only Nandadāsa who used the longer and more intricate forms of verse.

(vi) *Rītikāvya* or the Poetry of Mannerism. Shiva Singh Sengar has mentioned on the strength of Colonel Todd, that in the assembly of Rājā Mān Singh, an ancestor of King Bhoja, there was a captive called Punḍa, or Pushpa, who translated into Hindi a book of Sanskrit rhetoric, but nothing definite is known about him. The works of Munital another writer are also non-extant. The first Rītikāvya poet of whom definite information is forthcoming is Kirpārāma, who wrote his *Hittaraṅgiṇī* on the subject of love. Kirpārāma himself mentins that while other poets before him described the emotion of love in long verses, he used small stanzas out of consideration for elegance. From this observation of his it is apparent that other books had also been written on love poetry, but if there were any, they are not now in existence. Thereafter Gopa wrote two books on this subject, *Rāmabhūṣaṇa* and *Ahaṅkāra Chandrikā*, but details about these too, are not forthcoming. The same is the case with Mohanlāl Mishra's book *Śṛṅgāra Sāgara*, in which he wrote about love, and the different kinds of *nāyikās*. In this period Rahīm wrote his book *Barvaī Nāyikābheda*, and poet Nandadāsa wrote *Rasamañjarī* about the different types of *nāyikās*. Poet Karnes who was a friend of Narahari produced three works on rhetoric, namely *Karṇābharaṇa*, *Shrutibhūṣaṇa*, and *Bhūpabhūṣaṇa*. Keshavadāsa's own precursor Balabhadra Mishra wrote two books—*Dūṣana Vichāra*, and *Nakhashikha*.

(vii) Influence of Sanskrit Works on Keshavadāsa.—Though prior to Keshavadāsa a number of works on rhetorics had appeared in Sanskrit, love-poetry and rhetorical verse were developed in his time. Famous writers like Bhāmaha, Daṇḍin, Udbhaṭa etc. stressed the importance and beauty of rhetorical verse. Jayadeva went to the extent of saying that if one considered poetry to be shorn of rhetoric and even then thought himself to be wise, he may well consider fire to be devoid of heat. Appaya Dīkshita, Keshava Mishra and other poets too stressed the importance of rhetoric. In Keshavadāsa's time, therefore, these two tendencies viz. love and rhetoric, had taken hold of poetry, and so he wrote *Rasikapriyā* in fulfilment of the former, and *Kavipriyā* as a rhetorical work on the rules and conventions of the poetic art.

Keshavadāsa's poetry shows unmistakable signs of being influenced by these tendencies. In the mode of the heroic poetry which had been written before him, he composed his *Ratanabāvanī, Vīrasiṁhadeva Charita* and *Jahāngīr Jas Chandrikā.* Following the tradition of poets who wrote about Rāma he wrote *Rāmachandrikā* and influenced by devotional poetry of the saints he wrote *Vijñānagītā.* By writing *Rasikapriyā* and *Kavipriyā* he virtually started a new tradition in Hindi poetry, for none before him had assayed to write in such a systematic manner about the canons of poetry, and about conventions and rules of poetic composition.

3 Religious

The rule of the Afghāns, which came before the Mughal rule, was based on Muslim religion and theocracy. Apart from extending their domain, the Afghān rulers also preached Islam to those whom they conquered, and converted them to their faith by the sword. They continuously attacked and decried Hindu religion and made it so hard for the Hindus that many of them were forced to adopt Islam. They desecrated temples, destroyed idols, and tortured those who would not accept their faith. Under such conditions a mighty religious unheaval took place all over India. This movement, called Vaiṣṇava Bhakti, was not something new or sudden. Starting from the south it spread gradually towards the north of India, and by the time Akbar came to the throne it had enveloped the whole country.

Amongst the monarchs of the Gupta period from the fourth century, right upto the middle of the sixth, the Vaiṣṇava and Bhāgavata religions had a large following. After the Gupta period their influence waned in the North, but in the southern part of India their hold became more and more. The religious books of the Vaiṣṇava faith were written for the first time in Tāmil and contained Arvar songs, of which mention has been made by Dr. Dīndayāl Gupta in his book *Aṣṭachhāpa aur Ballabha Sampradāya.* After the Arvars some scholars wrote about the

Vaiṣṇava religion in Sanskrit. The chief amongst these were Nātha Muni and Yāmunāchārya. After them in the eleventh century came Rāmānanda who propagated the Vaiṣṇava doctrine in northern India. The south too was not behind and there Mādhavāchārya, Viṣṇusvāmī and Nimbārkāchārya preached this faith. Due to their efforts the Vaiṣṇava religion spread far and wide in India from the twelfth to the fifteenth century.

Rāmānuja was born in Paramvatur in southern India. He refuted Shaṅkarāchārya's theory of Brahman being the reality as pure consciousness and infinite (*satyam jñānam anantam brahma*) as being pure intelligenc (*chinmātra*) and the ultimate reality (*paramārtha*). Rāmānuja held that there could not be any state of pure revelation without an object. Just as light means both the source of light, and also the rays coming from it, so the self is both consciousness and that which possesses such consciousness. The scriptures do not deny that *Brahman* has qualities, but only that it has undesirable qualities (*heya-guṅān pratiṣidhya*) Rāmānuja held that the existence of god can be known only by the testimony of the scriptures (*shāstra pramāṇaka*). He discarded Shaṅkara's view that cause alone is true and all effects are false. He denied that there is something like pure being more ultimately real than god. God has created the world for the good of the beings in it, or through his playful activity. The scriptural injunctions are merely his commands, and all morality is obedience to these commands and his worship. It is by god's grace alone that emancipation can be achieved. He makes those persons do good actions whom he wishes to reward, and makes those do evil actions whom he wants to punish. Man is merely a tool in his hands.

Rāmānuja emphasised the personal aspect of god, and his worship and meditation. He believed that god is the dweller within the soul, and hence without knowing him the nature of the soul cannot be known. Rāmānuja added warmth and appeal to religion by his concept of god. He gave his followers a living god who could be served, worshipped, and loved; who could give them strength in moments of weakness and hope in moments of despondency.

Vallabha—was born in a village near Madras. He got

his education in Vārāṇasī and thence went all over India, finally settling down to preach in a village only two miles from Allāhābād. Like Rāmānuja, Vallabh also criticised the advaita doctrine of Shaṅkara. The highest reality according to him is Kṛiṣṇa who is full of sweetness (rasa) and joy. Thus for Vallabha the highest reality possessed a form (*sākāra Brahman*). Such a god is eternal, unchanging, omnipresent, omniscient, and omnipotent, and possesses powers such as knowledge, action, evolution and involution. The world and the souls therein are in essence one with him. There are three forms of *Brahman* : (i) *Puruṣottama* (ii) *Antaryāmin* and (iii) *Akshara Brahman*. Kṛiṣṇa is Puruṣottama and the object of love and worship. Vallabha considered the scriptures as the most authoritative. He emphasised god's grace and showed preference for the emotional form of worship. He turned people again towards god, and brought men's soul nearer to their maker. He taught men to serve god and even to lose their individuality in the ecstasy of instant union with him.

Nimbārka—lived in the eleventh century. He admits three real substances viz. *Brahman*, *chit* or the sentient, and *achit* or the non-sentient. *Brahman* means 'one which possesses greatness' and is according to Nimbārka, Kṛiṣṇa, or Hari, the greatest being who has no superior or equal. The system expounded by him is known as *dvaitādvaita*. According to it the cause-effect relationship is neither a relation of difference nor of non-difference. It is rather identity-in-difference. The jar is different from the clay of which it is made for it serves many purposes—like carrying water etc., which the clay cannot, but at the same time it is also of the nature of the clay from which it is made. In the same way the universe is one with *Brahman* but also different from it. Though *Brahman* is different from the world, the difference is only of forms, attributes, and activities, and it only implies the transcendence of *Brahman* over the world. This is Nimbārka's famous doctrine called *svābhāvika bheda*, *bhedavāda*, or doctrine of natural difference and non-difference between god and the universe. According to Nimbārka the reason of creation of the world is god's *līlā*, or sport. The creation of the world is not necessitated by any imperfection on his part but is mere sport to him just as a king should indulge in sport even when he has all his desires fulfilled. At the same time this sport is not erratic or unreasoned, but based on justice and moral order, for each individual soul reaps what it has itself sown, though the field of action covers many lives. While Rāmānuja and Mādhava had emphasised reverence to god, Nimbārka was the first Vaiṣṇava philosopher to stress love and devotion—*mādhurya pradhāna bhakti*. He laid stress not only on external ritualism but also on the ethical virtues of self-control, simplicity, purity, and the like. It is not necessary for one to leave the life of a householder, but that he should perform his allotted duties conscientiously and in a disinterested manner.

The most valuable contribution of Nimbārka is his spirit of compromise and adjustment. He avoids conflicts and reconciles differences like those between the rigid intellectualism of the *advaita* and too much emphasis on the personal aspect. His philosophy is both for the ascetic and the householder, for the practical worker as well as the scholar. He gave dignity to love and worship without stifling them with ritualism, ennobled feeling, and enriched reason, without throttling them in the noose of sophistry and argument.

Mādhavāchārya—Mādhava's philosophy is known as *dvaita*. Mādhava was born near Udipi in the year 1199. He emphasises scripture (*āgama*) as being a spiritual text which is essentially a source of knowledge. The *Vedas* and the *Upaniṣads* he considered as verbal testimony and holds that *vedic* scripture alone can give complete knowledge of reality. The *Veda* is the language of reason. To know it is to see the inner harmony and the all-pervading truth which lies in it. The *Brahma Sūtra* of Bādarāyaṇa is, according to Mādhava the key to the wisdom of the *Vedas*, and each is indispensable to the proper understanding of the other. The *Veda* is the highest source of knowledge and *Brahman* is the highest reality. The philosophy of *Brahman* is marked by freedom from passions, and makes for spiritual progress. Mādhava considers that philosophy is the highest discipline. It is joy in itself and the expression of the divine in man, and the result of the grace of *Brahman*. Thus philosophy of *Brahman* is really the philosophy of Viṣṇu. The active self is that which has the power of doing, undoing, and of doing differently. This power must have the ability to avoid evil and do good, freedom from exhaustion, anxiety, failure of memory, misery, and the like, freedom from dependence, the ability to accomplish what is desired, intelligibility, absence of dissipation of energy, and self-sufficiency. None of the things of the world except *Brahman* possesses such power and so cannot be said to be the doer. *Brahman* alone is therefore the all-doer. *Brahman* which is Viṣṇu, is according to Mādhava, complete, defectless, object, and goal. Individuals have diverse approaches to philosophy. First there are those who are interested in philosophy, second those who are indifferent to it, and lastly those who are opposed to it. Those of the latter two kinds are not real knowers. The philosophy of *Brahman* can be followed only by the grace of Viṣṇu, and so there are different kinds of knowers. These are of five grades, the first being controller (deva) of the world, the second, teacher (*ṛiṣi*), the third father (*pitṛ*), the fourth protector (*pā*), and the fifth man (*nara*). The study and teaching of the philosophy of *Brahman* frees the soul from bondage. Mādhava believed that such study and teaching should be pursued by all men, by the lowest castes, the *Shūdras*, and by the untouchables (*antyajas*). He thought it was the duty of the government to create an environment for such teaching. Political organisation must have such study and education as one of its principal objects. Emancipation means attaining Viṣṇu by his grace. It means enjoying the bliss of Viṣṇu as the highest bliss.

In the wake of these Vaiṣṇava philosophers and scholars, five main schools of Vaiṣṇava thought arose between the fourteenth and sixteenth centuries. These were of Rāmānanda, Chaitanya Mahāprabhu, Vallabhāchārya, Hitārivaṁsha, and Haridāsa. Of these it seems that Rāmānanda and Haridāsa alone had any influence on the poetry of Keshavadāsa.

Rāmānanda—was a highly placed Vaiṣṇava who gave up his status and position on getting spiritual realisation. His chief contribution was to spread religion to all persons irrespective of caste and creed. He saw humanity as one huge family, and all men as brothers. He believed that it was not birth which made a man high or noble, but love and sympathy, and he began to preach this love to all without distinction. He gave up the use of Sanskrit and preached in the language of the people. Thus his great achievement was that he laid the foundation of the modern vernacular literatures. A poem of Rāmānanda incorporated in the *Granthasāhib* says: 'Where shall I go ? In my own house there is music and festivity. My heart wishes not to move , and my mind has folded up its wings and is still. One day my heart was filled to overflowing and I desired to offer worship to *Brahman* with sandal and perfume. But my *guru* showed, that *Brahman* was in my heart. Wherever I go I see water and stones worshipped but thou hast filled them with thy presence. Vainly they seek in the *Vedas*. If thou art not to be found here we must seek there. My true *guru*, thou hast ended my illusion. Blest art thou! Rāmānanda is lost in his master, *Brahman* ! The *guru's* word destroys the million bonds of action.'

The first twelve disciples of Rāmānanda were Ravidāsa, Kabīr, Dhannā, Sena, Pipā, Bhavānanda, Sukhānanda, Āshānanda, Sarasurānanda, Barmānanda, Mahānanda, and Shrī Ānanda. The last six were of the Rāmānuja school, which they later left. There were a number of other disciples also, some of whom were women.

Haridāsa—was a high caste *Brahmin* family. He was a singer, poet, and divine of a high order, and a contemporary of Akbar. In the beginning the cult of Haridāsa had as its objective the practice of meditation and prayer and did not inculcate any specific doctrines or teachings. From an account of Nabhādāsa, however. we know that Haridāsa used to worship Rādhā and Kṛiṣṇa in the manner of a friend (*sakhībhāva*), and used to obtain bliss by such devotion. It is of interest to note that it is traditionally believed that Haridāsa gave guidance to Tānasena, the famous musician at Akbar's court.

Keshavadāsa represented in his writings the various influences and tendencies of the age in which he lived and wrote, though this influence was not very marked in some directions.

The cult of Kṛiṣṇa worship left him more or less unaffected. The religious ecstasy and devotion to Kṛiṣṇa shown by

Sūradāsa and his followers is absent in Keshavadāsa's verse. There are only a few stanzas here and there in which such devotion is evident, for the rest he has depicted the worldly love and passion of Kṛiṣṇa for Rādhā and the cowherd maidens in the spirit of Jayadeva and Vidyāpati.

In *Rāmachandrikā*, Keshavadāsa has written on a subject which had been dealt with in a more deep and masterly manner by Tulasīdāsa. The depth of his adoration for Rāma and Sītā are not found in Keshava's book, nor his simplicity and aptness of words. In fact Keshavadāsa is inclined to be pedantic, and treats the subject as a peg on which to hang his learning. Rāma becomes in his hands just another Mughal Emperor, who sometimes sits amongst his courtiers to listen to music and song, and sometimes watches the water-sport of the women, or delights in the ravishing accounts of Sītā's beauty given by her companions. This is far removed from the Rāma which Tualsī had in mind, and of whom he says:

'As woman for the lustful man, and for the greedy as gold is,

E'en so do thou eternal Rāma, loved in my heart for ever live.'[2]

Though Keshavadāsa wrote *Vīrasiṁhadeva Charita* in the style of the Sūfī poets, it cannot be said that Sūfīsm had any marked effect on him. In *Vijñānagītā* he described the soul's emancipation and its merging into *Brahman* in the tradition of devotional poetry which shows some influence of Kabīr and other poets. Like them also he occasionally dilates upon moral behaviour.

The social and political influences manifest themselves in Keshavadāsa's *Vīrasiṁhadeva Charita*, *Jahāngīr Jas Chandrikā* and *Ratanbāvanī*. In the first book the poet eulogises his patron Vīrasiṁha, the undaunted ruler of Orchhā, whom Akbar failed to crush. In the second book he extols the virtues of the Emperor Jahāngīr, his patron, and in Ratanbāvanī he narrates the heroism of Ratansiṁha, son of Madhukar Shāh.

In the books above mentioned, Keshavadāsa was in some measure following the traditions of writing existing in his period. In *Rasikapriyā* and *Kavipriyā*, especially in the latter, however, he forged a new path. In *Rasikapriyā* he gives us descriptions of the beauty of different kinds of women as we find in the literature of *Rītikāla*, and also an account of poetical composition by means of the nine kinds of emotions and their illustrations. In *Kavipriyā* he describes the different constituents of poetry with special attention to the use of metaphor. While other outstanding poets of his time like Sūra and Tulasī had laid emphasis on worship and spontaneous devotion and had an emotional approach, the stress of the poets of the *Rīti* period was on art, style, and construction. Keshavadāsa's *Kavipriyā* is a rhetorical composition of the latter type. The difference is much of the kind between the romantics like Shelley and Wordsworth and the eighteenth century poets, in English poetry. Though some poets before Keshava had tried to polish up verse with art and artifice, no one had described the different divisions and species of verse in such great detail as he did in *Kavipriyā* and therein he can be said to have started a new tradition in Hindi poetry.

(B) Life

(1) Sources—The sources from which we can know about Keshava's life are, firstly references to himself and those connected with him in his own works, secondly the testimony of others about him including that of ancient writers and of modern research, and thirdly rumour and hearsay.

(a) Keshavadāsa's own works—Amongst references made by the Poet to himself are chiefly those which are contained in his works *Rasikapriyā*, *Kavipriyā*, and *Rāmachandrikā*. In *Kavipriyā* we are told thet Keshavadāsa was born in the family of *Sanāḍhya Brahmins*. His grandfather Kṛiṣṇa Dutta Mishra had studied the *Purāṇas* very well and was honoured for this by Rājā Rudra Pratāp. His father, Kāshīnāth, was a great favourite of Madhukar Shāh. Keshavadāsa had two brothers. The elder one was Balabhadra and the younger Kalyāṇa. Even the servants in Keshava's family spoke in the Sanskrit language. Though born in such a household, Keshava had to write his poetry in the local dialect due to the peculiar circumstances then prevailing. Once Indrajīt singh, the ruler of Orchhā told the Poet to ask for whatsoever he wished. Keshavadāsa merely wanted the ruler's continued favour. On a similar occasion Rājā Bīrbal once asked him the same question, to which the Poet replied that he wished that no restriction should be placed on his entry to his durbar. Mahārāja Indrajīt considered Keshavadāsa to be his *guru*, and he gifted the poet twenty one villages. Because of Indrajīt, his elder brother, Rāma Shāh also honoured the poet as a dear friend and advisor.

In *Rasikapriyā* we find mention of Keshavadāsa's sojourn in Bundelkhanḍ in the city of Orchhā near Tuṅgāraṇya, on the banks of the Betwā River. It is also mentioned that he was a poet of a high order and known far and wide.

In *Rāmachandrikā*, there are references to the Poet's life, though they do not add anything new to the information given in the two books mentioned above.

In *Vijñānagītā* we are told that Rājā Vīrasiṁha once asked the Poet to let him know what he desired. Keshavadāsa requested him to give to his sons the subsistence which the Rājā's ancestors had bestowed on his forefathers. Hearing this reply Vīrasiṁha gave him both prerequisite and position. Later, we are told, Keshavadāsa began to live on the banks of the Gaṅgā, which might mean that becoming displeased with him the *Rājā* deprived him for a time of the property he had given. From the information contained in *Vijñānagitā*, we also know that the Poet's wife died while the book was being written and that she left him more than one son.

In *Vīrasiṁhadeva Charita* we are told that during the conflict between Rāma Shāh and Vīrasiṁha, the Poet acted as a mediator and achieved partial success. From the talks held between Keshavadāsa and Vīrasiṁha on this occasion one can gather that both Rulers greatly honoured and trusted him.

(b) Secondary Testimony (i) Ancient—Tulasīdāsa's, disciple Benīmādhava Dāsa wrote the saint's biography in *Mulgasainī Charita* in which there are some references to Keshavadāsa also. This work, however, is not authentic, and cannot be wholly relied upon. It is mentioned in this that Keshavadāsa went to meet Tulasī who was then residing in Kāshī (Vārāṇasī). When the latter was informed of his coming, he exclaimed, 'Send in this unrefined poet, Keshavadāsa.' Hearing this Keshavadāsa immediately left, after informing the servant that he would come again next day. On reaching home he composed

Rāmachandrikā during the night, and after having done so, met Tulasīdāsa at the same spot next morning. This, however, appears to be a fanciful story without any truth. One could never expect a man of Tulasī's gentle nature to utter such words. Chronological evidence too does not support this tale, and it is certain that the account of Benīmādhava Dāsa is mythical and unreliable.

There is also mention about Keshavadāsa in a book describing the loves of the Prince and Princess of *Kāmarūpa*, called *Kāmarūpa kī Kathā*, which was written by a descendant of the Poet, namely Harisewak Mishra, but this adds nothing new about him.

In Deva's *Vairāgyashataka* we find some references to Keshavadāsa, from which it is apparent that the Poet was greatly respected and was counted amongst poets of the top class. Deva mentions that Keshavadāsa's service of the *Rājās* and *Mahārājās* proved of no avail to him in his last days, and he had to repent for having fallen prey to greed. This recalls the famous words of Cardinal Wolsey, 'If I had served my god with half the zeal I served my king, he would not have given me over in my gray hairs. We cannot however take seriously Deva's remark in his book that despite Keshavadāsa's ascendancy amongst poets he was reborn as an evil spirit.

(ii) Modern—There is reference to Keshavadāsa in three works—*Shivasingh Saroj*, *Mishrabandhu Vinod*, and *Hindi Navaratna*. Shivasingh Sengar has written in *Shivasingh Saroj* that Keshavadāsa was an old resident of Tehrī. He came to Madhukar Shāh, Ruler of Orchhā who greatly honoured him. Rājā Indrajīt Singh gifted him twenty-one villages, and from that time he began to live in Orchhā along with his family. Elsewhere Sengar says that when the Emperor Akbar, being displeased with Indrajīt for his disobedience and for failure to present the courtesan Privīnarāye, imposed a fine of a *crore* rupees (about 1333333 dollars) on him, Poet Keshavadāsa met Bīrbal secretly, and read over to him a poem he had composed in his praise. Bīrbal was so moved by it that he got the fine excused, though the courtesan had to present herself in the durbar.

In *Mishrabandhu Vinod* we find about Keshavadāsa that he

was a grandson of the *Sanāḍhya Brahmin* Kṛiṣṇadatta, and son of Kāshīnāth; that he was born in Orchhā near about *saṁvat** 1612, and the famous poet Balabhadra was his brother; and also that he was greatly honoured in the durbar of Indrajīt Singh, the brother of Mahārājā Rāmasingh, King of Orchhā. The book also mentions the incident about the fine of a *crore* rupees levied on Indrajīt. From this time Keshavadāsa began to be greatly valued in the Orchhā durbar.

In the *Hindī Navaratna* the birth of Keshavadāsa is given as saṁvat 1608. It is also mentioned that Keshavadāsa went to Āgrā where he recited a stanza which he had composed in Bīrbal's praise before him, which pleased the Rājā so much that he presented the poet bills of exchange of the value of six lakhs rupees (80000 dollars) which he had that time in his pocket. Moved by this generous reward Keshavadāsa recited some more stanzas.

(c) Tradition—Some traditional tales are prevalent about Keshavadāsa, which though not meant to be taken seriously , do illustrate some aspect or the other of his character, and were perhaps invented for this very reason.

The first story runs as follows; One day the Emperor Akbar was camping in Vishvanāthapurī Kāshī, and eager to meet some saints, he sent his eminent ministers to entreat all the sages to come to Mankankā Ghāt on the river Gaṅgā to give him their benediction. The sages came and obliged the Emperor with their blessings. Akbar met them with reverence, and thereafter all of them went away, except those whom he beseeched to stay on a little longer. Amongst these were Tulasīdāsa, Sūra, and Keshava. By chance the Emperor, all of a sudden, said, 'Today, it seems difficult to decide who is really a poet amongst the three of you. So Keshavadāsa, you tell me. Keshavadāsa replied. 'I, sire.' Though the Emperor repeated his question thrice, he got the same answer each time. Hearing this, Akbar was greatly pained for having needlessly asked a question which led to disrespect being caused to the two other poets, namely Tulasī and Sūra. Reading the Emperor's mind, Keshava said, 'I have only

* *Saṁvat* is the Hindu year of the *Vikrama* era. The present year 1971 is *saṁvat* 2027-80 So to find out the corresponding English year substract 56 from the *saṁvat* year.

replied to your [question, and not slighted these honoured and revered saints. They are not poets, but rather saints of a high order, and divine persons who have descended on the earth as men. Sūradāsa is the incarnation of Uddhava, and Tulasīdāsa of Vālmīki who is even more adored than Rāma. I cannot dishonour them by calling them mere poets. They are in fact gods fit to be worshipped, but I am only a poet.' The Emperor was greatly pleased at Keshavadāsa's quick-witted reply.

Another traditional account has it that it was Keshavadāsa who broke the news of Bīrbal's tragic death to the Mughal Emperor. Birbal was the most dearly loved of Akbar's ministers. It is said that when Bīrbal started on his campaign to wage war with the Yusufjais on the north-west border, Akbar made it known that whoever said anything derogatory about Bīrbal would be severely punished. When news of Bīrbal's death reached the court no one dared break it to the Emperor and this delicate task was entrusted to Keshava. The Poet conveyed the news to Akbar in the following stanza:

'Yāchak sab bhūpati bhaye, rahyau na koū len ,
Indrahu ko icchā bhaī, gayo, Bīrbal den.'

(All the beggars became kings and not one remained to take him. Then the god Indra also became desirous, and Bīrbal went to fulfil that desire).

Hearing this, Akbar exclaimed, 'Ah ! is Bīrbal then dead? Keshavadāsa answered, 'Your majesty, I could not say so clearly because of your royal command ! Filled with sorrow the Emperor spoke these lines:

'Sab ko sab kuchh dīnhh, dukh na kāhu ko diyo
So mar hamko dīnh, bhalī nibāhī Bīrbal !'

(You gave everything to everybody but never gave pain to anyone, which you gave me indeed by so dying—so well did you treat me, oh, Bīrbal)

Another such story has been mentioned by Dwivedījī in his *Sukavi Saroj*. One Keshavadāsa passed through a village called Phuṭerā on a palanquin carried by kahārs (palanquin bearers), who by reason of the heat, it being the summer month, grounded the palanquin near a well called Paṭā, and were minded to quench their thirst. There took place some altercation between the *kahārs* and the *ahīrs* (herdsmen), who lived in that village and the *ahīrs* treated the palanquin-bearers very badly. When Keshavadāsa reached Orchhā, news of this incident came to the ears of Maharājā Indrajīt Singh who was greatly pained because of it, and ousting the *ahīrs* from the village, he made it known that he would give them harsh punishment. But the kind-hearted Poet got them pardoned. Thereafter this village too was given by the Ruler to Keshava, and even to this day the descendants of the Poet are prominent in the village. The other villages which were given to Keshavadāsa as *jāgīrs*, were later taken away from him. We also learn that in *saṁvat* 1900 some family members of Keshava were given *sanads* for their *jāgirs* went with them to request the ruler of Tīkamgarh to either allow them to exercise their rights according to the *sanads*, or to take the *sanads* back. No one, however, gave them a hearing, so much so that they were not even allowed to see the Ruler. Frustrated and enraged, they threw the *sanads* into the river and went back. There is, however, no confirmation of such an incident in the historical records of Orchhā or of Tīkamgarh.

The account of Keshavadāsa's ghost is also quite popularly known. The story runs that once the thought entered Indrajīt's mind that the splendour of his court should last for ever. Keshavadāsa advised him to carry out a sacrificial worship of evil spirits to accomplish this end. The sacrifice was carried out, and in it Keshava also offered his life, and became an evil spirit, but he did not find this state to his liking. One day Keshava's evil spirit was sitting near a well, when by his good fortune, the sage Tulasīdāsa also happened to come there to draw water, and lowered a pot in the well for the purpose. The spirit of Keshava recognized Tulasī and caught his *lotāh*. When the sage entreated him to leave it the Poet said that he would do so only on condition that he was released from his ghost existence. Tulasīdāsa asked him to recite his own *Rāmachandrikā* twenty-one times, but by mischance the Poet could not remember its first stanza even though he had himself composed it. Tulasīdāsa refreshed his memory, and after he had so recited the entire poem the prescribed number of times, the Poet got rid of his ghost existence. This fanciful tale has significance only because it proves that Keshavadāsa died before Tulasī.

The most popular and noteworthy tale about the Poet is one which brings out his romantic nature and his abhorrence of old age. It is said that once Keshavadāsa was passing by the village well when some beautiful girls too came that way to fill water. Seeing him one of the girls greeted him by calling him *bābā* which means 'grandfather'. This reminded the Poet of his old age and caused him much grief, which he conveyed poignantly in the following stanza:

'Keshava Kesan as karī, jas arihū na Karāhiṁ
Chandrabadanī mṛigalochanī, "bābā" kahi kahi jāhiṁ.'

(Oh! Keshava, your grey hair have done for you what even your enemies would not have wished to do, so that these antelope-eyed maidens with limbs fair as the moon, pass by, calling you 'grandfather')

With the help of the foregoing source materials we can reconstitute the figure and the personality of the Poet and know much about his life.

2. Birth—About the date of birth of Keshavadāsa there remains much doubt and controversy. Some scholars like Rāmachandra Shukla, Dr Rāmakumār Varmā, Rāmanaresh Tripāṭhī, the Mishra brothers, and Shrī Kaye would have it as *saṁvat* 1612 or thereabout. Others like Gaurīshankar Dvivedī and Lālā Bhagavāndīn think it to be *saṁvat* 1618. Bābū Govind dāsa of Chatrapur holds the year of the Poet's birth to be *saṁvat* 1594, Gaṇeshprasāda Dvivedī as *saṁvat* 1508, and-Shivasingh Sengar as *saṁvat* 1624. None of these scholars advanced any proof in support of his conclusions, but it seems that the view of the scholars who consider it as *saṁvat* 1612 is nearer the truth, because we can fit in the year of the composition of *Rasikapriyā*, which we know for sure as *saṁvat* 1648, best with this date, for by this calculation Keshava would be about thirty years old when he wrote it, and that would be quite logical.

We have already seen that Keshava was born in a cultured

family of *Sanāḍhya Brahmins* of Orchhā, and was the son of Kāshīnāth. His elder brother Balabhadra Mishra was a good scholar of Hindi, and wrote some books : *Nakhshikh, Bhāgavatabhāṣya, Hanumannāṭaka-ṭīkā* and others. His younger brother was Kalyāṇa. We also know that he was married and had children and enjoyed a long and mostly happy domestic life.

Some stray verses which are ascribed to the wife of the son of one 'Keshava' are also in existence in the literature of Bundelkhaṇḍa. There were only two eminent persons of this name living at this period. One was Keshavarāye Babuā and the other was Poet Keshavadāsa. It seems that this lady was the wife of Poet Keshavadāsa's son.

3. Keshava and Bihārī—A point on which much controversy has been raised is whether the eminent Poet Bihāri, was a son of Keshavadāsa or not. This possibility was for the first time explored by Shrī Radhākṛiṣṇa Dāsa Later, some more scholars like Paṇḍit Gaurīshankar Dwivedī, Jaggannāthdāsa Ratnākar and Chandrabalī Pāndey supported him in this stand: On the other side are those who do not believe Bihārī to be Keshava's son, and these are the Mishra brothers, Dr. Shyāmsunder Dās, Māyāshankar Yājnik, Gaṇeshprasāda Dwivedī and Dr. H.L. Dikśhit. It will be fruitless to consider in detail the arguments advanced by all these scholars in support of their respective stands, which would be out of place in an outline of this sort. The points for and against may however briefly be mentioned for the sake of those who are interested enough to undertake a deeper study.

Points to prove that Poet Bihārī was Keshavadāsa's son:

(i) Both of them were contemporaries.

(ii) In a verse (which is not found in *Bihārī Ratnākara*), the Poet Bihārī has stated that he was born in Gwālior, spent his childhood in Bundelkhanḍ, and his youth in Mathurā, the home town of his in-laws. (Keshava was also a resident of Bundelkhanḍ).

(iii) Bihārī used words of Bundelkhandī dialect in his poems.

(iv) In one of his verses Bihārī praises one Keshavadāsa (who may be the Poet Keshavadāsa).

(v) In one of Bihārī's verses there is a reference to Madhukar', which may mean Madhukar Shāh of Orchhā.

(vi) To disprove that Bihārī was Keshava's son it is said that he had little to do with Orchhā, but the reason for this is that he loved his maternal grandfather very much and so remained mostly at Gwalior with him.

(vii) It is said that Bihārī was a *Chaube*, and Keshava a *Sanāḍhya* which is a different sub-caste. But Bihārī may have called himself a *Chaube* due to long association with his maternal grandfather. In any case it is not certain tha he was a *Chaube*.

(viii) Phuṭerā village was the old residence of Bihārī and since many villages near about Jhānsī (in Bundelkhaṇḍ) remained for long in Gwalior, it is quite possible Bihārī said it was in Gwalior, though really it was Bundelkhaṇḍ.

(ix) It is pointed out that Keshavadāsa never mentions Bihārī as his son, which he would have done in view of Bihārī being such a famed poet, but Keshava made it a point not to mention about those younger than him. Bihārī did not also mention Keshava as he did not want to flatter anyone, even his famed father, and cared only for poetical expression.

(x) There is much in common between the manner and language of the poetry of the two poets. It is thought that Bihārī read Keshava's poems at Bundelkhaṇḍ.

(xi) Bihārī mentions the word '*paturrai*' in his poems. This might refer to the courtesan Pravīṇārāye, and if this is so, it could only have been with Keshava's influence that Poet Bihārī gained admission to the Orchhā durbar and learnt about her.

(xii) Perhaps Bihārī met the saint and scholar Naraharidāsa through his father Keshava. The saint's father had connections with the Orchhā ruler.

(xiii) There is mention of a wife of Keshava's son who was a poetess. Maybe she was the wife of Bihārī.

Points which go to show that Biharī was *not* Keshavadāsa's son:

(i) There is nothing to show that Keshavadāsa ever lived at Gwalior where Bihārī was born.

(ii) Had Bihārī been the son of the famous Poet Keshavadāsa there would be some allusion to this in the traditional tales of this period, which is not so.

(iii) Critics and commentators interpret writings of writers differently, and so no reliance can be placed on any alleged similarities in the writings of the two poets.

(iv) In *Kāmarūpa kī kathā* written by a descendant of Keshava, there is no mention of Bihārī, which there would have been if he was Keshava's son, in view of Bihārī being a prominent poet also.

(v) Keshavadāsa was a *Sanāḍhya Brahmin*, while Bihārī was *Chaube*. Even if it is believed that Bihārī was also a *Sanāḍhya*, then too the *gotras* (clans) of the two were different and this cannot be so in the case of father and son.

(vi) The name of Bihārī's father was not Keshava or Keshavarāye but Keso Kesorāye.

(vii) Bihārī was born near about the time Keshava died, so he cannot be his son. Also according to some calculations Bihārī had been born even before Keshavadāsa.

(viii) Bihārī himself gave his birthplace as Gwalior and his wife's residence as Mathurā. Orchhā, the residence of Keshava, was far removed from these. There is no proof of Keshava's ever living either at Gwalior or at Mathurā.

(ix) Had Keshavadāsa been the father of Bihārī he would have mentioned this somewhere or the other, seeing that he has given so many details of himself and his family in his own writings.

(x) Regarding the mention of the word '*paturrai*' in Bihārī's poems, this word can relate to any accomplished courtesan, and not necessarily to Pravīṇārāye only, as considered by some critics.

(xi) Keshavadāsa has given the name of his father as Kāshināth Mishra, while, Bihārī's grandfather was Vāsudeva, though some scholars do not believe this to be so.

(xii) Had Bihārī been son of Keshavadāsa, this would have been known right from the beginning, and at least that son of Keshava who enjoyed the property gifted by Vīrasiṁha, ought to have known about it. There is nothing to show why this fact escaped mention by him and by so many others who could clearly say so if it was a fact.

The matter is, as we see, controversial, and the main difficulty seems to be that while there can be many surmises, there are few specific facts on which to rely. However the question is purely academic. Both the poets—Keshava and Bihārī—hold an eminent position in Hindi poetry, a position which cannot be affected by their being, or not being, father and son.

We will now go on to consider the attainments and the nature of the man Keshavadāsa.

4. Keshava's Love For His Native place and Race—Like most other men, Keshavadāsa had a great love for his native place—Orchhā. His description of Orchhā in *Rasikapriyā* is much in the strain of Goldsmith's wistful and poignant description of Auburn. Keshava was attached to the woods, rivers, and soil of his native town, which was for him an ideal place, before which other places faded into insignificance. The men and women of Orchhā appeared to him as gods and goddesses, and the River Betwā which flowed through it surpassed the Gaṅgā and the Yamunā in its sacredness and merit; for while a bath in these washed off one's sins, the very sight of the Betwā was enough to do so. In *Vīrasiṁhadeva Carita* he says, 'By merely seeing the River Betwā the body's fever is cooled, by its touch all sins are completely removed, and by bathing in it wisdom dawns in the minds of beings'.

In like manner, Keshavadāsa also took pride in his caste. Speaking in praise of *Sanāḍhya Brahmins* he says in *Rāmachandrikā*, 'The worship of *Sanāḍhyā Brahmins* destroys all sins and bestows all the pleasures of Indraloka, or heaven, Not only this, all the fourteen worlds are attained by it, and it slays all the wrong-doing of kings'.

In other places in *Rāmachandrikā*, too, the virtues of *Sanāḍhya Brahmins* are extolled. Most probably Keshava did this because he knew that the favours of kings were short-lived and were governed by their erratic nature. They could be taken away as suddenly as bestowed, and so he took good care to publicise the need of serving *Brahmins* like him, for, as he says further in the same work, 'He who forcibly takes away the property of a *Sanāḍhya Brahmin* will burn in everlasting fire. He will die of starvation and be cast into different kinds of hells'.

3. Keshava's Patrons—Keshavadāsa enjoyed the special patronage of kings and rulers. It seems that his ancestors too had been getting such royal patronage. Not only Kṛiṣṇa-

datta his grandfather, Kāshīnāth his father, and Balabhadra Mishra his elder brother, were thus honoured by the rulers of Orchhā, but in addition Keshava's ancestors too received such honours from time to time. The Poet has himself written that his ancestor Jayadeva received the patronage of Mahārāja Prithvī Rāja. Jayadeva's son Diwākar was honoured by the Emperor Alāuddin. Trivikram Mishra, another ancestor of the Poet, was greatly respected by Gopālgaṛh Durgapati. His son Shiromaṇi was given twenty villages as a gift by the Rāṇā, and in like manner Shiromaṇi's son Harināth got the patronge of Tomarpati.

Keshavadāsa's first patron was Mahārāja Chandrasen. He was the son of Rājā Māldeva of Jodhpur. Māldeva was content to be under the Emperor Akbar, but Chandrasen was for ever thirsting to be independent. So collecting a number of princes of the Māru country who were like-minded, he determined to maintain his independence, and fleeing from Jodhpur he took the fortress of Sivānā, and faced the Mughal armies undaunted for seventeen years, at length dying an honourable death. Keshavadāsa has praised his valour in *Kavipriyā*. It appears that the Poet also visited Sivānā sometime, and personally met Mahārāja Chandrasen.

Keshava's other patron was the famous Maharāja Indrajīt Singh. He was the younger brother of Mahārāja Rāma Shāh, the ruler of Orchhā, and the entire administration of the State was in his hand. Indrajīt was a very solemn, charitable, and wise ruler. He was greatly gifted, a lover of poetry, and himself a poet. He had a special aptitude for music, dance, and song. Keshava wrote *Rasikapriyā* for his patron Indrajīt.

Keshavadāsa's third patron was Mahārāja Vīrasiṁha, brother of Mahārāja Indrajīt Singh. In the beginning he was in possession of only one *Jāgīr*, namely Baraunī, but after the death of Akbar, Emperor Jahāngīr gave him the entire kingdom of Madhukar Shah. He was greatly favoured by Jahāngīr, because he had taken sides against Akbar when Jahāngīr (then Prince Salim) rebelled and waged war with his father. Vīrasiṁha was very just, learned, broadminded, generous and brave. He had wrested many fortresses from the Mughals and defeated their armies repeatedly. Akbar could not vanquish this brave Ruler. Keshava eulogised Vīrasiṁha's valour in *Vīrasiṁhadeva Charita* and wrote *Vijñānagītā* also with the Ruler's encouragement. Even to this day stories about Vīrasiṁha's valour are told in Bundelkhaṇḍ.

Another person whose protection Keshava had was Amarsingh, in whose praise the Poet has written a few lines in *Kavipriyā*. There are two persons by the names of Amarsingh who were Keshavadāsa's contemporaries. One of these was Amarsingh, the Rājā of Rewārī who had waged war against the Orchhā king Jujhar Singh in support of Emperor Shahjahan. The other Amarsingh was the eldest son of the famous Mahārāṇā Pratāp who after the death of his father, succeeded to the throne of Mewār. Most probably, Keshavadāsa's patron was this second Amarsingh. He was the most powerful of the rulers of Mewār, had many virtues, and was famed for his valour and generosity. The Emperor Jahāngīr sent his armies several times to crush this valiant Ruler, but each time he repulsed them. Unfortunately in the final combat when there seemed no way out of captivity except surrender, he had to give way. Dejected and sorrowful at heart, he finally left his Kingdom to his son, and abandoning Chittor he went away to Nauchaukī where he lived till his death. Keshavadāsa has written about Amarsingh too, in *Kavipriyā*.

6. Keshava's Friends and Disciples. The closest and most affectionate friend of Keshava was famous Maheshadāsa Dube, better known as Bīrbal. We have already seen that Bīrbal gave Keshava much money in the form of gifts. Bīrbal's pre-eminent position in Akbar's court must have been a great source of help to the Poet in establishing his fame. Because of his friendship with Bīrbal he had easy ingress into the Mughal Emperor's durbar.

During his visits to the Court of Akbar, Keshavadāsa must have come into contact with the other learned and prominent men there. Toḍarmal, who had gained a position of eminence during the reign of Shershāh Sūr, and who was Akbar's notable revenue minister, was not liked by the Poet. Abdur Rahīm Khānkhānā, Abul Fazal, Faizi, Mānsingh, and other gifted men who were in Akbar's durbar, were Keshavadāsa's acquaintances. We have already spoken of the close connection between him and Tulasīdāsa. Another of Keshava's close friends was the goldsmith Ratirām, about whom he has mentioned in

Kavipriyā. According to this account Ratirāma was illiterate, but (in all probability due to Keshava's company) he could understand and appreciate poetry. Apart from plying his goldsmith's trade he also distributed medicines for common ailments. He was very cunning in stealing gold and could do it successfully even under the very gaze of his customers. He was so adroit and fearless that he even pilfered the gold of women of the palace. He was also jealous of Keshavadāsa's good fortune.

The earliest of Keshavadāsa's disciples was the singer at the court of Indrajīt Singh, the accomplished lady, Pravīṇārāye. It was to teach her the poetic art that he wrote *Kavipriyā*. Keshavadāsa wrote very highly about her in his book, and compared her beauty to that of a goddess. Pravīṇārāye was not an ordinary courtesan. She was also an accomplished poetess, and was in fact a courtesan in name only, for when she was summoned by the Mughal Emperor Akbar, she was not tempted by the better prospects which would be her's there, but remained faithful to her liege and master Indrajīt, and tried her best to avoid going to the Mughal durbar.

Mahārāja Rāma Shāh, the ruler of Orchhā also considered Keshava as his guru, and gifted him twenty-one villages.

Of the *Rītikāla* poets who came after Keshava all must be considered his disciples, for it was he who laid down the canons of rhetorical poetry in *Kavipriyā* for them to follow.

7. Keshava's Travels—Although Keshavadāsa does not appear by nature to be fond of travel, largely because of his attachment to Orchhā and its rulers, yet we do find proof in his writings that he visited prominent places of Northern and Central India. He seems to have visited Prayāga (Allāhābād). Kāshī (Vārāṇasī), Delhi, Āgrā, and other towns sometime or the other. His association with Bīrbal must have taken him to Āgrā often, and from *Kavipriyā* we know that he once accompanied Indrajīt to Prayāga on pilgrimage. Tulasīdāsa, he met at Kāshī. From the vivid description the Poet gives us of the contemporary social conditions of Delhi and Vārāṇasī in *Vijñānagītā* we can be sure he visited these two cities. We have also seen that Keshava visited Sivānā in Jodhpur to meet mahārāja Chandrasen and Mewār (Udaipur) in order to see Rāṇā Amarsingh.

8. Keshava's Nature and Accomplishments—As we have seen, Keshavadāsa extolled his own caste of *Sanāḍhya Brahmin* to the skies. Though this was partly to maintain his own influence in the inconstant minds of princes, it was also due in a large measure to his vain and egoistic nature. It was this vanity which made the Poet call himself 'a diadem amongst poets'. and 'knower of the whole world'. He knew his own merit and did not conceal it in a veneer of humility. He did not have the meekness of Tulasī or Sūra. At the same time he cannot be called narrow-minded for he had a generous heart and was sympathetic to men of races and beliefs other than his own, though he would give prime importance to persons of his own caste, creed, and nationality. This can be seen by his observation in *Rāmachandrikā* about the giving of gifts : 'Give the wealth earmarked for charity first to your own dependants, then to the residents of your city, then to the citizens of your country, if after giving all these, something still remains, then give it to foreigners.'

Due to his large-heartedness Keshavadāsa did not hestitate to meet the most poor and humble person. He befriended even the unscrupulous goldsmith, Patīrāma. In *Kavipriyā* he also mentions the door-keeper of the palace of Bīrbal called Chānd and praises him. He could in Kipling's words 'walk with kings, and yet not lose the common touch'. Although he never lacked wealth, Keshava had no greed for it, and considered respect and honour much more valuable. He was also very fearless and straightforward, and knew not the art of flattery. This can be seen by the counsel he gave Rāma Shāh to hand over the reins of administration to the valiant Vīrasiṁha, and by advising the latter to fall on the feet of Rāma Shāh when he was sent to intercede between the two Rulers. While being straightforward he was also tactful, a quality which stood him in good stead in maintaining the uncertain goodwill of the kings and rulers amongst whom he moved. His fairness of mind and clarity of vision can be seen in the attitude taken by him in controversial issues in the story of Rāma as expounded by him in *Rāmachandrikā* in which he does not allow judgment to be warped by emotion. He did not, for example. justify Rāma's abandonment of Sītā. On the contrary, he considered it a great wrong-doing on Rāma's part. So when the news of the victory of Lavakusha over Shatrughna and Lakshmaṇa came, Bharata is made to say to Rāma: 'For what sin did you abandon Sītā, whose character was so pure that hearing of it the world becomes purified? Misfortune is sure to befall him who finds fault with one who is faultless.' While Tulasīdāsa had, out of devotion to Rāma, overlooked his injustice in abandoning Sītā, not so Keshava. Again, about Bibhīṣaṇa, the brother of the demon king Rāvaṇa, who came over to Rāma's side before the two armies attacked each other, Keshavadāsa does not mince words. Tulasīdāsa had harped upon the nobility of Rāvaṇa's brother and depicted him as true friend of Rāma, not Keshava. He looks upon Bibhīṣaṇa's act with suspicion. Why didn't he come over instantly when Rāvaṇa committed the ignoble act of Sītā's abduction? Why had he to wait till Rāma's army began to get across the sea to Laṅkā? And why after the slaying of the demon king did Bibhīṣaṇa wed his dead elder brother's widow, whom he should rather have regarded as his mother? These questions are brought by Keshava into prominence and he doesn't at all support Bibhīṣaṇa in these acts. He says : 'Oh! Bibhīṣaṇa, come, you indeed are the jewel of your family. You are the brave man who at the start of the battle abandoned his brother and allied himself with the enemy. Why did you not leave Rāvaṇa and come to the protection of Rāma at the very instant Sītā was abducted? When the battle began, then to save your own life you came to Rāma. Oh! you man of low caste, you have besmirched the name of your family. According to the *shāstras* an elder brother, a master, a king, and a father—all these are to be given equal respect, but you have taken the wife of Rāvaṇa your elder brother and made her your own. Was she not like a mother to you?

Keshava was full of laughter and merriment, and did not lack the capacity of viewing things in a light vein. He would have fully agreed with Sir Toby when he says: 'Dost thou think, because thou art virtuous there shall be no more cakes and ale?' His constant association with the durbars of kings and emperors must have inculcated in him the mood for enjoyment, for there the wine flowed to the strains of sweet music and the melodious jingle of dancing feet. We can see this merriment and jollity even buffoonery, in some of his verses, as for example, where he rains sallies on the harsh voice of a shrewish woman, 'How melodious is her voice, even finer than that of a cricket. She has outdone the pewit in her repetition. Her speech beats that of the female jackal, and is greater than that of a female demon. Her voice is better than a buffalo's, sharper than an ass's, and more intelligible than that of a female camel. Her voice has crossed the limit of that of an ewe and broken the vanity of the female mongoose. Her speech is lovelier than that of a goat, and the cawing of the crow seems to have melted away before it. Hearing her voice the female pig feels abashed and the bitch falls into silence. What is the owl's hoot compared to her voice? Even the female elephant is charmed when she hears it.'

There was no dearth of emotion and amorousness in Keshava. Even when he was old and his hair had turned gray he could not help being piqued when the young girls passing by addressed him as 'grandfather'. Age could touch his body but not his mind and heart, which was ever inspired by a beautiful face or some new thought of love.

Keshavadāsa was familiar with all branches of learning and accomplishment. Not only was he a great poet having command over the Brajabhāṣā language, he was also expert in the art of poetics, rhetoric, and the intricacies of versification. He was a good scholar of Sanskrit, and had special knowledge of botany, astrology, medicine, and *Vedānta*. He was skilled in politics, geography, sociology, and religion. We find traces of his learning in all these subjects in the poetry he wrote.

In *Rāmachandrikā*, on the occasion of the wedding of Rāma, the Poet writes about a woman: 'that maiden earth-shaped is lying on the bedstead shaped like the gem-studded hood of Sheṣanāga with her head towards the south and her feet towards the north. According to geographical knowledge the earth spreads from the south to the north poles and hence Keshava has called his damsel 'earth-shaped' i. e. spreading her body from south to north. So Keshava has shown his acquaintance with geography in these stanzas.

We see his astrological knowledge expresed in the lines in *Rāmachandrikā* where he is describing the loveliness of Rāma. He says, 'Ear-rings shaped like fishes are resplendent in the ears of Rāma's splendid face. It appears as if the moon is shining in the twenty-second lunar mansion in makara, the tenth sign of the zodiac.' According to Hindu astrology some portion of the lunar mansions of *uttaraṣāḍha, shravaṇa* and dhaniṣṭhā fall in the *makara* zodiac and this knowledge has been used by Keshava in the description of Rāma. Keshavadāsa's ancestor Bhaurāma had written a celebrated treatise on *Āyurveda*, the Hindu system of medical science, called *Bhāvaprakāsha*, and Keshava, too, was familiar with it. During the course of the exchange of repartees between the excitable Lakshmaṇa (Rāma's younger brother), and the hot-headed sage, *Parashurāma*, we find Keshava using his *Āyurvedic* knowledge when, addressing his hatchet, the enraged sage exclaims: Oh ! my battle-axe ! you have cut into the flesh of Haihayarāja Sahasrārjuna, and by so doing you have, as it were, eaten morsels of most deadly poison. In order to cure you of the poison I have made you drink the melted fat of many kings, as if it were clarified butter, but even then your heart was not assuaged. Therefore, oh ! friend hatchet, if you wish to live for long, listen to me. You will not get satisfaction till you drink the blood-like essence of Rāma. According to Hindu medical science the antidote for poison was considered to be fresh blood, clarified butter, or lime-water.

Keshavadāsa's knowledge of botany can also be seen in his poetry. *Jawāsā* is a prickly grass used in medicine, which remains green in the summer season but dries up in the rainy months. To express the heat and the oppression of dense clouds gathering all round the Poet says, it is as dry and sultry as the *Jawāsā* plant'. It was also believed that the small tender fruit of the pumpkin creeper withers away if one points his finger at it. Tulasīdāsa had used this popular conception in *Rāmāyaṇa* where Lakshmaṇa is made to say to Parashurāma when he is threatened by the latter: 'There is no small unripe fruit here, which seeing the foremost finger of the hand, will wither.' Keshavadāsa uses the same metaphor in *Rasikapriyā* where the *nāyikā* says to her lover: 'If seeing our love, people raise their finger, may it not wither away like a small tender fruit?'

In the same manner it is said that after sixteen years the *champā* (jasmine) creeper yields flowers with extremely sweet scent. In *Kavipriyā* describing the young *nāyikā* Keshavadāsa says: 'That girl is sixteen years old; and as the *champā* flower is greatly scented on a creeper of this age, so is she increasing one's pleasure'.

By coming into contact with the accomplished Pravīṇārāye, and the other ladies of the court, Keshava learnt much about music and dance. In *Rāmachandrikā* and *Vīrasiṁhadeva Charita* describing the assembly of Rāma and of Vīrasiṁhadeva, Keshava shows that he was fully acquainted with the intricacies of music. In *Rāmachandrikā*, describing the music and dancing in the palace of Rāma he gives the various kinds of notes, sounds, gamut, scales, musical measures, modulations of voice, etc. of music, and also describes seventeen types of dances. The detailed and accurate description he gives can leave no doubt in the mind that he had carefully studied the arts of music, and dancing, and was familiar with the expert exposition of both.

Keshavadāsa's writings also show that he had intimate knowledge of the various kinds of arms then used in wars. This knowledge he must have gathered by his close association with kings and princes and visits to courts. In *Rāmachandrikā*, describing the assault made by the demon king, Rāvaṇa, having ten heads and twenty hands, he gives a list of nineteen weapons which were being used by him against the warriors of Rāma's army, which would do credit to any historian. The weapons mentioned by the Poet are pounder, sword, pole-axe, javelin, lance, halberd, pike, spear, club, sling, mace poniard, spike, rock, tree-trunk, goad, discus, sabre, and bow and arrows.

We know that not only Keshava, but most of his ancestors and family members were deeply learned in religious books like the *Purāṇa*, *Rāmāyaṇa*, and *Mahābhārata*, and we find this learning also reflected in much of what Keshava wrote. In *Kavipriyā*, for example, Keshava mentions several incidents in the life of *Kṛiṣṇa* which are described in *Mahābhārata*, like his taking the form of a mendicant for the sake of Rājā Balī, a gate-keeper at the palace of Ugrasena, a servant in the form of the devotee Senā, a messenger for the Pāṇḍavas, a charioteer for Arjuna, and a hewer of wood for the *Ṛiṣi* Sandīpani. Elsewhere in the same book he alludes to the assistance given by Kṛiṣṇa to Shabarī, his instruction to Tāḍaka, his deliverance of Gaṇikā and of the she-demon Pūtanā.

Due to his constant touch with kings and courts we can be sure Keshava acquired much knowledge about statecraft. In *Rāmachandrikā* when Rāma has parcelled out his kingdom amongst his sons and nephews he gives them lessons in good government. 'No enemy, ally, or neutral power, can harm a king who has by degrees tackled and well arranged thirteen kingdoms along with the one which is his own. He should thus arrange relations between his kingdom and each of the three lying in all the directions viz. north, south, east and west, of his own. With the kingdoms adjoining his, he should wage war; with those lying further he should maintain peace, and with the kingdoms on the outermost limit he should keep a system of mutual friendly exchange of gifts. The king who arranges so with the kingdoms lying around his right upto the Sindh country, sleeps the sleep of contentment.'

Allied with his knowledge of statecraft was the Poet's knowledge about horses and horsemanship. At that time the cavalry was one of the most important sections of the army, and horseback the most popular mode of travel. A horse was as important as in the times of King Richard III of England who had said 'A horse ! a horse ! my kingdom for a horse !' Keshava's *Vīrasiṁhadeva Charita* shows the poet's familiarity with horses. At one place in this poem he says: 'The horse who has blue and yellow spots in the eyes will live only ten months, if god so lets him live.'

9. Keshava's Views On Religion—Keshavadāsa's conception about *Brahman* and *Jīva* is more or less the same as found in the *advaitic* doctrine. *Brahman* is beginningless and endless. It is desireless and faultless. The world is produced from it, is sustained in it, and dissolves into it. Its light is ever constant and unfettered. It is limitless, unrestrained, having no limbs and shape. It is not liable to decay or death, motionless, colourless, supreme, imperishable, free from all defect, stainless,

bodiless, invisible, and detached. Brahmā, Viṣṇu, Śiva, and the *Vedas* call it by the epithets 'yosi, sosi'. The same *Brahman* inhabits outside and inside and in each body. It is of the nature of truth and is seen as all the three *guṇas* viz. *rajas*, *sattva*, and *tamas*.

According to Keshava the mundane existence or the visible world is illusion (*māyā*) which is the spouse of Attachment. Blunder and Confusion are the two sons of Illusion which are procreated by her. The working of *māyā* is like the condition of sleep in which the person asleep remains influenced and deluded by many dreams which for the moment he thinks as real; but the effect of *māyā* is long lasting, and one cannot so easily get rid of it.

Imprisoned by *māyā*, the Soul attains various forms. Just as flower even though having shape, form and scent, does not itself understand their nature, so the Soul bound in the net of Illusion and Infatuation does not know his real nature. Just as grains of gold when mixed with iron take the shape of the iron itself, or as a child riding a wooden toy horse begins to imagine he is riding a real one, as girls playing with dolls fancy them to be their sons and daughters, even so is the Soul imprisoned in Infatuation's net. Just as a blind man falling into a well overgrown with weeds does not feel sorry at heart, even so the Soul does not feel sorry though fallen in the darkness of Delusion. Those who bind him with the bonds of love the Soul thinks to be his brothers; and mistaking the poison of worldly pleasures as tasty sweets, he partakes of them. In this manner even though being the controller of worldly pleasures and desires he becomes their slave, and forgetting his real nature begins to find pleasure in these bonds. Just as sound is a quality of the ethereal fluid, but the latter itself knows not the splendour of sound, as the bits of the tree do not know the nature of the fire in the wood even though they burn, as portraits even though having form and shape cannot relate them, even so the foolish souls do not know the power of *Brahman* though it pervades them all.

The unfettered Souls are described by Keshava as those who are extremely pure both externally and internally. These Souls believe in disinterested action. To others they seem on the surface ignorant, but they are really full of wisdom. They think all the creatures of the world one with themselves and have forsaken egotism. Such Souls even though bound in the coils of action are really free. In the *Vijñānagītā* Keshava describes the unfetterd Soul as one who considers joys and sorrows as the same, who remains removed by both desire and desirelessness, who has abandoned egoism, who realizes the real nature of all worldly things, who remains innocent as a child and an enlightened sage, who looks with even-mindedness on himself and other moving and unmoving things in the world.

Higher than the unfettered state of the Soul is its incorporeal state. In this state the Soul begins to understand both the seen and the unseen, and realises that the world is merely an idea. Not desiring anything he considers how he should be one with *Brahman*, and devotes all his endeavour to that end. In this state he is absorbed neither in action nor in non-action and like a lotus in water, remains removed from the world even though being in it. In this state the Soul remains rapt in the Supreme Being.

Keshavadāsa has divided all Souls into three kinds—high low, and middle. The high noble Souls are those who consider god's will as supreme and work according to his desire. These Souls remain ever detached from the world. If for some reason they accidently commit an action which is contrary to the spirit of god's command they punish themselves. They also urge others to tread the good path which they themselves have taken.

The middling Souls are those who are in some measure under subjugation of their minds. When troubled by sorrows and diseases they take shelter in the *Vedas* and the *Purāṇas* and are emancipated through the giving of charity, vows, abstinence, austerity, prayer, and renunciation.

The low, or fallen Souls, are those who have totally forgotten god, and in whom egoism is predominant. Even while giving ear unto the injunctions of the *Vedas* and the *Purāṇas* they cling to various kinds of sinful actions. These Souls are of various classes. According to their actions they keep taking different birth till at their appointed times they attain to god.

According to Keshava the mind is the basis of the entire

creation including things seen and unseen. Creation arises due to the association of god and *māyā*. This association gives birth to mind. The mind has two partners—activity and inactivity. From activity are produced the three worlds, attachment, passion, rage, greed, egoism, thirst, and so on. Wisdom, evenness, contentment, thought etc. are the children of inactivity. The seed of creation of bodies is the good or evil desire which according to love or hatred experiences joy or sorrow.

The various forms existing in creation are not real. The world of illusion and attachment does not contain real truth. Just as a pearl oyster is taken for silver, but when the illusion is removed it is known as an ordinary pearl oyster, even so is the fallacy of this world. All the relations of sons, friends, children, acquaintances etc. are illusory. These relations are established in varying ways, times out of number, and as they are established so also are they ended. Keshava holds that these relations have no significance. As Shrī Kṛiṣṇa says in the Bhagavad Gītā : 'In fact there was never a time when I was not, or when you or these kings were not. Nor is it a fact that hereafter we shall all cease to be.' In like manner, attachment, passion, greed, anger and rapture, do not have any reality, or any firm foundation.

Keshava believes that all the things and relations of the world are transient and momentary. Brahmā, Viṣṇu, Śiva, and others, right down to all visible creatures are all going swiftly towards destruction, the same way as the water of the sea runs of itself towards a submarine fire. Elephants, horses, servants, wealth, the entire earth, and other such things, in brief all material things, are liable to decay. Father, mother friend, son, and even one's own body, abandon us in the end. Considering anything as one's own in this world is foolish. Flies, mosquitoes, mice, cats, worms and birds, all consider the house they inhabit as their own, but in reality it belongs to no one, and to think that it belongs to any is mockery. The associations of this world are as momentary as the company of men who sit for a time on the same boat, or as the clouds which momentarily gather in the sky, or like blades of grass and sedge which come together for a moment and then separate. The Souls of this world come together for a while only and then go their own way as people momentarily collect in some market, road, or marriage party, and then disperse.

Following the traditional view of religious and philosophical thinkers Keshava also considers the world full of sorrows. According to him there is not an iota of happiness in the world, rather endless grief. Even after death, the Soul is not freed from sorrow. It has to take many births and experience great suffering. Right from the time life is formed in the womb, till death, through childhood, youth, and age, the soul undergoes manifold sorrows. Keshava has given a graphic description of the world's suffering in both *Rāmachandrikā* and *Vijñānagītā*.

In order to achieve *moksha*, or emancipation, four things are essential viz. the society of good and pious men, equanimity, contentment, and discernment. According to Keshava, even by cultivating any one of these four, one can gain entry to god, and if one follows by thought and deed all the four with open heart he is freed of all desires and attains his true and pure state.

The good and gentle person, according to Keshavadāsa, is one who remains free from blemish even on entering this dark, dreary, and bottomless, worldly maze. The company of pious men is better than bathing in holy rivers or pilgrimages. Equanimity consists in not being perplexed in any condition whatsoever—whether seeing, talking, hearing enjoying, sleeping, or walking. Contentment is that state in which the mind does not desire to possess anything, or grieve at having lost something gained. To ponder over questions like, 'Who am I ? From where I have come, and where will I go ? What is the truth of it all ? What is my true relationship with my wife, father, and others ?' this is wisdom and discernment.

Another practice which is advocated by Keshava is the control of breath. On this he has laid stress both in *Rāmachandrikā* and *Vijñānagītā*. He did not believe it necessary to abandon the world and live the life of a forest recluse in order to achieve emancipation. The important thing is to have control over mind. If one has right ideas, speaks the truth, remains away from sinful deeds, gives ear to religious discourse, moves in the society of pious men, if there is compassion in his heart, if even while enjoying things he does not become wrapped in them, and if in this manner he has sway over his mind then for such a man both home and forest are the same, and if these things are not in him it is of no avail to take a vow and go into the forest.

Keshava's Rāma is the all-powerful *Brahman* whom the *Vedas* call 'not this, not this'. His light shines as one throughout the entire world. He is revealed by Shaṅkara, the Destroyer. The Creator, Brahmā, keeps beholding his qualities. The great Sarasvatī, goddess of learning, keeps investigating his nature, and the mighty Sheṣanāga cannot grasp him fully even while singing his praises through his many mouths. He has neither form, nor shape, not colour. The *Vedas* call him beginningless and endless. Keshavadāsa's Rāma, however, has a shape and form when he takes birth as man for the sake of his devotees. In the form of Brahmā of *rājasic* quality he creates the world, in the form of the *sāttvic* Brahmā he protects it and as the Brahmā of *tamas* he destroys it. Thus Keshava's Rāma is higher than the *Trimūrti* of Brahmā-Viṣṇu- Mahesha. He is much like the Kṛiṣṇa of the *Gītā* who comes down to earth to help his devotees, to punish the evil-doers, and to re-establish the reign of righteousness upon the earth. According to Keshava chanting of Rāma's name has great significance. He believed that when due to the fall in moral standards in the *Kaliyuga* age, books of religion like the *Veda* and the *Purāṇas* are no longer effective, when people lose faith in prayers and pilgrimage, then the soul finds salvation merely by the chanting of the holy name of Rāma; even if a sinner takes the name of Rāma sincerely he can be saved. Every person can worship the lord and enjoy his grace irrespective of his caste and creed, whether he is a *Brahmin*, *Kshatriya*, *Vaishya* or *Shūdra*, whether a man or a woman—provided he does so with purity of devotion. If he does so he can achieve everything, like wealth, sons, and the like. The chanting of Rāma's name destroys sins, removes desires, and makes one worthy of going to heaven. Keshava himself was more a believer in a god with human form than the formless *Brahman*. He believed in the religion of worldly devotion, in which prayer and worship had foremost place.

10. Keshava's Views About Women—Keshavadāsa follows

the orthodox view about women as existing in his time—that they are an impediment in the realisation of god and the attainment of wisdom. Since passion is against such an end, and the instrument of passion is woman, she is decried and condemned by the devotee. Wherever there is woman there is enjoyment of the senses and pleasure. So by the abandonment of woman only can there be true renunciation, without which happiness is not to be attained. Loving another man's wife is the greatest of all sins, and has been greatly condemned by Keshava. He says that the huge flames of the sin of coveting another man's wife are always burning the lover. Even if there is no physical contact between such a woman and her lover she can captivate him merely by her sight. The crooked mischievousness of the lustful woman's mind is the hook, the carnal desire in her heart is the fleshy bait upon it, and her entire body is the steady string in the hands of Passion the fisherman, for catching the men-shaped fish.

From the customary point of view Keshavadāsa acknowledges the importance of the wife in the social pattern. According to him the man who lives in his house without his wife does not perform his duty. Keshava is also not in favour of a man's becoming a recluse by abandoning his wife. For a man who thus forsakes his wife, residing in the forest is fruitless. A wife without her husband, and a husband without his wife, is like the night without the moon, or the moon's brightness without night.

The position of woman in Hindu *dharma* is inferior to that of man. Man is the master and worthy to be worshipped, and woman is his dependent and slave. This traditional view, which was taken up by Vālmīki, Tulasī, and other outstanding poets, was also endorsed by Keshava. According to him, the husband should be worshipped by the wife in thought, word, and deed, and without serving him, all charity, austerity, and prayer, is of no avail to her. Even if the husband brings sorrow to her, she should think it as her good and so receive it. In the entire world she should consider only her husband as her friend. Only by laying her mind, body , and wealth, at her husband's feet can she achieve emancipation and blessedness. She cannot abandon or forsake her husband, however diseased, incapacitated. or wicked he may be—whether crippled, dumb, deaf, old, a dwarf, diseased, unshapely, pale, or a libertine, gambler, or thief. Even after his death she should not forsake him but rather ascend his funeral pyre and burn herself with him.

For widows Keshava has stern and harsh injunctions, for in this too he adopted the orthodox view. A widow should not seek enjoyment, or take part in laughter and merriment. She should abandon all pleasure-giving things, and all adornments. Leaving all bodily pleasures aside, she should pursue religion with her whole mind, word, and deed. She should control her senses by vows and austerities, and remain subservient to her son for the remaining period of her life. A widow is prohibited from listening to music or songs, from desiring honour or homage. She should not joke or jest with anyone, or use anything pungent, like perfume and the like. She should not drink cold water, not apply oil, and should refrain from all amusements. She should not bathe with cool water, or desire warm water, or sleep on a cot, eat sweets, or wear shoes on her feet.

Keshava's Views On Princely Duties and Good Governmant—Keshavadāsa had full knowledge of the art of government, because he moved intimately in royal assemblies and high political circles. He had opportunity to closely observe the structure of various administrations under the Orchhā rulers—Madhukar Shāh, Indrajīt Singh, and Vīrasiṁhadeva. In Delhi the great Mughal Emperor Akbar and Jahāngīr reigned and Keshavadāsa had the opportunity of observing the progress made by them, too, in this regard. Enriched by this experience the Poet has left a fairly comprehensive account of nature of kings, their policies, and their methods of government.

Keshavadāsa makes King Rāma give some admonitions about good government which largely has its basis on moral principles. Accordingly he charges his sons and nephews not to speak untruth, not to be friends with fools, not to take back a gift of charity once it is bestowed, not to break the bonds of affection once having formed them, not to injure the feelings of a minister or a friend, not to gamble, not to reveal a secret to anyone, not to be obstinate, to visit foreign countries but not to trust the enemy, to give support and protection to the *Vedas*, to be careful of what one eats in an enemy country, not to needlessly trouble the subjects in his Kingdom, to discriminate between the guilty and the innocent before awarding punishment, not to take by force the wealth which belongs to a minor, or a woman, or a respectable person; not to have enmity with *Brahmins*; to consider another's wealth and property as poison, to consider another's wife as his own mother, to remain removed from passion, anger, greed, attachment, vanity, and agitation; to win renown in battle, to cultivate the company of sages and wise men, to consider as well-wishers those who give instruction connected with morality, not to converse with the unrighteous man, not to consider worthy of charity one who is ungrateful, sophistic, lecherous or greedy; to give gifts of charitable donation willed by oneself with his hands to *Brahmins*, and not to get it given to another. The itinerary is long and exhaustive, and can well be an excellent guide not only for kings but for all men.

In *Vīrasiṁhadeva Charita* the duties and responsibilites of kings have been described in even greater detail. The king has been admonished to be truthful, valorous, and pious. If he is brave, men will fear him, if he is truthful he will enjoy everyone's trust, and if he is in addition charitable, he will gain repute. It is expected of a king that he should not take to heart the defects of his ministers and friends. He should not make a foolish and ignorant person a minister, friend, councillor, priest, physician, astrologer, writer, messenger, chamberlain, preacher, and the like. It is the duty of a king to keep his counsel to himself, and to abstain from intoxicating drinks. According to Keshavadāsa the rule of a king who fails to do this is not abiding.

The king should rightfully acquire wealth and look after its safety. Wealth should be expended only for righteous purposes. The king should look after his subjects as though they were his own children, and keeping their happiness and betterment in mind, plan flower-gardens and cisterns throughout his kingdom, and arrange for their benefit, flowers, fruits, medicines, foodgrains, and apparel. The king should appoint suitable officers and officials at various places according to need. The officers so appointed should be courageous, of high and noble character, and loyal. Those who fly from the field of battle or those who submit, should not be killed by the king. The king should distribute the wealth obtained from other kingdoms, by conquest or otherwise, to *Brahmins*, brothers, sons, and friends. Keshava also advocates that a king should , in order to acquaint himself with the true state of affairs in his kingdom, send secret spies, and call them aside in the night and listen to their reports. Messengers should be called into the king's presence one by one, and in order to ensure safety they should not bear arms, but the king should remain armed while receiving them. There should be spies also for keeping an eye on the conduct of the officers of the realm. Good officials should be rewarded by giving them rank, and the wicked ones should be adequately punished.

It is the king's duty to exterminate thieves, highwaymen thugs, unscrupulous and rash persons, and lay down proper punishments in order to check increase in crime in his kingdom, and to punish every evil-doer. While giving punishment he should have no consideration for relationship or caste and should punish even a near relation if he does a wrong. But a *Brahmin*, one's own parents, or a *guru*, should not be punished. Also crime committed by a diseased person, a poor man, an orphan, or a guest, should be punished by banishment or dispossession of property instead of the capital punishment of death. A servant, a mendicant, a debtor or a trustee, a uterine brother, and a disciple, should be treated with consideration, and if in bringing home to them the seriousness of the crime they have committed, they repent, they should not be slain for it.

In *Vijñānagītā*, too, Keshavadāsa has described the principal qualities of kings in the words spoken by Rājadharma to Vivekarāja,— Charity, mercy, understanding, courage, truthfulness, knowledge of the ethics of government and the ability to protect his subjects are, according to Keshava, the main virtues to be looked for in kings. The persons who need to be assisted by the king's charity are those who are learned, the subjugated, the poor, friends, and *Brahmins*. Those who require his mercy are the poor, *Brahmins*, women, and cows. The king should constantly know and be concerned about his domain, wealth, sons, progress etc. He should show courage not only in suppressing his enemies but also in subjugating his senses. In misfortune he should be calm. Both in *Vīrasiṁhadeva Charita* and in *Vijñānagītā*, Keshava makes the king responsible for protecting his subjects from criminals and the anti-social elements, for evolving a rational system of punishment for the guilty, and for enforcing it justly without partiality or favour.

Contemporary Society as depicted by Keshava—In Keshava's time society had fallen into depravity, and there was a decline in moral standards. Kings and courts were plunged in opulence and sensual pleasures. Hypocrisy, ostentation, theft, and licentiousness, were on the increase. The castes had relinquished their respective duties. These conditions have been described by Keshavadāsa in *Rāmachandrikā* and *Vijñānagītā*.

Keshava notices how kings have become greatly attracted towards worldly enjoyments and have forgotten religion and truth, abandoned courage and calmness, and begun to deride preceptors and the injuctions of *Vedas* and *Purāṇas*. They pride themselves only on drinking wine and dallying with wives of others. Their courage lies only in hunting, accounts of which are related by poets with much gusto. Their looking towards anyone means sympathy, and their speaking even a word means affection.

The kings of his time, drunk with power, consider it a great favour on their part if they merely meet someone. Merely talking to one implied respecting him, and considering one near was as if infinite wealth was bestowed. For such kings rightful counsellors were enemies, and flatterers became ministers and friends.

In *Vijñānagītā*, while describing life of Delhi, Keshava tells us that there were a number of people in that city who in the night were engaged in dallying and in flattering, and speaking words of love to coquettish women; and in the morning these same people bathed and put on white dresses and applying *ṭikā* marks on their forheads went round preaching to people to undertake vows and austerities, prayers and sacrifices, pretending to give religious instructions. In Delhi there were a large number of persons who hardly ever gave heed to the injunction of their preceptors, and who knew almost nothing about religious duty, rightful action, oblations, and worship. As a rule people were ignorant of the virtues of charity, ablution, abstinence, and *yoga*, and considered pampering the body and enjoyment of the senses alone as worship of god. The *Brahmins*, who were given the task of expounding the *Vedas* merely rattled off the words without understanding them. Wearing a cloth around the neck such as ascetics wear, having an antelope skin, putting on a garland of beads, having matted hair, and covering the body with ashes, were considered to be signs of worldly detachment. Ascetics who prattled with false and empty reasoning thronged public places. People of low castes proclaimed their excellence by tattooing their bosoms, foreheads. ears, and waists. In this manner, says Keshava, ostentation and prudery were rampant in the society of the times.

In Kāshī (modern Vārāṇasī), the religious centre of Hinduism, too, conditions were not much different. Innocent pilgrims were robbed, and villages were set on fire without compunction by unscrupulous people who outwardly feigned to be holy men braving the bitter cold to bathe in sacred rivers and chanting religious *mantras*. Keshavadāsa mentions that there were a large number of men who would commit theft and adultery, and drink wine in the company of strumpets, and yet have the arrogance to consider themselves interpreters of truth.

Narrating about the *Kaliyuga* in *Vijñānagītā*, Keshavadāsa says that the *Brahmins* of that period behaved like Shūdras while seeming to be engaged in doing lofty and noble actions. Women were attracted to men other than their own husbands whom they left off serving. People began to worship and give charity with hypocrisy and ostentation. The worship of Viṣṇu was on the decline and that of Durgā was gaining vogue. *Brahmins* cared little for the *Vedas*, and were engaged in serving outcastes. The *Kshatriyas* had left off protecting the people, and did not hesitate to plunder the property of *Brahmins* for no fault of theirs. The *Vaishyas* had left off trade and business and had started bearing arms and weapons like the warrior class. The *Shūdras* put ordinary stones in place of idols, and began worshipping them. They would rob and steal and have no fear of the law.

Conditions in the temples had also deteriorated. In *Rāmachandrikā*, Keshava has described their state in the words spoken about a head-priest who was resident of Kannauj. This priest used to adorn the idol well when a wealthy person came into the temple, but on the days no such man came, he would not even lift him from the palanquin. He had collected a large sum of money by accepting gifts, and was always engaged in libidinous activity.

Due to such behaviour on the part of temple priests, the Poet had no regard for them, and considered their very touch to be evil and contaminating.

(C) **Works and Commentators.**

1. Works—There is dfference of opinion amongst various scholars of Hindi literature regarding the number of books Keshava wrote. For the first time the Poet's works were referred to by the French scholar Garcin de Tassy in *Histoire de la litterature hindouie et hindoustanie*. Tassy has mentioned the names of eight works of Keshavadāsa, namely *Rāmachandrikā, Kavipriyā, Rasikapriyā, Vijñānagītā, Ekādashī cha yantra, Bhakta Līlāmṛita, Jaiminī Bhārata* and *Satsaī Dohrā*. Of these the last four have obviously been ascribed by him to Keshava due to some misunderstanding.

Thereafter in *Shivasingh Saroj* there is the following account of Keshavadāsa's works : Keshavadāsa, the *Sanāḍhya Mishra* produced his first work called *Vijñānagītā* for the benefit of Madhukar Shāh, and his work *Kavipriyā* for the prostitute *Pravīṇāraye*. He wrote *Rāmachandrikā* for Indrajīt, Madhukar Shāh's son, and *Rasikapriyā* and *Rāma alaṅkṛita mañjarī piṅgala* for the benefit of scholars. Thus *Shivasingh Saroj* gives the number of works of other scholars like Dr. Grierson, Dr. Suruyakānta Shāstrī, Pandit Kharagjīt Singh Mishra, Sūryanārāyaṇa Dikshit and F. E. Kaye.

Then there are those who have attributed seven works to the Poet. These are the Mishra brothers in *Hindi Navaratna*, GaurīshankarDwivedī in *Sukavi Saroj* (Part I), Dr. Rāmakumār Vermā in *Hindi Sāhitya kā Ālochanātmaka Itihāsa*, and Govindāsa of Chattrapur. Scholars who consider Keshava's works as eight in number, are Panḍit Rāmanaresh Tripāṭhī and Gaṇesh Prasāda Dwivedī. Others, as Lālā Bhagwāndin and Dr. Shyāmsunder Das, have attributed as many as ten works to the Poet.

According to the research reports of the Society for Promulgation of *Devanāgarī* the number of works ascribed to the Poet are mentioned as five or six, while some works are mentioned as belonging to three other poets of similar name, viz. Keshorai, Keshavarāye, and another Keshava (*Jaimun kī kathā*, of Keshorai, *Hanūmān Janmalīlā* and *Bālicharitra* of Keshava, *Kṛiṣṇalīlā* partly written by Keshava, and *Rasalalita* of Keshavaraye). Another small work which the reports of this Society have attributed to Poet Keshavadāsa is *Amighūṁṭ*.

Despite these differences in the views of various scholars regarding Keshava's works, there are nine which firm evidence points as being definitely his. These are as follows :

Works of *Rītikāla* Poetry.

(i) *Rasikapriyā*.
(ii) *Kavipriyā*.
(iii) *Shikhnakh*.
(iv) *Chhandamālā*.

Works of Religious Poetry.

(v) *Rāmachandrikā*.
(vi) *Vijñānagītā*.

Works of Historical Poetry.

(vii) *Vīrasiṁhadeva Charita*.
(viii) *Jahāngīr Jas Chandrikā*.
(ix) *Ratanbāvanī*.

(i) *Rasikapriyā*. This work was primarily written for Indrajit, son of Madhukar Shāh, Keshavadāsa's patron, but the Poet seems also to have had in mind the entertainment of readers of amorous verse. In this book Keshavadāsa has described different kinds of sentiments or emotions which he has classified under nine heads, and also the different kinds of defective sentiments. The sentiments are nine in number, viz. merriment, compassion, fear, valour, dread, wonder, loathing, calm, and love, but prime importance is given to the love sentiment which throws all the others into shade, and the major part of the book is concerned with the various aspects. of love and lovemaking. The defective sentiments are those which are avoided by poets, and these are the conflicting or opposite ones, the insipid nauseous ones, and the vexatious and confounding ones. In the beginning the Poet depicts Kṛiṣṇa (the chief amongst nāyakas) as possessing all the nine different kinds of sentiments, but as the narrative proceeds all the others give place to the primary one of love. Love is described as that state in which the mind dwells on desire for lovemaking and on Kāmadeva, the god of love, who controls all amours. Love has two aspects, viz. union and separation.

The Poem begins in the traditional manner by an invocation to Gaṇesha—the auspicious god of wisdom and the remover of obstacles. Thereafter the Poet goes on to give a vivid description of his native state of Orchhā, and of his benefactors and patrons, after which there is the ninefold classification of sentiments and the twofold aspects of love—viz. parting and meeting. The second chapter deals with the different kinds of *nāyakas.* The third chapter, which is the longest, describes the various types of *nāyikās* grouped according to class, action, arrogance, and age. This includes the famous classification of women which *Vātsyāyana* had made, viz. *Padminī*, *Chitriṇī*, *Shaṅkhinī*, and *Hastinī*. While describing the maiden of wondrous amorous dalliance, the Poet has mentioned two kinds of lovemaking. The first is the external kind like kissing, embracing, touch, and the like, while the other is internal, which finds expression in varied moods of the women. Each of these, viz. external dalliance and internal moods, have seven divisions, which along with the two of which they are parts, form the sixteen types of adornments in which amorous maidens. indulge. In the next chapter of the book we are told about different kinds of union between the lover and the beloved. These are meeting one another personally, seeing a portrait or picture of the loved one, meeting one another in dreams, or hearing the loved one's voice. The fifth chapter begins by describing the passionate desire of a newly-wed wife and goes on to narrate the various ways which the young lovers devise to meet each other, when even after many attempts they are unable to do so. In this chapter also the Poet describes the different places and situations in which lovers meet for the first time. In the sixth chapter the nature and kinds of gestures and expressions are enumerated. Expression is defined as that which is produced by speech, eyes, and mouth, and is said to be of five different kinds. The many types of dalliance are also described. The seventh chapter deals with different kinds of *nāyikās* according to their ages and natures. The types of women with whom conjugal connection is forbidden are mentioned, viz. a relation, the wife of a friend or *Brahmin*, and one who may be willing because of being sorrowful or hungry. Those with whom dalliance should be had after due consideration are said to be a woman of lower or higher caste, one deficient of a limb, a widow, and a pious woman. The eighth chapter deals with the feelings of separated lovers. Love at first sight is described as that feeling which is instantly produced when newly-wed couples see each other, and when not seeing each other they remain sorrowful. Yearning is that condition which arises when the eyes, the heart, and speech, having already met, the bodies, also yearn to meet. The ten states arising from the separation of the beloved are also described. The ninth chapter describes the various kinds of arrogance which are born in women and which keep them away from their lovers, and the tenth gives the different methods by which such arrogance can be removed. The eleventh chapter continues the theme of separation of lovers and defines the nature of such separation when born of compassion, and because of the residence of the lover in a foreign land. The twelfth chapter describes the different kinds of women who serve as bosom companions to the lovers, and assist them in advancement of their suit. The thirteenth chapter describes the different types of behaviour of bosom friends and the ways they adopt in bringing lovers together. Thus the foregoing chapters (which form the major portion of the book), speak in one way or the other of the emotion of love. A description of the remaining sentiments like merriment, compassion, valour etc. is given in the fourteenth chapter. The fifteenth describes other states of emotion consisting of mixed sentiments of the minds. The sixteenth (the concluding chapter) is devoted to a description of defective sentiments which good poets avoid in their writings.

Thus we see that *Rasikapriyā* is mainly devoted to giving an account of the love sentiment in its various aspects, conditions, and possibilities, and this is its paramount importance. The study of this work is of special significance for students and poets writing in Hindi and is an outstanding work on poetic art.

(ii) *Kavipriyā*--This book was written by Keshavadāsa for the instruction of the courtesan—Pravīṇārāye, the beloved of Mahārāj Indrajīt Singh, and his own disciple. The Poet had a special liking for this work, so much so that he called it, 'the beloved of poets, and the very life-breath of their lives'. The book is divided into sixteen parts. It begins with the usual invocation and an account of the time of composition, the king's lineage, and a description of the assembly in the court of Mahārāj Indrajīt Singh and the six courtesans who lived in it. In the second part we have an account of the Poet's lineage. Thus the Poem really begins from the third part which enumerates the defects of poetical composition. The fourth part deals with poetic styles and varieties, and of the sixteen adornments much in the styles of *Rasikapriyā*. The fifth part describes the adornments or embellishments of poetry which are said to be mainly of two kinds—one simple and the second exquisite, the former having four more divisions. Parts five and six describe simple embellishments. In the seventh part we have an account of the early domain with descriptions of the natural scenery and things existing on the earth's surface. The eighth part gives a description of kingship and allied matters, with instructions and admonitions to kings, queens, princes, priests, generals, messengers, ministers, advice regarding counsels and voyages, horses and elephants, huntings and sports in water. Parts nine to fifteen give an account of specific and exquisite embellishments, while the sixteenth and last part deals with uncommon embellishments depending on placement of sounds and words. Examples and illustrations are liberally given throughout the entire book which bring home to the reader clearly the different embellishments and figures of poetic expressions sought to be expressed. The book is an analysis of the poetic art showing much scholarship and erudition. In it Keshava sought to lay down the canons of poetical composition for all time to come, and in this sense there is much of originality in the work.

(iii) *Shikhnakh*. In this small fragment, the date of

writing of which is not free from doubt, Keshavadāsa has described the beauty of various parts of a *nāyikā's* body with the help of examples and metaphors in the old Sanskrit tradition. Thirtyone parts of the body and description of articles used by women, like sarees and ornaments, have been described. These include the female hair, lips, teeth, waist, brow, breasts, waist, etc. Keshava's descriptions of aspects of feminine beauty are charming and interesting, and make pleasant reading.

(iv) *Chhandamālā*. This is Keshava's poetical treatise on the science of prosody in which stanzas containing both long and short vowels have been dilated upon. More consideration has been given to stanzas of longer vowels, presumably because this was the tradition in Sanskrit verse, the influence of which was quite strong when Keshava wrote. The Poem opens with the usual invocation, after which examples and characteristics are given of various stanzas beginning from those of single words to those containing as many as twenty-six. The generic character of *daṇḍaka*, a Sanskrit metre, is then discussed.

This is a specialised work which goes into the technicalities of Hindi poetry, and is of special interest to scholars and critics of verse.

(v) *Rāmachandrikā*. The proof of Keshavadāsa's permanent and undisputed place in Hindi literature is *Rāmachandrikā*. Being Tulasī's contemporary Keshava must have met him sometime or the other. According to popular belief he wrote the book in one night as a rejoinder to Tulasī's calling him an unrefined poet. But this is not borne out by Keshava's own account, according to which the sage Vālmīki appeared to him in a dream and asked him to write it. The sage gave him the *mantra* of Rāma saying, 'Rāma is the only truth, there is no other'. When Keshava asked the saint, 'How can sorrow be removed?' he replied, 'it is Harī (Rāma) who will remove it'. The Poet therefore chose Rāma as his deity and took upon himself the pleasant task of singing the praises of 'that Rāma whose splendour ever shines in the whole universe'.

Though Keshavadāsa based his book on the story of Rāma's banishment, the abduction of his wife Sītā by the demon king Rāvaṇa, the resultant war between the two, and Rāma's final victory and return to his kingdom—yet there is much difference between him and Tulasīdāsa in regard to the treatment and presentation of the theme. Keshava's account is rather unconnected and disjointed, and the incidents in the story are used by him to air his own view about various matters which interested him, like the art of government, the virtues of a good king, the sorrows of youth and age, and the vices of priesthood. While this takes away from the continuity of the narrative and mars the story interest, it makes the work more subjective and introspective. Tulasīdāsa wrote with devotion, and portrayed the characters of his Rāmāyaṇa in the highest and noblest manner. Rāma is the ideal king, Lakshmaṇa and Bharata ideal brothers, Sītā the ideal wife, and so on. Keshavadāsa does not hesitate to criticise the actions of his characters. When after Rāma's banishment, he along with his brother Lakshmaṇa, and his wife Sītā, are going in the forest, Keshavadāsa says : 'Sītā puts her feet on the footprints of her husband Rāma so that her scorched feet may be comforted by their coolth.' How different is this from Tulasī's Sītā who out of consideration and respect for her lord walks so carefully that her footprints fall in between his, for fear of marring them. Where Tulasīdāsa had exhausted his vocabulary in describing the splendour of Rāma, Lakshmaṇa, and Sītā, Keshava describes them in metaphors which throw suspicion on Rāma. He says, 'Seeing them (Rāma, Lakshmaṇa and Sītā) go, people say to Rāma "Either you have forcibly married this royal Princess (Sītā) or she has married you herself of her own desire against the wishes of her parents, and for this reason the two of you are wandering about in hiding in the forest, or have the reputation of being victorious over love, passion, and the entire world, and for fear of Shiva's enmity you are going to reside alone in the forest or you have been cursed by some saint, or you are minded to do some sinful act against a *Brahmin* and will kill someone with a mortal blow.." At another place the Poet compares the exiled state of Rāma to that of a lion, a serpent, a ruddy goose, a *Jawāsā* plant, a black bee, and even to an owl. Keshava cannot forget statecraft while speaking of Rāma. Describing Rāma's method of spying on wrong-doers in his kingdom he says that he used to enter the room where dried fruits were stored, disguised as an indigent beggar, in order to ensure that they were not being pilfered, and in the treasury-room he would enter as a cunning thief. All these epithets and comparisons are derogatory and quite improper when used for a divine personage. Sītā, whom Tulasīdāsa considered the ideal of womanhood, Keshava has compared to a hawk. On the whole Keshava's Rāma is a prototype of the Mughal Emperors, and a person given to sensuous pleasures and human weaknesses. He instantly kills a demon merely because he makes Sītā afeard. He fans Sītā when she is in the forest, and entreats Hanumān to show her to him. While in the royal palace he behaves like the Orchhā rulers or the Mughal Emperors, playing polo, seeing feats of arms, witnessing feasts of love, strolling with Sītā in the arbour, watching the ladies of the court sporting in the water, or enjoying music and dance. Sometimes he is awakened by the thrush, and then he surreptitiously watches lovely women playing in the forest; sometimes he listens to descriptions of the beauty of Sītā's serving maids. Thus Keshavadāsa departs from the devotional view in his depiction of the two main characters of narrative, viz. Rāma and Sītā. The same attitude is noticeable in the other characters of his story, like Bharata, Rāma's brother, Kausalyā his mother, Dasharatha his father, and the like. Keshava pulls down his characters from their high pedestals and divests them of much of their drapings and finery. He castigates Rāma for abandoning Sītā in the forest, and calls Bibhīṣaṇa a coward and a traitor for going over to the enemy side, and an immoral libertine for marrying his elder brother's widow. With all its poetic merit Keshava's book lacks the universal appeal of Tulasī's with the result that while the *Rāmāyaṇa* has come to mean to the Hindus what the *Bible* is for the Christians and the *Korān* for the Muslims, Keshava's *Rāmachandrikā* is mainly a work of poetical erudition for scholars and students of Hindi literature. It is greatly popular even now in the divisions of Bundelkhaṇḍ and Rohilkhaṇḍ, and one of the prominent kings of Bundelkhaṇḍ, Rājā Chatrpāl, is said to have constantly kept a copy of the book by his side.

(vi) *Vijñānagītā*—Keshava's *Vijñānagītā*, which he wrote in *saṁvat* 1667, is a book of metaphysics. It is said that Vīrasiṁhadeva, the ruler of Orchhā, encouraged him to write this book.

The work has twenty-one parts, the first twelve of which

narrate the conflict between Wisdom and Great Delusion, and the remaining nine, the nature of Understanding as depicted through the characters of Prahlād Shikhidhvaja, and Rājā Balī etc. The whole narrative is allegorical in nature.

Wisdom and Great Delusion are two Kings. Sight of Falsehood is the Queen of Great Delusion, and Hopelessness, Thirst, Worry, Scorn etc. are her handmaids. Anger, Passion, and the like are the friends, advisors, and generals of Great Delusion; Sloth and Disease are his warriors, and Duplicity and Guile his messengers. On the other side, Knowledge is the Queen Consort of King Wisdom, and Faith, Compassion and the like are his other queens, while Charity, Attachment, Calmness, Contentment, Even-mindedness, and Self-restraint are his family members. Victory, Good Company, and Kingly Duties, are the ministers of King Wisdom, and Courage his messenger. Great Delusion has made all preparations to annihilate Wisdom, and war is imminent between the two rival forces along with their respective helpers. Great Delusion along with all his allies, moves to storm the citadel of wisdom which is Kāshī (Vārāṇasī). He sends Duplicity, Guile, and his other messengers, ahead, who manage to win over a number of the warriors of the other side. In order to fully depict the greed and covetousness of Great Delusion, he is made to describe expansively how he desires to conquer all the seven islands and the prominent parts of Bhārata (India). In the end King Great Delusion along with his entire force reaches Kāshī, where fierce fighting breaks out between the two armies. Great Delusion is Vanquished, and the Victor, King wisdom, establishes his reign.

In this allegorical account Keshava has treated a serious subject like philosophy with great ease, and has also in parts drawn a vivid picture of society and manners as existing in his time.

(vii) *Vīrasiṁhadeva Charita.* This book was completed by Keshava in the spring of *saṁvat* 1664. The work takes the form of a conversation between the famous idol of Durgā in Orchhā, Charity, and Greed, the object of which is primarily to sing the praises of Vīrasiṁhadeva, the author's patron. There are thirty-three chapters in the book. The first and second are taken up with a debate between Charity and Greed in which each is bent on asserting his eminence. The end of the second part is occupied with an account of the lineage of the rulers of Orchhā. Parts three to fourteen describe the friction and rivalries between the sons of Madhukar Shāh, the Ruler of Orchhā, in order to extend their power, and the various wars waged between the armies of Vīrasiṁhadeva and Akbar. The death of Akbar, and Jahāngīr's ascension are described, and the raising thereon of Vīrasiṁhadeva to the rulership of the entire kingdom of Orchhā. From the fifteenth to the thirty-third chapter we have an account of Vīrasiṁhadeva's daily routine and of his opulence. We have detailed descriptions of the town, lake, flower, garden, palace, the bed-chamber, the beauty of women in their limbs and parts, and the playing of polo by the King. The last few chapters of the book describe the virtue of charity, the duties of kings, and statesmanship. *Vīrasiṁhadeva Charita* is mainly a work in the heroic strain, though there is much more in it also. Its importance is from the historical point of view.

(viii) *Jahāngīr Jas Chandrikā*. This book was written in *saṁvat* 1669 in the form of a dialogue between Effort and Destiny. Each of them tries to establish his ascendancy over the other, and ultimately both go to the god Shiva for his verdict. Shiva asks them to go to the Mughal Emperor Jahāngīr and so both of them repair to Āgrā, the capital of the Empire which is graphically described by the Poet. After going round the city, the two go to the Emperor's assembly. At this stage, the assembly, the ministers, and councillors, and the various *Rājās*, and *Mahārājās* who keep flocking round the Mughal court are described. Finally both Effort and Destiny assume their respective forms and appear before Jahāngīr, who suitably does honour to them and inquires the reason for their coming. On hearing the purpose of their visit he rules that both are equal and have equal place. Thereafter Effort, Destiny, the *Qāzī*, and Poet Keshavadāsa recite stanzas in the Emperor's praise.

This work is of ordinary merit, and while being of historical import, does not tell us anything more about Jahāngīr than we know from the chronicles of his reign.

(ix) *Ratanbāvanī.* This book was written in praise of Kunwar Ratanasena, son of Madhukar Shāh, the Orchhā Ruler. Ratanasena was an undaunted, and courageous prince, extremely conscious of his duty. He opposed the armies of Akbar and died a valorous death in the affray. A singular episode is said to have been the reason which led to Akbar's sending his forces against Madhukar Shāh. According to this story, once the Orchhā Ruler had gone to the court of the Mughal Emperor wearing a robe which did not trail low enough. On the Emperor's asking him the reason for this, the Ruler is reported to have said that the land of his Kingdom was full of thorns and prickles. The Emperor thought his words to be sarcastic and exclaimed in anger that he would see his Kingdom. After a few days Akbar's army invaded Orchhā. This incident has been mentioned by Poet Keshavadāsa in his book.

Ratanbāvanī is written in *Ḍingal*, the language of the poetry of *Rājapūtānā*. Much of it is in verse of six feet, and the entire poem is full of vitality and fervour, and it is the main source of study of the brief but eventful life of Ratanasena.

Of the works of Keshavadāsa, *Jahāngīr Jas Chandrikā*, *Ratanbāvani* and *Vīrasiṁhadeva Charita* are panegyrics of historical value and import, *Vijñānagītā* is a metaphysical work, while *Rasikapriyā*, *Kavipriyā* and *Nakhshikh* are works in the *Rītikāla* tradition, dealing with love, beauty, and the structure of poetry. *Rāmachandrikā* is a work of learning of the highest class, throwing an interesting sidelight on a popular theme.

2. Commentators—Barring Tulasīdāsa's *Rāmacharitamānasa* Nābhādāsa's *Bhaktamāla* and Bihārī's *Satsaī*, Keshava's works have found the largest number of commentators: and in fact seeing their terseness, this was necessary. The commentators on *Rasikapriyā* are, *Sukhavilāsikā* of Sardār Kavi. *Jarovar-Prakāsha* and *Rasagāhakachandrikā* of Surat Mishra (both of which are handwritten). Commentaries on *Kavipriyā* are *Kāshīrāj Prakāshikā* of Sardār Kavi which was written by command of Ishwarī Nārāyaṇa Singh, Mahārāja of Kāshī, *Kavipriyābharaṇa* of Poet Haricharaṇadāsa, *Dhīrakṛita Kavipriyā Tilak* of Poet Dhīr, *Kavipriyā* Saṭīka of Surat and *Kavipriyā kī ṭikā* produced through Pandit Daulatrāma Bhaṭṭ of Asnī. The commentators on *Rāmachandrikā* are Jānakī Prasāda, who in his book *Rāmabhakti*

Prakāshikā (hand-written) has given meaning of difficult words only, and Sardār Kavi of whom mention has been made by Krishnashankar Shukla in his *Keshava kī Kāvyakalā*.

All the above commentaries are in Brajabhāṣā, which was the language prevalent at that time, and they do not have the clarity of modern Hindi. There are no punctuation marks in them, which makes their reading difficult. While being of interest to scholars they do not have much utility now, because most readers are unfamiliar with Brajabhāṣā. In order to make up this deficiency Lālā Bhagwāndīn wrote his commentaries on *Rāmachandrikā* and *Kavipriyā* entitled *Keshavakaumudī* and *Priyāprakāsha* respectively. These commentaries are in greater detail than the ones before, and contain copious notes. The writer has done a great service to readers of Keshava's works by writing them. Another good commentary is by Lakshmīnidhi Chaturvedī (on *Rasikapriyā* and *Kavipriyā*) published by Mātṛi-bhāṣā-mandvi Dārāganj, Prayāga.

(D) Nāyaka and Nāyikā

In Sanskrit love poetry a meticulous classification was made of ladies and lovers called *nāyikās* and *nāyakas* respectively. *Nayikās* were catalogued according to different situation and circumstances, beauty and form. A woman could be one's own wife or another's or a virgin; she could be either young, adolescent or middle-aged; or she could be in different situations in relation to her husband or lover, as for example estranged from him, or preparing to welcome him back, filled with longing for him or deceived by him, and in a fretful mood.

Similar was the classification of lovers and husbands known as *nāykas* (literally 'an eminent person') who were sometimes divided into fourteen types.

Vātsyāyana's famous book *kāma Sūtra* and Kalyāṇa Malla's *Anaṅga Raṅga* were mainly works of erotics, and though they did make certain classifications of men and women according to their build, ardour, and the like, there was no such poetic and imaginative treatment of these as in the later Sanskrit literary works which not only mentioned such classes but also illustrated them by examples of selected verse.

Before Keshavadāsa wrote *Rasikapriyā*, in which he described the various kinds of *nāyakas* and *nāyikās*, some Sanskrit books of this type had already been written, the chief amongst which were *Nāṭyashāstra* of Bharatamuni, *Rasamañjarī* of Bhānubhaṭṭa, *Sarasvatī kula kaṇṭhābharaṇa* and *Shriṅgāra Prakāsha* of Bhojadeva, *Rasārṇava Sudhākara* of Bhūpāla and *Sāhitya darpaṇa* of Vishvanātha. It cannot however be said that Keshava took his conception of the *nāyaka* and the *nāyikā* from any of these writers, because his classification is different from that found in them. Similarly, though Keshava takes some points from *Kāma Sūtra*, *Anaṅga Raṅga*, and *Rasamañjarī*, as for example his description of the types of women (*Padminī*, *Chitriṇī*, *Shaṅkhinī*, *Hastinī*) the literary concept always remains different from the erotic one found in these works. Keshavadāsa has classified all his ideas about love, meeting, separation, moods, arrogance, *nāyakas*, and *nāyikās*, under two main heads, viz. 'hidden' and 'manifest'. This sort of classification is not found in the works of any Sanskrit scholar except Bhojadeva, who in his *Shṛiṅgāra Prakāsha* has mentioned 'hidden attachment' and 'manifest attachment' in the sixty-four kinds of attachments listed by him. It is possible that Keshavadāsa may have followed Bhoja in this, though some scholars do not think so. The other Sanskrit books do not give such a classification at all, and Keshavadāsa could not have adopted them as a model.

(i) *Nāyakas*—According to Keshavadāsa, a *nāyaka* is one who has pride in himself, and who is youthful, yielding, handsome, forgiving, wealthy, prosperous, of virtuous taste, noble descent, and skilled in the art of love.

It would be interesting to compare Keshava's concept with others. According to Vishvanātha (in *Sāhitya-darpaṇa*) a *nāyaka* has the following qualities:

Liberality, gratefulness, wisdom, noble descent, forbearance, handsomeness, youth, exuberance, cleverness, splendour, gentleness, and such excellence as is worthy of imitation by others.

According to Bhūpāla the qualities which are essential in a *nāyaka* are—politeness, bounteousness, firmness, dexterity, splendour, religiousness, noble descent, eloquence, gratefulness, purity, lustre, and skill in the arts.

According to Bhoja the *nāyaka* should be of noble descent,

bounteous, lucky, grateful, handsome, youthful, gentle, proud, commanding respect, and the like.

Keshavadāsa does not appear to have followed any particular scholar in his definition. Rather he seems to have picked out some of the qualities from each of them. In *Rasikapriyā* he classifies all *nāyakas* to be of four kinds—agreeable, upright, deceitful, insolent. He gives their attributes as follows :

Agreeable—According to Keshava the agreeable *nāyaka* is devoted in mind, speech, and action, to his wife, and does not favour other women. He is, therefore, a faithful husband who does not believe in illicit amours. In this Keshava seems to be in agreement with other Sanskrit scholars like Bhūpāla and Vishvanātha, and his characterisation is clearer than theirs.

Upright—Keshava considers an upright *nāyaka* to be one who is devoted to his first love out of fear of inviting opprobrium. Even when his heart is unsteady he does not allow it to be fickle and thus withstands the temptation of being false to his first love. Vishvanātha and Bhūpāla, however, have a different view. According to them an upright *nāyaka* shows equal devotion to different women and thus lacks the constancy of Keshava's *nāyaka*.

Deceitful—Keshava's deceitful *nāyaka* is one whose heart is full of guile, but who disguises his inner feeling by outwardly speaking sweet words, and who has no fear in doing wrong—much like Shakespeare's hypocrite who may 'smile and smile and be a villain'. This view is similar to that of Vishvanātha and Bhūpāla. The former considers a deceitful *nāyaka* as one, who while being attached to another women, outwardly shows devotion to his first love even though he really does not care for her. According to Bhūpāla a deceitful *nāyaka* is one who is foolish and prone to wrong-doing.

Insolent— Keshava's view of an insolent *nāyaka*, which agrees with that of Vishvanātha, is one who has abandoned fear altogether and who does not hesitate to abuse, or even beat his beloved, and who does not acknowledge his fault even when it is clearly pointed out to him.

(ii) *Nāyikās*— The word *nāyikā* literally means, 'a beautiful young woman.' Sanskrit scholars and writers of erotic works like *Kāma Sūtra* and *Anaṅga Raṅga* classify such women into many types according to their looks, characteristics, and passions. Keshava has also divided women into four types, much on the lines of *Anaṅga Raṅga* on the basis of form and other characteristics. Other Sanskrit scholars, however, have omitted such a classification. The different classes mentioned by Keshavadāsa are :

Padminī—The love of a *Padminī* is pleasure-giving and completely engrossing. It conforms most exactly to Lord Byron's idea about a woman's love:

> 'Man's love is of man's life a thing apart
> 'Tis woman's whole existence'.

A *Padminī* woman is beautiful in appearance, her body has natural loveliness and a sweet odour, and her complexion is of the hue of gold. She is bashful, wise, generous, and tender-hearted. She is cheerful, and keeps her body and clothes clean. She eats and sleeps little, and has less of arrogance, anger, and desire for lovemaking than other women. Her private parts are hairless.

Chitriṇī— A *Chitriṇī* type of woman has a liking for dance, song, and poetry. Her mind is calm but her eyes are restless. She is fond of making love. Her seminal discharge is profuse. Her breath is sweetly-scented. She has very few hair on her body and on her private parts, and her odour pleases all. A *Chitriṇī nāyikā* is fond of pictures. Some of the qualities mentioned by Keshava are found in *Anaṅga Raṅga* and a few in *Ratirahasya* of Kokā *Pandit*.

Shaṅkhinī—According to Keshava the *Shaṅkhinī* is expert in showing deceit and displeasure. Her body is moist and beautiful. She has a liking for red garments and finds satisfaction in being marked by nails in lovemaking. She is shameless, fearless, and petulant. Her seminal fluid is pungent and she is much inclined for lovemaking. Some of the qualities of the *Shaṅkhinī* given by Keshava resemble those given in *Anaṅga Raṅga*.

Hastinī— Keshava's *Hastinī nāyikā* has coarse fingers, feet, face, and lips, and her hair is brown. Her speech is biting. Her mind is restless, and her gait slow. Her sweat and seminal fluid smell like the ichor of an elephant in rut, and she has great fondness for amorous dalliance. The account closely resembles that given in *Anaṅga Raṅga.*

The above division is according to physical and emotional characteristics. Keshava has further made a division according to behaviour, and from this point of view he has classified *nāyikās* to be of three kinds—*svakīyā*, *parakīyā*, *sāmānyā*. All scholars, like Dhanañjaya, Vishvanātha, Bhānudatta, and the like, also give a similar classification, but Keshava has not written about the *sāmānyā* (ordinary) *nāyikā* because he has throughout depicted Rādhā, the beloved of Kriṣṇa himself, as a *nāyikā* in his writings, and she cannot be considered at par with an ordinary woman.

Svakīyā—A *svakīyā nāyikā* is one whose behaviour towards the *nāyaka* remains the same in mind, word, and deed, while passing through different circumstances in wealth, during suffering, and in death. This quality of a *svakīyā* is mentioned by Bhūpāla also in *Rasārṇava*.

Of the *svakīyā* Keshavadāsa has given three kinds-- the *mugdhā*, *madhyā* and the *pragalbhā nāyikā*. This division is also traditional and followed by all scholars. The characteristics of these three types have, however, not been mentioned by Keshava.

Mugdhā—Of the *mugdhā nāyikā* Keshava has given four further sub-divisions. These are *navavadhū*, *navayauvanābhūṣitā*, *navalaanaṅgā*, and *lajjāprāyarati*. The characteristics of these different kinds of *mugdhā nāyikās* have also been given by him. The *navavadhū mugdhā* is one, the beauty of whose body increases day by day, the *navayauvanābhūṣitā mugdhā*, who has passed her girlhood and has entered into youth, the *navalaanaṅgā* who talks and plays as children do, and laughs and shows fright amorously. The *lajjāprāyarati mugdhā* is a maiden who is bashful in love-making. Further speaking of the *mugdhā nāyikā* in general Keshava says that even in a dream she finds no pleasure in entering into amorous dalliance, and that mostly she does not show any arrogance, and even if she should, her arrogance can be removed like that of a child's by frightening her.

Vishvanātha has given five classifications of a mugdhā, and Bhūpāla six. Despite some similarities they are on the whole on different lines.

Madhyā— Keshava mentions four kinds of *madhyā nāyikās*, *madhyārūḍhayauvanā*, *pragalbhavacanā*, *prādurbhūtamanobhavā*, and *vichitrasuratā*. The first kind is one who is in the prime of life, full of good fortune and prosperity, and loved by the *nāyaka*. The second kind is one who makes complaints and shows alarm; the third kind is whose mind and body is wholly employed in the arts of lovemaking, and the last, the *vichitrasuratā*, is one who tries curious methods of lovemaking. Vishvanātha has given five kinds of *madhyās*. He too mentions the *surativichitrā* who is the same as Keshava's *vichitrasuratā*. Of her Vishvanātha says :

'At the time of lovemaking that lustful woman, whose passion was aroused, showed such uncommon ingenuity, that many a time her tamed pigeons, imitating her cries of ecstasy, seemed as if they were her disciples.'

Keshavadāsa, too, describes in *Rasikapriyā* the lovemaking of his *vichitrasuratā* in a similar vein: 'In which there is playful soft laughter, the supreme pleasure of sight and love-talk, seven kinds of lovemaking in thought and action, and reversed roles of the lovers; in which bashfulness is forgotten, clothes and ornaments lie scattered, hearing the shouts of ecstasy of which even the birds begin to shout—that indeed is true lovemaking, all else is mere observance.' From these similarities it seems that Keshava followed Vishvanātha in his divisions of the *madhyā*. Three further divisions have been made of the *madhyā nāyikā* from the point of view of behaviour. These are *dhīrā*, *adhīrā*, and *dhīrādhīrā*. According to Keshava the *dhīrā* uses sarcasm in her dealings with the *nāyaka*, the *adhīrā* speaks sharply to him, and the *dhīrādhīrā* reproaches him. While the conception of *dhīra* and *adhīrā* is found in the work of Vishvanātha that of *dhīrādhīrā* is found neither in his work, nor in that of Bhūpāla.

Pragalbhā— Of the *pragalbhā nāyikā* (the bold type of woman), Keshava has mentioned four kinds— *samastarasakovidā*, *vichitravibhramā*, *ākramatī*, and *labdhāpati*. The nature of the first has not been clearly defined. A *vichitravibhramā* is one who has subjugated her lover by means of her speech, mind, and actions, and the *labdhāpati nāyikā* who regards her elders as much as she does her husband.

Bhūpāla has given only two classifications of a *prauḍhā*, viz.

sampūrṇayauvanonmattā and *rūḍhamanmathā*, the former being one who while making love clasps her lover so tightly that it seems she would enter into his body. The *rūḍhamanmathā* is one who swoons with pleasure even at the beginning of lovemaking. Vishvanātha has given six classifications. Parallel to Keshava's *vicitravibhramā* is Vishvanātha's *bhāvonnatā*, the nature of whom he has narrated thus: 'Chiding by her soft words, contractions of her eyebrows, and by her fingers that *nāyikā* assists Kāmadeva (the god of love), in winning all the three worlds by the various contacts of her body, by her love cries at the time of lovemaking, and by her sidelong glances. Describing his *vichitravibhramā prauḍhā*, Keshava says, 'Her gait is gentle and bewitches the mind, seeing which desire arises in the heart of Kṛiṣṇa. He is attentively viewing the playfulness of her eyebrows, her soft laughter, and the splendour of her limbs. Seeing her sidelong glance, Kṛiṣṇa is becoming verily Kāmadeva, who forgetting his arrows of flowers thinks that her eyes themselves are passion's darts. Scholars have given three more classifications of a *pragalbhā nāyikā* (as for the madhyā) viz. *dhīrā*, *adhīrā* and *dhīrādhīrā*. The *dhīrā nāyikā*, according to Keshava, hides her anger and pretending to be friendly, conceals dishonour in honour, the *adhīrā* considers her lover to be a wrong-doer and does not befriend him, while the *dhīrādhīrā* speaks harshly to her lover even though she loves him from her heart.

Vishvanātha has also given such a classification. His *dhīrā*, like Keshava's, hides her anger and reveres and honours her husband by external words, but remains indifferent in lovemaking, the *adhīrā* chides and admonishes, while a *dhīrā-dhīrā* speaks in a tone full of sarcasm. We can see that there is considerable similarity between Keshava and Vishvanātha about these kinds of *pragalbhā nāyikās*.

Parakīyā—Keshava's view of the *parakīyā nāyikā* is rather singular. According to him her lover is not an ordinary person, but the supreme Brahmā himself. There are two kinds of parakīyās, *ūḍhā* (married) and *anūḍhā* (unmarried). Though other Sanskrit scholars describe the *parakiyā* also, they too do not give any further sub-divisions except the ones given by Keshava.

Nāyikās according to Situations—Sanskrit scholars

have classified nāyikās according to situations as being of eight types, viz. *svādhīnapatikā*, *virahotkaṇṭhitā*, *vāsakashayyā*, *kalahāntaritā*, *khaṇḍitā*, *proṣitapatikā*, *vipralabdhā*, and *abhisārikā*. Keshvadāsa has to a large extent followed this classification. There are minor differences between various scholars in their descriptions about such *nāyikās*, but by and large they follow the same pattern.

Keshava describes the *svādhīnapatikā* as one whose husband is devoted to her, and always lives with her. The *virahotkaṇṭhitā*, whom Keshava calls by the name of *utkā*, is one whose lover cannot for some reason come to her house, and she remains thinking about him. The *vāsakashayyā* (or *vāsakasajjā*) keeps glancing at the door of her house, each moment expecting her lover back. The *kalahāntaritā*, whom Keshava calls *abhisandhitā* does not pay any regard without him. The *khaṇḍitā* is the *nāyikā* whose lover, not coming at the appointed time, comes early next morning bearing signs on him of the enjoyment of another woman. The *proṣitapatikā* is one whose lover goes away on some business for a fixed period. The *vipralabdhā* is one whose lover summons her to the appointed place of meeting through a messenger, but does not come, and not finding him there she becomes sorrowful. The *abhisārikā* is one who impelled by love, elation. and passion, goes to meet her lover.

Having described his *nāyikās*, Keshava goes on to say how different kinds of women go to meet their lovers. The *svakīyā abhisārikā* decorated with ornaments etc. walks to her tryst with faltering steps, accompanied by her friends, with great bashfulness. The *parakīyā abhisārikā* walks bashfully, her feet avoiding the path she goes on, accompanied by her maidservant, bosom companion, and trusted friends. The *sāmānyā abhisārikā* dresses in blue clothes and with surprise and boldness goes to the meeting place at mid of night. The *sāmānyā nāyikā* goes decked with cosmetics and ornaments, dauntlessly, laughing, and staring all around, captivating people's minds. She walks slowly with a flower in her hand accompanied by her paramour, friends, and companions.

In these descriptions Keshava seems to have followed Vishvanātha to some extent, but the characteristics of the *nāyikās* mentioned by him are his own.

Nāyikās According to Arrogance—Keshava has mentioned yet another three classes of *nāyikās* viz. *uttamā*, *madhyamā*, and *adhamā*. The *uttamā* shows arrogance on being affronted, and on being honoured relinquishes it, and is pleased when she sees her lover. The *madhyamā* shows arrogance even on a minor transgression on the *nāyaka's* parts and leaves it only on great entreaty, while the *adhamā* shows arrogance many a time, but is appeased very soon.

Bhoja and Vishvanātha have made a passing reference to these *nāyikās* but have described their characteristics, while Bhūpāla has given their qualities as well, which, however, do not agree with those given by Keshava, except, to some extent, for the *uttamā*.

Women with whom Cohabition is Prohibited.—At the end of the seventh chapter of *Rasikapriyā* Keshava has enumerated those women with whom amorous alliance is forbidden. No such description is forthcoming in the books of Sanskrit scholars, and in all probability Keshava has taken as his source material for this, the account of such women in *Kāma Sūtra* and *Anaṅga Raṅga*. According to Kalyāṇa Malla the women who should not be enjoyed are, the wife of *Brahmin*, of a priest, of a *Kshatriya* (the warrior class), of a friend or foe or relation, or a virgin who is not one's wife, a widow, a chaste woman, the wife of a pupil or disciple, a defiled or a mad woman, a woman older than oneself, the wife of a *guru*, a pregnant woman, a woman whom one does not know, a sinful woman, and a woman whose complexion is black or yellow. According to Vātsyāyana women who are not to be enjoyed are, lepers, lunatics, outcastes, a woman who reveals secrets, who is extremely white, or black, or evil-smelling, or one who openly expresses a desire for sexual congress, a friend, a near relation, a pious woman, the wife of a relation, friend, learned *Brahmin*, or of the King.

(iii) Meeting Places of Lovers.—The places and occasions where lovers meet for the first time have been enumerated by Keshavadāsa. These are the homes of a servant, bosom companion or nurse, or some other lonely house, on pretence of merry-making or disease, on the occasion of invitation to a feast, or in a forest abode. Bhūpāla and Bhoja have not mentined about such places. Vishvanātha however has given some places where the *abhisārikā nāyikā* meets her lover. These are fields, large wells in which there are steps to descend and bathe, funeral places and cemeteries, forests, temples, the house of a female messenger, riversides, lonely houses far from the roadside, and so on. While some places are those mentioned by Keshava, others are new.

(iv) Signs of a Woman's Amorousness— The *Rasikapriyā* mentions ways in which a young woman expresses her love. When her lover looks somewhere else, she looks at him fearlessly, and when he chances to gaze on her, she embraces her bosom companion in order to let him thereby know the desire she possesses for him. In like manner, sometimes she scratches her ear, and at times stretches her limbs lazily, and yawns over and over again. She often laughs while speaking to her friend, and on some pretext or the other bares her limbs for her lover to see. We find an account of such devices used by women in *Kāma Sūtra* and *Anaṅga Raṅga*. In Anaṅga Raṅga the signs of a woman's amorousness are mentioned thus: 'She smooths her hair often, and scratches her head to attract her lover's attention. She strokes her cheeks. She draws her dress over her bosom, and under pretence of adjusting it leaves her breasts partly bare. She bites her lower lip, looks as if she were ashamed, and sits in a corner pretending to be engrossed in some thought. She embraces her bosom companions, laughing loudly the while speaking sweely, joking, and jesting. She often kisses any young children who are nearby, and hugs them to her bosom. She smiles, walks indolently, and stretches herself, often looking at times at her shoulders, or under her arms. She stammers, sighs, and sobs, without any apparent cause, and yawns. She puts herself into her lover's way to attract his attention.' Vātsyāyana mentions the following main signs in woman who shows her love. 'She does not directly look at her lover, and when he gazes at her she becomes abashed. She shows him her limbs on some pretext. and when he moves away she casts a covert glance at him. When he speaks to her she looks down and answers indistinctly in incomplete sentences. She shows delight in his company, speaks to her maid-servants strangely, so that her lover's attention may be drawn to her. She draws him into long conversation to be able to talk to him for as much time as possible, and makes him interested in objects all around. She kisses and embraces a child in his presence, and marks the foreheads of her maids with the auspicious mark, and when they jest with her she makes sportive movements of her body'.

(v) Helpers and Go-betweens—In *Rasikapriyā* Keshava has described the different kinds of friends and helpers of the *nāyikā* who are useful in bringing her to her lover. These are her nurse, maid-servant, a barber's wife , a neighbour, an actress, a gardener's wife, a female betel-leaf seller, a female bangle-seller, a female artist, a female goldsmith, a woman of mixed caste, a female ascetic and the wife of one who works on ornaments with gold thread. Vishvanātha mentions such go-betweens, classifying them into a friend , a female nurse, an actress, a maid-servant, a neighbour, a female ascetic, a washer-woman, a female artist, and a young girl. Kalyāṇa Malla and Vātsyāyana too describe them on similar lines, the former mentioning in addition a widow, a domestic servant, a dyer's wife, a female beggar, and a cowherd maiden.

Keshavadāsa also gives us an account of the conduct of the bosom friends of *nāyikā's* and the relations existing between the two of them. In the Hindu society of that time in which men and women could not freely mix, friends were very helpful in bringing about a meeting. In *Rasikapriyā* Keshava mentions the services done for the *nāyikā* by her near companions. They instruct her in the art of love, appease her when she is sulky, reunite her with her lover, adorn her body, and bend her into humility when she is beset by arrogance. Other Sanskrit scholars have made no mention of this.

Vātsyāyana has given the ways in which the go-between turns the mind of the lady towards her lover. She should talk so to the man's wife that she becomes indifferent towards her husband, praising her beauty, wisdom, and generosity, and condemning his dullness, meanness, and other faults. When she has thus created a rift between the two she should extol the virtues of the lover. Thereafter she should show the woman all the expensive gifts which her lover has sent, expressive of his desire, like rings, perfumes, ornamental figures and the like, and persuade her to send gifts in return. After presents have been exchanged thus, she arranges a meeting between the lovers at a suitable place, as in a fair, a theatrical performance, or bathing-*ghāṭ*.

(vi) Arrogance and its Removal—One of the main hurdles in 'the course of true love' is arrogance. When this takes hold of the *nāyikā* she cannot freely express her love which is stifled in her as a beautiful flower in thorny weeds. When the consciousness of loveliness creates vanity in the mind of the woman, arrogance arises, and this acts as a screen between her and her lover. Such arrogance has three types or degrees of intensity, namely great, small, or middling. Such a conception is not found in any of the Sanskrit scholars. According to Vishvanātha arrogance is of two kinds, viz. the one arising due to respect and the other due to jealousy. Of that arising from jealousy there are three further types, *utsvapnāyita*—when the *nāyaka* mumbles in his sleep about another woman, *bhogāṅka*-sambhava—when the *nāyikā* sees on her lover signs of his having enjoyed another woman, and *gotraskhalanasambhava*—when she hears her lover utter all of a sudden, by chance, the name of some other woman. According to Bhūpāla arrogance is of two kinds: *sahetu* and *nirhetu*. The former arises from jealousy, which is of four types viz. produced by sight , by knowing of another woman's enjoyment, by hearing about another woman from the *nāyaka* himself, and through hearing from another. The divisions are more or less those of Vishvanātha. Keshava too has followed these two writers to some extent in his definitions of various kinds of arrogance viz. great, small, and middling. Great arrogance is that which is produced in the *nāyikā* when she observes on the *nāyaka* signs of enjoyment of another woman, or hears him take her name. Small arrogance arises in the lady when she catches the *nāyaka* looking towards another woman, or hears through her friend of his fondness for such a woman. Middling arrogance arises when the *nāyikā* observes her lover conversing with some other maiden.

Then we come to the ways in which arrogance arising in a *nāyikā* can be removed. In this too, with minor deviations, there is agreement between Keshava and the Sanskrit scholars Bhūpāla and Vishvanātha. Arrogance can be removed by speaking gentle words, giving gifts, sowing disunion, by humility, by indifference, and by destruction of attachment. When arrogance is removed by captivating the mind in some manner it is the way of gentleness; when it is done by giving gifts on some pretext it is the method of giving gifts; when by winning over the bosom friends of the *nāyikā* to one's side, the way of sowing discord. When the *nāyaka* falls on the lady's feet, either out of passionate desire or to own up his fault, it is the method of humility. When arrogance is removed by leaving off all entreaty for its removal and diverting the woman's mind by other talk, it is the way of indifference, and removing it by instilling fear in the beloved's mind is the method of destruction of attachment.

Apart from these specific methods, Keshava says that arrogance can sometimes be destroyed easily by hearing melodious music, beholding things full of loveliness, seeing places, and by the use of scents.

In his treatment of the *nāyaka-nāyikā* theme Keshava has mainly followed the old Sanskrit scholars— Bharata Muni (*Nāṭyashāstra*), Bhūpāla (Rasārṇava-Sudhākara) and Vishvanātha (*Sāhityadarpaṇa*), though at the same time it cannot be denied that he made some deviations from the pattern laid down by these writers which prove his originality. We do not find mention of Keshava's deceitful *nāyaka*, the *madhyā dhīrādhīrā*, and *prauḍhā adhīrā nāyikās* anywhere in the writings of Sanskrit scholars. So also the classification of *nāyikās* into *uttamā*, *madhyamā* and *adhamā* is peculier to Keshava. Sanskrit scholars too did not classify their *nāyikās* according to physical and emotional characteristics like the *Padminī*, *Chitriṇī*, *Shaṅkhinī* and *Hastinī*. Keshava introduced this new element in his poetry, following closely the example of the erotic writers *Vātsyāyana* and Kalyāṇa Malla. So too is the case with his account of women with whom sexual relation is forbidden.

(E) Emotions

In the sixth part of *Rasikapriyā*, Keshava has defined emotion, or sentiment, as being the heart's message expressed through the mouth, eyes, and the voice. Sentiment is related to be of five different categories, viz. disjointed, positive, virtuous, steady, and unchaste. The disjointed sentiment is that by which the various pleasures of the world increase all of a sudden. These are further subdivided into two types, namely supporting and exciting, the former aiding pleasure and giving more bliss, and the latter creating excitement. The former (viz. supporting disjointed emotion), is produced by sights of nature such as blossoming flowers , blue lakes, the sky, spring groves, dark rain-bearing clouds and the like; while the exciting disjointed emotion has its birth in the various items of love-making like inflicting nail-marks, kissing, loud cries of love, conversation, sight, and touch. The significance of the second sentiment mentioned by the Poet (viz. the positive) is not clear. The steady emotions are love, laughter, sorrow, anger, zeal, fear, scorn, and amazement. The eight virtuous emotions are firmness, those causing perspiration and horripilation, loss of voice, trembling, exposition, tears, and conversation. The unchaste emotions are remembrance, fickleness, shame, contempt, indifference, weariness, doubt, labour, intoxication, care, rage, pride, joy, excitement, scorn, sleep, debate, stupor, craving, dream, wisdom, sorrow, epilepsy, violence of the mind, hope, argument, great perplexity, frenzy, death, fear, and bodily disease.

Keshavadāsa also describes two kinds of emotions which are peculiar to Rādhā and Kṛiṣṇa. One is the emotion of delight which makes bashfulness fly at the touch of perfect love, and the other is the emotion of amusement in which the lover and the beloved cause much amusement by disguising themselves as each other.

The elegant emotion is produced in speaking, laughing, and beholding the elegant gait of the beloved; that of ecstasy is born with the passage of childhood into youth; that of perplexity when due to excess of love the lady wears all her ornaments the wrong way, and intense pleasure causes her to melt as it were. Then there is the emotion in which bashfulness is so great that the lady cannot speak; the emotion of amorous gestures, where pride, laughter, joy, rage, and fear, all arise at once; the emotion of slight where due to the vanity of love and beauty the woman shows disrespect to her husband; the emotion of breaking up, where the maiden decked with all her ornaments yet causes dishonour ; the emotion of suppression where the pure sentiment of bashfulness is suppressed by the use of wisdom; the emotion of quarrelsomeness where the lovers pretending to quarrel, engage in the sweet give and take of lovemaking; and finally the emotion of perception where the secret intent of one is understood by the other.

Thus Keshavadāsa has given us a panoramic view of the various emotions which arise in the minds of lovers. In his interpretations he has followed more or less the Sanskrit scholars Bharata, Bhūpāla and Vishvanātha.

Keshavadāsa has given top place to the emotion of love. He has called it 'the leader amongst emotions'. This view finds support in both Hindi and Sanskrit scholars. Bharata Muni the earliest commentator wrote, 'all those things of the world which are pure, eminent, and agreeable, fall under the domain of love,' thus choosing Shelley's famous stanza:

> 'All thoughts, all passions, all delights,
> Whatever moves this mortal frame,
> Are all ministers of love
> And feed his sacred flame.'

Maharṣi Vedavyāsa, too, has given prominence to the emotion of love in Agnipurāṇa. He says 'From the *ahaṅkāra* of the Parama Brahma Paramātmā arose egoism, and from the transformation of egoism arose love. Therefore love is the primary emotion, and all others were born after it. Love is the source of creation and the basis of the illusion of the world.' Although some scholars have given equal importance to the emotions of compassion and heroism, most have put love over them all, while some have even held love to be the only emotion, and all the others merely its products. Hindi scholars like Deva and Keshavadāsa, follow the same tradition. Describing the characteristic of love, Keshavadāsa says, 'it is where thoughts are expressed about the desire for enjoyment of love, and about Kāmadeva who is love's partner.' Other emotions have also been described by Keshava. Special attention has been given to that of laughter which is said to be born where delight is produced by the endeavours of eye and speech. Four kinds of laughters are described—feeble, sweet, violent, and loud, and the detailed nature of each is related. Tenderness is described as the emotion following separation from one who is beloved, violence is produced by rage in which the body becomes heated and at strife, the heroic sentiment arises from enthusiasm, dread from fear, the loathsome from abhorrence, wonder from astonishment or surprise, and evenness when the mind being dejected from all quarters settles at one place. According to convention in Sanskrit and Hindi literature, emotions are given colours which go with their natures. Following this tradition Keshava has assigned black to love, white to laughter, a pigeon's hue to compassion, red to violence, white to heroism, black to awe, blue to loathsomeness, and yellow to wonder. The same is the view of Bharata Muni in *Nāṭyashāstra.*

In his treatment of emotion and of estrangement of lovers, Keshava takes a new line. Similarly the narration of various devices and artifices resorted to by lovers in meeting each other, and the assistance given therein by their friends and helpers (for which again Keshava went to the writers of erotics), enriched his poetry and showed a departure from the tradition set by previous poets. This can be seen in his description of the various opportunities and places for the first meeting of lovers, the instruction in love given to the *nāyikā* by her close female friends, their pleadings and appeasement, their ways of bringing her close to her lover, beautifying her with ornaments, making her listen to her lover's suit, and chiding her when she is proved wanting. In all these descriptions, and also in narrating certain types of amorous dalliance, Keshava treads new ground.

(F) The Kinds of Poetry

Towards the end of *Rasikapriyā* Keshavadāsa describes all verse to be of four kinds— *Kaushikī*, *Bhāratī*, *Ārabhaṭī*, and *Sāttvikī*. The first is that in which merriment, love, and tenderness are blended together, and in which simple and expressive words are used. The *Bhāratī* verse is one in which feelings of heroism, wonder, and merriment are contained, and whose meaning is delightful. The *Ārabhaṭī* is that in which there are violence, dread, loathing, and alliterative words having double meanings. *Sāttvikī* verse is that in which wonder, heroism, and calmness, mingle in equal measure, and whose sense is understood instantly. This is poetry of the purest kind. Various illustrations of these four kinds of verse have been given by Keshavadāsa.

Vishvanātha has not given any account of verse patterns. Bhoja has mentioned them but he has not given the emotions comprising different types of verse. Bharata Muni and Bhūpāla have, however, described the types of verse with all these details. Keshava seems to have followed Bharata Muni in his description.

Defects noticeable in poetry have also been enumerated by Keshava with the caution that they do not deserve too much attention lest one be obsessed by them. These defects are mostly due to the presence of contrary or irreconcilable emotions in the same piece of verse.

Keshava made the study of the poetic art more systematic by thoroughly investigating in detail the various kinds of divisions of poetry in a scientific manner—an investigation which was continued by poets who came after him, like Matirāma, Deva, Bhikhāridāsa, and Padmākara. In this way Keshava can be said to be the founder of the Technical and Scientific School of Hindi Poetry.

(G) Rādhā and Kṛṣṇa

The Hindi *Rītikāla* poets use the words *nāyaka* and *nāyikā* symbolically. Literally *nāyaka* means 'a guide', 'a leader' or 'an eminent person', and *nāyikā* means 'a beautiful young woman'. Thus the words can be used for any man or woman having good and outstanding qualities. Sometimes, however, a poet writing about a *nāyikā* would think of some woman whom he himself loved, and then his descriptions would be based on his ideas about that particular woman. Then again it was possible that neither an unknown woman, not a particular one beloved of the poet was meant, but Rādhā, the beloved of Kṛiṣṇa, herself. Bihārī's *nāyikā*, for example, stood for some unknown woman, and at times for Rādhā, while that of Ghanānanda was often for a courtesan in the Mughal court, whom he loved and gave the name of Sujān. In Keshava's *Rasikapriyā* the words *nāyaka* and *nāyikā* implied Kṛiṣṇa and his beloved Rādhā. This was nothing new, for a lot of poetry had been written round the loves of Rādhā and Kṛiṣṇa before him.

Jayadeva's *Gīta Govinda* which was written towards the close of the twelfth century, was mainly about the rift between Rādhā and Kṛiṣṇa, caused by the latter's love for other cowherd maidens, the sorrow of Rādhā due to this, and her subsequent rapture when her lover came back to her. In the beginning of the poem we are told how Kṛiṣṇa, his foster father Nanda, and Rādhā the daughter of Vṛiṣabhānu, whom Kṛiṣṇa loves, are going through a dense forest, when all around dark clouds begin to gather. Fearing that the boy Kṛiṣṇa may lose his way, Nanda asks Rādhā to guide him home. Being inflamed with love, the two begin an amorous dalliance in the forest. Later, Kṛiṣṇa forsakes her, and begins to sport with other cowherd girls, which gives Rādhā great sorrow and anguish. She broods over this change, and keeps desiring for Kṛiṣṇa in her heart. Ultimately Kṛiṣṇa repents his cruel behaviour and leaving the cowherd girls, comes back to Rādhā and they enjoy their bliss together.

Jayadeva's poem, which was written in Sanskrit, described poignantly Rādhā's longing, her jealousy, her bitterness at Kṛiṣṇa's abandonment, and her passionate fulfilment when she is reunited. The poem soon became well known and was imitated by a number of poets. During the fifteenth and sixteenth centuries there were many poets writing on this theme, prominent amongst them being Vidyāpati and Chaṇḍīdāsa, who took up the subject of the loves of Rādhā and Kṛiṣṇa much in the manner of Jayadeva. In a different strain, and writing with devotion, were Mīrābāī, Sūradāsa, Kṛiṣṇadāsa, and others. Keshavadāsa followed closely on Sūra, and in *Rasikapriyā* carried on the same tradition. These poets however widened their scope, and depicted all the various aspects of lovemaking while describing the Rādhā-Kṛiṣṇa attachment, like meeting, separation, descriptions of the beauty of limbs, love lessons given to Rādhā by her near friends and by her serving maids, arrogance and how to remove it, trysts, assignations, coquetry, love pangs, and amorous dalliance.

The source of the Rādhā-Kṛiṣṇa cult lies in the *Vedas* and the *Upaniṣads*, and its germs are the *Bhakti* movement and the devotion of Chaitanya. The *Vedic* hymns sing the praises of the gods. In the *Kaṭha Upaniṣad* and the *Muṇḍaka* we are told that god can only be attained by one whom he chooses: 'God is not reached through discourses, nor by intelligence, nor by much learning. He can only be realised by him whom he chooses. To such a one he reveals himself.'

The *Upaniṣads* describe *Brahman* as bliss and the source of all human joys. The *Bhagavad Gītā* also enjoins complete devotion to god:

> To me for shelter come, be not aggrieved—
> All works abandoned; unto me alone;
> And from all burdens thee I will release.

The Bhāgavata religion, which is the religion of devotional love for god, lays stress on grace. The *Mahābhārata*, too, teaches that only he can see god to whom he becomes gracious. In the south of India the Bhāgavata religion gave rise to the *Alvars*, who flourished in the seventh or eighth century. The word *Alvar* means one who having a deep intuitive knowledge of god, is ever contemplating him. According to them one of the ways of expressing devotion to god is through the relationship of the lover and the beloved. Mammarvar, one of the *Avlars*, was so intoxicated with the love of god that he behaved like an expectant bride going to meet her husband. Vallabha, the Indian philosopher, conceived of *Bhakti* as being intense love for god. The highest type of devotee, according to him, is filled with the love of Kṛiṣṇa alone, and surrenders everything else—wife, home, children, and friends—to him. *Bhakti* comprises of service and love.

The doctrine of *Bhakti* was given a concrete shape by Chaitanya, a saint of Bengal. He devised the way of *Saṅkīrtana* i. e. singing the name of god loudly in chorus, which is even now a popular method of worship. He renounced the worldly life at an early age and travelled all over northern India, making disciples, and chanting the name of god. The sight of a blue sky would bring to him the remembrance of Kṛiṣṇa (who was dark of hue), and throw him into a trance. The last twelve years of his life passed thus almost incessantly in joyful communion with Kṛiṣṇa, but often in excruciating pangs of separation from him—identifying himself with Rādhā the beloved of the god. Chaitanya believed that Kṛiṣṇa performed *līlā* (or love play) with the *gopīs* (milkmaids) of Vṛindāvana. This sport was called *rasa* that which is relished, signifying that he relished the love play with the maidens. According to the intensity of their love the devotees were divided into four classes: (i) *Dāsya bhaktas*—those who love as a servant would love his master. (ii) *Sākhya bhaktas*—love of comrades who are nearly of the same age as Kṛiṣṇa. These consider themselves equal in all respects to him, and sing, dance, eat, and sleep together. (iii) *Vātsalya bhaktas*—the love of those who consider themselves the parents of Kṛiṣṇa, and love him as they would their own child. (iv) *Kānta bhaktas*—the love of youcthful maidens known as *gopīs*, the chief of them being Rādhā. In the *gopīs*, love has reached its utmost limit, and the state of their love is called *mādhurya* (i. e. love of god as one's lover). It must not be supposed that there is anything carnal in the love of the *gopīs*. It is not a love for the sake of personal pleasure, but one in which there is annihilation of the self. It is not a love which restricts, but one in which there is unrestricted bliss, only a brief glimpse of which is experienced in sexual satisfation. The sport of Kṛiṣṇa with the *gopīs* has two aspects, the manifest and the unmanifest. Usually such sport cannot be seen by the worldly-minded, hence it is unmanifest; but some are pure of heart and can see it through his grace, and then Kṛiṣṇa comes down to earth in human guise, and they pass through all stages of human life. This is manifest *līlā* (sport). In this latter type of sport, the *gopīs* imagine themselves to be the wives of the cowherds, though this is not actually so. This mythical belief enhances their eagerness for meeting Kṛiṣṇa, resulting in their hastening to the woods for clandestine meetings. Their caresses are not carnal, for the *Bhāgavata Purāṇa* tells us that Kṛiṣṇa performed these sports before he left Vṛindāvana for Mathurā, and that was when he was only eleven years old. The *rāsalīlā* described in the *Bhāgavata* in which the *gopīs* go out to meet Kṛiṣṇa attracted by the sound of his flute, and are suddenly abandoned by him to be met joyfully later on, took place when Kṛiṣṇa was only eight years old. Rādhā is the embodiment of the highest love known as *mahābhāva*. The characteristic of this is a maddening delight for both the lover and the beloved. In this state even a touch or a sight of Kṛiṣṇa is enough to cause thrill which usually follows a kiss or an embrace. Along with this there are also the pangs of separation which increase the desire of union with him.

It must also not be forgotten that the entire happenings mentioned in the *Bhāgavata* are on a transcendental plane and have an allegorical significance. The *Bhāgavata* tells us how Kṛiṣṇa held his love-sport with the *gopīs*. When the autumnal night came, and the *mallikā* flowers began to break into blossom, he played on his flute. Attracted by the sweet sound the *gopīs* came running to him, leaving whatever they were doing at the moment, some even leaving their infants half-fed at their breasts. Those who could not get out of their houses began to meditate on him where they were. Kṛiṣṇa sported with them for some time on the bank of the river Yamunā, but when the *gopīs* saw themselves so greatly favoured, pride entered their hearts, and they began to think themselves better than the other woman of the world. In order to cure their conceit, Kṛiṣṇa abandoned them, and suddenly disappeared along with Rādhā, the most favoured of the *gopīs*. But Rādhā too had to be taught a lesson, for when she found Kṛiṣṇa treating her differently from the others, she was filled with pride and even asked him to carry her on his shoulders. So Kṛiṣṇa again disappeared leaving her alone, and it was thus that the *gopīs* found her. Together they lamented and sang hymns in his praise. Kṛiṣṇa appeared again in their midst and celebrated the union with dance and sport, bringing back the lost bliss to the *gopīs* and to his beloved Rādhā.

The entire episode, as will be apparent to anyone who follows it with insight, is an allegory. Kṛiṣṇa is the eternal Lord, and the *gopīs* are human souls. The union of the souls with the divine Lord is the *rāsalīlā* or love-sport. When there is the slightest pride or egoism, god suddenly disappears and the souls feel miserable without him. But when they again approach him with overpowering love, after being cured of egoism, he takes compassion on them and readily grants them reunion. The final sport is the intense bliss of the reunion from which there is no more parting.

Considered in its proper light the love play of the *gopīs*, and of Rādhā with Kṛiṣṇa, is highly spiritual. The use of conventional terms and expressions of lovemaking are there only because in our small human way it is only by these words of ardour and love that we can convey some little idea of that eternal bliss which in its entirety is indescribable and beyond words.

It is against this background that we have to consider the love poetry of Keshava. In *Rasikapriyā* he never leaves the reader in doubt that Rādhā is his *nāyikā* and Kṛiṣṇa the *nāyaka.* He gives definitions and characteristics of various persons, things, and situations, and illustrates them by examples from episodes of the loves of Kṛiṣṇa and Rādhā. When Keshava is describing a *Padminī*, the best type of womanhood, he says, 'this daughter of Vṛiṣabhānu (Rādhā) is like the bud of a *champā* flower'. When he speaks of the *labdhāpati prauḍhā* then too it is Rādhā who beams with splendour by the side of Kṛiṣṇa. When he is describing the meeting of the *nāyaka* and *nāyikā* it is Rādhā who is casting amorous glances on Kṛiṣṇa. 'When Rādhā, the daughter of Vṛiṣabhānu, sat after adorning herself, all her adornments were very attractive. When she looked at the *nāyaka*, Kṛiṣṇa, with desire-filled eyes it seemed as if the *nāyaka* of love, Kāmadeva, rained arrows from his bow'. When the meeting of lovers at the house of a maid servant is described it is again the amorous meeting of these two:'Today the maidens of Braja fearlessly decked Kṛiṣṇa as a girl and made him cast his arms around Rādhā, the lady of many loves, who seemed like a creeper of desire. By running hither and thither and hiding in many places, he fulfilled a million longings of her for amorous dalliance.'

Illustrating the sentiment of tenderness the Poet chides Nanda for making a son as lustrous, delicate, bounteous, powerful, and handsome, as Kṛiṣṇa, a mere keeper of cows; and also for making a woman of divine speech who is a creeper of beauty and bright as lightning, (Rādhā), sell milk.

Examples can be multiplied, for almost all through Keshava's book it is Kṛiṣṇa who is the *nāyaka*, and Rādhā the *nāyikā.* In choosing Kṛiṣṇa and Rādhā as his *nāyaka* and *nāyikā*, Keshava is somewhat different from other poets. In doing so he has given refinement to *Rasikapriyā*, and his verses lose nothing of love's delight while remaining exalted.

(H) Keshava, the Artist

(i) Forceful narration— The test of a good writer is whether in his narratives and descriptions he has been able to depict the proper emotional atmosphere. If this is not achieved, the work does not have that depth of vision which is the hall-mark of all good writing. Although it may sometimes appear from Keshava's verse that he has not reached that extent of sympathetic insight which occasion demands, we can be sure that this is the exception rather than the rule. When Rāma is going along with Lakshmaṇa his brother, and Sītā his wife, in the forest, folk are captivated by their transcendental beauty, and they begin to wonder who these heavenly beings are. Keshavadāsa has captured their innocent wonder splendidly in making them ask many questions about the three, all in the same breath. 'Who are you, from where have you come ? Where are you going and for what work? Whose daughter is this lady ? Whose daughter-in-law ? Whose wife ? Are you all residents of one village and one family, or are you merely chance companions ? These simple questions are more expressive of the onlooker's surprise and fondness than a whole lot of descriptive words, and recall Lear's famous soliloquy.

Keshava's descriptions of distress and sorrow are poignant. We find such descriptions in *Rāmachandrikā*, particularly where the Poet is describing the anguish of Rāma in not finding Sītā in her hermitage when he returns after slaying Mārīcha, the illusive deer. Addressing his brother Lakshmaṇa, whom he had left to look after Sītā, and in whose brief absence she was abducted, he says: 'I do not see my lovely Sītā here? What is the reason for this ? Tell me at once. Hearing the words (of the dying deer), and being affected with instense love for me, has she gone away to that part of the forest where I slew him? Or having said some bitter words to you she now hides in shame and fear on my coming ? Is this my cottage or someone else's? Are you not my youngest brother Lakshmaṇa?' The words of Rāma are full of shock and anguish, recalling Tennyson's famous lines:

'Tears, idle tears, I know not what they mean,
Tears from the depth of some divine despair
Rise in the heart and gather to the eyes.'

Later when he learns of Sītā's abduction through the bird, Jaṭāyu, it maddens him, and he wildly wanders about putting vain questions to the birds and trees. Addressing a pair of *chakravāka* birds he says: 'Whenever you saw Sītā by my side you felt sorry to think that you were not so beautiful, but now forget your jealousy, and if you have seen her, let me know which way she has gone.' Proceeding a little further on, he says to the *chakor* bird (which according to popular belief is said to be enamoured of the moon): 'Oh! *chakor*, that Sītā, looking on whom you kept alive, forgetting the moon, has gone. Now remembering your debt to her assist me in finding her.'

His sorrow not assuaged, Rāma goes on to speak to the tree bearing the name ' Compassion', and says: 'Oh ! kind Compassion tree ! pray tell me where to seek for Sītā? You are of pious nature, so I ask you. Why are you silent ? If you say why I don't ask other trees, then hear why I don't do so: I have not asked the *champak* flower because he is an enemy of the suppliant, and he does not allow the nectar begging black bees to come near. (Black bees do not alight on *champā* flowers). So he cannot understand my sorrow. I do not ask the *ashoka* tree because his name is *ashoka* i. e. "one who is griefless," and being so how can he appreciate my grief? I do not ask the *kevṛā*, *ketakī*, *nutmeg*, and *rose*, because they have thorns, and so I think them to be of sharp nature, and those who are sharp are fearful. Therefore, thinking you to be gentle, I ask you alone'.

The above examples show that Keshavadāsa could depict sorrow and anguish in the most appropriate words without verbiage and useless prolixity.

In the same manner the Poet has expressed vividly the feeling of elation. When Rāma's messenger, Hanumān, meets Sītā and gives her Rāma's ring in the exuberance of her joy, she addresses the ring itself and says, 'The royal power of kingship abandoned Rāma in Ayodhyā, I abandoned him in the forest, and you have abandoned him on the way—then, O ! Ring, say, who is the man who will retain belief in the faithfulness of womankind. Tell me, O ! Ring, is Rāma in good health ? And Lakshmaṇa, my eternal well-wisher; the self-respecting, dear Lakshmaṇa, is he well ? Oh ! wise and gentle Hanumān, tell me yourself, for this Ring speaks not. Oh! Why does it not speak ?

Hanumān replies with wit and cunning: 'Oh ! mother, the Ring answers not, for you address it by the wrong name. Due to separation from you, Rāma has become so thin with grief that he wears this ring now as a bracelet and calls it by that name. So not being addressed by its correct name it does not respond.'

We can see in this dialogue the overpowering joy of Sītā by suddenly seeing before her a token of love from her husband Rāma. Overcome with emotion she keeps raving to the ring instead of speaking to its messenger, Hanumān.

At another place Keshava describes the bashfulness of the women of Rāma's household. The beauties of the palace have wandered into the flower garden. At one spot they see love-filled black bees kissing the *mālatī* flowers not minding the presence of the female black bees. Even this is enough to fill the maidens with bashfulness, and covering their faces in their veils they smile. The concept of humility has also been aptly depicted by Keshava. Hanumān, Rāma's valiant messenger, is entrusted by him with the difficult mission of going to the captive Sītā in Laṅkā and telling her about Rāma's preparations to free her. Hanumān not only accomplishes the mission, but in addition sets fire to Laṅkā, gives a good thrashing to Rāvaṇa's warriors, despoils his land and groves, and even humbles the great demon king. When Rāma praises him for his daring exploit, he meekly replies: 'Oh ! my lord, you praise me all for nothing. What have I done ? By the power of your ring I could fly across the ocean to the other side, and the strength of Sītājī's gem returned me back. What prowess did I show by burning Laṅkā, which was in fact already destroyed ? The warrior Akshaya Kumāra whom I killed was a mere weak child. Thereafter I was bound by the enemy. Had I been powerful why should I have allowed myself to be bound ? Trees indeed I uprooted, but they were lifeless. In this way I did not act with valour at all, while you are praising me so.'

Examples of verses depicting courage and enthusiasm are not lacking in Keshava's works. In the battle between the armies of Rāma and Rāvaṇa there was a warrior on the demon king's side, Kumbhakarṇa, who woke up only once in six months, and that too when elephants were made to walk over him. When he came on the battlefield to fight with Rāma, Keshavadāsa makes him say: 'Oh ! Rāma, do not think me to be Tāḍaka or Subāhu whom you could kill with ease. I am not the bow of Shiva which you broke as it were the stalk of a flower. I am not Tāla, not Bālī, not Khara, whom you grievously pierced with many holes. Nor am I Kharadūṣana who became a target for your arrows. Just look at me closely, I am Kumbhakarṇa, devourer of demonesses and celestial nymphs, and the destroyer of even the great Shiva. 'O ! Rāma ! I challenge you to combat. You have become vain ever since you came to Laṅkā. Today everyone will see how strong you really are.'

At another place when Sītā laments over Lava who has been made unconscious by Shatrughna's arrows, his brother Kusha says to her, 'Mother ! you sorrow needlessly. Even if it is Yamarāja (god of death)himself who comes against me I will kill him, and destroying his forces, rescue Lava. Oh ! mother, then only will I return and take the dust of your feet'. The same Kusha challenges a warrior like Lakshmaṇa with resounding words : 'Oh ! Lakshmaṇa, do not commit the mistake of thinking me to be Makarāksha or Indrajit whom you made a target for your arrows. I am not the one to be cowed down by you. Why do you seek to lose that fame which you have enjoyed till now ? Lakshamaṇa ! do not make your mother childless by entering into combat with me'.

The heroic sentiment occupies a place in Keshava's writing which is second only to that of love. This is evident in much of his verses in *Ratanbāvanī* and *Vīrasiṁhadeva Charita*. In the former we find it in the exhortation given by Ratansen to the warrior and general in the army to oppose the Mughal forces of Emperor Akbar, and in the latter in Bhūpālarāya's valiant words to decry the advice given to the effect that Akbar's army shall not be opposed.

Other emotions are also represented in Keshava's works.

The fearful emotion we find depicted in several places in *Rāmachandrikā*. For example, when Rāma's beloved brother Lakshmaṇa is wounded in the battle against Rāvaṇa, and Bibhīṣaṇa has the audacity to suggest that he would die as soon as the sun rose, the otherwise gentle Rāma assumes a fearful mood. He says he will destroy all the twelve Ādityas and the fourteen Yamas and the eight Vasus, drown all the eleven Rudras in the sea, and sacrifice all the Gandharvas as animals. He will make captive Kubera and Indra forthwith, and hand them over to Rājā Bālī, remove the wisdom of the Vidyādharas, and snatch away all accomplishments of the Siddhas. He will make Aditi slave of the Diti and destroy wind, fire, and water. If the sun arose (over his dead brother) he will hand over the entire creation to the Asuras!

The dreadful emotion is depicted in Keshava's writings, for example in the description of the confusion caused in the enemy ranks by the news of the coming of Rāma's army which struck so much terror in them that they hid in rocky caves and caverns, and left clothes and ornaments lying scattered about!

The emotion of gentleness is depicted in various verses here and there—as for example, the description in *Rāmachandrikā* of the foolish souls sunk in the ocean of sin: 'Oh ! foolish mind ! borne on the boat of passion, you keep afloat on the sea of sin, and though burning in the conflagration of rage, oh! ignorant soul, you do not abandon this game. Even though caught in the billows of untruth you enter deeper into the current of greed. Keshavadāsa says, why do you not learn that by which you can get out from this sea of sin?'

The sentiment of laughter has been given expression to in some places in *Rāmachandrikā*. But its best examples are to be found in *Rasikapriyā*. One day Kṛiṣṇa puts on a woman's dress. The cowherd maidens go to Rādhā and announce the arrival of a girl who is as beautiful as the wife of the god of love, who sings so well as it would appear that the goddess Sarasvatī herself had come. Rādhā is intrigued, and asks the cowherd maidens to bring her in. When the maidens bring the girl, (who is no other than Kṛiṣṇa disguised), Rādhā clasps her close to herself affectionately, at which the mischievous maidens break into uproarious laughter! At another place it is Kṛiṣṇa who is tricked. A cowherd maiden comes the way he is standing with an earthen jar on her head which though splashed with curd outside has really nothing in it. Kṛiṣṇa, who is fond of curd, stops the maiden and takes down the jar from her head, hoping to enjoy a good feed, when lo! he finds it empty, and seeing it so becomes abashed, at which the other maidens looking on begin to giggle beneath their end-cloth!

In *Rasikapriyā* the development of love is traced out. The lovers are Rādhā and Kṛiṣṇa. The *nāyikā*, Rādhā, hears about the virtues of the *nāyaka*, Kṛiṣṇa, and desire to meet him grows in her heart. When they meet, Kṛiṣṇa grows so fond of her that he comes to stay in her heart for ever. 'Oh my dear friend! you told me of Kṛiṣṇa, giving me many oaths. Thereafter I know not by which path he entered into my eyes. Then all bashfulness was of no avail and the eyes caused him to be united with the mind. Now what should I do, how should I save myself? Slowly Kṛiṣṇa has entered into my heart!'

When one is a prey to love he becomes completely engrossed in it. All merriment and laughter is forgotten. Everything around him reminds him of his unfulfilled love. This is the state of the lovelorn Kṛiṣṇa as related to the *nāyikā* by one of her bosom friends. 'Kṛiṣṇa neither plays nor laughs, nor does he listen to any song, for it pierces him as an arrow. He even forgets to wear his clothes and walks about as though naked! He is afflicted by the pain of passion as much as Shaṅkara was by Kāmadeva, the god of love. He does not ever smell a flower even by mistake, because his body, tender as a flower, withers if he does so! He neither eats betels nor talks to anyone, and keeps staring at your face as the *chakor* at the moon!'

In such a state of love, a sharp or bitter word of the lover, even though spoken in jest, hurts the beloved's heart, and this indeed is what happens to a lovelorn cowherd girl one day. One bosom friend of the *nāyikā* relates the incident to another: 'At one time Kṛiṣṇa said jestingly to a cowherd girl, "when your father has turned you out how can you persevere in your love for me?" Oh! dear friend, what reply could that maiden make? Tears began to flow from her eyes. Seeing this Kṛiṣṇa hurriedly clasped her to his bosom, but even then, till midnight her sobs did not cease!'

Love cannot stand a rival. When by chance the name of another woman escapes Kṛiṣṇa's lips while conversing with his beloved cowherd maid, it causes her so much unrest that she breaks into tears. Telling about it, one of the *nāyikā's* close friends says: 'Today when that cowherd girl was laughing and conversing with Kṛiṣṇa, I know not how by accident he uttered another woman's name. Hearing this the betel which that girl was about to chew, remained in her mouth, and she became so greatly agitated that tears welled up in her eyes.'

With love comes arrogance, and this creates a wall between the lovers. When the *nāyikā* shows her arrogance, she cannot be appeased however much her lover tries to cajole her. The *nāyaka* has to go away disheartened. But soon after the *nāyikā* repents of her doing, and thus confides in her bosom friends : 'Even when my beloved fell on my feet I did not so much as glance at him. Oh ! my bosom friend, I did not do as you instructed, but followed instead the dictates of anger. Now my limbs even though anointed with sandal, burn, and even the moonlight and the lotus cannot cool me ! Due to manifold sorrows my body has become devoid of pleasure. God has rightly punished me for my wrong-doing.

Along with repentence, boldness enters the *nāyikā's* mind, and throwing caution and fear to the winds she goes out to meet her lover of her own accord, seeing which he is charmed, and wholly won over. He says to her, 'You have charmed me by coming over to me without my calling.' The *nayikā* bashfully answers that it was the dark clouds which called her, and there follows an affectionate exchange of words. But this love is intercepted by parting, when the lover goes away to a distant land on some business, and the pangs of separation trouble the *nāyikā*. The night never seems to end. Laughter is forgotten. Sleep comes and goes like lightning. The body burns, and the *nāyikā* cries for beloved incessantly like the sparrow-hawk. As time passes and the days of estrangement lengthen, the state of the *nāyikā* becomes as that of a mad woman. Her own shadow startles her, and she looks all around as one who has lost her mind. Describing this condition of hers, Keshava says : 'Her mind remains disjointed, her feet stagger, and even her shadow startles her. She says one thing and understands another, and changes with each moment. I know not whether some witch has cast a spell on her, or she suffered exposure to the wind, that she so raves, or whether someone has done something to perturb her. Oh ! Kṛiṣṇa today Rādhā cares neither for her veil, nor for her earthern jar, nor for her dress !'

The *nāyikā* has reached a stage when even her near friends, tired of her impatience, abandon her. One such friend says to another : 'If she (the nāyikā) does not listen to me, and is bent upon giving up her life, let us come away, and leave her to do as she likes. One should pay heed only to a person who listens to advice. What this woman wants is that her beloved should come to meet her immediately today, or else she will die. Tell me, my bosom friend, can water ever be found the very instant fire breaks out ?'

When her lover calls her, the *nāyikā* goes to meet him with a determination which only long-suppressed passion can give. The Poet describes vividly her going : 'When the *nāyikā* went to keep an assignment with her lover, snakes got entangled in her legs, and many were crushed under her hurrying feet ! Beholding her go thus, demons began to peer at her from all sides. She minded not the heavy downpour, thought little of the chirping of the beetles, or the thunder of the clouds. She heeded not her falling ornaments, her torn clothes, and the thorns which pricked her breasts as she hastened along. Seeing her go like this the female evil sprites began to ask her, "Oh ! licentious woman ! where did you learn this way of keeping your tryst ?" ' Thus she goes, the lovelorn lady, to meet her no less eager lover. They meet at whatever place offers itself—the house of a maid-servant, or of a dear friend who does them a good turn by bringing them together, in some abandoned hut, or at some show or function, or perhaps they meet in the forest where trees are thick and shady so that they can remain hid from prying eyes ! 'Pulling him towards her with the magnetic glance of her love-filled eyes, Rādhā put the noose of love around his neck. She met him alone in the moonlight, with soft laughter and sweet fragrance. In this way making him drink the nectar of her lips, and winning him over, the young maiden engaged him in talk and took him into the forest, her mind set on enjoyment !'

Love could also be at times tempestuous and passionate—a love that carries all before it :

> 'Shame has quite abandoned her.
> Her clothes and trinkets strewn do lie,
> Hearing her lustful shouts and cries
> Even birds coo—such should one deem
> Lovemaking—all else is routine !'

Thus in Keshavadāsa's works we find an expressive and complete account of the different aspects of love—its arising, its longing, and its fulfilment.

(ii) Dialogue—Keshava is expert in writing effective dialogues, and they enliven his works with their swift repartee and pleasant wit. Though other poets like Tulasīdāsa, Jāyasī and the like, used the dialogue form in their works, none could do it so well as Keshava. We have seen that Keshava had complete knowledge of the stratagems of statecraft, and was well acquainted with all aspects of diplomacy, due to his constant touch with the courts of emperors and princes. He was also an expert in the art of writing, and so we find innumerable instances of pithy and expressive dialogue in his works. In *Rāmachandrikā* especially there are examples of such dialogues between the various main characters of the story, the most outstanding being between Rāma and the sage Parashurāma, and between the warrior Aṅgada and the demon king Rāvaṇa. When Rāma breaks the bow which marks him out for wedding Sītā, Parashurāma gets annoyed and begins to upbraid him for it. Rāma manages to invite the sage's anger and he says, 'You have broken Shaṅkarajīs' bow and have wedded Sītā in the *svayaṁvara*. By doing so, the vanity of your mind has greatly increased. Say, had you no fear of me even while breaking the bow?' To this outburst Rāma gently replies: 'Yes, this wrong has certainly been done by me. Pray then what shall I do to set it right?' This leads the sage to say that he would cut off Rāma's hands with his axe, which forces the latter to say that the sage's strength would be a mere straw. We can at once see the forcefulness of Rāma's reply, though of course the sage's anger is not appeased, and he continues railing till Rāma finally discloses to him his true nature. *Rāmachandrikā* is replete with such effective dialogues which prove Keshava's skill in this form of writing.

(iii) Descriptions—We find descriptions of nature throughout Keshava's writings, and they have richness and beauty. His accounts of natural beauty excite the mind and are full of embellishments and appropriate comparisons. Even in works like *Rāmachandrikā*, *Vijñānagītā*, and *Vīrasiṁhadeva Charita* we find descriptions of nature interspersed with the main story, showing the Poet's great affinity to nature.

In *Vijñānagītā* speaking of a lovely lady separated from her beloved, the Poet compares her grief-laden body to the blue sky : 'Tears flow from her eyes constantly so that she cannot know the difference of day from night. When she speaks some words the glimmer of her teeth is like a flash of lightning, and she repeats "my love ! my love !" as the *chatak* bird says "pi ! pi !" in the rainy season.' The description is full of beauty and pathos. In *Rāmachandrikā* the Poet has given a charming and vivid description of the rainy season : 'The white and black clouds are pleasing to the eyes, and the swan-like fleeces flying hither and thither amidst them are captivating. It appears as if, while drinking the water of the ocean, the clouds had swallowed a number of conch shells also, and are now disgorging them with their whole strength. The rainbow is giving great splendour, and the clouds are appearing many-coloured. It seems as if the gods have tied a frill of precious stones on the gateway of heaven to welcome the rainy season ! All around dense clouds have gathered. It were as if seeing the sorrow of the earth the god of rain, Indra, has invaded the sun for needlessly oppressing her with summer's heat ! The clouds are thundering loudly as if battle-drums are sounding, and the crack of lightning is as the noises of Indra's thunderbolt. This is not a rainbow which has come out, but the bow of god Indra, and the raindrops are the arrows rained from the bow ! These are not the sparrow-hawks, toads, and peacocks making noise, but warriors of Indra who are challenging the sun to combat! This is not lightning which flashes but great kings who are wandering about with drawn swords! Due to being wrathful on the sun they have brought trouble on the bright and shining stars. They have even captured the ladybirds and made them over to the earth to wreak their vengeance!'

Apart from descriptions of nature we find vivid descriptions of places and things in Keshavadāsa's poems. In *Rāmachandrikā* giving a description of the maid-servants of Sītā, he narrates the beauty of their various limbs. Speaking of their waists he says 'As in this world we hear about *dharma* and *adharma*, truth and untruth, but do not understand which is right and which wrong, so fine is the difference between them; so is the condition of these women's waists! It is heard that they have waists, but on seeing it seems they haven't, so slender are they!'

Further, speaking of the hips and thighs in relation to the waist of a maid-servant, the Poet says, 'The hips are swollen with joy, and the waist is thin, as if the hips have robbed all the wealth of the waist. Due to this the hips blossom out with joy (having got the wealth), and the poor waist has hid itself due to fear of public dishonour! The greatly priceless, fair, and robust thighs appear as if they were two toys for the god of love to play with at the time of sexual enjoyment!'

In describing the bed-chamber of Rāma the Poet has not omitted a single article of luxury and comfort. The description is complete and picturesque: 'There is a single lamp alight in the room, but by its brightness the gems studded in the walls are set a glimmer, as ministers getting glory by the splendour of the King! Beautiful gem-studded jars filled with unguents, kept in shelves in each compartment, look as if they are articles for the use of the god of love. Under a smooth white canopy of pearls there is a studded bedstead which pleases the mind. On that bed is spread a lovely mattress of red satin, and above is a canopy with a frill of pearls. This bedstead appears so as it seems the moon is raining drops of nectar on the sun! On the pegs in the bedroom many garlands of various kinds are hanging, and in between there are strings of sapphire which have been compared by some friend thus : the god of love having won over the entire world, but oh ! Rāma, having admitted defeat from you, has taken off the string from his bow and hung it there. Having admitted defeat he has handed over his arms to you. The various flowers and fruits of land and sea are there, and also scented powders to make fragrant cloths and apparels. There are unguents and cosmetics of sandal-wood to apply which gods crave. There are scented pastes containing saffron, and the women have filled the metal box with betels scented with camphor and musk !'

Keshava's description of women sporting in water in *Rāmachandrikā* is also lovely and captivating. 'At the time of sporting in the water one girl laughs and catches hold of the swans, as did Damayantī, another picks out a lotus root like a swan, and wears it round her neck. A maiden catches hold of her ornament as soon as it drops, even in the midst of the waves, and does not let it fall to the bed. If one says she is swift as a fish that would be an inept comparison, for she is more agile than even the mind ! Some of the women clasp each other and dive as if to see who can keep down the longest, and they stay in the water as if it was their home ! On seeing them even the celestial nymphs are fascinated. At the time of their water sport these moonfaced women seem like lotus flowers, and being deceived, the black bees keep hovering around them !'

We find Keshava's descriptions vivid, picturesque, and entertaining. Some of them are the result of personal experience, as those describing some aspect of kingly life, others are imaginative as when he describes the ocean, but all have that depth and grandeur which are found in the narrations of good writers. His metaphors are generally happy and his comparisons homely, though at time he becomes somewhat obscure, as when speaking of a woman's waist he says, it is 'sweets meant for a ghost !'

(iv) Language—Keshavadāsa was born in an age in which the Sanskrit language had a strong hold on contemporary literature, and the higher class of people used it in writing. Though circumstances led him to break from this tradition and to use the Hindi language for his works, we find the impact of Sanskrit strong on him.

When Keshava began to write, there were two languages (apart from Sanskrit), in which the poets of his time wrote—Avadhi and Braja. Keshava chose Braja. This was mainly because it was closer to Bundelkhaṇḍ, the language of the province of his birth. Besides this, Braja had an innate richness and melody which Avadhi did not have, and it was more suitable for incorporating and adopting foreign words.

Since Keshava was scholar of Sanskrit we find many words of that language in his books, specially in *Rāmachandrikā* and *Vijñānagītā*. He did not stop short of Sanskrit words, and in places used Sanskrit inflexions also. Thus describing his own devotion to Rāma and Sītā the Poet says:

'Rāmachandra pada padma vṛindāraka vṛindābhivandanīyam
Keshavamati bhūtanayā lochanaṁ chañcharīkāyate.'

(As the black bee is devoted to the lotus, so is the wisdom of Keshava to the lotus feet of Rāma).

Sanskrit words predominate in the description of the *svayaṁvara* of Sītā in which the kings coming from various lands are described:

'Sītā shobhana byāha utsavā sabha sambhāra sambhāvana.
Tatta tkārya samagra vyagra mithilāvāsī janā shobhanā.
Rājā rāja purohitādi suhṛidā mantrī mahāmantradā
Nānā desha samāgatā nṛpagaṇā pūjyāparā sarvadā.'

(Respectable and honoured kings of many lands are collected in Janakapura. King Janaka, the court Priest, and all the beautiful inhabitants of Mithilā are busily engrossed in their work, for the arrangements in connection with the auspicious *svayaṁvara* of Sītā are in the minds of everyone).

We also find many Bundelkhaṇḍī words in Keshava's writings. This was natural, for Bundelkhaṇḍ was his birthplace and he spent the greater portion of his life there. In fact there are so many Bundelkhaṇḍī words in his writings that it would not be inappropriate to call the language used therein as Braja mixed with Bundelkhaṇḍī. Describing the gathering in Sītā's *svayaṁvara* the Poet says:

'Devāṁ syauṁ janu devasabhā shubha sīyasvayamvara dekhan āī.'

(It seems as if the assembly of gods itself, along with all the gods therein, have come to behold Sītā's *svayaṁvara*).

In this stanza the word *syauṁ* (*Sahita* i.e. 'along with') is Buṇḍelkhaṇḍī. Words like *kuchī* (*kuñjī*), meaning 'key', *ghorilā* (*khuṁṭī*), meaning 'peg', and *gourmadāin* (*Indra dhanuṣa*), meaning 'rainbow', which are Bundelkhaṇḍī, have been freely used by Keshava.

Though Braja had been selected by Keshava in preference to Avadhi, we also find some words of Avadhi being used by him as e.g. *ihāṁ* ('here') *uhāṁ* ('there'), *dikhāu* ('show') and so on.

Apart from these words of local origin, Arabic and Persian words were also used by Keshava, but in a slightly modified form. Since Keshava belonged to an era of Muslim rule in which, due to the tolerant policy followed by Akbar and Jahāngīr, there was amity between Hindus and Muslims, it was natural that this influence should leave its mark on the Hindi literature of the time. Prominent literary persons like Bīrbal, Ṭoḍarmal, Tānsen, and Khānkhānā, used to flock to the Mughal court, and so Arabic and Persian words entered in their writings and of those who, like Keshava, came into contact with them. Words like *sirtāj* (crown), *fauj* ('army'), *shor* ('noise'), *fīl* ('elephant'), *durbār* ('court'), *firmān* ('royal edict'), *kune* ('march'), and the like, are frequently used by Keshava.

Some variations have also been made by Keshava in normal words by slightly altering their sound. For example, instead of the word *sādhu* ('a pious man') he has used *sādha*. *Paravāha* ('concern') he alters to *Pravāha*, and instead of the familiar word *veshyā* for prostitute he uses *visvā*.

Other words he coins on his own, like *balakta*, *jeya*, *leya*, and the like. Some he has used in an entirely novel manner, as for example for *bāpa ko mārane vālā* i.e. one who is the murderer of his own father, he has *bāpamār* (*bāpa*=father, and *māra*=

killer). Yet other words he uses in a sense now no longer used. These we mostly find in *Vīrasiṃhadeva Charita*(like *unmān, vibūche* etc). In some cases he combines two separate words to form a new one. Such compound words are mileb + milai (mirgle) + *ab* (now), and *bhayeb=bhaye* (have become) + *ab* (now).

In order to embellish language Hindi poets used idioms and proverbs. Keshava's poetry is replete with both. In *Rasikapriyā* it is said of Kṛiṣṇa, *he Harī āṭhahū gāṃṭh haṭhāye* meaning that he is a great mischief maker. In *Rasikapriyā* the female bangle-seller giving instruction to the *nāyaka* says that if the *nāyikā* is enraged or displeased he should first appease her. To illustrate this she uses a popular saying: '*tāto hai dūdha sirāin pījai* i.e 'the milk is hot, cool it and then drink'.

We find Keshava's use of words in their onomatopoeic sense most appropriate. He seems to convey by them the exact mood of the situation. For example when Rāma breaks the mighty bow of Śiva at Sītā's *svayaṁvara*, we can almost hear the sound of its breaking. This he accomplishes by using words having the hard sounds 'ṭa' and 'ḍa' and also the sound 'na' which denote the twanging of the bow-strings:

> '*Prathama ṭankora jhuki jhāri saṁsāra mada,*
> *Chaṇḍa kodanḍa rahyo manḍi navakhaṇḍa ko.*
> *Chāli achalā achala ghāli digapāla bala,*
> *Pāli ṛiṣirāja ke bechana parachaṇḍa ko.*
> *Sodu daī Īsha ko bādhu Jagdīsha ko,*
> *Krodha upājaye brigunanda bāri-banḍa ko.*
> *Bāndhi vara svarga ko sādhi apavarga, dhanu*
> *Bhaṅga ko shabda gayo bheda brahmāṇḍa ko.*'

Even the first twang of this mighty bow removed the arrogance of the entire world, and resounded in the nine countries (which along with Bhārata were the known world). Shaking the whole earth, destroying ths strength of the guardian deities of the different quarters, fulfilling the grand promise of Viśvāmitra, informing Mahādeva, telling Viṣṇu that the work of the universe was being carried out according to his desire, creating rage in Parashurāma, astounding and disturbing the heavenly host, bringing emancipation to the kings and sages (of whose bones it was made), piercing the entire universe, that sound of the breaking of the bow went into the upper region of space.

Similarly in order to show how the earth appears to sink at the approach of Rāma's army, the Poet has used words like *dachkani*, *dachkati*, *machkat*, *thalthal* etc.

'Uchaki chalata kapi dachkani dachkat,
Manch sise machkat bhūtala ke thala thala
Lachaki lachaki jāta sesa ko asesa phana
Bhāgi gaī bhogavatī atala bitala tala

(The earth shakes due to the jostling and the jumping of the monkeys upon it, and goes up and down as it were a machān. All the fangs of Sheṣa's extended hood droop down because of the weight, and the habitation of the top surface of the earth sinks into that of the one below).

The writings of Keshava show that he was equally skilful in melodious verse, which had strength and vitality and was pleasure-giving and gentle. Examples can be found in most of his compositions. As regards the first kind, viz. verse possessing sweetness and melody, the invocation of *Rasikapriyā* which forms the very opening stanza is a perfect example. The choice of musical and soft sounding words makes it exceedingly pleasing to the ears. Another example is the description given by the Poet in *Kavipriyā* of a maiden afflicted by the pangs of separation:

'Meṁhke haiṁ sakhi-āṁsu usāsani, sātha nishā suvisāsini bāḍhī
Hāsa gayo uḍī haṁsini joṃ chapalāsama nīṁd gaī gati kāḍhī
Chātak jyoṁ pivapīv raṭai, caḍhi, tāpataraṅ giṇī jyom ati gāḍhī
Keshava vākī dashā sunihau aba āgi binā aṁgangani ḍāḍhī'

(Oh! dear friend, her tears are not tears but showers of rain! This treacherous night has lengthened with her long sighs. Her laughter has flown away like the swan somewhere, and her sleep comes and goes like the brief lightning flashes. She keeps crying for her beloved like the *chātak* bird, and fierce flames of separation are burning her body. Keshava says, how shall I relate her condition, the limbs of that poor lady are burning away even without fire !)

Equally vivid is Keshava's narration of the vigorous type of verse. When Rāma had broken the bow at Mithilā in Sitā's *svayaṁvara*, the sage Parashurāma, not recognising Rāma's divine nature, vents his anger at his being so presumptuous as to break the mighty bow of Śiva. He says: 'Today I will slay and destroy with my hatchet all the race of Raghus along with elephants, horses, and chariots. I will make Lakshmaṇa fly on the breeze created by my arrows, and will pierce the strong Shatrughna as one pierces a target. Driving away Rāma, along with his wife, to the forest, I will roast Bharata in wrath's furnace, and if Rāma lifts up his bow and fights, I will kill him also and make Dasharatha, his father, childless.

Examples of the pleasure-giving and gentle kind of verse are widespread in Keshava's writings. In *Kavipriyā* we have a good instance of such verse in which Keshava relates the effect of the seasons on lovers: 'Hearing the cry of peacocks in the rainy season, who is there whose mind does not become restless? Their cry is a path for the going of the chariot of passion's longing. In the spring, the cry of the cuckoo resounding in the forest instantly increases the heart's passion and when in the same season parrots and starlings chirp of love, even maiden girls are captivated, not to speak of women! But in this autumn season, who is the woman who has a heart such, that taking off the garland of her arrogance she speaks not to Kṛiṣṇa?'

Keshava had such great command over language that often his verses had double meaning, and sometimes were open to even five or six different interpretations, a feat which few poets can accomplish. For example, in *Kavipriyā* the Poet makes a bosom companion say, 'In lovemaking first fear is produced, but on the *nāyaka's* giving courage to the *nāyikā* her timidity goes away and passion, appetite, warmth, and trembling of the body, etc. arise. The strong *nāyaka* made virile by herbs becomes violent in love even on being denied. Then according to the kind of lovemaking various kinds of words are uttered by the lovers and the lips are sucked by the teeth. The *nāyaka* becomes brutal and he shows no kindness, but at the same time remains dignified. The breasts of the maiden thereafter withstand well the attack of the lover's nails.

At such a moment, lovely necklaces and other ornaments, do not seem good, as they come in the way of the lover's clasping and embracing. Oh! dearest friend, this manner of love-making is excellent!'

After having said this, when the friend of the bosom companion asks if she is telling about making love, the woman says, 'No! dear friend, I describe war!' and she goes on to interpret the words of the stanza to fit them accordingly.

Thus we can see that Keshavadāsa had full command over the Braja language, and surpassed other poets in this. Some critics consider Keshava's writings terse, and have called him 'the evil spirit of terse poetry!' So much so that according to popular belief, when a king wished to deprive a departing poet of his customary reward he would ask him to interpret some poem of Keshava—which the unfortunate poet would not succeed in doing!

Kavi ko dīna na chahai bidāī,
Puchai Keshava ki kavitāī.

(Not desiring to give the poet a reward, he (the king) would ask him abont Keshava's poetry.)

The terseness of Keshava's poetry is however noticeable only in parts of ***Rāmachandrikā***. His other works are not so terse, and the language used in them is plain and expressive. In fact Keshava's terseness would not have been bothersome, were it not for the fact that sometimes due to lack of depth in meaning, when the reader, after much effort, reaches the core of sense, he finds the reward disproportionate to the effort. None-the-less, on the whole Keshava's language, and his use of idiom and metaphor, is praiseworthy, and few poets have used the instrument of language to such great advantage. As Dr Shyāmsunder Dāsa says, 'I firmly believe that Keshava has given much grandeur and dignity to the Hindi language. Just as Tulasī is to be praised for plainness and simplicity, and Sūra for depth of vision, similarly, and indeed to a greater extent, Keshava is to be extolled for strength and virility of language.'

(v) Metre and Stanza—The history of Hindi prosody

is very old. The *Vedas*, which are said to be the oldest compositions in the world's history, are composed in stanzas. In the use of metrics Hindi poetry remains unsurpassed. The importance attached to prosody can be seen from the fact that it has been considered as one of the branches of *Vedic* study, and called 'the feet of the *Vedas*'.

Stanzas have been considered to be of two kinds—scriptural, and conventional. The former are those kinds which have been used exclusively in the *Vedas*. Conventional stanzas are of three types—those containing short vowels called *mātrika*, the second the *varṇika* or *vritta* and the third *akshara*, which is formed of letters only. In Hindi only two stanzas are acknowledged viz. *mātrika* and *varṇika*, and the third kind, namely *akshara* is included in the classification *varṇika*. Keshava has used both the *mātrika* and *varṇika* stanzas. No other poet before him has written in so many different metres as Keshava. In this respect he outshines even Tulasīdāsa, and it is this malleability of his verse which has given it such great charm and variety. This is noticeable especially in *Rāmachandrikā* in which the use of many metres has been made, some in a novel manner. By the use of different metres Keshava has made his words vividly convey the atmosphere and mood of the occasion he describes. For example, describing the monkeys as they jump about this way and that when they move in search of Sītā, he has used a short metre, called *hīraka*, with small words and alliteration. On reading the lines it seems as if the monkeys are dancing about before our very eyes!

> '*Chaṇḍa charana, chaṇḍi dharanī, maṇḍi gagana dhāvahiṁ,*
> *Tatkshaṇa hui dacchina disi lakshyahi nahiṁ pāvahīṁ,*
> *Dhīra dharana bīra barana sindhutaṭa subhāvahīṁ,*
> *Nāma parama, dhāma dharama, Rāma karama gāvahīṁ.*'

(As soon as Rāma gave his permission, those monkeys immediately proceeded to jump up and down, and to rush in the sky towards the east. They searched and searched but were not able to find Sītā. Then those calm and valiant monkeys, sitting docilely on the seashore, began to humbly sing of Rāma's deeds).

At another place Rāma is minded to see flower-garden, and a horse is fetched for him. The poet has described Rāma's going on horseback in such an appropriate metre (called *chañchalā*), that we can almost hear the prancing of the horse, recalling Browning's famous stanzas in 'How They Brought the Good News From Ghent to Aix':

> *'Bhora hota hī gayo surāja loka madhya bāga.*
> *Bāji āniyo su eka iṅgitajñas ānurāga.*
> *Shubhra summa chāri hūna aṁsha reṁṇu ke udāra.*
> *Sīkhi sīkhi leta haiṁ to chitta chañchalā prakāra.'*

(As soon as morning came all the ladies of the palace went to the garden. A devoted and intelligent horse was brought for Rāma. All the four hooves of this horse were white. The dust particles which were on those hooves seemed as if they were the minds of munificient persons which had resided therein so that the hooves may learn restlessness from them, i.e. there was more agility in the horse's hooves than in the minds of such persons).

The same effect can be seen where Keshava describes the routing of Rāma's army after being troubled sorely by the arrows rained on them by the brave Lava and Kusha. To create the effect of sudden confusion caused on the army thus, Keshava has used a metre called *nārācha* in this stanza :

> *Bhage chaye chamū chamūpa chhoḍi chhoḍi Lakshmanai.*
> *Bhage rathī mahārathī gayananda vranda ko gaṇai.*
> *Kushai Lavai niraṅkushai biloki bandhu Rāma ko.*
> *Uṭhyau risāya kai balī bandhyo ju lāja dāma ko.*

Seeing the great prowess of Lava and Kusha, many brigadiers of the army left Lakshmaṇa and fled away. Great and small chariot warriors and countless elephant riders deserted the field. Seeing Lava and Kusha stand undaunted, the powerful Lakshmaṇa, who was till now tied with the rope of shame, (i. e. who was not attacking them thinking them to be boys), became filled with rage and came out before them.

Finally, an example may be given of a melodious stanza

in which maidens with voice sweet and low as starling's, are singing. For this Keshava has used the gentle *haripriya* metre. The soft sibilants and the sweetness and smoothness of the word increase the effect :

'Jāgiye trilokadeva, deva deva Rāmadeva,
Bhora bhayo bhūmideva bhakta darasa pāvaeṁ
Brahma mana mantra varṇa Viṣṇu 'hṛidaya-chātaka ghana,
Rudra hṛidaya-kamala-mitra, jagata gīta gāvaeṁ
Gagana udita ravi anata shukrādika jotivanta,
Chhana chhana chhavi chhīna hota, līna pina tāre,
Mānahu paradesha desha, Brahmadesha ke pravesha,
Ṭhaura ṭhaura te vilāta jāta bhūpa bhāre.

(Oh ! master of the three worlds, Cakravarti Mahārāja Rāma, now awake. It is morn. Arise and give charity to *Brahmins*, and show yourself to your devotees. Oh ! Rāma ! you are the undecaying and eternal being of Brahmā's thought-shaped vow, the giver of satisfaction to the *chātaka* of Viṣṇu's heart, the sun for the heart-shaped lotus of Mahādeva; in this manner the whole universe sings your praises !. The sun has dawned in the sky, and the various shining planets get dim each moment. Other big stars are also becoming extinct from view. Their disappearance seems like the destruction of big kings of near and foreign lands due to the sin of killing a *Brahmin*).

Keshava's use of metre was happy and appropriate. He experimented with many kinds of stanzas and in some respects was an innovator. It is this factor which gives a flexibility and freshness, and in this respect his contribution to Hindi literature was considerable.

(vi) Embellishment—The belief of Hindi poets was that just as a girl's beauty was increased by ornaments, so was the charm of Poetry made more when the language used therein was polished and embellished. This feeling was expressed by Keshava himself too, in *Kavipriyā*.

'Yadapi sujāti sulakshaṇī suvaranasarasa suvṛitta
Bhūṣaṇa bina na virājai kavitā vanitā mitta.'

(Oh! friend, even though Poetry be of the highest order, of good quality, full of good and juicy words, and of excellent metre, it does not appear attractive without embellishment. Just as a maiden may be of good race, of good characteristics, fair, and amorous, and sweet-tongued, but she will not appear charming without ornaments).

Sometimes however, the poets overdid this ornamentation of verse, and often even though it was decked so, it lacked emotion and depth. It would then seem as a woman wearing ornaments, but not having that innate beauty without which all ornaments are vain. Without depth, beauty, and emotion, embellished poetry would be like such a coarsely over-dressed woman. In *Agnipurāṇa*, Vyāsajī says: *'vapuṣyalalite strīṇāṁ hāro bhārāyate param.* (For the increase of beauty embellished poetry, too, should not be qualitiless, because on an unlovely woman's body a necklace also appears to hang heavy). Though ornamentation adds to the grace of poetry, it cannot be a substitute for depth, emotion, or quality, and without these elements mere ornamentation is not only valueless in increasing its charm, but makes it seem dull and pedantic.

In *Rasikapriyā*, Keshava says that without the expression of emotion, poetry remains as devoid of splendour, as sightless eyes. In other words he wished poetry to be simple, and to be the vehicle of emotion. In practice, however, Keshava does not himself follow this precept, and he loads his verses with embellishments and ornamentation. The age in which he lived was one of kingly grandeur, and the Mughal Emperors who were on the throne patronised painting, music, architecture, and other fine arts. This created an atmosphere of show and dilettantism which was reflected in much of the art and literature of the times. Keshava, who was in direct touch with the Orchhā court, and through it with the court of the Mughal Emperor, could not remain unaffected by this pomposity. Besides this, he was at heart a scholar, and loved to flaunt his learning in the reader's eyes. Again, the poets who wrote before him had used ornamentation widely in writing their verses. All these factors led to Keshava's ornateness, much as he wished to be simple. Sometimes this ornateness was his undoing, and he is in fact at his best where he cuts through the mist of ornamentation and appeals directly to the heart.

Some examples may be given of the ornateness of language

in Keshava's writings. Describing the desires of Kṛiṣṇa in *Rasikapriyā*, the Poet uses the ornamentation of disposition or mood in his verse.

'You tie your turban after untying it again and again, and with laziness, look strongly into the mirror. Who is she with whom you sever all connections one moment, and then touch her feet, like one deranged ? Sometimes you snap your finger and sometimes scratch your ears ? To whom do you offer again and again a necklace, and for whom do you sing contrary songs ? Tell me, O! Kṛiṣṇa, how fares it with you today ?'

At another place in *Rasikapriyā*, Keshava has described the meeting by night between Kṛiṣṇa and the cowherd girls. In this description he uses the *samāhita* ornamentation, which is used where a work is accomplished by chance. The cowherd girls and youths along with Kṛiṣṇa go to Gokul. On the way back, night falls, and dark clouds cover the sky, so that they cannot see each other. Taking advantage of this accident Kṛiṣṇa makes love to the maidens and dispels the sorrow of their separation.

In *Rāmachandrikā*, describing the canopy in the courtyard of Sītā's apartment, the Poet says, 'In that courtyard there is a golden canopy on which cloth is spread. That canopy appears as if on the summit of Mount Meru an assembly chamber of the gods has been built.'

Describing the tear-filled eyes of the Emperor Akbar on hearing the news of Abul Fazal's death in *Vīrasiṁhadeva Charita*, the Poet says, 'Tears trembled in his restless eyes as the lotus shivers when shaken by the wind.' The Betwā River is described in the same book thus; 'It flows along murmuring and rippling as if the beloved of Rāma Shāh, being displeased with her lord, goes away mumbling in anger! At another place the Poet is describing the march of Vīrasiṁha. He takes the help of the adornment of metaphor and describes the King's going thus: 'On Vīrasiṁha's departure each spot is being lost to him one after the other, as on the rising of the sun the stars !'

It is true that at times Keshava flaunts his learning and his scholarship. At the same time there are many instances in his writings where he has used the art of embellishment with success and has enriched his verse by apt metaphors and comparisons, and produced thereby the appropriate atmosphere, mood, and situation.

(I) Conclusion; Keshava's Achievement

Keshava's poetry was many-sided and significant from a number of angles. He was not only an eminent poet, but also a scholar and historian. He was greatly adept in composing short poems, and in these he occupies a supreme place. He had command over Braja language. He was adept in embellishing his verses by metaphors, similies and figures of speech, and in the use of metres no poet in the history of Hindi literature can stand comparison with him.

Though future poets did not follow the traditions or the rules of poetical composition to which he subscribed, it cannot be denied that he opened new paths and enriched Hindi poetry.

As a historian of his times, Keshava has indisputable importance. Though he did not add much to the contemporary account of the Mughal rule and administration, he certainly wrote with authority about the Kingdom of Orchhā in which he largely lived and moved. His books *Kavipriyā*, *Vīrasiṁhadeva Charita* and *Ratanbāvanī* contain much information about events which took place there, and in learning about Orchhā rulers the works of Keshava cannot be ignored.

Above everything Keshava lived a full life. The magnificence of courts and palaces, the wiles of ministers and chieftains, the idiocyncracies of kings and emperors, and the treacheries of plotters and assassins, were all within his field of experience. He had devotion, but was not blinded by it, and did not demur to point out the weaknesses of those whom tradition considered faultless (as Rāma and Bibhīṣaṇa), and yet he did not forget wherein they were noble. He worked on a wide canvas, and excelled in his narrations, whether he was describing lovemaking or the soul's emancipation. He wrote about war and he wrote about peace, and in both he was equally expressive. He wrote with equal facility about the march of Vīrasiṁhadeva's forces, and the clash of armies; about first love, about the laughter of women, their longing, their fulfilment and their innocent wiles. His vast experience of various facets of life made him write on almost all subjects-religion, philosophy, court amours, love, hate, and horror; and gave him the gift to speak about everything—from the signs to be looked for when buying a horse, to the qualities of the enlightened soul. Age did not bend him, and to the end he remained the amorous poet which he ever was. He did not like to be reminded of the sorrowful passing of youth, and cursed his grey hair. He could, 'walk with kings nor lose the common touch' and while on the one hand he had as his friends the great Madhukar Shāh and Vīrasiṁhadeva, he also befriended a common and illiterate goldsmith. His wisdom kept pace with his exuberance, and he knew how much honour could corrupt, greed debase, and intimacy despoil.

'Ati ādara ati lobha taiṁ, ati saṁgati taiṁ mitta
Sādhun hūṃ ko hota hai, Keshava chañchala chitta.'

(Keshava says, by excessive honour, excessive greed, and excessive association, the nature of sages even becomes unsteady).

Some critics have discounted him as terse, others have dismissed him as a charlatan parading in borrowed clothes. He was neither. As any other writer he could not escape the impress of his age and times, but whatever he wrote was full of strength and vitality, and in some respects he was a pioneer.

Chapter I

Invocation and Blessing

This is the Introductory chapter of the book. Hindi poets usually begin their work with a prayer or invocation to a god. Keshavadāsa addresses his invocation to Gaṇesha, the god of wisdom, wealth, and prudence. Gaṇesha is said to be the remover of obstacles, and is propitiated at the beginning of all undertakings, whether it be building a house, going on a journey, starting the new year, or writing a book or a poem. This power of his is believed to have come to him from his father Shiva. It is said that when Gaṇesha was born he was a youth of such dazzling beauty that his mother Pārvatī became jealous of him and cursed him to have a pot-belly and an elephant's tusk. Her husband Shiva however countered the curse by pronouncing that Gaṇesha would hold a high position amongst the gods, have an overpowering influence in all worldly affairs, and be invoked first on all occasions, failing which the task would be doomed to failure.

After the invocation there follow three verses which narrate the difference between benediction of faith and the humble offering made in the ordinary manner without religious significance. Then there is a verse which summarises the exploits of the god Kṛiṣṇa, whom the Poet has taken as his model lover right through the book, followed by a long verse in which Keshavadāsa narrates a little of the contemporary history of Orchhā, his native city, and the circumstances which led him to write the *Rasikapriyā*. This verse gives exactly the year in which the Poet wrote his book.

The remaining portion of the chapter describes briefly the nine emotions as conceived by poets, the ascendancy of love amongst them, and the nature of meeting and parting of lovers.

The mention of love, and a description of its nature, is a fitting prelude to the book, which goes on in subsequent chapters, to elucidate what love means, who the different kinds of lovers are, and how they meet and part.

Invocation

Thus Keshavadāsa prays : 'Victory
To Shrī Gaṇesha[1] who has tooth one,
Of wisdom who the storehouse is
The slayer of Kāmadeva[2], and the son
Of Shrī Shivajī and Pārvatī[3],
Of bliss the source, who sign of the moon
Upon his forehead wears, who gives
Great happiness—of much repute
Whom Viṣṇu[4] himself has decreed
As first of gods, who does devour
The wicked, and the poor does free;
The principal and greatest power,
Eternal, wealthy, fortunate,
Abode of treasure, pot-bellied :
The sorrows of the world who slays,
And shelter gives to those who need.

The benediction of adoration

Remembering the household deity
When one his salutation makes,
Of adoration, as men see,
The benediction there takes place.

The benediction of blessing

Where coupled with the deity's name
The word 'victory' is put in,
'Tis called by poets of good fame
The benediction of blessing.

The benediction descriptive of an object

Amongst the words writ in a book
Where '*namaskāra*'[5] or 'Victory'
Find not a place, and which is full
Of supplication, this merely

Describes an object, and so should
Such benediction good poets see.

The exploits of Kṛiṣṇa

Who did assume a form so that
Shrī Vṛiṣabhānu's daughter, Rādhājī[6],
Could seek love in him; who begat
Such merriment when he did steal
The clothes of bathing cowherd girls:[7]
Who showed much winning tenderness
Bound by his mother, and who was
Fearful when Keshī he suppressed;
And full of valour when he killed
Vatsāsura;[8] and of dreadful shape
When he the forest fire did swill[9],
And loathesomeness who did create:
The breasts of Pūtanā[10] in death's hold
Who held—astounded Brahmā too,
When he the stolen calves restored :[11]
The sentiment of wonder who
Brought forth; that very same Shrī Kṛiṣṇa
Of nature who is ever calm :
Of sentiments nine, O ! lovers, him
You should e'er serve, says Keshavadāsa.

The writing of *Rasikapriyā*

Upon the river Betwā's[12] banks
Where places of pilgrimage are,
Which the Tuṅgāraṇya forest[13] spans,
There lies the city of Orchhā[14]
Which in the world does thriving stay,
And men of all four castes[15] are there,
And of the *āshramas* four[16]—engaged
In pious acts, worship, and prayer,
And study of the sacred *Vedas*:[17]
Where merit always does increase,
And wealth made more in many ways;

And compassion and charity
Do every moment greater grow.
Lives in that town a poet of fame
Called Keshava, whom the world does know.
The people of that place remain
Happy in their own duties, they
Have conquered mighty monarchs all;
In that place Brahmā[18] did create
With understanding, Madhukar Shāh[19]
The blessed king, who was the light
Of Gaharwārs[20] of the Solar race,
And Dūlāh Rāma his son—the bright
Adornment of the world, whose brave
And pious younger brother was
Indrajīt Singh,[21] whom Viṣṇu[22] gave
A generous mind, and body strong,
Success in war, and all that makes
A noble man; and he esteemed
His elder brother as Lakshmaṇa
Shrī Rāma;[23] and his reign all things
Progressed; he took the *guru mantra*[24]
From Keshavadāsa, whom giving much
Of joy, he made him undertake
The *Rasikapriyā*; thus in *saṁvat*
Sixteen hundred and forty-eight[25]
On the seventh day of the bright half,
Of eighth, Monday, to be precise—
With love and wisdom to the task
Summoning, Keshavadāsa did write
The *Rasikapriyā*, with knowledge filled,
For persons of the amorous kind.
As big eyes splendour do not give
If in beholding they be blind,
E'en so without succulent words
The poets elegance do not know.
Therefore one should, considering well,
Says Keshavadāsa, such poems compose
Which by their sweetness will the mind
Of the dear dark beloved mate[26]

By their melodious music bind,
And in a moment captivate.

The nine emotions

Love, laughter, compassion, and wrath,
Wonder and dread; the awesome, brave,
And silent—nine emotions[27] are
Which diverse forms and meanings take.
Says Keshavadāsa, of these the prime
Is love—which has over others sway,
And mighty Hari[28]—Lord divine
Is love's own chosen god for aye.

The emotion of love.

Those thoughts which surge with love's desire
Or of Kāmadeva[29]—of love the spouse,
Such feasts of love which lovers tire,
Have skilful poets soon aroused:
Of love's essence twofold there be—
Meeting and parting—yet appear
Of these two kinds, as poets see,
One is concealed, the other clear.[30]

An example of hidden love

Once in the woods when Kṛiṣṇa[31] did sport
With Rādhā, seeking pleasures sweet,
And shouts of joy did issue forth
As oft when lustful lovers meet,
When she did take the active role[32]
Her necklace studded with dark gems
Did wildly shake thus to and fro,
Says Keshava, as it were the sun
Had taken Saturn on his lap
And joyfully him he had swayed
In swing of black silk—so did flash
Those dark gems with each move she made.

Hidden meeting

To lover or beloved known,
Or those who meet in secrecy,
Or to the woman's friends alone
Such meeting, parting, hidden is.

Open meeting

That union and parting is deemed
Open, which known to all men seems.

An example of open meeting.

Once Shrī Kṛiṣṇa sat with Rādhā[33] near
On the same couch, with pleasure swayed,
And she in mirror held did peer
To watch the splendour of her face..
Her form reflected he did see
In her red gem on forehead worn
Which seemed as with her husband's leave
Sītājī sat, in fire, adorned.[34]

An example of secret parting

The nāyikā says to her friend:

'O, friend ! the harsh words I did speak
In arrogance, now my ears do vex
As by worms bit, and deafen me.
When he arrives: those eyes which wept,
At his departure long have lain
On lonesome Braja[35] of him bereft
For whom wait I, O! soul, in vain?
I live, a challenge unto death !'

An example of open parting

Rādhā says to her maid-servant:

'O! fan me not with breezes cool
And keep the moon's soft light away,

For these my pleasure have removed
And sorrowful have made my days.
Scatter the flowers, dust camphor off[36]
From me, this sandal me afflicts,
A dying fish from water cast
Can be by water saved—not milk!
My suffering do you comprehend?
Or knowing not, you tend my pain?
Who by this fire is burnt, my friend
Is by that same fire cooled again!'

Concluding verse[37]

Thus have been told the twofold modes
In which the lovers part and meet,
Open and hid—and now I will
Describe the kinds of *nāyakas* that be.

NOTES

1. All Hindi poets start their work with an invocation, generally addressed to one of the gods and goddesses like Sarasvatī—the goddess of speech and learning, Viṣṇu—the Preserver or, as in the present case, Gaṇesha. Gaṇesha, who is son of Shiva and Pārvatī, is paid special homage in any new writing or undertaking because he is the remover of obstacles and also god of wisdom. He is said to have written the Mahābhārata from the dictation of the sage Vyāsa. He is represented as a short fat man, of yellow complexion, with a protuberant belly, four hands and an elephant's head having only one tusk (hence 'one-toothed'). In one hand he holds a shell, in the other a discus, in the third a club or a goad, and in the fourth a water-lily. His vehicle is a rat. On his forehead he wears the sign of the moon. Viṣṇu, the Preserver, had given him a boon, that he, (Gaṇesha), would take precedence over all the other gods.

All ceremonies start with a prayer to Gaṇesha. In fact to start a thing is to 'do *Shrī* Gaṇesha'. When guests are invited to a feast, and when the food is served, the host even today says '*Shrī Gaṇesha kījiye*', i. e. 'start eating please'. *Shrī* is used as a prefix to a name, (like 'Mister').

2. The Hindu god of love——like Eros or Cupid. He has a son named Aniruddha and a daughter Tṛiṣṇā. He is lord of the Apsarases or heavenly nymphs. He is armed with a bow, a quiver of arrows—the bow is of sugar-cane, the bowstring a line of bees, and each arrow is tipped with a distinct flower. He is usually represented as a handsome youth riding on a parrot

and attended by nymphs, one of whom bears his banner displaying the *Makara*, or a fish, on a red ground.

There is a famous incident about Kāmadeva which is mentioned in the *Rāmāyaṇa* and forms the plot of Kālidāsa's *Kumārasambhava*. Once when Shiva—the Destroyer, and famed ascetic, was sitting in *samādhi*, the gods sent Kāmadeva to disturb him, so that Pārvatī could marry him and beget a son who was to slay Tāraka—a demon, and relieve the gods of their distress. Kāmadeva sent many tantalising women to disrupt Shiva's penance, but to no avail, and as a last resort he himself approached the ascetic god and showered on him his arrows. This so enraged Shiva that he opened his third eye from which flames came out and reduced Kāmadeva to ashes. Ratī, his wife, bemoaned his death before Shiva, and out of compassion the god revived him, but henceforth he was bodiless—Ananta. And so he is to this day.

3. Shiva or Mahesha is one of the gods of the Hindu triad. As Rudra he is the great destroying and dissolving power. As a restorer he is worshipped by his symbol of the *liṅgam*, or phallus. He is also known as the great ascetic and frequently displays his mastery over austerities and rigorous penance. He is represented as a fair man with five faces and four arms, seated in profound thought, with a third eye in the middle of his forehead surmounted by the moon's crescent. His matted locks are gathered up into a coil like a horn, which bears upon it the symbol, of the river Gaṅgā, which he caught as it fell from heaven. His wife is Pārvatī, daughter of the Himālaya mountain. *Jī* is a suffix added to a name in Hindi as a mark of reverence.

4. Viṣṇu is the second god of the Hindu triad—the unconquerable Preserver. He is called Nārāyaṇa, 'moving on the waters', and represented as a human form slumbering on the serpent Sheṣa, and floating on the waters. The holy river Gaṅgā is said to have sprung from his feet. As Preserver, Viṣṇu is represented as having four hands, each of which holds a conch shell, a discus, a club, and a lotus. He is sometimes shown as seated on a lotus with Lakshmī, his consort, beside him, or reclining on a lotus leaf.

5. *Namaskāra* is a greeting made by joining the palms of the hands, which is the customary greeting amongst Hindus.

6. Daughter of Vṛiṣabhānu. the favourite mistress and consort of Kṛiṣṇa while he lived as Gopāla amongst the cowherds in Vṛindāvana. She was the wife of Ayanaghoṣa a cowherd. The Sanskrit Poet Jayadeva, the court poet of King Lakshmaṇasena, made Rādhā the central figure and heroine of his poetical work *Gītagovinda* (which has been translated into English by Keyt). Later on, Poet Chaṇḍīdāsa of Bengal and Poet Vidyāpati of Mithilā wrote beautiful songs about Rādhā and made her immensely popular.

Like Kṛiṣṇa, Rādhā has a dual role—one as the pretty cowherd girl who made love to Kṛiṣṇa, and the other the divine Rādhā, Shrī Rādhā, as she is called. Caitanya—the sage and poet, the Rādhā-Panthiīs, Vishṇusvāmīs and Nīmbārkars accepted her as a goddess and divine spouse of Kṛiṣṇa.

7. The incident is mentioned in the *Bhāgavata*. The gopīs (cowherd girls) had been complaining often to Kṛiṣṇa's mother about his stealing their

milk and butter. So Kṛiṣṇa thought of a new joke. With mischief in his mind he went to the river-bank where in a secluded spot, pretty young cowherd maidens, both old and young, were bathing in the river, having taken off their clothes and heaped them near the trunk of a tree. He quietly gathered up the clothes, and tying them into a bundle went up the tree. When the girls came out, imagine their horror when they found all their clothes gone ! Glancing up they found Kṛiṣṇa, who was at that time about seven years old, sitting with their clothes in a bundle. When they begged him to return them he began indifferently to play on his flute. Later, seeing their desperation he asked them to plead his forgiveness for making complaints against him, and seeing them do so very piteously, dropped their clothes one by one. It was great fun to see their embarrassment, and though the girls had promised not to do so, they still complained about the incident to his mother, and the boy Kṛiṣṇa got a good spanking for it !

8. Demons who were killed by Kṛiṣṇa.

9. The incident refers to the swallowing of the forest fire by Kṛiṣṇa which broke out, threatening the cattle and huts of the cowherds. In order to save them from destruction Kṛiṣṇa swallowed the flames of the fire and thus ended it.

10. Pūtanā was Kaṁsa's cousin and confidant. She was entrusted by Kaṁsa, the tyrant of Mathurā, to poison the child Kṛiṣṇa. She tried to do so by giving him suck to her breasts, the tips of which she had anointed with arsenic-paste. But instead of the child being poisoned, she herself died in the attempt, for the infant Kṛiṣṇa sucked out her very soul.

11. The reference is to an incident in the *Bhāgavata* which relates the various happenings in the life of Kṛiṣṇa. When Lord Kṛiṣṇa was born, all the gods went to Gokul to have his *darshana* (blessings). Brahmā; the Creator, followed them soon after, but his wisdom being confounded, he thought he would test Kṛiṣṇa. So he took away the calves which were there and hid them in a cave. But when he reached the infant Kṛiṣṇa, lo! the calves were there just the same! Kṛiṣṇa had duplicated the calves by his power of illusion, and Brahmā was astounded to see the same calves near the infant Kṛiṣṇa which he had hidden away in the cave.

12. A river in Central India, which passes through Orchhā, the native place of Poet Keshavadāsa.

13. A deep forest which runs along the banks of the Betwā river, near the city of Orchhā.

14. The native city of Poet Keshavadāsa. It was a small state or principality during his time ruled by Hindu rulers.

15. The four castes are, *Brahmins* the priestly caste, *Kshatriyas* the warrior class, *Vaishyas* the business class, and *Shūdras* the servant class. The division is laid down by the code of Manu.

16 The four stages in a man's life according to the *Upanishads*—1) *brahmacharya*, the stage of bachelorship, 2) gṛihastha, the family stage, 3) *vānaprastha* the life of retirement from the world, and 4) *sannyāsa*—the final stage of renouncement.

17. *Veda* is from the root *vid*—to know i. e. divine knowledge. The

Vedas are holy scriptures which are the foundation of Hindu religion. They were revealed to the ancient *rishīs*, or sages, whose names they bear. For this reason they were called *Shruti* i.e. 'what was heard'. They are four in number—*Rig*, *Yajur*, *Sāma*, and *Atharva*—the last one being of recent origin. They were written in Sanskrit between 1500-1000 B. C.

18. The Creator and the first god of the Hindu triad. He is the god of wisdom, and the four *Vedas* are said to have sprung from him. Brahmā has a red skin, wears white garments, and rides on a goose. He has four heads, and four arms, each holding the *Vedas* and a sceptre, a string of beads, a bow, and a water jug. Unlike the two gods of the Hindu triad—Viṣṇu and Shiva— he is not widely worshipped.

19. Madhukar Shāh was the ruler of Orchhā when Akbar was Emperor on the Mughal throne. He stubbornly resisted Akbar's attempts to conquer the state, and finally when hard pressed by the Mughal forces fled to the hills where he died. His son was Dūlah Rāma.

20. Gaharwārs were a branch of the solar race from whom the rulers of Orchhā had descended.

21. Indrajīt Singh was the younger brother of Mahārāja Rānāshāh, the Ruler of Orchhā, in whose hands the entire Orchhā administration rested at Keshavadāsa's time. Indrajīt was Keshava's patron, and it was for him that the Poet wrote his *Rasikapriyā*. He was a lover of poetry, music, dance, and song, and a number of lovely women graced his court.

22. The second god of the Hindu triad. (See note 4 of this chapter).

23. Two of the four sons of Dasharatha king of Ayodhyā. The story of Rāma is told in the Rāmāyaṇa, the most sacred book of the Hindus. Rāma broke Shiva's bow and married Sītā, daughter of Janaka, King of Mithilā. Later, due to a palace intrigue, he was banished to the forest for twelve years. His brother Lakshmaṇa and his newly-wed wife Sītā accompanied him. Sītā was abducted by Rāvaṇa the demon-king of Laṅkā, and later rescued after a battle between his army and Rāma's. Lakshmaṇa had great affection and regard for his elder brother, Rāma. The poet therefore compares the love of Indrajīt for his elder brother to Lakshmaṇa's love for Rāma.

24. *Guru mantra* is the holy formula given by a preceptor or sage to his disciple. According to Hindu belief such a formula was essential, and being initiated by a *guru* or master was considered one of the fundamental steps towards divine realisation.

25. *Saṁvat* means 'year'. It refers to the era of Vikramāditya dating from 57 B. C. Hindus work out their calender from this point of time, as Christians do from the birth of Christ. The current Christian year, 1971, corresponds to *Saṁvat* 2028.

26. For Hindus a dark complexion is no disqualification for beauty. Draupadī, who is considered to be the paragon of beauty, was dark. Hindus pay more attention to grace and features than to complexion.

27. Nine emotions—According to Bhoja, poetry is beautiful because of the presence of *rasa* (emotion). It is by reason of the experiences of many births that we get it in our souls. It is the germ from which other qualities grow. It is the inner quality of the ego, the idea of I-ness in man. It is man's

love for his own self, and that which makes him take even pain as pleasure. Hindi poets have given different classifications of the *rasas* in poetry. Keshava gives us nine, as in this verse. The primary emotion, according to him and the other Hindi poets, is love, called by Keshava the leader of emotions.

28. Usually an epithet for Viṣṇu, the Preserver but sometimes used for other gods too. The Poet says that love is the leader of all other emotions and its god is the Lord Viṣṇu himself.

29. Kāmadeva—See note 2 to this chapter.

30. Concealed and clear—Keshava divided various ideas about love, meeting, separation etc. into two main heads (a) hidden (b) clear, or manifest (*pracchanna* and *prakāsha*). This classification is novel and peculiar to him. It has been adopted throughout the book.

31. The most celebrated hero of Hindu mythology. Kṛiṣṇa was of the Yādava race who were settled in Vrindāvana and Gokul. The story of Kṛiṣṇa is given in detail in the *Bhāgavata Purāṇa* in which he kills the female demon Pūtanā, humbles the great serpent Kāliyā who lived in the Jamunā, steals the clothes of cowherd maidens when they go to bathe, lifts the mount Govardhana to save the people of Vrindāvana from the wrath of Indra, the god of rain when he poured down a heavy deluge, and finally kills the usurper Kaṁsa and puts the rightful king, Ugrasena, on the throne. The *Bhāgavata Purāṇa* also describes Kṛiṣṇa's exploits with his beloved cowherd maids (*gopīs*) the chief of whom was Rādhā, whom he wedded. His favourite dance was the *Rasamaṇḍala* in which the cowherd maids danced around him and Rādhā. Kṛiṣṇa had other wives too, including the famous Rukmiṇī, the betrothed of Shishupāla, whom he carried off by force, but the most heard of was Rādhā. A whole literature has developed around the loves of Rādhā and Kṛiṣṇa, and Hindi poets have used their romance as a peg on which to hang all their stories of love. The episodes of Rādhā and Kṛiṣṇa form the nucleus of most of the Hindi love poetry of the *Rītikāla* period. Other names of Kṛiṣṇa are Hari, Gopāla, and Shyāma. In the Mahābhārata, Kṛiṣṇa gives the message of the *Gītā* to Arjuna who acts as his charioteer, but in this Kṛiṣṇa shows his religious aspect, which finds place in Hindu religion and religious poetry as distinct from his romantic aspect.

32. The active role—Arabian writers on erotics do not favour the reversed role in sexual intercourse. *The Perfumed Garden* says : 'Do not let the woman perform the act of coition mounted upon you for fear that in that position some drops of her seminal find might enter the canal of your verge and cause a sharp urethritis'. Again, 'If you do it with the woman bestriding you, your dorsal chord will suffer and your heart will be affected; and if in that position the smallest drop of the usual secretions of the vagina enters your urethral canal, a painful stricture may supervene'. (Burton's translation).

The reversed position, however, has fascination for Hindu erotic writers who classify postures into three main divisions. (i) Normal (2) Reversed, and (3) Fellatia. Under these three broad classifications Vātsyāyana describes about eighty-four postures; others even more. Kalyāṇa Malla the author of *Anaṅga Raṅga* calls the reversed role *Purushāyitābandha* and describes it thus : '*Purushāyitābandha* is the reverse of what men usually practise. In this case the man lies upon his back, draws his wife upon him and enjoys her.

It is especially useful when he, being exhausted, is no longer capable of muscular exertion, and when he is ungratified, being still full of the water of love. The wife must therefore place her husband supine upon the bed or carpet, mount upon his person and satisfy his desire.' (Burton's translation).

In *Kāma Sūtra*, Vātsyāyana says about the reversed roles as follows :

'When a woman sees that her lover is fatigued by constant congress without having his desire satisfied, she should with his permission, lay down upon his back, and give him assistance by acting his part. She may also do this to satisfy the curiosity of her lover, or her own desire of novelty.

There are two ways of doing this, the first is when during congress she turns round, and gets on the top of her lover, in such a manner as to continue the congress, without obstructing the pleasure of it; and the other is when she acts the man's part from the beginning. At such a time, with flowers in her hair hanging loose, and her smiles broken by hard breathings, she should press upon her lover's bosom with her own breasts, and lowering her head frequently should do in return the same actions which he used to do before, and returning his blows and chaffing him, should say, "I was laid down by you and fatigued with hard congress, I shall now therefore lay you down in return'.

In *Chaurapañchāshikā* the Poet speaks of the reversed posture thus: 'I remember my beloved's face when she took the reversed role—her gold ear-ring, brushing against her cheeks, and drops of perspiration shining on her face like pearls'. The Hindi poet Bihārī describing the reversed role of the lovers says :

'Now vigorous is the loveplay with many cries and sighs.'
The lovers on love's battlefield are bent on glorious war,
Their roles reversed becoming, she raised above him lies
For the waistband bells are jingling, and the anklets silent are.'

The fourteenth century poet, Vidyāpati, has also given vivid descriptions of the reversed mode of lovemaking. In one of his verses he says :

'The *nāyikā* is enjoying making love in the reversed role. The necklace dangling upside down from her breasts appears as splendid as though streams of milk were sprouting from golden jars. Abandoning shame she crushes the lips of her lover as the moon sucking the lotus. The tinkling of her waistband bells appears as melodious as the musical instrument of the Kāmadeva-like warrior. The garland entwined with her loose hair is as though the swift waves of the Gaṅgā and Yamunā Rivers have met. Her face glistening with beads of perspiration looks as if the moon is being offered pearls having the splendour of the god of love.'

At another place describing the lovemaking of the lovers in reversed roles, the Poet says :

'The jingle of the *nāyikā's* waistband bells, the tinkle of the bracelets, and the clink of her anklets are so loud as it seems the god of love had admitted defeat in the battlefield of love, and his victorious opponents were loudly exulting in their triumph.' For a moment there was the sound of the rubbing of their thighs; then love's battle had ended and all was quiet and the lovers separated.'

Describing the lovemaking of Rādhā and Kṛiṣṇa in reversed roles one bosom companion says to another : 'Oh! my friend, how shall I describe their lovemaking, I know not whether it was real or merely a dream I saw, whether it is a thing I saw from near or from afar. O! friend, I can hardly describe the scene. It seemed as if Shrī Kṛiṣṇa lay like a cloud beneath the creeper of lightning that was Rādhā. She could be distinguished only by her necklace glittering like the waters of the River Gaṅgā. It seemed as if her dark tresses, dense and bright, had swallowed her beautiful moonlike face and the vermilion sunlike auspicious mark on her forehead, and as if the flower-like stars of her tresses lay scattered in all directions. Due to the motions of lovemaking her sky-blue garment was displaced, her heavy breasts were loosened, and her body began to move as one. The breeze of her deep breath began to blow, and the melodious sound of her ornaments was like a swarm of bees. The bodies of the lovers were drenched in the sea of love, but still there was no end to their lovemaking. (*Poems of Vidyāpati* : translation author's).

33. See notes 6 and 31 of this chapter.

34. The story of Sītā is told in the Rāmāyaṇa. Sītā was the daughter of Janaka, King of Videha, and wife of Rāma. Rāma won her by bending the great bow of Shiva. Later, she accompanied her husband to the forest in his banishment from Ayodhyā but was carried away by Rāvaṇa, King of Laṅkā, and confined there. Rāvaṇa made many attempts to win her over, but without success. When Rāma had slain him and freed Sītā, he refused to accept her as he could not convince the people of her purity. This, however, she asserted in a touching manner by undergoing ordeal by fire. A pile was raised and she entered the flames in the presence of gods and men. But she remained unharmed by the fire and the god of fire brought her forth and placed her in her husband's arms. The words in these verses refer to Sītā's ordeal by fire. Rādhā's form reflected in the mirror is compared to Sītā sitting in the blaze of fire.

35. The land of the *Yādavas*—the family to which Kṛiṣṇa belonged. It lies in the fertile valley of the Yamunā-River, and is full of shady trees, flowering creepers and pasture land. The central place in this country was Mount Govardhana which was worshipped as a holy mount by the *Yādavas*.

36. Camphor and sandal were used by Hindu women as cosmetics for beautifying the body. Both have a pleasant smell, and that is the reason why their use as unguents for anointing the limbs was popular with women. Sandal (Sanskrit—*chandana*) is an evergreen tree. Its wood is hard, and very close-grained and oily. The branches are slender and dropping. Sandal-paste is still commonly used in India especially in summer, for its cooling effect. The separated Rādhā feels the grief of estrangement so much that she adjures her handmaid to scatter the flowers from her hair and remove the camphor-dust and sandal which deck her body; for just as a fish which is caught can be saved only in dropping it in water again and not in milk, even so her separation can be cured by the presence of her lover, Kṛiṣṇa, and not by such adornments of the body.

37. The concluding verse—Each chapter of the *Rasikapriyā* has a concluding verse like this one stating what the reader has been told therein, and hinting at the subject matter of the next one.

CHAPTER II

The Nāyaka

The dictionary meaning of the word *nāyaka* is 'an eminent person'. While writing about love, Hindi poets used the word to signify an ideal lover. In *Kāma Sūtra*, when Vātsyāyana describes the life which a citizen should lead he had in mind such an ideal man. Though the Hindi poets do not tell us as much about the *nāyaka* as about the *nāyikā* (the ideal woman), most of them do mention him in their works, and enumerate what according to them are the characteristics of such a man. Poet Keshavadāsa follows the traditional pattern, and in this chapter he gives us his conception of what a *nāyaka* should be. He also classifies all *nāyakas* into four types—agreeable, dexterous, deceitful, and brazen, and gives examples of such kind. As usual he classifies each kind of *nāyaka* into his favourite division of hidden and manifest. This is a short chapter unlike the next one, in which, after having described the different kinds of *nāyakas* the Poet goes on to write of the *nāyikās*. In line with the fashion of other poets who wrote before him, Keshavadāsa's analysis of women is much more exhaustive and meticulous than that of men.

Who is a *nāyaka*?

Know him a *nāyaka*, says Keshava,
Renouncing, young, vigorous, vain,
Forgiving, and adept in love;
Handsome, wealthy, skilful, plain;
Such *nāyakas* of four kinds there are—
Genial, brazen, crafty, clever.

The agreeable *nāyaka*

Who loves with action, speech, and thought,
His wedded wife with faith deep sown,

For other women caring not
Agreeable *nāyaka* is known.

Example of a hidden agreeable *nāyaka*

The nāyikā says to Kṛiṣṇa:

'Without me, love, you do not sit
To laugh and sport; to maids untrue
Inclined not: yet 'tis as befits
A gentle nature—one should do
That which for ever can be done,
And yet not reach men's prying ears:
Clothes, ornaments, and a good home,
Are somehow got: Oh! Kṛiṣṇa, I fear
Without me you no betels[1] take,
O! tell me why do you abstain?
Is it for love of me, or hate?
This would I know, for I am pained.'

Example of a manifest agreeable *nāyaka*

The nāyikā's handmaid says to her:

'Your eyes are straight, and straight your sight,
Straight things you hear and understand,
Plain words you speak, and from your bright
Mouth, moon-shaped, pure laughter does come.
'Twas as if you have gathered now
In you the plainness of the world'
O! friend, when straight you are, then how
Have crafty Kṛiṣṇa you so enthralled?'

The nāyikā answers:

'My eyes are restless not, O! friend,
Nor my speech graceful, ne'er I did
With ornament myself adorn,
Nor learnt I e'er my brows to knit.
With cunning I ne'er on him looked,
Then why should I be slandered, pray?

Deceitful ways have I forsook,
Why he's still bound I cannot say.'

The dexterous *nāyaka*

Who loves his other wives as much
As his first wedded, and whose heart
Is never fickle—*nāyaka* such
Of steady love is dexterous called.

Example of a hidden dexterous *nāyaka*

Hearing through her bosom friend of the fascination of the nāyaka for some other woman, the nāyikā, addressing her mind, says

'O! mind e'en by mistake show not
Conceit to lovers as Shrī Kṛiṣṇa,
If him you love not from the heart
No good will this perverseness bring.
In this world tongues will falsely speak
As for Sītā the messenger,[2]
So trust the eye for what they see
And not the ears for what they hear!
The Gokul[3] hussies e'er deceive
With prattling tongues, but to this day
My lover Kṛiṣṇa with me is pleased,
And of the morrow who can say?'

An example of the manifest dexterous *nāyaka*

The nāyikā says to her intimate handmaid:

'Friend still his gaze with ardour stirs
As 'twas before; his fears as old,
And so the tender words that were,
Caressing yet my love-filled soul,
And so his laughter and love-sport—
Oh! how much more should I relate!
His faithlessness[4] have your eyes told,
Or has your fancy wrought this tale?

The deceitful *nāyaka*

Who says sweet words, yet is in sooth
A hypocrite; who has no dread
Of doing wrong; removed from truth—
Nāyaka deceitful, he is said.

Example of a hidden deceitful *nāyaka*

Seeing the redness of anger in the eyes of his nāyikā the nāyaka, trying to conceal his wrong-doing, says to her :

'The redness of your eyes is like
Bright lilies red, red sandal-paste
No whit their splendid redness vies
With burnished gold, or *champā*[5] pale.
O ! why do you thus on me glance?
Who is that man on whom you throw
Your gaze, with eyebrows made aslant?
Seeing your eyes red, I guess they glow
Not from night's rage: my body burns
Red hot with parting; e'er your eyes
Dwell in my heart, and heated turn
Bright red; so in them redness lies'[6]

Example of a manifest deceitful *nāyaka*

The *nāyikā* maid says to Kṛiṣṇa :

'In your ear's hue your eyes are steeped
They haste to see of whom they hear,
And you too wander as black bee[7]
Tongue's bliss to taste; more things I fear
Hid there be—I would not disclose—
Which even a witless man would guess!
Both good and bad right well you know
O ! Kṛiṣṇa; your limbs by one possessed
Are; by another is your soul !
And guile and cunning in you reign

She you have tamed, and me too hold !
O ! lord of *Braja*, *you* who has tamed?'

The brazen *nāyaka*

Whom beating and abuse shame not,
Says Keshavadāsa; who fear forgoes;
Who owns not even a noticed fault,
Him brazen *nāyaka*, wise men know.

Example of a hidden brazen *nāyaka*

Who steals the pots with butter filled[8]
Not counting curd and milk; who smiles
When he is cursed, and when forbid
Does come as if one him invites !
What more should I speak of his name?
All virtues in him long have died;
Friend ! Shrī Kṛiṣṇa is of all the bane,
And who shall for him make reply ?

Example of a manifest brazen *nāyaka*

Who demurs not an oath to swear
Who steals, and yet is unconcerned!
Of village council[9] has no fear,
Whose eyes with sensual passion burn :
Who knows no shame, nor fears to lose
His well-being, who me artless knowing
Does closer come; who faithless proves—
Why tire your mouth to speak to him?

Concluding verse

Thus have the poets wise described
Who *nāyakas*; and now I will tell
In the same strain, the diverse kinds
of *nāyikās* that are known to dwell.

NOTES

1. Leaves of a creeper which are chewed after being smeared with a paste of catechu and lime along with betel-nuts. The catechu paste is applied to the back of the leaf on one side, and the lime paste on the other. The betel-nuts are then placed on the leaf, and for those who like tobacco, and the leaf is folded in the form of a cone. The betel-leaf is chewed usually after the principal meals but those who have developed a habit of chewing it, do so at all times, and keep the betels ready-made in a small metal box. After chewing, the mixture turns a maroon colour. While normally the betel is offered after meals to improve taste Vātsyāyana has a novel use for it in the *Kāma Sūtra*. Speaking of the method of creating confidence in a newly-wed wife, he says the husband should first embrace her, and when she accepts his embrace he should persuade her to bite off part of a betel which he has in his own mouth. Under this pretext he should kiss her lips softly and with grace without making a sound. Also according to Vātsyāyana the offering of leaf with a slit in the middle means 'breaking off' in the language of love. A betel-leaf with an arrow out in the middle signifies passionate love.

2. We are told in the *Rāmāyaṇa* that when Rāvaṇa, the demon king, carried away Sītā, the wife of Rāma, he lodged her in a garden near his place closely guarded by she-demons. He also sent messengers to her bringing her false news of Rāma's banishment and death in an attempt to win her over for himself, but Sītā kept faith in her lord. The reference here is to these messengers who conveyed false news to Sītā.

3. A village in Braja, the native village of Nanda, the head of the *Shūra Yādava* class, in which many of the cowherd men and women lived. It forms the centre of Kṛiṣṇa's early exploits.

4. Vātsyāyana has something to say about faithlessness both in men as well as women. He details the signs by which a woman can know that her lover has ceased to care for her. These are not giving her what she wants, making false promises, deceit, failure to fulfil her desire, talking secretly with his own servants and those of a previous beloved of his, and sleeping in some other house on a false pretence. After giving the signs of the wane of love the author counsels the lady to get rid of such a lover, for accomplishing which he gives twenty-eight methods, by following which she can gradually show her indifference and finally get rid of him. Before doing so however she should get hold of all his wealth by stratagem, and if her lover is a rich man she should ever after treat him with respect, and if poor forget about him.

Regarding an unfaithful wife. Vātsyāyana observes that a good method to avoid incontinence in her is to engage a young woman to keep an eye on her and inform him about her chastity from time to time. According to him if a clever man is fully acquainted with the methods of winning other people's wives, that knowledge should also help him in not being deceived by his own. According to Kalyāṇa Malla, the writer of *Anaṅga Raṅga*, the main causes for faithlessness between lovers, are lack of variation in sensual pleasures, and the monotony which settles down after some time. This monotony leads to satiety, and aversion to sexual union, which drives men and women into the arms of others, and the result is adultery, polygamy, abortion, and a thousand such ills which cast a slur on them and their ancestors.

5. *Champā*—mischelia campacca or Spanish jasmine, is a small flowering tree about ten feet high. During the hot and rainy season it bears large corymbs of big white exquisitely fragrant flowers with the interior of their cups yellow.

6. The *nāyaka* says, 'I do not think your eyes are red due to last night's anger, but the fact is that your eyes ever reside in my heart and when my heart becomes heated due to the fire of your separation they (the *nāyikā's* eyes) become red with heat!' The *nāyaka*, who has been enjoying himself with another woman, tries thus playfully to detract the *nāyikā's* attention from his fault.

7. Hindi poets dwell frequently on the black bee in love-poetry. This is a big black insect of the humming variety which hovers round flowers for their pollen. The affinity of the black bee to flowers is compared to the attraction of the lover to the beloved. In describing a woman's beauty it is often said that black bees gather round her, taking her for a sweet scented flower. Poet Bihārī has a beautiful description of a woman who assays out stealthily to meet her lover. On the way, to her chagrin, the moon rises and lays her bare to prying eyes. She is considering whether she should go back or not, when lo ! black bees hover round her attracted by her scent, and provide her the much-needed cover :

'While halfway on the path that lady was,
The moon rose in the sky, whereat perplexed,
If she should forward go, or yet turn back.
She halted doubting; when lo! all at once
The black bees round her gathered, by the scent,
Sweet of her body drowned, and all was dark!'

(Bihārī, Satsaī.)

So is a woman described in Bāṇa's *Harṣacharita* :

'A thick swarm of bees settling eagerly upon her eyes beautiful as a pair of blue lotuses, hid half her face, which thus appeared as if it was covered with a dark blue silk veil.'

8. The reference is to Kṛiṣṇa. As a child he used to steal butter, curd, and milk. In the *Bhāgavata* an incident is described in which the boy, Kṛiṣṇa, enchanted by the sight of a pot of butter on a rope-hanger could not resist the temptation to sample it. He threw a stone at the pot and broke it and not only enjoyed as much of it as he could himself, but also invited his pet monkeys to have the rest. On seeing this his mother, Yashodā, became very angry and gave him a good beating, and bound him to a mortar.

When Kṛiṣṇa grew up he did not forget his old habit, and would sometimes steal curd from the jar carried by a passing cowherd girl. Because of this Kṛiṣṇa is also called by the name *Mākhan chor* i. e. 'pilferer of butter', (*mākhan* = butter : *chor* = thief)

9. The village council is a body of the village elders which considers and decides all local matters of the village. Often matters of a personal nature are also considered by it. Thus it is a powerful body which is feared

and respected by village folk. The village council can even ostracise a person for a wrong-doing or turn him out of caste, which means that persons of his own community would then have nothing to do with him. The village council still exists in modern India in the form of the *gaon samāj* which looks after the village land and property and keeps accounts, and through the *panchāyatī adālat* even decides cases involving minor offences.

CHAPTER III

The Nayika

The dictionary meaning of *nāyikā* is 'a beautiful young woman'. Hindi poets classify *nāyikās* under various heads according to qualities, moods, or age, in relation to their husbands or lovers. Some writers like Bharata give as many as fourteen classifications. From the point of view of looks and figure Keshavadāsa follows the fourfold classification of Vātsyāyana (*Padminī*, *Chitriṇī*, *Shaṅkhinī* and *Hastinī*). From the point of view of qualities he has three divisions of *nāyikās*, namely—*svakīyā*, the *parakīyā*, and the *sāmānyā*. Of the *svakīyā* there are three types viz., *mugdhā*, *madhyā* and *prauḍhā* with their various sub-divisions, while of the *parakīyā nāyikā* there are two. Of the *sāmānyā*, or ordinary kind of *nāyikā*, Keshava does not say anything at all. Examples of women in diverse situations are given throughout to illustrate the concept of each variety of *nāyikā*. In these, for the most part, the lover is Kṛiṣṇa, and his beloved is Rādhā.

Apart from describing the different kinds of *nāyikās* the Poet narrates the seven ways of making love, the seven positions which are adopted by lovers in sexual intercourse, and the sixteen ways in which women adorn themselves. Having described the various kinds of women in this chapter, which is the longest in the book, Keshavadāsa goes on, in the next, to narrate the ways in which they meet their lovers and enjoy the pleasures of union.

Nāyikās according to body build

Poet Keshava says, diverse there be
Of women, as have been described,
The *Padminī* and *Chitriṇī*
Shaṅkhinī, *Hastinī*—of four types.

The *Padminī*

Of mien auspicious, odour sweet
Whose love is joyful and complete,
Who little sleep and hunger knows,
And rage and arrogance too less shows.
For lovemaking who little cares,
Who bashful is and wise, who bears
A bounteous heart and tender mind;
Who cheerful is, whose body shines
As gold; who raiment clean does wear,
Whose private parts have not a hair:
A women with these qualities
Is known to all as *Padminī*.

Example of a *Padminī*

When speaking, she so sweetly[1] smiles,
It seems as fragrant flowers would fall !
Her flirting is mysterious; wise
Is she in all the arts of love.
Of snake-maidens,* celestial nymphs,
And singing girls, I offering make
Unto her beauty; women seem
But vulgar when against her placed.
Says Keshavadāsa for her I die,
Darling of Braja—her Brahmā[2] made
One of her kind; lo ! round her fly
So many with their longings swayed,
As black bees; of Vṛiṣabhānu[3] this child
As lovely *champā* bud does lie.

The *Chitriṇī*

For verse, and song, and dance, who pines,
Of restless gaze, but steady mind :
Who likes to make love, whose love-seed
Is copious, and mouth smelling sweet :
With scanty hair on private parts,

Whose body's odour pleases all :
Whom pictures charm—such qualities
Are noticed in a *Chitriṇī*.

Example of a *Chitriṇī*

To listen unto all, but speak
Oneself; to gaze into eyes deep;
To dance, sing, on the *vīṇā*[4] play,
To please oneself, and captivate
Others; to love, to laugh one's fill
To make sweet love while time there's still
And such like—if these were outlined
In Hari's[5] portrait, all would find
Solace to merely on it gaze,
And who would pine to meet him, pray?

The *Shaṅkhinī*

Adept in showing wrath and guile,
Whose body moist and hairy is,
In wearing red clothes who delights
And for nail-marks who has relish :
No patience has, nor shame, nor fear,
Whose love-seed has a salty smell,
To whom the game of love is dear—
By these a *Shaṅkhinī* one tells.

Example of a *Shaṅkhinī*

The camel goes not into rows
Of plantain trees, but chews instead
The thorny plum tree, nor bestows
His longing on the *champā* bud:
And to the lotus he goes not
Viewing it foul; if he is grazed
On clove creepers, says Keshavadāsa
And gooseberries, and betels frail—
However one may seek to feed

Him—raisins or dates—yet he must
Turn from these dainty things, and seek
The prickly leaves of thorny shrubs[6]!

The Hastinī

Whose fingers, feet, and face, and lips,
And eyebrows, coarse are; sharp whose tongue;
Mind restless, and whose gait slow is,
Whose sweat and love-seed smells as one—
The ichor of an elephant; whose
Tresses are dirty brown; limbs all
Bristle with hair, sharp and profuse—
Such woman *Hastinī* men call.

Example of a *Hastinī*

Foul smells she, how have poor fools sought
Their pleasures with her? Like thorns rear
Her bristling hair, says Keshavadāsa;
She speaks words harsh which pain the ear,
As if a black bee lotus left
Elephant's cheeks to hover round;
Or as to live in wicked hell
One preferred to a worldly crown!

Nāyikās according to qualities

Three kinds of *nāyikās*—know that are[7]
Of that *nāyaka*—the *svakīyā*
The *parakīyā* and *sāmānyā*.

The *svakīyā*

In wealth, misfortune, and death too,
Who constant faith in her spouse keeps
Throughout, with mind, and word, and deed—
Her should one a *svakīyā*[8] view.

The kinds of *svakīyā nāyikās.*

Of *svakīyās* there are three kinds
Mugdhā, *madhyā*, and the *prauḍhā*[9]
And four types of each we find.

The *mugdhā nāyikā*

Of *mugdhās* four kinds are there known
The newly-wed; the girl who's grown
To puberty; the maid unused
To making love, and one who's used.

The newly-wed *mugdhā*

The splendour of the wedded *mugdhā*
Each day redoubled is, and so
A new bride, learned men her call,
And so skilled poets do her know.

Example of a newly-wed *mugdhā*

One handmaid says to another about the nāyikā:

'The ways to win her Kṛiṣṇa she knows,
But for his words she careth not!
The tips of her young breasts do grow
With each new day, O! friend, so fast,
I know not what will them contain!
Her chemise hides them not[10], her eyes,
Mysterious and restless, remain
Now here now there, and scan the sky:
If so her splendour will increase
From day to day, then where, O! friend,
Will its radiance imprisoned be
Which bathes her limbs from end to end?'

The adolescent *mugdhā*

A *mugdhā* maid adolescent
Is one whose girlhood day by day
Is by her youthfulness displaced.

Example of an adolescent *mugdhā*

The handmaid says to the nāyaka about the nāyikā:

'Her eyebrows dance with pleasure filled,
Her hips her waist at last has robbed;[11]
Her voice now agitated is,
And with shyness her eyes do pause:
In movement now she knows no rest,
You may demur to meet her, friend,
But youth has met her ripening breasts
And driven out her ignorance.'

The *mugdhā* unused to lovemaking

The *nāyikā* who speaks and plays,
And laughs and fears as young girl,
Says Keshavadāsa, her men do say
A *mugdhā* is, unused to love.

Example of a *mugdhā* unused to lovemaking

'Do not pull at my clothes, my love!
Be not so restless! slumbering deep
The parrot is already, thus
Let starling also fall asleep.
Turn low the lamp, my moonlike face
You still may see; the deer and geese
From this bedchamber let me take,[12]
What you desire, me too does please!'
Thus when that maiden's timid prayer
The *nāyaka*, Shyāma, heard, he did feel
A hundred times more charmed with her,
Than if to make love she did yield.

The *mugdhā* used to lovemaking

Who with the greatest bashfulness
Makes love, thus winning the regard
Of her dear husband—such a girl
A *mugdhā* used to love is called.

Example of a *mugdhā* used to lovemaking

He called and called, I did not speak,
Then to win me my feet he touched,[13]
I covered myself with a sheet,
Then my denial to repulse,
He crushed me close in his embrace,
But still I did not yield to him;
And then to lift my eyes to gaze
Into his, up he forced my chin
With thumb, but still this wretched shame
My eyes possessed so, that e'en then
His efforts futile did remain,
My glance to him I could not send.

The joy given by a *mugdhā*

At first the *mugdhā* does not lie
Beside her lover, but when she is
By her maid persuaded to comply,[14]
No rapture vies with the one she gives!

Example of the joy given by a *mugdhā*

Speaking of the nāyikā's lovemaking, one maid says to another:

'The *nāyaka* on her feet did fall
Beseeching her in many ways,
Then with a flutter of her heart
Upon the bed her foot she laid:
'Twas only when a million oaths
He swore, that she did courage take

With him to lie[15]; then venturing forth
She laid her lips on his, which gave
Much pleasure to him—then indeed
In her one breath all fragrances
Within a moment were released
That on him did their rapture shed'.

The *mugdhā's* lovemaking

The *mugdhā* likes not love to make
Nor joy finds; and if pressed to do
By strength and wile that which she hates
No bliss or charm from it accrues.

Example of the *mugdhā's* lovemaking

The handmaid says to the nāyaka:

'With all the maidens looking on
You pleased her, and oaths made her take,
Then drugging her, *nāyaka* stubborn!
Forced her to sleep with you; that maid
Slender as lotus root, and sweet
As jasmine garland, you have pressed
So roughly; are you man or beast ?[16]
She knows not when morn comes, nor says
A word: see how her body is
As a spoilt picture, by you marred:
O! novice lover, pray in this
What pleasure have you got from her?'

The *mugdhā*'s arrogance

The *mugdhā* girl no arrogance shows,
And if she does then well it were
By frightening her, to make it go,[17]
As done to those who foolish are.

How to remove the *mugdhā*'s arrogance

Sunk in arrogance sat the *mugdhā*
And spoke not even when spoken to,
But with her nails she lines did draw,[18]
Seeing which the knowing *nāyaka* threw
His palms up, saying, god has made
Lines short and long upon my hand,
Which one, tell me, is the line of age?
With love filled, this she could not stand,
And in a frightened voice did say,
'Dear love! how is it, let me see?'

The kinds of *madhyā nāyikās*

Four kinds of *madhyās* know there are
Ārūḍhayauvanā pragalbhavachanā
Prādurbhūtamanobhavā surativichitrā.

The *ārūḍhayauvanā madhyā*

The *nāyikā* whose youth shines from far
Full of fortune and married bliss
Who loves her husband with all her heart,
Ārūḍhayauvanā madhyā is.

Example of an *ārūḍhayauvanā madhyā.*

The hand-maid says to the nāyikā:

A goddess-like *gopī*[19] I espied
Today, Gopāla,[20] whose crescent brow
As half-moon was, whose piercing eyes
Were Kāmadeva's arrows, and eyebrows[21]
As bows; and perfumed was her breath
As scent of lotus flowers, her teeth[22]
As seeds of sweet pomegranate:
Her laughter bright as lightning,[23] feet
Like lotuses; her neck[24] and arms,

As jars, and belly as betel-leaf:[25]
As swan's her gait,[26] and limbs that shone
As burnished gold[27]—and her smell sweet[28]
As does from earthen vessel rise
When water first is poured inside.

The *pragalbhavachanā madhyā*

Says Keshavadāsa the *nāyikā* bold
With tongue who oft complains, and threats,
Her *pragalbhavachanā madhyā* know.

Example of a *pragalbha vachanā madhyā*

O ! Kṛiṣṇa, fine you are ! and have learnt
Strange ways—your eyes so seem distraught !
I know you, and those whom you tempt,
Oh ! go away ! Why go you not ?
O ! Kṛiṣṇa, in garden and in grove
Who will by day be led ? Oh ! how
Glance you with false conceit: all know
Your secret; see what happens now ![29]

The *prādurbhūtamanobhavā madhyā*

The *nāyikā* who with body and mind
Towards lovemaking is inclined,
With all the signs of love adorned,
Is *prādurbhūtamanobhavā madhyā* known.

Example of a *prādurbhūtamanobhavā madhyā*

A *gopī* I did light upon
Much different from a cowherd girl,
Such splendour from her body shone
My eyes remained transfixed on her.
Ne'er one so charming met my gaze
The loveliness of all worlds three[30]

In her one sidelong glance I'll stake
To moon or Kṛiṣṇa she'd wedded be.

The *surativichitrā madhyā*

Whose lovemaking takes various ways,
Of hearing whom men her desire,
Whom poets find hard to delineate,
She is a *surativichitrā madhyā*.

Example of a *surativichitrā madhyā*.

Soft laughter full of coquetry
In her there dwells, and endless bliss
Is to see her or speak; she knows
The seven kinds of love[31] that flow
From act and pose, and mode reversed,
And shame has quite abandoned her.
Her clothes and trinkets strewn do lie,
Hearing her lustful shouts and cries
Even birds coo—such should one deem
Lovemaking, all else is routine.[32]

The seven ways of making love.

Embracing,[33] kissing,[34] rubbing, touch—
Marking with nails[35], and by the teeth,[36]
Sucking the lips when drunk with love,
Are seven ways which lovers seek.

The seven postures of sexual union

The firm, the slanting, face to face,
And turned away, above, below,
And supine—these are seven ways[37]
In which fond lovers bliss do know.

The sixteen adornments for women[38]

First come ablutions of all kinds,
Second the bath, then raiment clean;

Fourth braiding[39] hair, and then applying
Cosmetics; putting vermilion in
The parting of the hair[40]; on brow
Crescent of sandal-paste—then paint
A black mole on the cheek, enow
With sandal-paste[41] the limbs anoint,
And palms with paste of myrtle leaves,[42]
With flowers and ornaments then deck,
Chew betel-leaves to sweeten breath,[43]
And cardamom—and then the teeth
With powder black stain,[44] lips paint red;
Last collyrium in eyes that tease[45]—
Thus with sixteen adornments helped,
Each moment you your spouse should please
By speech, laughter, and elegant gait:
Says Keshava, O! Rādheya yourself
With sixteen aids thus lovely make.

After the night of love

***One handmaid says to another*:**

'After the night of love,[46] my dear,
When the lovers lay awake in bed,
As lovely ocean they appeared,
Their beauty the water in it—the red
That decked her heels a fire which burned
Reflected—betel-juice, nail-marks
Upon her breasts as moons did run;
As nectar were sandal-paste spots,
Collyrium in eyelashes, venom;
The garland that had snapped and dropped
Seemed as it were a precious gem,
And sleep sojourning in eyes was
The sweet wine which them drunk did make,
So that with bliss the two did sway.

The three more kinds of ***madhyās***

Of ***madhyā nāyikās*** poets know
Three more kinds—***dhīrā***, adhīrā,

And *dhīrādhīrā*. From whom flow
Words crooked—she is known the *dhīrā*:
Adhīrā speaks words rough, uneven;
The *dhīrādhīrā* sore complains
Against her husband when she sees him.

Example of a *dhīrā madhyā*

O! friend you would convince me soon
As lotus his face is, but I
Do rather think it like the moon:
I saw in his heart dalliance lie,
At which my heart did tremble so
In fear, as if a chill I caught,
My peacock-like eyes, 'gan to close;
Like moon I knew then his face was,
Not like the lotus! for when near
The moon is then a chill does creep,
And when on the sky it appears
The lotus closes up and sleeps.[47]

Another example of a *dhīrā madhyā*

Chiding Kṛiṣṇa, the nāyikā says:

'Your limbs as your aged sire's I find,
As his they shake—yet virile still
As Balarāma's[48] who fans lust with wine!
And your face as your mother's is,
Your nature as earth, lazy; mind
As the wind restless; and unstained
As water, strong as fire; you shine
As brilliant skies; in love's fond game
Adept as Kāmadeva's wife; your form
As of love's god—then tell me why
The habit in you has been born,
To make you speak, oh! Kṛiṣṇa, such lies?'

Example of a *dhīrādhīrā madhyā*

The nāyikā says to Kṛiṣṇa:

Someone has counselled you alack!
So from you love like an ocean flowed,
His jewel-like mind who has got back
Once having put in another's hold?
Now converse only with your eyes,
The time to speak, alas! is gone;[49]
O! Kṛiṣṇa, in you do I confide
As you have in your handmaids done.'

The four kinds of *prauḍhā nāyikās*

Four kinds of *prauḍhās* know to be—
Samastarasakovidā, *vichitravibhramā*,
Akrāmati, and *labdhāpati*.

The *samastarasakovidā prauḍhā*

A mine of pleasure who can turn
Of whatever kind a man desires,
Such woman, pleasing everyone,
Is the *samasta rasakovidā*.[50]

Example of a *samastarasakovidā*

A cowherd maiden I have seen
Of form unequalled, Oh! Gopāla!
Her hue more lovely than gold seemed
Her scent like new-filled earthen jar's:
'Twas as though Splendour herself came
Upon the earth, or lightning took
A woman's form; no earthly dame,
Or goddess, or she-demon looked
With so much coquetry; 'twas if
Sarasvatī[51] on earth had stayed
So seemed that girl—key of all bliss—

Or lovely child sprung from Kāmadeva
Born of Menakā[52]—so I weened
That cowherd girl whom I had seen.

The *vichitravibhramā*

Attracted by whose splendour strong
The woman messenger does speed
To take her to her spouse lovelorn,
She *vichitravibhramā* is indeed.

Example of a *vichitravibhramā*

Her elegant gait his mind bewitched,
Waves of desire did in him course,
He gazed on at the playful bliss
Of her eyebrows, her laughter soft:
The fragrance of her limbs, her glance
Sidelong, entranced so Nandakumār,[53]
Kāmadeva he turned,[54] and so perchance
His flowerly arrows he forgot:
And her eyes burning with love's fire
Themselves his shafts were of desire!

The *akrāmati prauḍhā*

An *akrāmati prauḍhā* men say
Is one who by speech, deed, and thought,
Her husband's mind does subjugate.

Example of an *akrāmati prauḍhā*

The handmaid says to the nāyikā:

O! friend mine, Shrī Kṛiṣṇa sings and plays
And dances for you, you alone,
And decks himself in many ways,
Not thinking of another woman:
And yet contented you are not,

Do as you wish, but 'tis not meet
When one so straight as Kṛiṣṇa you've got
To make him fall upon your feet!'[55]

The *labdhāpati prauḍhā*

She who her husband's friends esteems
As she does him, such woman is
A *labdhāpati prauḍhā* deemed.

Example of a *labdhāpati prauḍhā*

Rādhā, the daughter of Vṛiṣabhānu
With splendour shines before Shrī Kṛiṣṇa
As though great Brahmā[56] had her formed
As he did those two handsome beings
Sarasvatī[57] and Kāma,[58] I've known
No other like her to exist.
In all the three worlds I have roamed,
But found not one as Rādhā is.

Three other kinds of *prauḍhās*—first the *dhīrā*

Who shows her love in outward wise,
Not from her heart; and disrespect,
Though in respect it be disguised :
Such woman false, men *dhīrā* tell.

Example of a *dhīrā*[59]

When Shrī Kṛiṣṇa came, she went to meet
Him, and with love she made him sit :
Then herself she did wash his feet,
And box placed with betels in it :
Then made two betels him to please,
And as the fan[60] she deigned to take,
Laughing, he caught her arm and teased,
'O ! love ! you warmly welcome make!'

Example of an *ākṛitiguptā prauḍhā*

You only see when forced to look,
And laugh when you are made to laugh,
And speak only when spoken to,
At other times you silent are :
And after many vows you rest
In his embrace, to love not prone,
And betels take only when pressed[61]
As girl now come to husband's home.
O ! maiden who taught you this way
To hold your lover's mind in sway?

Another example of an *ākṛitiguptā prauḍhā*

Look to your gain as all girls do
And hear what profits—what does bring
Existence to all; swear to him
'Lo! all these things have different proved.'
To him explain: 'All that I talked
O ! Kṛiṣṇa, was lies!' and if he slights,
Now who is there at you to scoff?[62]

The *adhīrā*

She who is on the surface harsh
But in her mind her spouse adores,
As sugarcane's rough outer bark
Shows not the sweetness in its core.
Or she who seeing her husband do
Great wrong, does not him favour show;
Such maiden who with caution moves
Keshava, *adhīrā prauḍhā* knows.[63]

Example of an *adhīrā*

The nāyikā says to her erring husband :

'My heart is sorrowful, do not speak
To me, and cease to laugh and chat,

Within the mirror glance and see
How drowsy are your eyes—alack!
Nice do they look! today to wound
Me, you have come again, distraught :
Your vows of yesterday, so soon,[64]
O ! husband mine, you have forgot!'

A *parakīyā*

Beloved of men who are most renowned,
The *parakīyā*,[65] wise men have found.

Two kinds of *parakīyās*

Ūḍhā anūḍhā, of two types
Are *parakīyās*—by them enslaved
Are, both the ignorant and wise !

The *ūḍhā* and the *anūḍhā*

The *ūḍhā* is a married woman,
Unūḍhā one not wed; and now
Says Keshavadāsa, so that you know them,
Their hid and clear charms I'll recount.

Example of an *ūḍhā*

With all her bosom friend adorned
Tha *nāyikā* in the assembly shines,
All eyes reflect her beauteous form;
When questioned she is not inclined
To plainly speak, but all things hid
She keeps, and to herself she laughs.
On the one hand her friends she quips
With playful frolic, telling all
With hints and gestures, and still keeps
Her spouse amused. Her secret none
Know—when and where her eyes do creep,
Roving on all, yet ever return

Her lover, Kṛiṣṇa, to gaze upon,
And having quickly gazed, pass on.[66]

Example of an *anūḍhā*

Amidst the belles of Braja one day
Sat Rādhā, daughter of Vṛiṣabhānu
The lovely game of dice[67] she played
With bosom friends; and when far gone
She was in it, perchance there stole
Softly behind, her lover, Kṛiṣṇa;
Whom hearing, restlessness awoke
Within her mind, and none took in
This secret; and they wondered why
So suddenly were roused her eyes.

Other characteristics of an *ūḍhā* and an *anūḍhā*

Her *secrets* who discloses not,
Anūḍhā is; who does disclose
To friends things hid and clear, is called,
An *ūḍhā*—thus the wise them know.

Discourse of an *ūḍhā*

The nāyikā says to her handmaid :

'Today to Gokul when I went,
O ! bosom friend, the maidens there
Did treat me as the moon new-bent
Upon the sky;[68] at me they stared
And fingers showed—as though above
At the new moon: and all did swear
I was the maid by Kṛiṣṇa beloved.
And wagering, some said, "I declare
She's so; and others she is not !"
Some looked at me and laughed or smiled;
With glances meaningful they talked,
And looked at me with chiding eyes.

Concluding verse

Says Keshavadāsa, thus have I given
The kinds of *nāyikās* known to Kṛiṣṇa,
And now I will go on to sing
Of their joys and unions, clear, and hidden.

NOTES

1. Kalyāṇa Malla, the writer of *Anaṅga Raṅga*, describes four types of women. First is the *Padminī* or lotus woman. Her face is like the full moon, her body is soft and fleshy, her skin fine and tender and her complexion fair. Her eyes are bright and like those of the fawn, with reddish corners. She has a hard and full bosom and her neck is like a conch shell, so delicate that one can see through it the saliva that she swallows!' She has a straight and shapely nose, and three folds across her body near the umbilical region. Her vagina is like a lotus-bud and her seminal fluid smells like a fresh lily. Her gait is graceful as a swan's and her voice melodious as that of a cuckoo. The *Padminī* likes expensive white clothes, and jewels. She eats and sleeps little, worships the gods with devotion, and enjoys the talk of learned men.

The *Chitriṇī* is a woman of sanguine temperament. She is neither short nor long, with jet black hair, thick neck, tender limbs, lean waist, and hard full breasts, well balanced thighs, and heavy hips. The hair about her pubis is thin, and her mons veneris is soft and raised. Her seminal fluid is warm, abundant, and smells like honey. Her gait is like that of an elephant, and her voice joyful as that of the peacock welcoming the rain. A *Chitriṇī* is fond of pleasure, cultured, and accomplished, and likes to tame pet birds. She has medium carnal desire.

The *Śaṅkhinī*, or conch woman, has a bilious temperament. She has a tawny complexion, large body, thick waist, small breasts, and thick hands and feet. She is always glancing through the corner of her eyes. Her seminal fluid has a salty smell, and her pubis is covered with thick hair. Her voice is hoarse and harsh, and her gait ungraceful. She eats little, and likes red clothes and flowers. She is choleric, rude, insolent, vicious, cruel, and is always finding fault. She is greatly passionate, and at the time of the sex act drives her nails into her husband's body.

The fourth kind of woman is the *Hastinī*. She is short and stout, having a coarse and pale complexion. She has tawny hair, large lips, a harsh and unpleasant voice, and a bent neck. Her gait is sloven and awkward. Her seminal fluid has the smell of the ichor of an elephant in rut. She is shameless and greedy, and difficult to satisfy in sexual congress.

In *Padmāvatī*, Poet Malik Muhammad Jāisī also gives his impressions of these four conventional types of womanhood. His descriptions are as follows :

The *Padminī* :

Who like a lotus, short nor tall,
Nor broad, nor slender, yet has all
The marks of beauty, and does speed
As cygnet—she is *Padminī*.

The Chitriṇī :

The smiling girl of subtle grace,
White as a lily, and moon-faced,
Who as a swan moves, graceful—she
Of beauty rare is *Chitriṇī*.

The *Shaṅkhinī* :

Of bosom large and narrow waist,
And stout, who walks with lion's gait :
With hair upon her thighs and chins—
And looks downcast is *Shaṅkhinī*.

The *Hastinī* :

Of narrow bosom, and wide waist,
Large feet and head, elephant's gait,
And arms well-formed, and breasts as be
And elephant's head is *Hastinī*.

(Jāisī, *Padmāvatī*).

Keshava's classification of women follows much on the same lines as the one made by Kalyāṇa Malla.

*Snake maidens—*nāga kumārīs*. The race of the *nāgas* (serpents) who were supposed to be a thousand in number, sprang from Kadrū wife of Kashyapa. Dwelling in *Pātāla* or the region below the earth, they were mythical semi-divine beings, having a human face, but with the tail of a snake. The females amongst the *nāgas* were called *nāga kanyās* or *nāga kumārīs*. (*kumārī* or *kanyā* means an unmarried girl). They were famed for their beauty, and some of them married men—as for example Ulūpī, the snake-maiden, who married Arjuna.

2. The first member of the Hindu triad. He is the supreme spirit and the creator of the universe. He was born from the mundane egg deposited by the supreme first cause, and is lord of all creatures. When Brahmā creates the world it continues so for 2,160,000,000 years at the end of which period it is consumed by fire, only the sages, gods, and elements surviving. Thereafter the world is again created, and this goes on till Brahmā's existence of a hundred years ends. After this he himself expires, and he and all the gods and sages and the entire universe are resolved into their constituent elements. Brahmā

has four heads and four arms. His vehicle is the swan, and his consort is Sarasvatī.

3. Rādhā's father.

4. The Indian lute.

5. Another name for Kṛiṣṇa.

6. The idea of this verse seems to be that the *Shaṅkhinī* woman, who is just as the camel, discarding plantain trees, *champā* flowers, lotus, gooseberries, clove creepers, betels, raisins, and dates, will chew instead the thorns of the plum tree, or the prickly leaves of thorny shrubs.

7. Kalyāṇa Malla enumerates eight types of *nāyikās*, namely :

Khaṇḍitā—the *nāyikā* whose husband comes from another woman with all the marks of enjoyment, like red eyes, scratches on his body, etc., and yet cajoles her into permitting sexual congress with him; and the *nāyikā* hesitates at first, but at last allows him.

Vāsakasajjitā—a fond bride who having spread her charming bed awaits with eager expectation the coming of her husband, her eyes constantly fixed on the door.

Kalahāntaritā—the lady who upbraids her husband when he falls on her feet in repentance for some wrong he has done her, and drives him away in anger, but when she is separated repents and begins to long for reunion.

Abhisārikā—the highly passionate woman who, when her desire is awakened, puts on an alluring dress, and goes brazenly, even at midnight, to the house of a stranger, looking for enjoyment with him.

Vipralabdhā—a woman who having sent a messenger to her lover, calling him to an appointed place, goes there, but finds only her messenger, not the lover with her, and becomes disappointed and agitated.

Viyoginī—The grieving woman whose husband has gone away to foreign lands, whom perfumes and good scenery serve only to increase her grief.

Svādhīnapūrvapatikā—the unfortunate woman whose husband gives her philosophical sermons when she needs gratification of her amorous desires.

Utkaṇṭhitā—the woman well-decked with ornaments with lively eyes who loves her husband to distraction and burning with passion awaits his coming with her head on a high pillow in her ornate bedroom.

Vātsyāyana's classification is threefold, namely :

Svakiyā—the highest type of womanhood, sharing the craving, the inclination, the pleasures, and the sorrows of her mate. She has the feeling of mutual interdependence, and at the same time she is free from the fear of social opprobrium. She is spontaneously prepared for dalliance and love.

Parakīyā—a woman who, while having all the above qualities, cannot have her pleasure due to fear or consideration of society. There is a slight difference between a youthful *parakīyā*, and one of middle age. While in the case of the former there is possibility of change in her attitude, this is not so for a woman of middle age. Another difference is that while the middle-aged woman is experienced in the art of love, a young *parakīyā* remains ignorant about it.

Veshyā— a woman having no fear or regard of society, and no ardour or craving for meeting her lover. She is constantly engaged in making money, and can almost be considered equivalent to a prostitute.

Apart from these major divisions other minor classifications have been made by Hindi poets. Poet Matirāma Rasarāja describes the *navoḍhā nāyikā* who is of the bashful and timid type :

'Extremely shy and timid, she does not come to her lover's arms; such a girl is called a *navoḍhā* by those well-versed in love.' Poet Chirañjīva has given a good account of the *kalahāntaritā nāyikā* :

'When Kṛiṣṇa came to me from one of his love haunts, I showed arrogance. This made him rise in anger, and alas ! I did not beseech him to stay. Oh ! how I curse myself now for not having done so !'

The *veshyā* is seldom described by Hindi poets, as she sells her love. In the Mahābhārata, however, we come across Urvashī who was deputed to tempt the great warrior, Arjuna. Poet Jāisī has given a beautiful description of the courtesans of Ceylon :

'From latticed windows do they glances steel,
The courtesans—with betel-reddened lips,
Within their saffron veils their forms concealed,
And on their ears the jewelled ear-rings peep.
The deer entranced are by their lute's sweet song,
Nor can the listener move another pace—
Brows bows, eyes archers; shooting arrows strong,
Upon the whetstone of their glances shaped.'

8. In *Satsaī*, *Bihārī* describes the fresh beauty of a newly married *Svakīyā* girl:

'Seeing the beauty of youth increase in her, the other co-wives feel jealous and are sad.' Describing another maiden whom chidhood has not quite left, he says :

'Ere childhood's glimmer has quite gone
The blaze of youth on her descends;
And mixing, they unto her lend
The brilliance of the shade and sun'.

Speaking of another *svakīyā nāyikā*, amorously inclined and keen to please, he describes the wile used by her lover to win her. The lady is lying with her face away from him on her bed of roses. He makes her afraid of the rose-petals, which he says will scratch her body, and she at once turns her face towards him :

9. Bihārī gives a charming picture of the *madhyā* type of woman. Describing the well-developed breasts of such a woman he says :

'With perfume o'erspread,
Her bodice plain and white,
Fails to hide her breasts,

Which stand out clear as the meaning
Contained in lines of verse.'

The *prauḍhā* woman, according to Bihārī, is one in whom the craving of passion is so intense that it has driven out all shame. Such a woman has no fear of her elders, or of what people think. She does not know what to say, and when. Such a *prauḍhā* woman has been described thus by him: 'the intoxication of her beauty has so taken hold of that *nāyikā* that night and day she remains drowned in it. It does not leave her for a moment. Drunk in this manner she has abandoned all fear. She does not have any sense of shame left, and all the time she prattles foolishly'.

The heavy breasts and the dimpled chin of the *prauḍhā* are described by Bihārī. 'Greatly tired by climbing her mountain-like breasts my gaze slowly moved onward, desiring to behold her face's loveliness, but on the way it came across the pit of her stomach in which it so fell that it could not come out again.'

Bihārī's *prauḍhā* is distinctive in her shamelessness, and even in her love-making. She cannot get up with ease in the early morning after a night of passionate love. Instead, 'the *nāyaka* and the *nāyikā* arise and sit with great difficulty when dawn comes; their eyelids are heavy with sleep and no longer able to sit, they embrace each other and fall back upon the couch'.

10. Similar is the vein in which Bihārī speaks of the breasts of his *nāyikā* which her bodice fails to hide :

'Numbed with her beauty, words cannot describe
Her body's loveliness, by clothes increased,
The splendour of her breasts her bodice hides
More than her bodice does her breasts conceal'.

Again, describing the rapidly developing breasts of a young girl he says:

'As in the summer, days increase,
And nights grow weaker—even so
The maiden's breasts with youth do grow
And slim her waist, the soul to please.'

Vidyāpati has also given us descriptions of the growing breasts of an adolescent girl. At one place, describing such a growing maiden he says : 'She often looks on her breasts at some lonely spot, and their sight gladdens her mind. Her breasts which were small as plums before, have now become large like oranges.' Or again, 'Now the loud laughter and merriment of her youth have been suppressed, and instead of that only quiet smiles linger on her lips. As if to make up for it, her breasts which had lain dormant till now have flowered and speak out in place of her forgotten laughter'. Elsewhere he gives a vivid and interesting description of the different stages of development of the breasts of a growing girl: 'In the beginning of youth the breasts of that girl were like small plums; thereafter increasing in size they became as big as oranges. Each day they began to increase, and the god of love also began to torment her. After some period they became large and hard and elongated like the big variety of lemons. Now they have taken the form of quinces or wood-apples. Searching for that lovely damsel, Kṛiṣṇa saw her bathing by the riverside. At that moment her thin saree, being wet, clung close to her bosom. The person who saw that beauty at such a rare moment should consider himself fortunate. The bosom of that girl was heaving, and her loose hair were scattered upon it...'

Describing the budding of a young maiden's breasts, Vidyāpati says : 'Now on tips of the rising breasts of the maiden small nipples like flower-buds can be seen.'

11. Compare the description of the girl ripening into womanhood given by Vidyāpati. 'The heaviness of her waist has been transferred to her hips, and her waist has become narrow.' Speaking of the beauty of a maiden, he says, 'On her pillar-like thighs shaped like golden trunks of plantain trees, is supported her waist thin as that of a lioness, and over it her heavy breasts are jutting like mountain peaks. Bihāri's *nāyikā* has a waist so thin that it can hardly be seen ! but,

'As if to make amends, god shaped
Her breasts and lions large.'

Ingenious is the description of Kādambarī's waist which was small and reduced as if by grief at not being able to see her face by reason of her lofty breasts:

In *Saundaryalaharī*, Rādhā's waist is said to be reduced to vanishing point by reason of her heavy breasts:

'O ! paragon of women ! your waist was
Too slender and curved, even at your birth;
'Tis now a vanishing line, what with your
Heavy breasts.'

The beloved of Sharkan in *The Arabian Nights* had a small waist, while her haunches were very heavy, so that, 'her body might have been thought to be a silver branch let into a wave of diaphanous crystal.'

12. Even now, in Indian villages, animals share accommodation with members of the family, especially cows, buffaloes, and pet birds. Here the abashed girl feels so self-conscious that she will not let her lover, Kṛiṣṇa, (Shyāma is another name for him), make love to her till the animals and birds either fall asleep and cannot witness their lovemaking, or are removed from the chamber of love. When Kṛiṣṇa, who was a confirmed and experienced lover, hears these guileless and innocent words of the maiden, he is more charmed with her sweet resistance than if she should have forthwith yielded to his desire.

13. In *Kāma Sūtra*, Vatsyāyana describes the ways of creating confidence in the newly-wed bride to make her agreeable to lovemaking. He says that the husband should approach the new bride gently, and according to her liking

and employ ways to win her confidence. He should first embrace her lightly with the upper part of his body and then put a betel-leaf in her mouth. If she does not accept this he should persuade her to do so by entreaties and oaths, and if these too fail, by kneeling at her feet, for however bashful or angry a woman may be, she cannot be unaffected by a man's falling on her feet.

14. Most Hindi poets would have their *nāyikās* keep maids, or depend on bosom companions to counsel them in affairs of love and assist them to meet lovers. This was so especially with ladies of the higher class, for example *Shakuntalā*, in Kālidāsa's play of that name. Poet Vidyāpati has devoted a number of his verses in describing such advice and assistance tendered by Rādhā's maids, when she approaches her lover Kṛiṣṇa for lovemaking. Vidyāpati's verses are notable for their frankness and vivid detail. Sample one in which Rādhā's bosom companion instructs her as follows. :
'O ! Rādhā do not harbour any care or doubt in your mind, but go to your lover Kṛiṣṇa. I say to you, abandon your useless thoughts. Oh ! foolish woman ! can one ever get pleasure without bearing pain? No, never ! it is true that at the time of sexual intercourse there is a moment's pain, but thereafter love's pleasure is there for the life-time. Therefore, oh ! my beauty, why do you turn away from such permanent pleasure merely due to fear of a little pain? You may shut your eyes a moment when you feel the stab of pain during the joyful congress, as a patient closes his eyes and swallows his bitter draught of medicine. Oh! my lovely one, get ready and make love.'

The bosom companion is considered so adept in her advice that poet Vidyāpati even makes her counsel such an experienced lover as Kṛiṣṇa, perhaps not so much to guide him, as to protect the interest of her *nāyikā* friend. The lady tells him, 'Oh Kṛiṣṇa, today I will test your amorousness. I have secretly brought you today, *Rādhā*, who is a precious gem amongst women. The girl is very tender like a *siris* flower, then too you should passionately embrace her and make love to her without fear, for everyone knows that a new shoot breaks not with the weight of the black bee. At first make her sit near you and speak to her words of love. Thereafter marking her naked breasts with your nails seat her in your lap. Do not give up if that maiden piteously says"no! no!" Her "no" means "yes".

Poet Bihārī says of his *nāyikā* :

'Although 'no ! no !'' is ever on her lips,
Yet from her eyebrows, laughter-filled she sends
Another message; while denial lies
In her uncertain words, her eyes consent !

Dūlāh, another Hindi poet, describing the bashfulness of a bride says :

'She says "no!" when his fond hands creep,
"No !" when to climb the bed he says;
"No !" when he wishes her to speak,
"No !" when to lift the veil he prays :

In kissing and embracing "no !"
In laughing and lovemaking "no !"
Oh ! lady wherefrom learnt you this
"No !" which far more than "yes" is sweet?'

Bihārī's *nāyikā* is also demure in lovemaking :

'Even a little untruth some would say
Is evil, but who would this counsel keep?
For when the work of love does start the "no !"
From the beloved's lips though false is sweet !'

Again :

'We met each other silently in love,
And spoke not; one day finding her alone
Within the house suddenly her hand I caught;
"No ! no !" exclaimed she, and yet all the while
Gazing with longing look; her sweet denial
Of that moment e'er has enslaved my soul'.

So also is the alluring *nāyikā* in another verse :

'Making her brow aslant she anger feigns,
Saying "no" yet in her eyes consent
Does clearly shine, and though she makes pretence,
Her hand to free, still drawn towards me comes !'

15. Much in the same strain Bihārī's *nāyikā* is abashed in the beginning, but gradually won over :

'At the beginning of love-play, her shame
Itself ashamed was, and away if fled :
Then bold she did become, and willingly came,
With sweet accord unto her lover's bed.'

A similar situation is described by another Hindi poet. After the wedding night one of the handmaids of the new bride notices the palm of her hand slightly burnt, and curious to know the reason therefor, asks another maid, who is closest to the bride, the cause of it. The second maid answers thus :

'Not knowing the meaning of love, the new lady,
To climb her lover's bed was afeared ;
When the words of love were spoken she smiled,
Seeing which he boldly caught her hands :
In the struggle when her waist-knot was loosened
The bashful lady extinguished the lamp
With the palm of her hand—and so, my friend,
In the battle of love her palm was burnt.'

16. Upbraiding the roughness of the passion-filled *nāyaka*, Bihārī says :

'Look how you have crushed this lady
Tender as flower : Oh ! heartless youth.
On her bosom place your hands and see
Her love-filled heart is palpitating still'.

Describing the meeting of the inexperienced Rādhā and her lover Kṛiṣṇa, Poet Vidyāpati says, 'Her lover dismissed all Rādhā's bosom friends and shut the door. His passion rose, and he began to remove Rādhā's clothes, while she clung on to them. She was frightened by Kṛiṣṇa's awakened passion, and was saying "no! no!" and weeping; but it had no effect on him, and he crushed her as black bees would crush a half-blown lotus. The girl's body started trembling as drops of water on a lotus leaf.'

17. In *Kāma Sūtra*, Vātsyāyana advocates gentle means of winning over new bride. He says that the husband should gradually win her confidence, embrace her, make her talk, and as if by accident touch her body and her breasts. By and by he should get so familiar that she allows him to place her in his lap. But if she does not yield, he advises the husband to frighten her by saying. 'I shall mark you with my teeth and put nail-marks on your lips and breasts, and then make like marks on my own body, and tell my friends that you made them. Then what will you do?' Thus Vātsyāyana advises the husband to take the help of force also and frighten the timid girl who will yield in no other way.

18. Poet Vidyāpati describes a *nāyikā* who, like Keshava's *mugdhā* makes lines on the ground with the nails of her feet to show her arrogance. But she too, (like Keshava's *nāyikā*), is won over by her lover at last. 'The lovely woman came near her lover's bed after much persuasion, and when she arrived she bowed her head and remained drawing lines upon the ground with the fingers of her feet. Oh ! dear friend, even when Rādhā sat near her beloved, and he began to plead his love, half the night passed off like this. When her lover caught her hands and pulled her in his lap, she went on repeating but one word and that was "no!" No sooner he takes her in his lap, she tries to twist away from him; but that lady is clever, for in her mind she is agreeable, only outwardly she resists.'

19. a cowherd girl.

20. another name for Kṛiṣṇa.

21. In the *Gīta Govinda*, too, Rādhā's eyebrows are compared to a bow : 'So your arrow of eye-play placed on your bow of an eyebrow wounds me'. In the story of Bheluā we are told of a girl whose 'crimson eyebrows are like a stinged bow prepared for use.' The brows of the courtesans of Ceylon are described thus :

'Brows bows, eyes archers, shooting arrows strong
Upon the whetstone of their glances shaped'.

The brows of Padmāvatī when she grew of age 'were bows from which she discharged conquettish glances'.

22. So also in a love-song, a Mopla girl is described as having teeth small

and white like the seeds of a pomegranate. Other things to which teeth are often compared are pearls, diamonds, small rice, jasmine flowers, snow-flakes hail-stones, and even a row of melon-seeds.

23. In an Oriental song a maiden's smiles are like soft lightning. Other comparisons are white flowers, petals of a lotus bud, a narcissus, rose-buds,and sunlight.

24. A woman's neck is usually compared to a conch shell, but sometimes also to a vase or a jar, as the neck of *Padminī* :

'Neck like a shapely conch, or as a vase
O'erlaid with gold thread, or turned on a lathe'.

25. The top of the betel-leaf is shiny, hence it is used as a comparison for the softness of the stomach. Softness is often emphasised in speaking of a woman's belly. Zuleikhā's belly was like a board covered with ermine :

'Her belly like a board with ermine spread,
So soft the midwife had her navel shoed.'

In *The Arabian Nights* the belly of the young girl in the Porter's Tale lay hid beneath her robe like 'some precious love-letter in a silken case.'

26. Of the comparisons used for a woman's gait, one is to an elephant's and the other to a swan's. Kālidāsa compares the gait of Queen Indumatī to that of a swan :

'Your low sweet voice to nightingales was given
Your idly graceful movements to the swans.

Rānī Damayantī is described as having a swan's gait and when Padmāvatī went out to meet Ratnasena, we are told, 'the swans departed when they saw her gait'.

27. The comparison of women's limbs to gold is common because of its resemblance to the golden brown complexion which the Hindus believe to be the ideal. In one of the ballads of Chhattisgarh a lovely lady is compared to the precious metal :

'My lovely girl is gold
Fresh from the goldsmith's house,
Golden are her hands and feet,
Golden her teeth.'

Describing Rādhā, Poet Govinda Dās says :

'She , the fair one,
Looks like a piece of jewelled gold.

28. The Hindus are enamoured of the peculiar smell which arises from a new earthen jar when water is poured in it, which is much like the smell of fresh earth.

29. Kṛṣṇa's efforts to draw the cowherd girls into the forest so that he

may woo them, are being derided. They all know his sly tricks. Who is the girl who will be persuaded to enter the grove with him by day, and thus risk being found out and lose her reputation ?

30. The three *lokas*, or worlds, are heaven, hell, and earth. Sometimes, however, there are more detailed classifications of the *lokas*, according to which the upper regions are seven in number, namely *Bhūr*, *Bhuvar*, *Svar*, *Mahar*, *Jana*, *Tapas* and *Satya*. Another enumeration calls the seven worlds, earth, sky, heaven, middle-region, place of birth, mansion of the blest, and abode of truth. The *Sāṅkhya* and *Vedānta* schools of philosophy recognise eight *lokas*, *Brahma loka*, *Pitṛi loka*, *Soma loka*, *Indra loka*, *Gandharva loka*, *Rākshasa loka*, *Yaksha loka*, and *Pishācha loka*.

31. The seven kinds of external and internal lovemaking. Kalyāṇa Malla says, 'external enjoyments are the processes which precede internal enjoyment or coition. The external enjoyments as given by him are embracing, kissing, marking by nails, stroking, biting, manipulating the hair, and inarticulate sounds produced by drawing the breath between closed teeth.

32. Poet Bihārī describing the essential nature of lovemaking says :

> 'Sometimes throbbing, sometimes filled with rage,
> Laughing, sobbing, pressing with sudden embrace,
> Lovemaking, in which these are, is pure bliss,
> In which these are not, sure vexation is.'

In *The Arabian Nights* there are similar descriptions of violent lovemaking e.g. 'She sighed and groaned among kisses and jumpings; I groaned and sighed with multiple couplings, until the noise of us filled the house and put all the street into a maze' (Trans, Mardrus and Mathers). Ovid, too, is all for vigorous lovemaking :

> 'Duty is all very well, but let's not confuse it with pleasure;
> I do not want any girl doing her duty for me.
> What I like to hear are the words of utter abandon,
> Words that say, "not too soon !" words that say "wait just a while",
> Let me see my girl with eyes that confess their excitement,
> Let her, after she comes, want no more for a while'.

33. Regarding the embrace Vātsyāyana says that it indicates the mutual love of men and women, and he enumerates four kinds of embraces— (i) Touching, when a man on some pretext goes alongside a woman, and touches her body with his. (ii) Piercing, when a woman bends down and seems to pierce a man with her breasts which the man clasps with his hands. (iii) Rubbing, when the lovers who are known to each other, go in a dark and lonely place, and rub their bodies against each other. (iv) Pressing, when one of the lovers presses the body of his or her partner against a pillar. Vātsyāyana also describes the embraces used at the time of sexual union and further the embraces of thighs, hips, breasts, and forehead.

The author of *Anaṅga Raṅga* describes eight kinds of embraces much on the lines of *Kāma Sūtra* involving clasping of the bodies, thighs, hips, loins, breasts, etc.

34. *Kāma Sūtra* devotes a whole chapter to kissing alone. For a young and inexperienced girl there are three kinds of kisses. Then there are the other kinds to be indulged by adept lovers—the straight, bent, turned, pressed, greatly pressed, a kiss of the upper lips, the clasping kiss, combat of the tongues, the love-kindling kiss, the awaking kiss , the kiss of intention, the transferred kiss, and the demonstrative kiss.

Kalyāṇa Malla enumerates ten kinds of kisses—the sustained or mixed, kiss of lower lip, neck-nape kiss, oblique kiss, kiss of the upper lip, kissing of the lumped lip, kiss of the inside mouth, toying kiss, awakening kiss, and pressed kiss.

35. Vātsyāyana enumerates eight kinds of nail-marks according to the shape which they make on the body. These are sounding, half-moon, circle, line-claw, peacock's foot, jump of a hare, and leaf of a blue lotus. He says that nail-marks should be made on private parts of a married woman to remind her of love. The sight of these nail-marks keeps her love fresh and new.

Kalyāṇa Malla gives six conditions, according to time and season, when nail-marks should be inflicted on the woman—when she is angry, when enjoying a virgin, when going away on a long voyage, when separating for a short time, when great financial loss is sustained, under the excitement of desire for sexual union, and at times when congress is not to be made. He gives seven different kinds of nail-marks.

36. Vātsyāyana enumerates eight different kinds of bites inflicted in lovemaking, and Kalyāṇa Malla seven. Vātsyāyana says that when a man bites a woman forcibly she should return his bite with double force, and when at some secret place her lover shows her the marks made by her she should smile and be unaffected, and then turn round angrily and show him the marks he has made.

The other ways of lovers, viz. rubbing, touch, and sucking of lips, have not received so systematic a treatment, but both writers mention them. The different ways of striking by the hand, the sounds produced and uttered by lovers in the sex act are described in detail.

The Perfumed Garden, the Arabian book on erotology, does not give such a detailed treatment of these matters, but the writer clearly realises their significance. He charges the lover to excite his lady by kissing her cheeks, sucking her lips, rubbing her breasts, and biting her arms. A connoisseur of love says in *The Perfumed Garden*, 'Believe me, the kisses, rubbing suction of the lips, the close embrace, the visits of the mouth to the nipples of the bosom, and the sipping of the fresh saliva, these are the things to render affection lasting.' (Trans, Burton's)

37. The *Kāma Sūtra* describes various methods of congress between a man and a woman like the rising position, clasping position, twining position, mare's position, yawning position, pressed position etc., and concludes that the kinds of congress may be multiplied after the manner of different kinds of birds and beasts, and should be according to the usage of each country and the

liking of each individual. He also says that the method should be varied according to the type of woman enjoyed. *Anaṅga Raṅga* mentions five main divisions: (i) *Uttāna-bandha*, or supine, in which the woman lies upon her back, (ii) *Tiryak*, or slanting, in which she lies upon her side, (iii) *Upaviṣṭa*, or sitting posture, (iv) *Utthita*, the standing position, (v) *Vyanta-bandha*, congress from behind. All these five main postures have various sub-divisions making twenty-nine different postures.

The writer of *The Perfumed Garden* also describes twenty-nine kinds of postures of which he praises the *dok el arz*, or pounding on the spot, the most. According to this the woman sits astride on the sitting man's thighs, crossing her legs behind his back, He tells a story about this posture. A man tried normal methods of congress with his wife without success. Then he was advised by an old experienced dame to try variations to the normal way. The husband tried each one in turn, and when he came to the *dok el arz* posture he was able to satisfy her, and she shouted in ecstasy,'This indeed is the real method of making love.'

38. There were no synthetic beautifying products like face cream, shampoo, etc. in those days, but women relied on things nearer to nature for beautifying their body. The step by step beauty aids form an attractive itinerary, and some of the items are still part of a Hindu woman's make up.

39. The modern trend is to wear the hair short, reaching upto the neck. But the orthodox way which has persisted amongst Hindu women from the earliest times, is to have long hair—the longer the better. The hair is twisted into two braids which are then twined to form one thick and long rope of hair, which some women keep dangling, and others tie it up in a bun in which they may place sweet smelling flowers.

40. As soon as a girl is married she gets the privilege of putting a line of vermilion mercury powder across her head where her hair part. An unmarried girl or a widow does not deck her hair so, and this provides a clear distinction between the two.

41. It is used to anoint the body because of its coolness and its perfumed odour. Nowadays sandal-wood is widely used on commercial basis in perfuming soaps, talcum powders etc. Wooden decorative articles like cigarette cases, ornamental boxes etc. are made of sandal-wood. Sandal-paste is also applied on the forehead by Hindu men as a sign of religious devotion and purity.

42. Paste made by grounding leaves of the henna plant, which is a large shrub, sometimes growing to a height of seven to eight feet. It bears, at the beginning and end of the cold seasons, numerous large compact panicles of small greenish-white flowers which have a delightful fragrance. Its leaves yield a red dye, with which Hindu women stain the palm and feet, making intricate and beautiful patterns with the fast dye.

43 Betal leaves have no scent, but it is the scented material within them which sweetens the breath when chewed.

44. Hindu women used to the stain spaces between their teeth black with a paste called *misi-* a practice which is losing popularity now, and is more or less confined to village belles. The application of the black *misī* paste to the

teeth was considered to be a beauty aid. In the love-song of a boatman of Thailand the *misī*-black teeth of a damsel are described thus :

'And the ebony bark, in its core beneath
Was never so black as thy shiny teeth.

The teeth of Princess Padmāvatī, blackened with *misī*, are picturesquely described by poet Jāisī as shining diamonds resting on black pedestals :

'With *misī* blackened are her teeth white,
As diamonds on a pedestal they shine,
As flash of lightning on an autumn night,
The two and thirty glistening in a line'.

45. Collyrium is lampblack, which is used in India for blackening the eyelids in order to add to their charm. The usual method of preparing it is to invert a small and flat earthen vessel over a sooty flame. The soot deposits as a thin paste, which is then applied to the inner eyelid by the finger. Eyelids darkened by collyrium are greatly admired. Sample Poet Bihārī's lines on his *nāyikā's* eyes:

'These ever moving eyes of thine,
Glance here and there, keep never still,
Oh ! whom are they about to rob,
These eyes of thine, collyrium-filled?

46. Hindi and Sanskrit poets have dwelt fondly on the picture of a woman on whom the effect of lovemaking is writ large. The most famous of these descriptions occurs in the *Gīta Govinda* of Jayadeva in the verse in which the poet describes Rādhā after her night of Love :

'In the morning most wondrous , the heart of her lord was smitten with arrows of love, arrows which went through his eyes, arrows which were his nail-scratched bosom, her reddened sleep-denied eyes, her crimson lips from a bath of kisses, her hair disarranged with flowers awry, and her girdle all loose and slipping.

With hair knot loosened and stray lock waving, her cheeks perspiring, her glitter of *bimba* lips impaired.

And the necklace of pearls not appearing fair because of her jar-shaped breasts being denuded.

And her belt, her glittering girdle, dimmed in beauty,

And all of a sudden placing her hands on her naked breasts, and over her naked loins, to hide them, and looking embarrassed;

Even so, with her tender loveliness ravaged, she continued to please.

The happy one drank of the face where the lips were washed with the juice of his mouth,

His mouth half-open uttering amorous noises, vague delirious, the rows of teeth in the breath of an indrawn sight delightedly chattering.

Drank of the face of that deer-eyed woman whose body lay helpless, released of excessive delight, the thrilling delight of embraces, making the breasts both flaccid and firm.' (Keyt, *Gita Govinda*).

Charming too is the description of such a maid by Kālidāsa :

'With rounded hips,
Whose grace is enhanced
By soft white silk, and girdle
Or gems and sandal-paste;
And masses of hair
With the lingering subtle perfume.
Mysterious breasts
With the fluid paste of sandal
And precious strings of snow-white pearls commingling;
And the region of the hips
With the quivering golden girdle;
Whose mind do they not allure
And fill with a wistful yearning ?'

(R. S. Pandit, Kālidāsa's *Ṛitusaṁhāra*).

So also the description of *Padmāvatī* by Poet Jāisī when she wakes after a night of tempestuous lovemaking :

'Awake, lady awake, the sun has sped
Beyond the eastern sky, now leave your bed.
The maidents unto Padmāvatī spoke,
And as unfolded lotus she arose.
Her eyes as lotus flowers glance on the day
Like frightened deer in forest gone astray.
'By nightlong vigil at your lover's side
Your eyes have reddened'—thus the maidens say,
'Where once the *champak* and rose-apple vied
The yellow oleaster has her way :
The orange garden of your budding breasts
The bee hath sucked; and lines of colour rise
Where nails have touched them; on your forehead rest
Thy rows of curls, all hoisted and awry :
And moistened by your lover's lips are yours
As if by chewing betel; and your face
As red as *raimunī* bird we find
Spent is the nuptial night O ! lady wake !'

The tipsy laughter and drowsy eyes of Bihārī's *nāyikā* bear witness to her night of love:

'O! buxom belle truthfully you say
That all night you have spent in making love,
For intoxicated with pleasure and joy you are

So too your laughter drunk and drowsy eye
Your wanton night of love do testify'.

47. The *nāyikā's* maid had told her that the face of her lover, Kṛiṣṇa, was like a lotus flower, but the *nāyikā* does not think so. She finds his face like a moon because its sight causes her heart to tremble and shake, just as the moon causes chills and tides. Her lover's face can certainly not be like a lotus which has no affinity for the moon, so much so that when it is night and the moon appears, the lotus closes up its petals. (The lotus flower opens its petals in the day and closes them at night).

48. Kṛiṣṇa's elder brother. It was with his help that Kṛiṣṇa defeated and destroyed Sunāman brother of Kaṁsa, and King of the Shūrasenas. He was very strong, heavy of build, and having the strength of giant. Balarāma's other names are Balabhadra and Baladeva. While Kṛiṣṇa was very dark, Balarāma was fair. It is said that Viṣṇū took two hairs, a white one and a black one, and of these the white one became Balarāma and the black Kṛiṣṇa. As soon as Balarāma was born he was carried away to Gokul to preserve his life from the tyrant Kaṁsa. He grew up with Kṛiṣṇa and took part in many of his pranks and adventures. He killed a number of demons. Once when he was intoxicated he called on the River Yamunā to come to him so that he may bathe. His command not being obeyed, he cast his ploughshare into the river and began to drag the waters wherever he went, till at last the Yamunā assumed human form and begged his forgiveness.

In the Mahābhārata he taught Duryodhana and Bhīma the use of the mace, and in the combat between the two when Bhīma struck a foul blow he was very indignant. This shows him to be fair-minded and of a sporting nature.

According to one view Balarāma was the incarnation of the great serpent Sheṣa, and when he died the serpent is said to have issued from his mouth (there is a famous Indian painting which so depicts his death).

Balarāma was much addicted to wine, and so he is called Madhupriya (*madhu*, 'wine': *priya* 'fond of') but despite this failing he was, contrary to his brother Kṛiṣṇa, a devoted husband and had only one wife, Revatī to whom he was faithful. His special weapons were a club, a ploughshare, and a pestle and he used a palm for his banner.

The *nāyikā* seems to be in an angry mood because of some lie which her lover has spoken to her, and so she utters whatever comes to her lips, sometimes speaking well of him, and sometimes evil.

49. The *nāyikā* depicted is a *dhīrādhīrā madhyā*, whose characteristic has been defined to be that she sorely complains against her husband when she sees him. This *nāyikā* is therefore in a complaining mood. She has come to know that her lover, Kṛiṣṇa, has been carrying on intrigues with her maids, so that he has become an ocean of love, bestowing his favours on all of them. She reminds him that love is not such a trifling affair, for once a lover gives away his mind to another he cannot get it back. Her lover has angered her so much by his amours that though he may look at her, she is too enraged to suffer him to speak.

50. The *samastarasakovidā* is a woman who can completely please all types of men, and therefore she has been called a mine of enjoyment.

51. Wife of Brahmā. The goddess of speech and learning, and patroness of the arts and sciences. She is represented as having a fair complexion, a graceful figure, wearing a slender crescent on her brow, and sitting on a lotus. As a river goddess, Sarasvatī is applauded for the fortifying and purifying powers of her waters and as the bestower of wealth and fertility.

52. An *apsarā* sent to seduce the sage Vishvāmitra from his devotions. She succeeded in her mission and became mother of the nymph Shakuntalā.

53. Another name for Kṛiṣṇa.

54. The sidelong glance of the captivating maid so affected Kṛiṣṇa that he felt like the god of love (Kāmadeva), who having forgotten the motion of his arrows of flowers, thought that her desire-filled glances themselves were such arrows. (Kāmadeva is supposed to have a bow of sugarcane, the bowstring of which is a line of bees, and each arrow of his is tipped with a distinct flower).

The eyes of a woman are described by Bāṇa in much the same manner:

'When she glanced sideways at me her black and pointed eyes looked as if Kāmadeva had shot his arrows of blue lotuses.'

The courtesans of Ceylon described in *Padmāvatī* have glances equally deadly :

'The curls swing on their cheeks, as their smiles dart;
Side-glances, striking men dead in a trice'.

The companions of Kādambarī had

'Side-glances which were like moving blue lotuses.'

55. The example given is of an *akrāmati prauḍhā* type of woman who holds her husband's mind captive by speech, deed, and thought. So here the *nāyikā* casts such a spell over her lover, Kṛiṣṇa, that though he gives all his time to her and does not care for other girls, she is not content, and wants to enslave her so much that he bows at her feet !

56. See note 20, chapter 1.

57. See note 51, Chapter 3.

58. See note 3, Chapter 1.

59. *The dhīrā prauḍhā nāyikā* has been described in the previous verse as being one who shows mere outward love. The woman whose description is given in this verse is one of that type. Her lover, Shrī Kṛiṣṇa, has come to meet her. Instead of showing the warmth expected from her at such a moment, she merely does the things which are to an honoured guest in a formal manner—like giving him a seat, washing his feet, offering betels, fanning him, and the like. Kṛiṣṇa is all the time thinking that she should treat him as a lover and not as a guest, and so when she starts fanning him, he catches her arm and says. 'What a welcome you are giving? Is this how a lover is to be greeted ?

60. There was no electricity in Keshavadāsa's days. The fan here is a bamboo fan which is rotated round and round by the hand to give breeze.

61. A newly married Hindu bride has to behave with circumspection when she first comes to her husband's home. She has to be bashful, conside-

rate, and careful of everything she does, so that she may make a favourable impression on her husband's people, especially on the women, who are inclined to be critical of her. Hence her taking betels only when pressed, so as not to show her eagerness for them, which would be considered bad taste.

In *Kāma Sūtra*, Vātsyāyana advises the husband to win over his newly-wed bride by putting a couple of betel leaves in her mouth and pressing her to accept them, and when she does so by kissing her softly and gracefully on the mouth—a sweet and ingenious way to overcome the new bride's bashfulness:

62. Here perhaps a dear friend or maid tells the *nāyikā* how to press her advantage with her lover. When he makes love she should swear and tell him how different she finds it from what she thought. She should tell her lover Kṛiṣṇa, that whatever she had spoken about love was all lies—so much better has he proved it to be : If he disregards her arrogance, even then she should smile, for now that she has won over her lover who can make fun of her?

63. In this verse two types of *nāyikās* are described. First, the one whose words show indifference to her husband but who desires him in her mind. She is the *adhīrā*—the opposite of a *dhīrā*, who has previously been described as one who shows mere outward love. The second and allied type of *nāyikā* is the *adhīrā prauḍhā* who on seeing some great wrong-doing in her husband (as for instance his affair with another woman), cannot bring herself to pardon him for it.

64. The *nāyaka* has returned after enjoying another woman. His eyes are drowsy with sleep. The *nāyikā* upbraids him for his faithlessness and says 'Do not try to hide your fault by laughing and talking to me. Look in the mirror and see how drowsy your eyes are. How nice do they appear indeed: Oh ! husband mine, you have again come to me bearing sign of your deceit. How soon you have forgotten the vows of love which you made only yesterday!' In *Satsai*, Bihārī gives us some delightful descriptions of the *nāyaka* returned with signs of having enjoyed another woman.

(i) 'To me beguiling words you vainly speak,
Your secret to betray not; but the drops
Of sweat upon your body gleaming, though
'Tis bitter cold in these cold winter months,
Are witness to the moments you have spent
Absorbed in the delightful bouts of love!'

(ii) 'Splendid shine the nails-marks on your bosom
Made newly by her, and drowsiness lies
Heavy on you; your eyes you cannot raise,
Then why, beloved, do you vainly swear
That another woman you have not approached ?'

65. Having described the different kinds of *nāyikās*, now Keshavadāsa goes on to describe the qualities of the *parakīyā*, whom he calls the most renowned and beloved type of woman. The *parakīyā nāyikā* is one who cannot have her pleasure due to fear of society and so carries on her lover-affair secretly. Poet Bihārī gives examples of *parakīyā nāyikās* in his verses. In one of his descriptions *nāyaka* and *nāyikā* are playing hide and seek, and under pretence of playing the

game they touch each other and embrace. Elsewhere, the lovers have to climb walls to hide their lovemaking from prying eyes.

'With their hands hoisting themselves o'er the wall,
On the other side they hang; then swiftly look
This way and that; and no one seeing in sight
With passion kiss each other's beauteous cheeks.

There is the other kind of *parakiyā* who is older and more adept in the knowledge of love. She does not share with her younger conterpart the fear of social opprobrium, and becoming impervious to slander, does not conceal her love, and throwing all discretion to the winds, runs to meet her lover :

'From house to house in secret vilified.
Not for a moment even then she stays
Within her house. Her disparagement
Remembering, does that lady turn,
But soon forgetting all, again she stands
Upon the doorstep of her lover's home',

66. Bihārī has given similar descriptions of a *nāyikā's* roving eyes. She is searching out her lover in the midst of a crowd, and the moment her eyes meet his, she ceases to look.

'Even through the denseness of the crowd they pierce
Unto her lover, somehow, him to greet
The *nāyikā's* eyes go, those of all avoiding,
And only when they meet his, they retreat.

At another place the *nāyikā's* eyes are compared to the *kibalnumā* or compass which Mohammadens take with them on their pilgrimage to Mecca. Just as the needle of the *Kibalnumā* always points towards Mecca, even so the roving eyes of the *nāyikā* stay towards her lover :

'Unto all do her eyes find a way,
But only for a moment, ere they turn
'Tis only with her lover that they stay—
As *Kibalnumā's* needle does revolve,
On every side, but towards Mecca stops'

67. *Chaupaṛ* was an ancient game, (rarely played now), somewhat resembling backgammon, played with three long dices. It was in the historic game of dice between Yudhiṣṭhira and Shakuni in the Mahābhārata, that the former pledged and lost all his kingdom and kinsmen, and even his wife Draupadī, which was the starting point of the great war between the Pāṇḍavas and Kauravas.

68. The new moon which appears on the second day of the lunar fortnight. The new moon which is just a thin arc, is visible with difficulty. It is also very lovely, and here it is mentioned in this sense. The maidens around Rādhā compare her beauty to that of the new moon.

Hindus frequently compare their women to the new moon to emphasise their beauty. A damsel, Anushayinī, is compared to the new moon appearing at dusk. 'And as he looked he saw her standing before him like the new moon at close of day, a pure form of exquisite beauty, a crystal without a flaw, tinged with the colour of heaven.'

In Kālidāsa's *Meghadūta*, the young wife of the *Yaksha*, who is sorrowful because she is separated from him, is compared to the slender moon :

'Resting one side upon the widowed bed
Like the slender moon upon the eastern height
So slender she, now worn with anguish dread,
Passing with stifling tears the long sad night.'

In the Song of Solomon, in the *Bible*, we have a description of a woman who is compared to the moon:

'Who is she that looketh forth as the morning, fair as the moon, clear as the sun, and terrible as an army of banners ?'

CHAPTER IV

The Meeting of Lovers

The different kinds of meeting between lovers are described in this chapter. Love begins from the eyes. It is born when a man and a woman look at each other with desire. Four kinds of meetings are described—meeting in person, seeing the beloved's portrait, dreaming of her, and hearing her voice. As usual, situations are given to illustrate the different types of meeting of lovers. Having narrated the various kinds of meeting, the Poet goes on, in the next chapter, to describe some ways in which the lovers woo their beloveds.

Definition of 'meeting' of lovers

When lovers send a mutual greeting
Through eyes, and thence desire is born
For one another, this is 'meeting'.

The four kinds of meeting

The first when she's in person seen,
The second to see her portrait dear,
The third to meet her in fond dreams,
The fourth her charming voice to hear.

Meeting in person

When wife and husband joyfully meet,
'Tis personal meeting; even to hear
Of which, drives off hunger, health, and sleep;
And what will happen when she's near !

Example of a hidden meeting in person of the *nāyikā*

When Rādhā, daughter of Vṛiṣabhānu,
Adorning herself, sat, she seemed

Thrice charming in all ways adorned;
And when her eyes on *nāyaka* Kṛiṣṇa
Desireful cast she, it appeared
As if Kāmadeva did arrows rain;
And when she in the mirror peered
To view her face, it beauty gained
As moon delightful does become
Hid in the halo of the sun.

Example of a manifest meeting in person of the *nāyikā*

First, sloth abandoning, I did peer
Within the mirror; then I rubbed
Myself with camphor, and did clear
It with rose-water perfumed; scrubbed
With towel plain—says Keshavadāsa,
My eyes with musk cleaned; then applied
Collyrium beautiful and fast;
But oh! my bosom friend, those eyes
When I on him did shyly cast,
All my devices were in vain,
With beauty armed those eyes, alas !
Their bashfulness did still contain.[1]

Example of a hidden meeting in person of the *nāyaka*

Her tangled hair on forehead curled,
By threads Kṛiṣṇa interlaced, and hung
From them a pleasing string of pearls;
The *nāyikā*, lotus-eyed, did turn
In mirror them to view—perchance
Shrī Kṛiṣṇa did at that moment come,
And hidden, on the *nāyikā* glanced
Just as she had her task begun:
Thus Keshava that moment describes:
As in the halo of the sun
The halo of the moon did lie,
And in between Triveṇī[2] ran.

Example of a manifest meeting of the *nāyaka*

Your breasts and nipples of delight
Unmatched are; as if to enhance
Their beauty, on that bosom lies
A necklace that the mind does charm,
Which seeing, restless maidens become,
And how much more so youth? What's right
I cannot help but speak! How long
Should I look on this charming sight!
As strange a woman as you ne'er
There lived who curd did churn; you still
Each moment at Kṛiṣṇa slyly peer
With fond eyes, in your end-cloth hid.

Meeting by seeing the loved one's portrait

Although her eyes she turns aside,
Her mind with deepening love is rent,
Beads of sweat on her face arise,
Her body's hair do stand on end:
Her heart does tremble—what shall I
Of this girl say, who in the deep
Of bashfulness is drowning? By
Shame so much overcome is she
Merely his picture to look on,
As though he had caught her forearm![3]

Example of manifest meeting by seeing the loved one's portrait

The bosom companion says to the nāyikā :

'O! friend mine! how can darkness flee
Without a lamp, by thinking on
A flame? Can hunger be appeased
By showing food to a hungry man?
O! Princess! how can thirst be quenched
By tales of water? Oh! moon-faced,
Say how can wealth to him descend

Who does on Lakshmī's picture gaze?[4]
So, foolish girl, waste not your days
In vain thus—how can fall to you
The pleasure of meeting your mate,
Merely his picture thus to view?'

Example of hidden meeting of the *nāyaka* by seeing the loved one's portrait.

How can her lifeless picture show
Her varying moods—sometimes displeased,
And then content? Her smile's fresh glow—
Her lovely eyes that sport and tease?
Can love without words be complete?
Can lovers speak not, yet remain
Close? How long shall my eyes I feed
On her insipid picture framed?
Deprived of water how can fish
Their restfulness retain? Even so
When on her picture I look, 'tis
As if my mind does burn fourfold.

Example of the manifest meeting of the *nāyaka* by seeing his loved one's portrait.

The glorious wives of demigods[5]
Past skies who move, *kinnarī* maids,[6]
Are nought before her; women all
At her feet bow—snake-women[7] frail,
Slim dancing girls, hill-women tall,
She-demons,[8] heavenly damsels pale:
As if lightning took form divine:
E'en Kāma's wife[9] poor beside her shows!
Like Lakshmī[10] or Sītā[11] she shines,
And even her picture steals my soul!

Meeting in dreams

Meeting in dreams is always hid,
Says Keshava, never manifest:
Lovers and wise men all know this.

Example of hidden meeting in a dream

Perplexed, she woke, and waking ran,
When in her dream her spouse she saw;
And as one stops a restless man
So that excited maid I caught,
And said, 'Oh! what madness is this?'
At which one moment she did pause:
And I said, 'Sweet! is it a witch
Or spirit, that so holds you in thrall?
Or does your lover's memory now
Move you?' Her so confused I found,
That beads of sweat shone on her brow,
And fast her heart began to pound.

The hidden meeting of the *nāyaka* in a dream

Before her nought is Draupadī,[12]
And Urvashī forgotten is,
Puloma's daughter, Lobhasī,[13]
And Tilottamā[14] are as linseed :
And Menakā,[15] the nymph, I rate
No more than dust—I did not see
The damsel who me did awake,
But I will know her certainly
When I meet her—for in her speech
She's gentle as Sarasvati,[16]
And Pārvatī's[17] nature she keeps,
And in love she's no less than Rati.[18]

Hidden meeting of the *nāyikā* by hearing her lover's voice.

Oh ! dear friend mine ! you gave me oaths
And tuned my ears to Kṛiṣṇa's sweet name;
I know not by which path remote
Thence into my fond eyes he came :
And through my eyes my mind he smote,
Vain all devices were of shame—
What shall I do, where shall I go,
When in my heart he home has gained ?

The manifest meeting of the *nāyikā* by hearing her lover's voice.

Till when will praise of him create
Enjoyment in you? For the thirst
To see him cannot thus be slaked
Till of his form you drink at first
With avid eyes. Dear friend, I'll say,
Guileless you are; by you I swear
On your one smile my life I'll stake :
A year shall find you made mature,
Such pleasures as you then shall yield[19]
Your dear friends, why give you not now ?
O ! artless cowherd girl, tell me,
When 'no' you love, why not your spouse ?[20]

The hidden meeting of the *nāyaka* by hearing his beloved's voice.

Addressing his mind, the nāyaka says :

'The worlds you span, but cannot cleave
From yourself, all beings you console,
Who shall console you? You would leave
The body, but shame firmly hold,
And wealth and friendship you would keep
Yet *pundit* be ! the paths do wind
Aloof of shame and sorrow—these
You cannot both tread; so, oh ! mind !
Pleasure and sorrow both forsake,
And keep afar; for who will show
Your eyes, of things the vivid shape,
Of which by speech the ears do know?'[21]

The open meeting of the *nāyaka* by hearing his beloved's voice.

How shall I say your wily love
For Kṛiṣṇa your passion has turned low ?
Desire it makes more, and rains lust,
And draws Kṛiṣṇa to you—as all know.
As ornament on lovely woman,

Thus should your passion I compare,
Or that which Braja belles have undone—
Your name, oh ! Rādhā, I declare
A chant of separation, such
That when the ears of Kṛiṣṇa it reached,
Both hearth and home at once he left,
And wandered in the forests deep ![22]

Concluding verse

Thus in these verses I've described
the various meetings that arise,
Pleasing to lovers; and now I will
show the sweet ways of love's delight.

NOTES

1. The *nāyikā* decks herself with all sorts of adornments, and determined to make an impression on her lover Kṛiṣṇa, boldly captivates his mind by her beauty. But when the time comes to meet him her eyes cannot abandon their bashfulness, and even though conscious of her adorned beauty she cannot lift them up and return her lover's gaze.

Describing the moment of union, a Hindi poet says that when the moment of meeting her lover approached, the eyes of the *nāyikā* became so full of tears that even though her lover was in front of her she could not see him. In a verse of Poet Ghanānanda a similar condition of the *nāyikā's* eyes is described. They are wet with tears when they are awake, and cannot see the lover whether they are open or closed :

'All is one
If closed or open eyes remain,
Such is their grief-afflicted state
When closed they are to see were vain.
Nor see they when they keep awake'.

And at another place Ghanānanda's *nāyikā* is so unfortunate that when she comes to behold her lover she cannot do so because of the tears of joy which flood her eyes :

'If perchance she her lover meets
The tears of joy do mar her eyes,
Thus seeing him not, desire to see
Unfulfilled in her heart does lie.

In a similar vein the eyes of Poet Bihārī's *nāyikā* cannot gaze on her lover when he comes before her, due to bashfulness :

'No comfort know these troubled eyes
For when their lover comes their way,
Ashamed, they cannot on him gaze,
And seeing him not, distracted lie.'

2. Triveṇī, literally means 'triple braid' and is the name given to the place where the Rivers Gaṅgā and Yamunā meet. The mythical river Sarasvatī is said to join at this place also by an underground channel. Hence Triveṇī is the place of confluence of the three rivers—Gaṅgā, Yamunā and Sarasvatī. It falls in Prayāga, (Allahabad), and is a place of holy pilgrimage. The ashes of all the great Indians, like Gandhi, Nehru and Shastrī were immersed there.

The comparison made in the last three lines is not very clear. There can be three interpretations. One can be that the pearl necklace of the *nāyikā* interlaced with her hair is like the sun's halo and her face below it is like the halo of the moon, and the locks of her hair in between are the Triveṇī. Another interpretation is that the *nāyikā's* face is like the halo of the sun, her reflection in the mirror is like the halo of the moon, and the braid of her hair in between her and her reflection in the mirror is like the Triveṇī. Yet another interpretation can be that the face of the *nāyikā* is like the moon, and its splendour like the moon's halo. This would be in keeping with the Hindu poetic tradition which compares a woman's face with the moon. The splendour of the body or limbs of the *nāyikā* is thus like the sun's halo and the hair interlaced with the necklace like Triveṇī between them.

3. This is a specially bashful *nāyikā*. Even the sight of the picture of her lover makes her feel shy, as though the lover had himself stepped down from it and had caught her by the forearm :

4. The *nāyikā* is gazing on the portrait of her lover. Her bosom companion says, Oh ! foolish woman, how can you get the pleasure of meeting merely by gazing on your beloved's picture ! Can a man's hunger be appeased by showing him food, or darkness fly without lighting a lamp, or thirst be quenched merely by speaking of water, or wealth be acquired just by gazing on the picture of wealth's goddess (Lakshmī) ? You are merely wasting your time in vain by looking on his picture.' Lakshmī is the wife of Viṣṇu, and mother of Kāma. She sprang, like Aphrodite, from the froth of the ocean, in full beauty, with a lotus in her hand, when it was churned by the gods and the demons. In one hand she holds lotus. Her other names are Hīrā, Indirā, Jaladhi from ja 'born of the ocean', Chañchalā or Holā, (the fickle goddess of fortune), and Lokamātā, (mother of the world). She is chiefly worshipped as the goddess of fortune and wealth.

5. Wives of *Yakshas*. *Yakshas* were a class of supernatural beings attending on Kuvera—god of wealth. These men were called Puṇya Janas i. e. good people. A *Yaksha's* message for his separated wife forms the subject matter of Kālidāsa's *Meghadūta* (Cloud Messenger). The women of the *Yakshas* were considered very beautiful.

6. Women of the *Kinnaras* were mythical beings with the form of a man and a head of a horse. They were celestial charioteers and musicians living in the heaven of *Kuvera* and Mount Kailāsha. Some consider them to have sprung

from the toe of Brahmā—the Creator, while others think them to be sons of Kashyapa.

7. Snake women were women of a mythical semi-divine race having a human face with the tail of a serpent and the expanded neck of the cobra Their females were considered to be very handsome, and some intermarried with men.

8. The females of the *Asuras*, or demons. The *Asuras* were enemies of the gods, and the *Brāhmaṇas* record many contests between the two, for example at the churning of the ocean. The gods having been worsted by the demons, went to Viṣṇu, the Preserver, who advised them to churn the ocean for nectar. Both the gods and the demons did so, and the latter forcibly carried away the cup of nectar, but Viṣṇu interposed and recovered the nectar for the gods. There are different versions of the origin of the *Asuras*—from the breath (*asu*), of Prajāpati, from his abdomen, from his lower breath, and from water. The *Daityas* and *Dānavas* are included in the *Asuras*, but not *Rākshasas*, who are said to be descended from Pulastya.

9. The wife of Kāmadeva, god of love is Rati, meaning 'love' or 'desire'. She is the Hindu Venus, goddess of sexual pleasures. Her father was Daksha. She is famed for her beauty and for her knowledge about love.

10. Goddess of wealth and fortune (see note 4 of this Chapter). Lakshmī is believed to be a very beautiful goddess. A vivid description of her has been given by Bain :

'Her neck resembled a shell, and on the pearl of its surface was reflected the dark shadow of the green emeralds that hung around it, and she held in one hand a dark blue lotus of exactly the same colour as her long cornered lashnetted, shadowy eyes. And the graceful creepers of her soft arms, and the extremities of her smooth and tapering legs, whose knees bent a little inwards, were loaded with rings of red coral that blushed with envy at the colour of her lips, which smiled, as if conscious of their own superiority : while her bosom, whose twin breasts were turned slightly away from each other like sisters that have quarrelled, rose very gently up and down as if keeping time to the music of the sea. And she held up with her left hand a coil of the blue hair which fell in masses from her head and encircled her like a cloud blown by the breezes, and its end trailed over the ocean waves. So she stood in silence bending a little forward, till a three-fold wrinkle showed in the soft fold of her slender waist, while the foam splashed and lapped over the back of the tortoise that supported her, hungry to kiss the arched instep of her tiny pearly tipped feet, and her eyes looked farway, fixed on the horizon of that sky-bounded ocean plain.

(F. W. Bain, *Indian Stories*).

11. Sītā is supposed to be the embodiment of purity, tenderness, and conjugal love. She is also famed for her loveliness. In the Mahābhārata she is described thus : 'The woman with lips soft and red as the *bimba* fruit...with eyes like those of a young gazelle...of sweet smiles and beautiful hips.'

(See also note 33 Chapter 1).

12. Daughter of Drupada, King of Pañchāla. Draupadī was a maiden of dark complexion but of great beauty; as radiant and graceful as if descended from the city of gods'. She was won by Arjuna in a *svayamvara* (contest), and became the common wife of all the five Pāṇḍava brothers. Yudhiṣṭhira, the eldest

brother, lost her, along with all his possessions, in a gambling match which led to war between the Kauravas and the Pāṇḍavas.

In the Mahābhārata, Draupadī is described thus :

'Slender-waisted like the wasp...neither low nor tall in stature...she has the fragrance of the blue lotus,...of eyes large as lotus leaves, of thighs fair and round, of dense masses of black curly hair...endowed with every auspicious feature, and of complexion like that of the emerald.'

13. Daughter of the demon Puloma and wife of Indra, god of the firmament. She is also called Sachī and Aindrī. Indra chose her for his wife from a number of competing goddesses, because she surpassed them all in voluptuous attraction. King Nahuṣa got enamoured of her, but she was able to escape his clutches.

14. The name of an *apsarā*. She was originally a *Brahmin* woman but was condemned to be born an *apsarā* because of the offence of bathing at an improper season. She was born to bring about the mutual destruction of the two demons Sunda and Upasunda.

15. In the *Purāṇas* she is wife of Himavat, and mother of Umā and Gaṅgā. She is also an *apsarā* who was sent to seduce the sage of Vishvāmitra from his devotions, and succeeding in this object, she became mother of the lovely maiden Shakuntalā.

16. See note 51 Chater 3.

17. Wife of the god Shiva and daughter of Himavat (the Himālaya mountains) In her milder form she is Umā...a type of beauty. As Durgā she is a beautiful yellow woman riding on a fierce tiger.

Bain's description of Pārvatī is picturesque, and brings out her charming loveliness. 'She drew herself, very slowly, up and back, till her two great rounded breasts seemed on the very point of parting in indignation from her body'.

18. Wife of Kāmadeva. (See note 9 of this Chapter).

19. The meaning is somewhat obscure. The *nāyikā* is young and inexperienced yet. When she becomes more ripe in age and mature, how much pleasure she will give her bosom companions : Why doesn't she give them that pleasure now! Apparently the bosom companions are women, and in that case the *nāyikā* would be a lesbian. The other . and more likely interpretation seems to be that when the *nāyikā* gets mature for enjoyment she will welcome her lover and keep her bosom companions pleased with accounts of her exciting moments of love with him. It was usual for a bosom companion to persuade her mistress to tell her about such amorous adventures.

20. There is a pun here: *nahīṁ*-no and n-*h*-husband. The bosom friend of the *nāyikā* asks her,'You love *nahīṁ* i. e. "no". Why not instead love nah i. e. "your husband?" (In other words) 'Why do you keep back your love; why not bestow it on a lover ?'

21. These lines have been addressed by the *nāyaka* to his mind and are meant to show its powers and limitations. The mind can span across the entire world but cannot leave itself. It can console others but cannot console itself. Even when surrounded by wealth and friends it can renounce both. The path of pleasure and sorrow should both be avoided by the mind, for there is no one who can bring it the picture of the beloved, of which the ears have heard so much.

(i.e. though the *nāyaka* has heard much about his beloved *nāyikā* he cannot form a picture of her in the mind, and there is no one who can show her to him).

22. The love of Kṛiṣṇa has become deep and passionate. The lovely maidens of the Braja country are drawn to it, especially Rādhā, whose name has become so enchanting for Kṛiṣṇa that he abandons his home the moment he hears it, and wanders in search of her into the deep forest.

Chapter V

Where lovers meet, and how

This is a short chapter but it is packed with information about the meeting of lovers. The Poet begins by relating the ways in which the bosom friend of the *nāyikā* conveys to the lover all that the *nāyikā* feels for him, and how sometimes the messenger herself becomes the loved one! At the same time the efforts made by the *nāyikā* herself to keep her love secret and hid from prying eyes are told. Examples are given of how the *nāyaka* and the *nāyikā* hint their love to each other, how despite the attempts to keep it hid it shows itself in an involuntary stretching of the limbs, a smile, a laugh, or a covert glance. The wiles and stratagems which lovers devise to meet each other are narrated, and in particular the ways invented by an experienced married woman and an inexperienced unmarried one (*ūḍhā* and *anūḍhā*). The spots where lovers meet for the first time are described. These are the abode of a faithful maid-servant, nurse, or bosom friend, on the occasion of some entertainment or invitation, on the pretence of illness, or under the influence of fright, or in a lovely house or a forest-dwelling. Accounts are given of the meeting of lovers at these places.

The endeavour of the *nāyikā's* friend

Sometimes the bosom companion tells
The lover what lies in the *nāyikā*'s heart,
And oft when telling him she herself
Feels restless, love thus to impart![1]

The bosom companion's account of the separation of the *nāyikā*

The cowherd girl whom you did see
Yesterday, has control not gained
Yet o'er herself; sometimes she feels
Great cold, and then she burns again.

She lives, and so lives her desire,
Afflicted both! Now seek her friends
A million ways to cool her fire,
And shower of cures upon her send—
But all in vain 'tis: oh! mischance!
Bear not ill with me if, O! Kṛiṣṇa,
I say your tender love-filled glance
Imbued with deadly poison is.

The bosom companion's account of the lovelorn *nāyikā*

Her hunger flown is, and her fear,
And night and day sleep she has scorned,[2]
Wisdom she shuns, nor yet she hears
My counsel; but e'er dotes upon
A tame caged parrot; songs appear
To her as poison, and no long
She faith has in amusements dear.
Love in her heart has short sojourn
As 'twere a guest: thus she appears—
I praise her not, with shame undone.

Endeavours of the *nāyikā*

Says Keshavadāsa 'now I'll describe
Endeavours which the *nāyikā* makes
Not to disclose to people's eyes
The love she bears for her lover's sake.

How *nāyikās* show their love

Her ears she scratches, then anon
With laziness does stretch her limbs,
Sometimes repeatedly she yawns
And laughs at nothing—then begins
To talk with her dear friend, thus she
With false pretence her body shows
Unto her lover—so do these
Loved maidens their deep love disclose—

Clear and hid, and their lovers please,
And by their wisdom win them o'er.

Rādhā's hidden endeavour

Rādhā's bosom companion says to her:

'Why glancing down you turn and start,
Me covertly to look upon ?
Why laugh, being pleased within your heart ?
Swear you by Kṛiṣṇa ! why oft you yawn?
Restless, your graceful limbs you stretch
And leave your splendid breasts unclothed,
And oftimes with excitement swell,
And 'gainst my bosom nestle close :
And with mind wandering you essay
To do this when that should be done !
Tell me, my friend ! have you this day
Accomplished something for your fun?'

Rādhā's manifest endeavour

Rādhā's bosom companion says to her :

'By kissing me how can you slake
Your passion? Can one's thirst be quenched
By licking dew? Your small hands place
Why so you on my bosom, friend?
If you must touch, then touch his breasts
For whom desire in you is strong:
If you have come me to caress
Then play the game as women long[3] !
Dear play-mate ! why with passion swayed
You clasp me so, time and again?
Why not your lover fond, embrace,
Who waiting for you nigh does stand?'

The hidden endeavour of the *nāyaka*[4]

'Your turban you tie and untie
Oft, as with sloth affected strong,

And strangely in the mirror pry,
Oh ! who is she with whom all bonds
You sunder at first, and then grasp,
As one deranged, her tender feet,
Your fingers snap, and your ears scratch ?
Whom offer you these strings of beads
So often ? Why do you essay
To sing such contrary songs? Tell me
How fares with you, O ! Kṛiṣṇa, today?'

The manifest endeavour of the *nāyaka*

For whom you many women bribed,
And vainly sent them here and there ?
And myriad love-chants did recite
To lure that maiden in your snare ?
And in vain stratagems devised ?
How far shall I recount, O ! Kṛiṣṇa ?
Yet failed all plans that you did try;
Say, shall I not my heart's wish win
If now that lady I unite
With you? Oh ! lover ! She's waiting :
Why do you not go forth ? Should I
Within my lap her to you bring?[5]

The lover's self-endeavour

Says Keshavadāsa, when having tried
All ways, the lovers cannot meet,
Then by their wisdom they devise
Themselves a way their love to plead.

The hidden self-endeavour of the *nāyikā*

To see you, from afar I sent
Love-letters oft; so we have met,
Now meet me to your heart's content,
When you met me my mind was set
On making love: O ! Kṛiṣṇa, perhaps

Some maid may look with evil eye,[6]
And then our schemes shall end, as snaps
A lotus stem, O ! jewel mine !

The self-endeavour of the beloved

Put not your hands against mine so,
For thus my ardour mounts on high
Each moment; and I do not know
What thoughts may in my mind arise,
And how shall they be cured: 'Tis well
With us, and with my craving sweet
Son of Nanda,[7] if our hearts have met
'Tis not uncommon—for hearts meet !

The manifest self-endeavour of the beloved

No female servant is within
With night blindness am I diseased,
And hard of hearing—and O ! Kṛiṣṇa !
Sore troubled—be fair unto me:
How long shall I my friends explain—
My bosom friends—that they should sleep
With me; and that it were nigh vain
For me their bed to share and keep?[8]

The *nāyaka's* hidden self-endeavour

One handmaid says to another:

'Know you the trick Kṛiṣṇa played today
To draw the *nāyikā* in the woods?
"My friends their brothers follow", he said,
"As servants, and me they reprove
For their own pranks—me frighten so,
Being off their minds, with Subāl's name,
That with my friends I cease to go,
And monkies my sole friends remain !"'[9]

The manifest self-endeavour of the *nāyikā*

'Come to the woods', the *nāyaka* said—
The *nāyikā*, 'Does one have the time?'
But hinted, 'Passion all affects!'
Yet he the hint could not divine,
And said, 'Have you no work left, say?'
The *nāyikā*, 'Come you here to fight,
As foe?' The *nāyaka* still not wise,
Said 'No! games we will play today!'
The *nāyikā*, 'This game know I not!'
But hinted, 'Does today not come?'
The *nāyaka*, 'Play; have you forgot?
Do not forget!' The *nāyikā* then
Said, 'Will you then force yourself thus?'
But hinted, 'Will you me embrace?'
But he still thought himself rebuffed,
And said, 'Does love for me yet stay
In your heart?' Then the *nāyikā* spoke,
'Will you fight if I say "no!" Yet
She hinted, 'Will you dalliance make?'
The *nāyaka* still did fume and fret
Not understanding; 'Such words dare
You say?' he said: The *nāyikā* loud
Did say 'I'll speak! do as you care!'
Then she her growing unrest did shroud,
And softly said, 'I've had my say,
I'll follow—now you go away!'[10]

The hidden self-endeavour of the *nāyikā*

From house to house the cowherd wend
Dancing and drunk—as good as dead
And drunk Balarāma and all his friends,
Whom shall I take? I beat my head:
I must go, for the feast of light[11]
Does summon me, though sing I may
Lonely the calves are; they will die,
If in my eyes you do not stay.

The way of loving of an *ūḍhā* (married woman)

The *ūḍhā* having love revealed
In many ways, her shame then leaves;
And with an agitated heart
How lover goes to meet at last.

The desire of an *ūḍhā*

Addressing her mind the nāyaka says :

'Even for a moment can't be stayed
My wishful chariot on its way;
It glimmers as in legends sung,
The Though-shaped wheels so fast do run
That even the wind astounded is !
Mounting this chariot I have flown
Through earth and sky, rain, cold, and sun.
My body now how long shall I
Keep still—like well, or tank, or pond ?
Without Kṛiṣṇa many days have gone :
Now like a river I will break
Through mighty mountains wisdom-shaped
And felling down of shame the trees
Mingle myself with the love sea.'[12]

Another example of an *ūḍhā's* desire

My honour and my caste have flown,
Love for my clan no more I know,
No pride in youth does now remain,
And faith in loveliness does grow
Each moment less—O ! Kṛiṣṇa, I swear
Seeing you all bonds I broke with shame,
And from all things myself did tear,
But your deceit is still unchanged ![13]

The way of loving of an *anūḍhā* (unmarried woman)

Should the *anūḍhā* not essay
To meet her lover through great shame,

Her friend to him somehow conveys
The passion that burns through her frame.

Example of the loving of an *anūḍhā*

The female friend of the nāyaka says to him :

'I know not who told her, and when,
That Kṛiṣṇa unto my swing did hie;
She chews not betel leaves since then,
Nor water drinks, but fills her eyes
With tears; I die on you, O ! friend,
Make haste to comfort her ! Oh ! why
Go you not forth her grief to end,
Which on her heart does heavy lie ?
For well I know she is a bud
On passion's tree which long has lain,
And if perchance it withers up,
Alas ! 'twill never flower again !'[14]

Places where lovers meet for the first time.

For the first time the lovers meet
Within the home of a serving maid,
Or bosom friend, or nurse discreet,
Or in some far and lonely place ;
Or when by chance events near thrown,
A function, illness, or some fear,
Or invitation by one known,
Or in some forest dwelling near :
All men who in this wide world are
From king to beggar, for the first time
Their loved ones meet, says Keshavadāsa,
In the spots which I have so outlined.[15]

Meeting at a servant's house

One handmaid says to another :

'Today the girls of Braja adorned
Kṛiṣṇa as a maid, and so conspired,

That his arms round Rādhā's neck were thrown,
Rādhā, the creeper of desire.
He ran where'er his fancy willed
And playfully hid in mock pretence;
A million cravings he fulfilled
Of hers, for making love—dear friend :
So in her servant's house today
Shrī Kṛiṣṇa did sport, and make the game
Of hide and seek, real lover's play,
When he so unto Rādhā came.'

Meeting through a bosom friend

Oh ! dear, within your eyes her keep,
As pupils thereof—press her now
As flute within your quivering teeth,
As garland worn upon the brow :
So think of her—as sandal-paste
Upon your limbs; as necklace cast
Around your neck: Oh ! dear, I lay
My life on you ! I somehow brought
This maiden to your house to know ;
Drink her perfume, as *champā* bud,
And in your mind her treasure so
As heavenly goddess—oh ! my love.[16]

Meeting through the maid

While games were played, and tales that pleased,
And riddles, told, the moon's light waned—
Children with sleepy eyes did leave,
And cowherd girls who still remained
Did homeward turn: dense clouds did spread
From all around. When Kṛiṣṇa arose,
The housemaid said, 'Share Rādhā's bed,
'Tis midnight, Kṛiṣṇa ! where will you go?'

Meeting by chance

When the art gallery Rādhā scanned
Devoid of pictures, she who seemed
A lovely garland, soon began
In spritely mood to sing a tune
Like to her anklets, and the soles
Of her feet so began to beat:
When lo! within her vision stole
The youthful Kṛiṣṇa; tongue cannot speak
Her body's state, when him she spied,
Her eyes which were listless and still,
Watery became, as if she cried;
And like clouds, full of tears were filled.[17]

Meeting in darkness

The cowherd girls and youths did hie
To Gokul once, and when night came
Back home they went: soon from all sides
Dark clouds arose, such darkness reigned
Upon the earth that when one spoke
Then only was his presence known.
Then Kṛiṣṇa sad separation broke,
And did those things which he was wont.[18]

Meeting by removal of fear

Hearing that fire had broken out
In Vṛiṣabhānu's house, all Braja poured in;
From all sides men did throng and shout,
And fear threw all shame to the winds.
When parrot and starling he had moved,
And woken the other maids—then Kṛiṣṇa
At last near slumbering Rādhā stood,
And kissed her lovely eyes and chin,
And quivering breasts; and clasped her close
As *champā* flowers in garland stringed—
Thus that fair maiden he awoke ![19]

Meeting at a function

On Balarāma's birthday belles divine
Of Braja all night did hold carouse,
Their bodies decked as gold did shine
Great crowd was there at Nandajī's house.
And everywhere people did throng
In all the three stories where they stayed,
No corner empty was ere long;
The women sang, and danced, and played,
As if a sea of pleasure had sprung;
'Twas then that sleepy Rādhā spied
Kṛiṣṇa's empty bed and dropped thereon,
And as she slept he himself hied
And seeing his Rādhā sleep alone,
He went to her as to a bride
First come unto her husband's home,[20]
And lay by his beloved's side!

Meeting on the pretext of disease

Gifts were given and cures applied
Still her disease did not improve,
Then offerings her ailment out to drive
Were made—oblations in fire too,
As did the *Vedas* enjoin, with care;
The malady went not still—I die
On you, oh! Kṛiṣṇa! with speed repair,
For Rādhā's mother, Vṛiṣabhānu's wife
Says piteously—that pain once more
With Rādhā has come back to stay,
With great endeavour which you drove,
And driving forth, did come away![21]

Meeting at an invitation

Yashodājī[22] once did invite
Vṛiṣabhānu's child, and herself brought her
Fully adorned, with great delight,

Into her house. When meals were over,
Chewing betels she upstairs did go
Alone, perchance some joy to seek,
When seeing her lover, Kṛiṣṇa, approach
She fled; whereat he fearlessly
Caught her and grasped her snake-like braid,[23]
Embraced her, and did as he chose;
Then rubbing saffron on her face,
Took her nose-ring, and left her so.

Meeting in a forest abode

Said Kṛiṣṇa, 'give me, O! pretty maid,
That curd you promised yesterday.'
And she replied, 'your garment spread
And take it!' Then again she said,
'Molest me not, stop not my way.'
'Your friend with bashful eyes should save
You!' he replied. She said anon:
'Be careful what you say, someone
May hear—know you whose daughter she is?'
Then Kṛiṣṇa did say, 'I know she be
Vṛiṣabhānu's child; *you* I know not;
Tell me, my dear ! whose slave you are !'[24]

Meeting by a lake

Shrī Kṛiṣṇa and Rādhā hand in hand
On the shore of Mānasarovar[25] stand;
On the head of the lover a turban twirls,
On the beloved's head a string of pearls;
Garlands adorn the necks of both,
Says Keshava, and silver waist-bands sport
Upon their waists: their bodies chaste
Are smeared with scented sandal-wood paste;
'Twas as if Lakshmī[26] and Viṣṇu[27] emerged
From the sacred sea of milk and curd.

Concluding verse

Know in this manner I have given
The spots of meeting of Shrī Kṛiṣṇa,
Apart from those there are many more
Which each knows as his wisdom shows:
The common *nāyikā* I've omitted
Purposely; and the reason is
That prominent amorists always say
Right from the beginning to this day,
When mentioning pleasures one should miss
Things which are tasteless and insipid.

NOTES

1. In the course of relating to the *nāyaka* the secret love which the *nāyikā* has for him, the bosom companion gets agitated herself with the passion which her narration excites.

2. In *Satsaī*, Poet Bihārī also describes a *nāyikā* in love who cannot sleep :

'O! love : what magic in you dwells
That if but once upon you gaze
These eyes, for ever restless they,
And not one wink in sleep they rest.'

3. These lines are a clear indication of the fact that lesbianism prevailed then as now. The female companions of the *nāyikā* not only helped her to meet her lover but also talked to her about love. These talks would doubtless set aflame the female companions (who were mostly young themselves) and they would spend their unquenched passion on the *nāyikā*, and 'play the game as women long,' but their thirst would only be quenched as much as a thirsty person's is by licking dew .

4. The previous verses have described the longing of the *nāyikā* for her lover. This verse, and the subsequent one describe the signs of desire in the *nāyaka* for his beloved.

5. The *nāyaka*, Kṛiṣṇa, has sent many bribed go-betweens to convey his message of love to his beloved, so that she may be persuaded to come to him. He has sent her many epistles and love-songs, and devised many stratagems, but all to no purpose. The bosom companion says to him, 'You have failed in all your attempts to get her. Now what will you give me if I unite you with her! Why are you standing like a dumb creature! Why don't you go and meet her! She is waiting for you at your doorstep ! Should I carry her for you in my lap !'

6. As amongst other races, superstitions exist amongst the Hindus also. One such superstition is that if some woman looks with admiration on another's

loveliness she will fall sick or come to grief. To counter this, mothers paint collyrium in the eyelids of children, and women apply it in theirs. This is supposed to ward off the effect of the gaze of an evil eye. The writer of *Anaṅga Raṅga* enumerates formulas or *mantras* for subjugating women of various types.

7. Kṛiṣṇa is Nanda's son.

8. The meaning of this verse is somewhat obscure. The idea however seems to be that the *nāyikā*, who is afficted by night-blindness and is deaf, wants that her bosom friends should come to her house and sleep with her. She cannot go to them as she cannot move out without the help of a serving woman, and there is none to help her. If her bosom companions sleep with her, Kṛiṣṇa may also be tempted to come there, for the other maidens will prove an attraction for him, and she can also now and then hope to receive his favours. So she devises this stratagem to bring Kṛiṣṇa close to her.

9. The *nāyikā* will not come into the woods with Kṛiṣṇa, so he tries a ruse on her. He tells her that all his friends have left off going with him and follow their own brothers instead, as though they were servants. They create mischief themselves and then blame him for it, and frighten him by uttering the name of Subāla. For this reason he has left off going with his friends and now wanders lonely in the woods, making monkeys his playmates. He tells the *nāyikā* all this, hoping to draw her sympathy. When she knows he goes alone to the forest she will offer to go with him.

Subāla was the father of Shakuni who was brother of Queen Gandhārī, and so an uncle of the Kaurava Princes. This Shakuni was a gambler and a cheat, and it was he who induced Yudhiṣṭhira to the game of dice at which he lost his entire kingdom. Subāla was obviously a terror.

10. This is a dialogue between the crafty *nāyikā* and dull-witted *nāyaka*. The *nāyikā* says something loudly, but means quite the contrary, and tries to bring home to her lover what she really means. First the *nāyaka* asks her to come to the woods along with him. As her female companions surround her she demurs, and outwardly answers that she has no time, but shows her willingness inwardly. The *nāyaka* does not take the hint and says, 'all of you are free, why don't you come!' The *nāyikā* says 'have you come to fight with me and my friends!' The *nāyaka* tells her that he wants to play games in the forest. Outwardly she answers that she knows no games, but hints her acquiescence. The *nāyaka* taunts her saying, 'have you forgotten to play also!' The *nāyikā* says outwardly, 'So you wish to force yourself on us!' But what she really hints is that she is ready for his embrace. The *nāyaka* still does not understand and asks her if she still loves him or not. To this she replies 'Will you fight with me if I say 'no'' ! But by her hints she invites him to make love to her. The poor *nāyaka* continues to be bewildered and says, 'How dare you say such words to me!' The *nāyikā* is fed up by now of the *nāyaka*'s failure to read her hints, and says in desperation 'I'll say what I like, do as you care but hiding her growing unrest she adds softly 'I've said what I had to say, now you go, and I will follow.'

11. *Dewālī*, the festival of the lamps, is one of the main festivals of the Hindus, in which oil lamps are lit and placed in rows on balconies and

roofs. It is to celebrate the return of Rāma to Ayodhyā, after his victory over the demon King of Laṅkā.

The cowherd men, and Balarāma amongst them, were great drunkards and took large quantities of wine. They used to hold bouts of drinking and carousals. The *Bhāgavata* describes the attack of Balarāma and his men on the city of Kushasthalī of the Puṇyajanas. After the city was vanquished the wine-shops were looted by the invaders, and Balarāma and his warriors drank to their hearts' content. Balarāma drank a lot and the more he took the better he began to feel. In his drunkenness he began to force Revatī (the damsel on whose behalf he had stormed the city) to drink but she quietly threw the liquor away. When it was evening Balarāma's men went about the streets drunk with wine.

On another occasion at a worship of the goddess Gaurī in which Kṛiṣṇa was present along with a young girl, Bhānumatī, boisterous festivity took place. The women danced wildly stopping now and then to drink wine, and to force it on the young men present there. Bhānumatī came now and then to press Kṛiṣṇa to drink, and he sipped a little wine to make her happy. The drinking led to sexual abandonment, and an orgy ensued in which the men and women enjoyed themselves crazily. It became so bad that Kṛiṣṇa could stand it no longer, and had to leave with the tipsy girl Bhānumatī to preserve her honour.

The *nāyikā* is half-inclined to stay on and enjoy the festivities, but she has to go, as it is Dewālī. She laments that there remains no sober person to escort her. Besides the calves are lonely and they need her care without which they will die. Being a cowherd girl the *nāyikā*'s sense of duty towards the cows and calves prevails.

12. These lines are addressed by the *nāyikā* to her mind. She says that the chariot of her desire, with wheels of thought, cannot be stayed even for a moment. On it she has gone through earth, sky, sun, rain, and cold. How long shall she suffer Kṛiṣṇa's absence and keep quiet. She will break through the wisdom-shaped mountains like a river, which uprooting the trees of bashfulness, mingles with the sea of love.

13. The *ūḍhā nāyikā* has defied her caste, spurned her honour, abandoned all faith and pride, and left aside bashfulness, but still the *nāyaka*, Kṛiṣṇa, does not relinquish his deceit.

14. Someone has told the *nāyikā* that Kṛiṣṇa has sat in the swing of one of her female friends. From that moment she is crestfallen, and refuses to eat betels, or even to drink water. Seeing her desperate condition the female friend goes to Kṛiṣṇa and asks him to comfort the *nāyikā* lest she may waste away with grief and die.

15. Vātsyāyana has some tips for lovers in regard to the places where they should try to meet their beloved ones for the first time. The lover should arrange so that he meets the woman either in the routine way or at a special occasion. The former is when he goes to her house, and the latter when he meets her at the house of a friend, or one of the same caste, or a minister or physician, or on the occasion of marriage ceremonies, sacrifices, festivals, funerals and garden parties.

16. The bosom friend has brought the *nāyikā* to the house of the *nāyaka* and is exhorting him to give her a lover's welcome.

17. Rādhā looks round the empty picture gallery and begins to daydream. Instead of real portraits she begins to see imaginary ones. Absent-mindedly she begins to beat out a tune with her feet, and her anklets sound to the movements; just then, her lover Kṛiṣṇa comes, and his sight affects her so much that she forgets her dancing, and her eyes become moist with tears of love.

18. Under cover of the pitch darkness Kṛiṣṇa made love to the cowherd girls and fulfilled their desires.

19. Word suddenly goes round that fire has broken out in the house of Vṛiṣabhānu, Rādhā's father and everyone who hears of it comes to help. While people are thronging around, and shouting, and removing one thing and another from the house, Kṛiṣṇa takes advantage of the general confusion, and goes quietly into the room where Rādhā is sleeping with her maids. He wakes all of them up, and bundles them out along with the tame birds in cages hanging above. Last of all, he stands by the sleeping Rādhā's bedside, and kissing her eyes, chin, and breasts, clasps her to his bosom as though she was a garland of flowers, and wakes her up in this pleasant fashion.

20. The old Hindu custom was that the ceremony of marriage took place early in childhood when the boy and the girl were children. But the girl went to her husband's home only after attaining puberty. This was called *gauna*. After this the couple began to have conjugal relations. The system is prevalent even now in the villages. Kṛiṣṇa sees Rādhā sleeping on bed and, filled with love, goes to sleep by her side as a husband would whose bride has come to him after the *gauna* ceremony.

Vātsyāyana advises the girl and her husband to sleep separately on first three days after marriage. Though he may do acts to win her confidence, he should abstain for some time from sexual intercourse.

21. When Rādhā's disease does not leave her despite all treatment her mother piteously summons Kṛiṣṇa, and says, "Oh Kṛiṣṇa, that pain has come over Rādhā again which you had cured and gone away. So please come back and remove it once more.

22. Wife of Nanda, and foster-mother of Kṛiṣṇa. Kṛiṣṇa was the son of Vasudeva and Devakī. The sage Nārada had foretold to Kaṁsa that a son of Devakī, (his brother's daughter) would kill him and overthrow his kingdom. So Kaṁsa kept Devakī confined to his palace, and ordered all her children to be put to death. But the eighth child, who was Kṛiṣṇa, was miraculously substituted for the female child of Nanda and Yashodā, and so he escaped from Kaṁsa, whom he later killed, as the sage had foretold.

23. Indian women usually braid their hair, which being jet black, looks then like a snake. So the braid of hair is frequently compared to a snake by Hindi writers and poets.

In Chaṇḍī Dāsa's description of Rādhā her hair is pictured thus :

'Like stilled lightning fair face
I saw her by the river.
Her hair dressed with jasmine,
Plaited like a coiled snake.'

In an Indian love song we have the following description :

'The curl of your lock has entwined my heart
And like a viper it has stung me.'

The braided hair of *Guzrātī* girls, we are told, 'look as if a cobra has nestled there'. When the serpent saw the lovely braid of Damayantī, humbled and shamed it crawled into the nether regions. In Jāisī's *Padmāvatī* hair is frequently compared to snakes. Speaking of maidens sporting in the water the poet says :

'Their glossy black hair on the waters lay
Like snakes which by their very looks did slay.'

The beautiful black hair of Princess Padmāvatī are picturesquely described :

Her tresses, black bees are, struggling to taste
Her nectar, soft and glossy—wave on wave.
As sinuous serpents on a rock do shine
Intoxicated by the sandal breeze
Of mount Malaya, they on her head do climb,
Thence wind around her deadly poison curls;
Love-chains which close on the beholder's neck—
The parting of her hair , as yet untouched
By vermilion, is a shaft of light
Through her mass'd tresses, black as is the night !

When her boat had sunk, and the unhappy Princess was cast on the merciless waves, her curling tresses lay

'as snakes climbing on
Her head, and leaving all her bosom bare'.

A Telegū poetess, describing a woman's braided hair, praises its sinuous length:

'Her braided hair was black and long like Rāhu the sky snake
Come to devour the full moon of her face which outshone it.'

24. Rādhā is going with another maid in the forest, the latter with a pot of curd on her head. Kṛiṣṇa waylays the maid, and asks her to give him the curd, which she had promised him the day before. She tauntingly says, 'spread out your garment and have it'. and adds, 'do not molest me or block my way'. The audacious Kṛiṣṇa, beckoning towards Rādhā, says, 'What if I molest you, will not your companion of bashful eyes save you! The maid is aghast at such impertinence and asks him, 'Did you know whose daughter she (Rādhā) is!' Kṛiṣṇa replies with greater insolence, 'Yes, that I know : she is the daughter of Vṛiṣabhānu, but I do not know whose slave *you* are'

25. A large lake in the north of the Himālaya mountains from which the River Gaṅgā takes its source.

26. See note 10, Chapter 4.

27. See note 4, Chapter 1.

Chapter VI

The Emotions

This is a long Chapter in which Keshavadāsa gives a thought-provoking analysis of various kinds of emotions by which lovers are swayed. Emotion is said to be expressed when the message of the heart is conveyed through a person's face, eyes, or voice. There are five kinds of emotions—disjointed, positive, auxiliary, steady, and that causing horripilation. The disjointed emotion is that by which there is sudden increase of pleasure. This is of two kinds—supporting, and exciting. The former is one which aids pleasure and enhances it, as for example, beautiful flowers, pleasant weather, shapely limbs shrouded by lovely clothes, the melodious notes of music, and the charming sights of nature. The exciting emotion, as its name implies, is one which creates and increases excitment of passion. Examples of things which excite are : sight, conversation, loud cries of rapture in lovemaking, kissing, rubbing, touch and marking by the nails or teeth. The supporting and exciting emotions are the chaste ones, and are sanctioned by convention for newly-wed lovers. The unchaste emotions are on the other hand those which though resulting in pleasure are not authorised by rule or convention. The list of unchaste emotions is long. They are thirty-four in all. These emotions are, indifference, weariness, doubt, laziness, poverty, delusion, recollection, contempt, shame, fickleness, labour, intoxication, care, rage, pride, joy, excitement, scorn, sleep, debate, stupor, craving, dream, awakening, sorrow, epilepsy, violence of mind, hope, argument, great perplexity, fear, frenzy, and death. Another division of emotions is from the point of view of amorous dalliance, especially, that of the traditional lovers, Rādhā and Kṛiṣṇa. Examples of such emotions are dalliance, amorous sport, elegance, merriment, coquetry, ecstasy, amorous gestures, and the like. The characteristics of these, and other emotions are described. As elsewhere, examples are given throughout to illustrate the various types of emotions. This is an unusual chapter, and the classification of emotions made by Keshavadāsa might be considered too meticulous and even sometimes tiresome, were it not for the fact that it is an important branch of study in Hindi poetry. None-the-less the significance of emotion in art, especially one so subjective as poetry, is obvious. In the words of H.R. Haweis: 'Emotion is the atmosphere in which thought is steeped, that which lends to thought its tone or temperature, that to which thought is often indebted for half its power.'

What emotion is

When what within the heart lay hid
Is manifested through the eyes,
Or by the face, or voice, that is
Emotion known by poets wise.[1]

Kinds of emotions

Emotions of five kinds methinks
Unto all poets are known to be,
Disjointed, positive, and helping,
Horripilating, and the steady.

The disjointed emotion

By which the pleasures of the world
All of a sudden show increase,
That is defined by Keshavadāsa
The emotion which disjointed is.
Of this two further types are told,
As poets skilled are wont to think,
The one is that which lends support,
The other which is exciting.

The natures of the disjointed and exciting emotions

By whose aid pleasure more becomes
That is the supporting: and by which

Excitement in the mind is born
That emotion exciting is.

Habitation of the supporting emotion

Young couples, bosom friends bound close
By ties of beauty, caste, and trait;
The cuckoo, lovely spring, and groves,
And blossoming flowers, delicious lake
With watery creatures, bumble bees,
The dainty lotus, *chātaka*,[2] sky;
The peacock's shout, a lightning's streak,
A lamp of oil, a bed that lies
Inviting; dark rain-bearing clouds,
A room sweet-scented, betels chewed;
A lovely dress fair limbs that shrouds,
The *vīṇā's* notes, guitar, and lute :
These are the things that pleasures please
And do emotion much increase.

Ingredients of the exciting emotion

Sight, conversation, and loud cries,
Inflicting marks of nail and teeth,
Rubbing and kissing, and the like;
And touch—these excitement increase.

Nature of emotions which follow convention

All acts which like the image lie
Of emotions that aid and excite,
Do sprout in newly-weds in love,
And bound by rules conventional are.

The steady emotions

Lovemaking, laughter, sorrow, rage,
Zeal, wonder, scorn—are known to be
By the authority of age
Emotions which are counted steady.

Nature of horripilation

Stupor, sweat, standing of hair
On end; trembling, and loss of voice,
Paleness, tears, and deliriousness;
Eight signs of horripilation are.

Unchaste emotions

Emotions in all pleasures that stay
Without a precept or a rule,
Are by good poets called unchaste.

The unchaste emotions

Indifference, weariness, and doubt,
Remembrance, fickleness, and shame;
Contempt, and poverty that bows,
Anxiety, fear, and sorrow vain;
Delusion, labour, pride and rage,
Sloth, intoxication, joy,
Excitement, scorn, sleep and debate,
Stupor, dream, cravings that cloy :
Awakening, hope, epilepsy,
Violence of mind, and worry grave;
Argument, frenzy, death, disease—
These are emotions all unchaste.

Emotions arising from the love of Rādhā and Kṛiṣṇa.

When for lovemaking of Shrī Kṛiṣṇa
And Rādhā, endeavours arise,
These are emotions such, wherein
The poets and poetesses surmise,
As is their understanding, these :
Love's amorous sport, and elegance,
Intoxication, dalliance sweet,
Deception, and bewilderment,
That which is planned, and coquetry;

The gestures fond which lovers use,
Bivvoka,[4] *moṭṭāyita,*[5] *kuṭṭamita,*[6]
And feelings which the heart can move.

The emotion of delight

Where power of perfect love does make
All bashfulness at once to fly,
And Kṛiṣṇa and Rādhā captivates,
That is emotion of delight.[7]

Example of the emotion of delight

She pulled him to her with the goad
Incomparable of her gaze;[8]
Thus Rādhā round his neck did throw
Her eyebrow-noose—alone she stayed
With her love in the moonlight dim.
Her fragrance, and her laughter soft,
Did linger—and she made him drink
The essence of her sweet lips oft,
Thus her beloved she did win:
Then him with talk she busy kept,
And to the forest she took him,
Her mind on sweet enjoyment set.

The emotion of amusement

When the lover and loved one devise
As one another to be clothed,
And so make love; then does arise
The sentiment of amorous sport:
Says Keshavadāsa, where both sojourn
As blissful lovers so engaged,
There amusement's emotion born
Is—thus do skilful poets say.[9]

Example of the emotion of amusement of the *nāyikā*.

Rādhā as Shrī Kṛiṣṇa being disguised
Learns low to bow, and touch his feet,

To bear insults in many wise,
To be wrathful, and to appease:
Betels to offer and to take
She learns; to be startled, and peep
In all directions in strange ways,
On drab and dirty floors to sleep:
To run at every crackle made
By dry leaves; and learns to blindfold
Her eyes, and still to make her way
From one grove to another grove.

Example of the emotion of amusement of the ***nāyaka***

Shrī Kṛiṣṇa,[10] as Rādhā being disguised,[11]
From casement peers, and his roof mounts,
To gaze; the cowherds he decries,
And sings Kṛiṣṇa's praises! looking on
His own portrait with joy much grown
So does he wander all the way
From home to courtyard, then to home;
And so does he spend all the day.

The elegant emotion

Where speaking, laughter, and fond sight,
And gait, becoming are described,
As they in truth are; there exists
The emotion which elegant is.

Example of the *nāyikā's* elegant emotion

Whose heart is spotless, and so tender,
Who has a worthy bosom friend
As Sarasvatī[12] to befriend her,
And lotus stalk within her hands,
As Lakshmī.[13] When the sound they hear
Of her toe-ornament,ducklings doubt,
And startled think that swans are near!
Whose waist with burden low is bowed

Of breasts,[14] and hair, and her shame deep!
That girl who walks with charming gait
And softly laughs, and sweetly speaks,
The mind of Kṛiṣṇa does captivate.

Example of the *nāyaka's* elegant emotion

Oh! see, my bosom friend, arise!
Ghanashyāma as cloud, today does go
From the woods to Braja—open your eyes
And drink your fill—his garments yellow
Like lightning are; his crown so glints
That the rainbow's splendour more it makes,
The charmed note of his flute methinks
Is as the cloud's beloved play-mate,
The peacock,[15] who with joy does dance
When he beholds his friend advance.

The emotion of ecstasy

When due to perfect love, conceit
Increases; and the change to youth
Does rapture bring—then 'tis in sooth
Emotion of sweet ecstasy.

Example of the emotion of ecstasy.

When graceful, and drunk with ecstasy
Of her sweet form, and arrogance,
Rādhājī sat—and oh! dear friend,
The handsome son of Nandajī,
Lovelier than Kāmadeva, to appease
Her did arrive; by Kṛiṣṇa I swear,
Oft laughed he, and at her feet there
Did fall, yet he did not succeed,
To win her: at that very time
Dark clouds arose: then in fear she
Like lightning did upon him leap
And round him her limbs close entwined![16]

Another example of the emotion of ecstasy

He has seen the daughter of Vṛiṣabhānu,
No winsome woman on this earth
Can now Kṛiṣṇa with her beauty charm:
The lightning has to him no worth,
And lovemaking has no repute,
And sporting in the moonlight stale:
Of others what it is to boot,
When Lakshmī too before her pales?
Drunk so with Rādhā's love is he,
Another girl he does not see !

The emotion of perplexity

Where ornaments are wrongly worn
In disarray under love's spell,
Where in meeting joy more becomes,
And mind and body starts to melt—
There is produced, as poets see,
Emotion of perplexity.

The emotion of perplexity of the *nāyikā*[17]

Her garland round her waist she hooked,
The waist-chain[18] hung around her neck !
Toe-ornaments[19] on fingers put,
With bracelets she her feet did deck !
Her skirt and bodice she forgot,
And with collyrium her breasts tipped !
The splendour of her eyes she sought
To make more with red dye for feet ![20]
When Kṛiṣṇa with ornaments adorned
Arrived, to meet him straight she ran !

The emotion of perplexity of the *nāyaka*

The son of Nanda, Shrī Kṛiṣṇa, did play
Within the woods; his body shone

With splendour of white sandal-paste,
When all at once Rādhā did come
Within his gaze; then his mind was
So unnerved that the betels placed
Within his hands did slip and drop
All unawares; he did mistake
The lotus leaves which wrapped them, for
The betels ![21] and them 'gan to chew,
Seeing which the cowherd girls did laugh,
And Shrī Kṛiṣṇa closed his eyes, confused :
Oh ! friend ! how sweet his closed eyes were !

The suppressed emotion

When bashfulness so hinders speech
That words do not come : Keshavadāsa
And other skilful poets that be,
Suppressed emotion this do call.

Example of the suppressed emotion of the *nāyikā*

A bosom companion says to the nāyikā :

'With sorrow burn you now, my friend,
Hearing me speak, but soon you'll burn
With fuel of your own obstinacy,[22]
Like timber which the sun does heat.
After so swimming in the sea
Of love, how long you 'll aided be
By others? All your friends are dying
To see you laugh and talk with Kṛiṣṇa :
The mind-like attic of your swain
You've climbed, how long will you remain
Now as a lifeless marionette
Within a picture drab, painted ?'

Another example of the suppressed emotion of the *nāyaka*

Vṛiṣabhānu's daughter, Rādhājī,
Today Shrī Kṛiṣṇa did much revile,

And called him names and him did beat
With lotuses; yet still awhile
She loved him in her mind, and he
All her behests with joy obeyed,
Whate'er new things sweet-scented she
Gave him, upon his breast he placed,
O ! bosom friend, with so much done,
To answer her how could he deign ?
For when Shrī Kṛiṣṇa his head bowed once,
He did not lift it e'er again !

The emotion of merriment

Where in playing, and laughing, and speaking,
And glancing, and walking, takes birth
Splendour; where various enjoyments
Are seen on the land and on earth,
In such is known to awaken
The emotion of merriment in verse.

Example of the nāyikā's emotion of merriment

The lustre of your lovely looks,
And of your *ṭikā* mark, proclaim
Your eyebrows have turned the abode
Of playfulness, and filled with shame
Your eyes are dancing all the way :
The brightness of your teeth has robbed
All reason; Shrī Kṛiṣṇa's mind enslaved
Have you by charming laughter soft,
And your mouth's fragrance; though I ween
He clever is: to captivate
Shrī Kṛiṣṇa's body and soul it seems
Your lips the vow of silence take.

Example of the *nāyaka's* emotion of merriment[23]

Those who your eyes have not beheld
To see them do entreat ; O ! Kṛiṣṇa,

Wise men and maidens newly-wed
And *nāgas*[24] love you; you sport within
The hearts of even faithful wives;
And bodies endless thus you bear
That even Brahmā[25] of their like
Searching, does give up in despair !
Your eyes do beauty's short-lived pride
And Kāmadeva's vanity remove,
And seeing those captivating eyes
Are women's vows forgotten soon.

The emotion of amorous gesture

Where labour, laughter, joy, and rage,
Desire, pride, and fear, do exist
All in a moment; this poets say
The emotion of amorous gesture is.

Emotion of amorous gesture of the *nāyikā*

On whom your joyful gaze you send,
And looking laugh? On whom you knit
With rage your brows, oh! bosom friend ?
Sometimes all bashfulness you quit,
Anon with your end-cloth your face
You cover! On whom do you pine?
Your sad state I like not, and pray
That god may yet preserve your mind!

The amorous gesture of the *nāyaka*

Of which clan is this Gokul maid
Who to herself has drawn you so?
Says Keshavadāsa, the soul she sways
As wagtail bird: she swinging goes
Upon the creeper, softly borne,
Of laughter and of merriment!
She speaks, she rises up, and bends,
Is quiet, and then with pleasure moans

All of a sudden; when around
Are women with such lovely forms,
Then why, oh! Kṛiṣṇa, are you forlorn?
And in what pleasure are you drowned?

The emotion of slight

Where due to vanity of love,
And beauty, disrespect is shown
By one deceitful—to men thus
Emotion base, of slight, is known.

The emotion of slight of the *nāyikā*

When she knew Shrī Kṛiṣṇa to approach
She feigned sleep, softly he essayed
To wake her—she would not be woke:
Then venturing forth, his hand he placed
Upon her rising bosom, so
That she did titillated feel;
Emboldened thus his hand did go
Her waist-band to untie, when she
Did start and rise, and knowing him close
Said, 'All day long, oh! boor ill-bred,
Your cows you tend and at night force
Yourself in another woman's bed!'

The *bivvoka* emotion of the *nāyaka*

One bosom companion says to another:

'At one time Shrī Kṛiṣṇa so did speak
Jestingly to a cowherd maid,
'Oh! what love can you now give me
When your own father left you, say?'
Oh! bosom friend, who could reply
To this? Soon tears began to flow
From that afflicted woman's eyes,
Seeing which perturbed, he clasped her close

Unto his breast, yet till midnight
That maiden's sobs knew no respite !'

The emotion of breaking-up

Where by ornaments beautified,
Dishonour, not respect, does rise—
There know for sure, says Keshavadāsa,
Is emotion of breaking-up caused.

The emotion of breaking-up of the *nāyikā*

The bosom companion says to the nāyikā :

The adornments with care you have chosen
According to your mind's desire
Are in truth no adornments, friend—
And useless, for they only tire
Him; and his heart they do not bind:
Can't you leave them, friend? They will
No favour with Brajabhūṣaṇa[26] find.
The world is by your perfume filled,
If scent you to yourself apply
'Tis meaningless : O ! my dear one !
Adornments when from you derive
Their grace, *you* how can they adorn?

The emotion of breaking-up of the *nāyaka*

To chew betels you have forsworn,
Nor turban wound; though you have changed
Your clothes, and obstinately thrown
The wreath of flowers, and ornament,
From off your neck; removed the mark
From forehead, sandal-paste from cheeks :
And from collyrium-filled eyes dark,
Collyrium; yet how can one seek
That natural fragrance to wipe off

O ! Kṛiṣṇa, which round your limbs does keep ?

The emotion of concealment

When body's trembling which exists
By amorousness, and woman's shame,
Suppressed by strength of wisdom is,
'Tis emotion of concealment named.

The emotion of concealment of the *nāyikā*

When Shrī Kṛiṣṇa sported in the grove,
A belle lovelier than Rati sat,
When all at once upon his back
Her eyes some manner fell to rove—
And saw, O ! fie ! Some woman's breasts
Their saffron marks had on him laid,
But she, poor maiden, as she stayed
Beside her mother, thought how best
Her body's bristling hair to hide :
With camphor-dust she sprinkled well,
Her eyes, and lotus flower did smell
And in her mantle hid did lie.[27]

Emotion of concealment of the *nāyaka*.

After meals in Vṛiṣabhānu's house,
Shrī Kṛiṣṇa, Nanda's pleasure-giving son,
Amidst a gathering sat, around
Him cowherds, and Balarāmajī thronged.
That moment to the casement came
Rādhā, and her gaze on him dwelt,
Which did so greatly him inflame
That with joy overcome he fell !
Whereat hue and cry there was much;
And his embarrassment to hide,
He shyly said, 'a betel nut
Perchance it seems has stuck inside !'[28]

The emotion of quarrelsomeness

Where love's sweet fray merely begets
False show of quarrelling, that is known
Emotion of quarrelsomeness.

The emotion of quarrelsomeness of the *nāyikā*

At first obstinate she did stay,
And sulkingly got up and went,
This act of hers I saw, my friend,
But you could not: Shrī Kṛiṣṇa then chased
And caught her : then she of herself
In his arms sought to be embraced;
He held her and her breasts did crush
Most savagely;[29] and so essayed
To hurt her by his teeth and nail,[30]
As one his enemy would treat,
But soon offered her betel-leaves—
Dear friend, what strange love he did make !

The emotion of quarrelsomeness of the *nāyaka*

Stubbornly silent she did stay,
When first she saw him; when she spoke,
Harsh words she said, nor towards him gazed,
And even when he gave her oaths
Her eyes to him she did not turn;
When he begged she did not bestow
Her favour; tired out and undone
Thus humbly his love to implore,
On her feet fell he, but she kicked
Him ! Yet now, lo ! he holds her face
Upon his lap, adorning it—
A strange love-lesson, friend, he gave !

The emotion of perception

One's secret intent when another perceives,
Perception's emotion the wise it believe.

The emotion of perception of the *nāyikā*

Once when the daughter of Vṛiṣabhānu
Amongst her bosom friends adorned
Did sit, a cowherd lad did keep
A withered lotus on her feet.
Then Rādhājī with yearning sighed,
And sandal-dust on it applied,
Offered him betels, and over-laid
His cheeks and mouth with sandal-paste :
And with collyrium did she stain
His eyes, and send him back again.[31]

The emotion of perception of the *nāyaka*

O ! dear friend, once Shrī Kṛiṣṇa remained
Amidst the cowherd boys, and shone
With splendour, as if the full moon came
After the poor hearts it had stol'n,
Of *chakor* birds; when a stranger gave
Him a water-filled inverted lotus,
Which Shrī Kṛiṣṇa saw, and returned the same
After folding its petals in the form of a bud.[32]
Oh ! tell me, my bosom companions why
Shrī Kṛiṣṇa did what I saw with my eyes ?

Concluding verse

Keshavadāsa says, thus I've detailed
Emotions Rādhā and Kṛiṣṇa have swayed,
As laid by rules; O ! poets excuse
My insolence great, so I pray you !

NOTES

1. Hindi and Sanskrit poets have made a systematic study of emotions. Keshava's characterisation is novel and not found in any other Hindi poet. According to him emotion is that which is produced by the various expressions

of the face e. g. contraction of the eyebrows, serious or frivolous looks, conditions of the eyes e. g. redness, moistness, and modulations of the voice, i. e. shrillness softness, loudness and the like.

2. A kind of cuckoo who is supposed to drink only drops of rain, also called *papīhā*, or hawk cuckoo. It is a small bird about the size of a pigeon which sends forth a plaintive note—pipeeha pipeeha. It can be heard from early spring to monsoon. According to ancient belief the *chātak* lives on raindrops and would rather die than drink anything other than this.

3. An Indian stringed instrument which is played as accompaniment to singing.

4. This term, and the two subsequent ones, have been left untranslated because they have no specific equivalent in the English Language. The Poet defines *bibboka* as that state, in which due to vanity of beauty and love, disrespect, is shown.

5. *Moṭṭāyita* is that condition in which a woman conceals by the power of her wisdom, the trembling of her body which is produced by bashfulness and amorousness (i.e. when an amorous feeling takes hold of her but her bashfulness will not allow her to show it, and she hides her trembling by controlling her mind).

6. *Kuṭṭamita* is that state where in amorous dalliance there is only outward show of lovemaking without the woman's mind being in it.

7. The emotion of delight is born when the hearts of Rādhā and Kṛiṣṇa are affected completely by love, all bashfulness in them being removed.

8. Just as a mahout guides the elephant with his goad, so did Rādhā draw her lover, Kṛiṣṇa, towards her with her gaze, and threw her eyebrow-shaped noose around his neck i. e. lifted her eyebrows towards him in such a manner that imprisoned him like a noose around his neck.

9. The emotion of amusement is produced when the lover puts on a woman's clothes and the beloved those of a man, and under their respective disguises the two seek to come close to each other.

10. *Shrī*—a prefix put before a name like 'Mister' in English (see note 2, Part 1).

In this verse Rādhā disguises himself as her lover, Kṛiṣṇa, and learns all his habits, so that she can escape prying eyes and meet him.

11. In the previous verse, Rādhā has disguised herself as Kṛiṣṇa, in this one Kriṣṇa disguises himself as Rādhā and goes round singing his own praises.

12. See note 51, Chapter 3.

13. See note 10, Chapter 4.

14. As Penser says in *Ocean of Story*, the Hindus have always admired full and heavy breasts—big and protuberant, and at the same time justing out and firm as depicted in the sculptures of Ajantā, Ellorā, and Khajurāho. Bhartṛihari, the Sanskrit poet says : 'breasts should be full, so that they make a woman bend with their weight. So heavy were the breasts of Urvashī that 'through the upborne burden of them, and the sharp movements of them, she was bowed down at every step. Those of another woman are described in a Hindu tale thus, 'Her body was straight and slender, and it swayed a little

as she walked like the stalk of the very lotus whose name she bore, as if it was about to bend, unable to support the weight of the beautiful full-blown flower standing proudly above it in the form of her round and splendid breasts.' The breasts of the women of Kāma's land are so heavy that they can scarcely walk :

'Their heavy-set breasts weigh them down
And make them walk gravely.'

15. In India the rainy season is the most welcome, for it ends the parching heat and the murderous *looh* (hot wind), which claims each year some victims. The coming of the monsoon fills everyone with joy. In *Satsai*, Bihārī, writes thus of the rain :

'Love awoke with the coming of the rain,
And filled with sudden longing the hungry soul
With women to sport with : dark clouds swiftly came
Low on the baked earth, as if to embrace,
That thirsty maiden, and to kiss her face.'

The peacock welcomes the first showers of rain with joyous cries, and in *Ṛitusaṁhāra* Kālidāsa, describing the rain's majesty, speaks of their joy :

'The silver clouds kiss the mountain tops,
And water rushes down valley and rill,
In the woods the peacocks move with joy,
And beautiful look the green-clad hills.'

At another place in the same poem, Kālidāsa describes the dancing of the peacocks in the rainy season :

'The thunder of the storm-laden clouds,
Fills with pleasure the peacocks, and their cries
Resound to welcome the rain's advance:
And opening out their bright-hued feathers,
With delirious joy they make love and dance.'

An anonymous Hindi poet thus sings of the rainy season in *Sāvan* (August) the month of heaviest rainfall, and its effect on lovers:

'With pleasure filled the cuckoo sings.
    the peacock cries with joy profound:
From all sides does the lightning streak,
    and from dark clouds the rain does pour:
The sparrow-hawk remains not quiet,
    and gales are speeding all around:
'Tis *Sāvan* when with bosom joined
    the lovers' bliss is blissful more.'

16. What Kṛiṣṇa is unable to accomplish by persuasion and begging he gets by an accident. Afraid of the dark clouds, Rādhā leaps into the arms of her lover and clasps him close.

17. The emotion of perplexity is depicted in the *nāyikā* who wears all her ornaments and makes all adornments in the wrong places. The garland which she should have worn round her neck she puts round her waist, and the ornament meant to be worn round the waist dangles from her neck. The ornaments to be worn on the toe of the foot she puts on her finger, and instead of putting the bracelets round the wrists she puts them round her feet. Her skirt and bodice she completely forgets to wear. (It should be remembered that Hindu women wear these beneath the *saree*, so not wearing them merely means that the *nāyikā* covered her body only by her *saree*). Collyrium, which she ought to have applied inside her eyelids she applies on the nipples of her breast, and the red henna dye which she should have put on her feet she absent-mindedly applies on the outside of her eyelids. When Shrī Kṛiṣṇa comes adorned, she runs to meet him at once even though all her ornaments had been worn topsyturvy.

18. A broad heavy inter-linked chain either of silver or gold, called *karadhanī* sometimes with tiny jingling bells suspended from it, so that when the woman moves they give a musical sound.

19. Toe-ornament, called *bichiyā*, is of silver, like a ring. It is slipped on to the toe, like the ring on the finger, and is considered auspicious for brides to wear.

20. The red dye made from henna or myrtle leaves. Painting feet and palms with this dye is also considered auspicious, and is done on certain festivals.

21. After being prepared, betel-leaves are wrapped in some outer covering to keep them fresh. Here the betels were wrapped in lotus leaves. Kṛiṣṇa was holding the wrapped-up betel-leaves in his hands when he suddenly saw his beloved Rādhā, This confused him so much that unawares the betels slipped out and fell down, and in his nervousness he thought the covering of lotus leaves which he still held in his hands were the betels and began to chew them in haste. What a comic picture for the watching cowherd girls. They simply laughed and laughed, and that embarrassed poor Kṛiṣṇa even more, so that he closed his eyes in shame. The incident is being related by one bosom companion of the *nāyikā* to another.

22. The bosom companion is upbraiding the *nāyikā* for her obstinacy. The *nāyikā* has won her lover's favour, but having done so, makes no further move. All her friends are eager to see her laugh and talk with her lover, Kṛiṣṇa, but are disappointed at her inaction. The bosom companion says that the *nāyikā* is burning at the moment with the sorrow of not having her lover's company, but soon she'll burn with the fuel of her obstinacy (in not making a move in ingratiating herself with her lover).

23. In this verse the worldly and transcendental aspects of Kṛiṣṇa have been blended together. On the one hand he is an incarnation of god (as Hindus believe), whose spirit enters into endless bodies in the universe, so that even Brahmā—the Creator, is baffled. His eyes remove the arrogance of beauty, i. e. they are so beautiful that they put earthly beauty to shame, and destroy the vanity of the god of love. Everyone from wise men to newly- wed wives and serpents are thirsting to see Kṛiṣṇa's lovely eyes.

Even faithful wives abandoned their husbands for Kṛiṣṇa. Rādhā, his mistress, was the betrothed of Aiyyān, and married cowherd girls forsook their husbands and homes to join him in the *rāsalīlā* dance. When women saw him they forgot their vows of faithfulness.

24. Mythical semi-divine beings having human faces with the tail of a serpent and the expanded neck of the cobra.

25. The first member of the Hindu triad, and the Creator of the universe. (See note 2, Chapter 3).

26. A name for Kṛiṣṇa (*bhūṣaṇa*-embellishment, and Braja- the Braja country). So *Brajabhūṣaṇa* the adornment of the Braja country, or the loved one of Braja. Much the same idea is conveyed in a poem in Bihārī's *Satsaī* in which the ornaments worn by the *nāyikā* compare so unfavourably with her body that they seem unsightly :

'Oh! lady wear not
Ornaments of gold,
For on your body
They unsightly seem,
As dirty spots
Spoil a mirror's gleam '

27. Suddenly caught off her guard, the girl tries her best to calm herself and conceal the visible signs in her body produced by noticing the saffron marks of another woman's breasts on the *nāyaka's* back. Women applied saffron on their bodies in those days, hence the *nāyaka's* clandestine affair left such marks on his back where the girl's breasts had touched. The *nāyikā* dusts herself with camphor powder, a box of which she must have been carrying (as it was an essential part of a woman's make-up), to conceal her bristling hair, which was the consequence of the emotion of horripilation. The lotus she smelt to steady her breathing, and finally cast her mantle around so that her mother may not see the state she was in.

28. The *nāyaka*, Kṛiṣṇa, fell down because of excess of pleasure on seeing his beloved, Rādhā, glancing at him from the casement. Everyone began asking him what the matter was, and so to hide his embarrassment he tells, them,... 'Nothing at all, friends, only a betel-nut, which seems to have stuck in my throat and made me breathless for a moment.' The betel-nut (Hindi *supārī*), is a nut which is sliced into bits and put inside betel-leaves and chewed along with it.

29. Both Vātsyāyana and Kalyāṇa Malla have given a list of embraces which couples can indulge in. The one resembling this most is of the *viddhaka* kind mentioned by Kalyāṇa Malla, in which the husband sits still and the wife coming near him places an arm over his shoulder and presses her bosom forcibly against his chest, and he returns the embrace with equal warmth.

Similarly Vātsyāyana describes the embrace of the 'mixture of milk and water,' in which the couple being much in love with each other, and not minding the causing of some hurt and pain, embrace each other so tightly as if they were entering into one another's bodies.

30. As stated previously (see notes 35 and 36, Chapter 3) Hindu erotic writers have made a systematic study of marking by nails and teeth, right from the mere touch of them to savage biting and marking, which is done under influence of deep passion. The former is, in the case of a young girl, when her lover wants to tease and excite her a little, and consists of touching the breasts, lips, or thighs, so softly by the nails that no scratch or mark is made, and only the hair of the body stand on end and a shudder passes through the girl's limbs. The other extreme of nail-marking is one made on the woman by her lover who is going on a journey called *nakhadāna* or token of remembrance, and is made by marking three or four lines close to one another with the nails on the breasts or thighs. These deep nail-marks serve as a token of remembrance.

Similar is the case with marking by the teeth. There are various types of such love-bites mentioned, right from the secret *gūḍhaka-dashana* in which the inner or red part of the woman's lips is bitten so that no visible mark is left outside for other eyes to see, up to the *kolacharchā* in which deep lasting marks are made by the lover in the heat of passion when going to a foreign land so that the woman may often see them and remember him thereby.

31. The exact significance of these actions is not clear but they are doubtless based on some totems of love. In Hindu eroticism such symbols are frequently mentioned. Vātsyāyana says that the biting of some things are signs of desire for enjoyment. These are : an ornament of the forehead or the ear, a nosegay of flowers and a betel or a *tamāla* leaf. Further while describing the ways of winning over a girl whose acquaintance has already been made, he says the lover should receive from her betel-leaves and ask for the flower she wears in her hair. If he himself gives her a flower it should be sweetly-scented one and marked with the marks of his nails and teeth.

The root of the lotus flower is one of the ingredients in many of the strange recipes mentioned by Vātsyāyana and Kalyāṇa Malla for charming and winning the favour of women, and the latter says that the *viyoginī* or separated woman, whose lover has gone away, looks upon the lotus flower and falls into a passion of grief.

Here all the acts of the *nāyikā* are symbolic of her loves. The withered lotus signifies that her lover is wasting with her separation, and Rādhā applies sandal-dust on it to convey that she would make him fresh again with her presence. Offering betel-leaves is often a gesture of love, and doing so to the messenger is symbolic of offering them to her lover. The other actions, like putting sandal-paste on his cheeks and mouths, and collyrium in his eyelids, signify the same deep love which Rādhā bears for the person who sent the messenger to her.

32. Here again love is expressed by symbolism. In the previous verse the symbolic object was sent by the *nāyaka* to his beloved Rādhā, and in this the maiden sends it to her lover, Kṛiṣṇa. The meaning of the symbolism is obscure, but it may possibly be that the *nāyikā* expresses her separation by sending the lotus with the petals open and separate, while the *nāyaka* Kṛiṣṇa closes the petals to signify that soon union will banish the pangs of her separation.

Chapter VII

More Nayikas

In the third chapter Keshavadāsa gave a list of different kinds of *nāyikās* and their characteristics. In this chapter some more kinds are described. The division of *nāyikās* is on the basis of behaviour and conduct only—not on the basis of physical characteristics, as in the case of the *Padminī*, *Shaṅkhinī*, *Chitriṇī*, and *Hastinī* described in chapter three. Keshava's division is eightfold :

1. The *svādhīnapatikā* who is greatly loved by her husband.
2. The *utkā*, who remains sorrowful because her husband being held up by some circumstances, fails to come home.
3. The *vāsakashayyā*, who, desireful of enjoyment, keeps glancing at the door of her house, each moment expecting her husband.
4. The *abhisandhitā*, who, on showing arrogance, affronts one who tries to appease her, and is thereafter sorrowful without him.
5. The *khaṇḍitā*, who reproves her beloved with many words, when having promised to come to her home in the night, he comes early morning instead.
6. The *proṣitapatikā*, whose beloved has gone somewhere to attend to business, giving her a time by which he will return.
7. The *vipralabdhā*, who feels sorrowful when her lover fails to arrive at the rendezvous arranged by the go-between.
8. The *abhisārikā*, who being affected by love, pride, or passion, goes to meet her beloved. When she is impelled by love she is called a *premābhisārikā* (*prema*—love), when by pride a *garvābhisārikā* (*garva*—pride) and when by passion a *kāmābhisārikā* (*kāma*—passion).

After having described these eight kinds of *nāyikās*.

Keshavadāsa goes on to give three divisions of the *parakiyā* (a married woman who is in love with another man), whom he had described in chapter three, as the most adorable kind of woman. These are the top, middling, and the low :

1. The top kind of *parakīyā* (*uttamā*) is a humble woman without arrogance, who esteems her lover even when he slights her, and always feels pleasure in his company.
2. The middling kind of *parakīyā* (*madhyamā*) is one who shows arrogance even on a small fault of her lover, and leaves it only when much cajoled and beseeched by him.
3. The low kind of *parakīyā* (*adhamā*) is one who gets angry without a cause, but can be soothed easily again and again.

These are only some kinds of *nāyikās* whose descriptions have been given. The actual number, considering all the meticulous divisions and sub-divisions, is three hundred, and sixty. If they were to be described in all their entirety, it would doubtless cover several volumes!

In the end Keshavadāsa gives, (in the tradition of the Sanskirt erotic writers), a list of women with whom sexual intercourse is prohibited. Such women fall into nine categories.

Having described the different kinds of lovers and their ways of meeting, the Poet goes on, in the next chapter, to describe their condition when they are parted from each other.

The eight kinds of *nāyikās*[1]

Eight kinds of *nāyikās* do I find
Says Keshava, as my wisdom shows:
Svādhīnapatikā, the first kind,
The second, whom all, *utkā* know,
The third, the *vāsakashayyā* is,
And *abhisandhitā* the fourth,
Next *khaṇḍitā*, and *proṣitapatikā*.
And *vipralabdhā* the seventh sort,
The last of all, *abhisārikā*.

The *svādhīnapatikā*

The *nāyikā* whose attainments bind,
Says Keshava, her husband for aye
A *svādhīnapatikā* is defined—
Of her lovemaking I'll narrate.

Example of hidden *svādhīnapatikā*

The bosom companion says to nāyikā:

'The very soul of those who live
In Braja; whom more than his own life
His father loves; whose mother will
Readily on him sacrifice
Girls true or false : by that beloved
Kṛiṣṇa, Oh ! daughter of an *ahīra* ![2]
By pumice stone you get your soles scrubbed,[3]
And with red dye get stained your feet !
Oh ! dear friend mine, me you dismiss
With a mere laugh, but if some day
Perchance another should see this,
An answer meet you'll have to make !'

Example of a manifest *svādhīnapatikā*

The bosom companion says to the nāyikā:

'As betel-leaves in basket are
So you with great care he does keep,
And in the mirror of his heart
Your image always shines, my sweet!
Though virtuous wives there many were,
Yet with vows austere of gods three[4]
A husband as your heart desired
You gained: Gopāla eternally
Behind your wish-shaped Bhagīratha[5]
Does wander, as the Gaṅgā will.
My Queen! say, is there any such
Wish of your's he has not fulfilled?

For what you say him so does bind
As though it were by *Vedas*[6] enjoined!'

The *utkā nāyikā*

The *nāyikā* whose dear spouse restrained
By some cause, comes not to his home,
And with this grief whose heart is pained,
She is an *utkā nāyikā* known.

Example of a hidden *utkā*

The nāyikā says to her bosom companion:

'Either in home affairs he is
Engaged, or with companions still
Or, 'tis his fast day, or he's sore
About some wrangling you've not told:
Or wisdom in his soul has dawned,
Or something with his health is wrong,
Or in his love is deceit, or fright
Of rain at middle of the night!
Perhaps he tests my love, oh! friend!
I know not why he does not come
Or what is passing in his mind,
That he keeps not the appointed time."[7]

Example of a manifest *utkā*

The nāyikā says to her bosom friend:

'Either my love he has forgot,
Or someone drove me from his mind,
Or the way he remembered not,
So that the path he could not find :
Or he's afraid, or in his heart
Some maiden sweet has found a place,
Oh ! friend mine, this to me impart
Has he come? Is he on the way ?

Or soon to reach? My Nandakumār
Has not come ! Why is he delayed ?
What keeps him from me so afar ?
Just think, and tell me, friend, I pray !'

The *vāsakashayyā*

The *nāyikā*, who longing for some
Pleasure, oft at her door does glance
With hope for her husband to come,
Is *vāsakashayyā*, says Keshavadāsa.

Example of a hidden *vāsakashayyā*

One bosom companion says to another about the nāyikā:

'Where the sandal-wood[8] tree does stand
With tender bright leaves, and entwined
By fair clove creepers—there she ran
And hid herself, that nymph divine!
Seeming the bright flame of a lamp[9].
In her blue dress she sought to hide
Her body's splendour; she does glance
This way and that with startled eyes:
At every soft sound of the breeze,
And leaves, and birds, and beasts, she yearns
For her beloved; thus concealed
In the network of groves and ferns
That maiden who for Nandalāl[10] waits
Looks like a bird within a cage.'

Example of a manifest *vāsakashayyā*

One bosom campanion says to another:

Who speaks such words as pleasure give,
And looks, friend, with joy in her heart,
Full of desire—who does bewitch
The soul with kindly laughter soft,
And merriment, and with perfume

Of her sweet body; who is she?
The holy basil plant, she seems
Incarnate; or Rati[11] may be
Reposing in a tulasi[12] grove:
Graceful this cowherd bride does shine,
As though radiant Lakshmī[13], adored,
In cottage where the creepers climb'.

The *abhisandhitā*

The *nāyikā* who shows arrogance,
Affronting him who tries to please her,
But soon does sorrowful become
Without him, is *abhisandhitā*

Example of a hidden *abhisandhitā*

Addressing her mind the nāyikā says:

'Oh! mind, when he addressed you oft,
Oh! thoughtless one, you did not speak,
Why like a child you weep so now?
The more he fell upon your feet
The harsher were you; now what gain
To be as butter soft? When you
From all things shorn did then remain
Save obstinacy? Now that too
Abandon; what harm can there come
By dying now? Your lover was set
In vain to please; should you have done
That, which now causes you regret?

Example of a manifest *abhisandhitā*

The nāyikā says to her bosom companion :

'Even when my loved one on my feet
Did fall, towards him glanced I not;
Your counsel, friend, I did not heed,

Instead by anger, I was wrought.
Even sandal, moon, and lotus, burn
My limbs,[14] and sorrows pleasures drive,
For wrong things that I have so done
God rightfully has me chastised.'

The *khaṇḍitā*

The *nāyikā* is *khaṇḍitā* known
Who her beloved much upbraids,
When pledged to meet her at home
At night, he comes at break of day.

Example of a hidden *khaṇḍitā*

Reproaching Kṛiṣṇa who has arrived early morning the nāyikā says :

'My eyes have seen, my ears have heard,
Much differently from what is told
About you; your flute's name is slurred,
And filth and offal like a crow
You pick; when told to keep away
You run to touch the feet instead,
And no distinction ever make
Between spots meet, and wrongful said.
Oh ! Ghanashyāma, in whose house you have
Passed all the night ? and now essay
To enter my abode, as would
A sly owl unseen make his way ?'

Example of a manifest *khaṇḍitā*

Addressing Kṛiṣṇa the nāyikā says :

'Today unusual I declare
Your eyes, oh ! Kṛiṣṇa, as if red made
With dye auspicious; by me swear !
Own up ! It seems they're red with rage
Which has so settled in your heart.
Oh ! Mohan to me they appear

Infatuated in some sort :
Yet still to captivate me are
They bent. Are these eyes so inflamed
By parting from your loved one true?
Or are they so with crimson stained,
Being by another's love imbued?'[15]

The *proṣitapatikā*

She is *proṣitapatikā* known
Whose loved one has gone to attend
His business, and does not return
By the hour appointed, to his home.

Example of a hidden *proṣitapatikā*

The nāyikā's bosom companion says to her :

'I know not by what good deeds done
In your former birth,[16] friend, you gained
A husband happy, as you longed :
Nor what the cause why late he came
By half a day, for which you speak
Not to him well: though Manmohan
Does fall so oft upon your feet :
Your obstinacy has become
Harder than is a wooden block,
So that even this parting's fire
Kindled of many days, cannot
Oh ! friend, burn it to ash entire !'[17]

Example of a manifest *proṣitapatikā*

The bosom companion going close to Kṛiṣṇa says to him on behalf of the nāyikā

'You promised her to come away
No sooner than you took your meals,
Somehow her mind I did engage

And with great toil put her to sleep.
Go ! why are you now sitting here ?
Who will tell you to go your way?
When once in her eyes start those tears
Have you e'er known those tears to stay?'[18]

The *Vipralabdhā*

When to the rendezvous arranged
By go-between[19], her lover defaults
To come; and this the *nāyikā* pains,
A *vipralabdhā* she is called.

Example of a hidden *vipralabdhā*

One bosom companion says to another about the nāyikā :

'This night the *nāyaka* being absorbed
In some work of his did not come,
Whereat the flowers seemed to her darts,
And perfumed things with evil stunk !
Her house a parcher's oven seemed,
Gardens to fearful forests turned,
Like fever were the cool moonbeams
Which all her body seemed to burn !
Songs were abuse, and betels made
Looked to her as if they poison were !
And all sixteen adornments[20] appeared
As if they merely were embers !'

Example of a manifest *Vipralabdhā*

When the nāyikā went to the place of rendezvous she found it empty; and when she looked towards the moon her sorrow was redoubled. Describing that moment of frustration her bosom companion says :

As soon as she the moon did espy
That woman glanced oft at her limbs,
And on a *champā*[21] leaf inscribed
Slowly some words : all perfumed things

Threw; and her garland of flowers broke,
And soundly thrashed the go-between !
Scattered the betels, laughed, nor spoke,
But moved with agitation seemed,
And deep sighs; then with sorrow looked
Upon the empty rendezvous,
And finding that place all forsook
Of Kṛiṣṇa's sweet voice, joined her hands two,
"O ! bosom friend," as if to say,
"By your instruction was I sent,
Ah ! well you did !" her sorrow made
Twofold, away that woman went.'

The *abhisārikā*

Her beloved when the *nāyikā* meets,
Impelled by love, or lust, or pride,
Abhisārikā[22] she is decreed;
Of this three kinds have been described—
She who with love is driv'n is known
Premābhisārikā, and she
To whom her pride the way has shown
Is *garvābhisārikā* indeed;
While she whom passion holds in thrall
A *kāmābhisārıkā* is called.

Example of a hidden *premābhisārikā*

The *nāyaka* to the *nāyikā* spoke :
'To captivate me so you've come
Without being called?' She answered, 'no !
Ghanashyāma, dark clouds have me summoned.'
'Much trouble you have undergone,'
The *nāyaka* said, 'when dark did hide
E'en you, the path so to discern !'
She said, 'the lightning was my guide !'
'Thorns and slush must have hurt your feet
On the rough road?'[23] the *nāyaka* said then :
She answered soon : 'My rashness, sweet,

And gait as of an elephant[24]
Much pleasure gave me !' He said, 'lo !
In this dark dreadful night you stay
Alone !' She said, 'beloved ! no !
'Tis not so ! love is my helpmate !

Example of a manifest *premābhisārikā*

The bosom companion of the nāyıkā says to the nāyaka :

'Whose eyes' unrest, and tongues' sharp wit
And body's fairness, and the grace
Of fair deportment can't be hid;
In diverse kinds who is portrayed
As are her moods, and by her side
A lovely cowherd girl who roams
In the litter of your doe-like eyes,[25]
Fair as the moon ! now to your home
Hies that same cowherd girl today,
Who yesterday did come—my dear !
Take as much water as you may
And betels, for the moment nears !'[26]

Example of a hidden *garvābhisārikā*

The bosom companion of the nāyikā says to the nāyaka :

'Where are you hid, your limbs beside
Some azure cow or heifer? Oh !
Keshava ! all measures I have tried
The calves yet to the cows won't go.
All the way running I've come now
To call you; in Gokul[27] all while
Oh ! Govinda[28] you have tended cows,
E'en by mistake show not your pride !'[29]

Example of a manifest *garvābhisārikā*

The maiden sandal did apply,
Donned lovely clothes, and necklace placed

Upon her breasts; to please the eyes
A garland of flowers she displayed,
On her lover sacrificed
Hundreds of Ratis;[30] when she played
Upon the *vīṇā*[31] it did vie
Sarasvatī's,[32] I have heard say;
And deer and swans by hundreds stayed
With her, that co-wives[33] startled were
As ruddy geese; and she did make
Their splendour dim as lotus flowers :
The eye-shaped *chakors*[34] quite forgot
The pain of parting when she rose
Her Kṛiṣṇa to meet; so she did start,
As moon to meet the moonlight goes !

Example of a hidden *kāmābhisārikā*

When she made haste her lover to meet
Shakes round her legs entangled were,
And many lay trampled under her feet !
And seeing her speed the demons stared
From all sides; the thick shower of rain,
She heeded not, nor the crickets' cry,
Nor thunder of clouds:[35] nor yet remained
Aware of ornaments falling aside,
Clothes rent, or thorns her breasts that hurt :
Seeing her the sprites said, 'Where did you
Oh ! lustful woman learn such love ?
This manner of keeping your rendezvous ?'

Example of a manifest *kāmābhisārikā*

The bosom companion of the nāyikā says to her:

Aged cowherd men who have gatherings seen
By millions, are in the assembly hall;
And mothers surprised, are gazing upon
Their children, who in lanes are playing:
From all sides do the women throng,

Watching your shadow through their veils;
Where are you going, your moon-like face,
Showing? See you not what goes on?'

Many kinds of *nāyikās*

Says Keshavadāsa, I have described
The *svakīyā nāyikā* of three types;
Of two kinds *parakīyās* are again,
And each of these of eight kinds known.
All these *nāyikās* are of three kinds
Says Keshava—middle, high, and low;
And more dividing them we find
In all their number eighteen score[36]!

The *uttamā* (high kind)

The *nāyikā* who her lover esteems
E'en though he slights her, and leaves all
Her arrogance; and seeing him does glean
Pleasure, she is an *uttamā* called.

Example of an *uttamā*

The bosom companion says to the nāyaka

'What boots it now to understand
When you did not then, even though
I tried to tell? One sidelong glance[37]
Of that fair lady is worth more
Than priceless wisdom, do not show
Ignorance, you'll know her I vow;
Why do you make excuses...go!
Appease her as you've done till now.'

The *madhyamā* (middle kind)

When even for a small fault, she
Shows arrogance, says Keshavadāsa,

And leaves it only when beseeched,
Madhyamā nāyikā she is called.

Example of a *madhyamā*

E'en by mistake she did not gaze
On him with favour, then Shrī Kṛiṣṇa
Submissive did become, and gave
Allurements diverse her to win.
When to implore her he despaired,
He humbly on her feet did fall,
Thus staying for long: Tell me from where
Such vanity that maiden got?
When god with long hair[38] her endowed,
And with slim body, would that he
Had made her eyes big[39], so that proud
Woman, her lover's love could see!

An *adhamā*

The *nāyikā* who is often angry
Without a cause, but every time
She can repeatedly assuaged be,
Her do great poets an *adhamā* find.

Example of an *adhamā*

Deceit which 'gainst the *nāyaka* is found
Should be cut into bits, words vile
Which cruel are as a butcher, ground
To powder, that veil wrenched aside
Which hides the dear beloved one:
That sight destroyed which is not good,
Says Keshavadāsa those bosom friends
Should slain be, who love ridicule
After counselling it! that rage
Burnt, which comes oft the heart to pain:
That empty wisdom cast away
Which bring sad parting in its train.

Women who should not be enjoyed

That woman should be ravished not
Who is a relation or appears
Of a friend's family or begot
Of *Brahmin*, or one who comes near
With hunger or sorrow distraught:
O! crafty amorist still beware
How with a maid of higher caste
Do you disport, or with one lower:
So should one not make love unto
A widow, or a woman pious,
Or one who lacks a limb or two—
Such are not meant to be enjoyed[40]

Concluding verse

Thus as I know I have described
Nāyakas and *nāyikās* of all kinds
With wisdom as them I did find
By country, time, and age, prescribed.
Says Keshavadāsa, I have portrayed
The manner in which lovers meet
With fondness: now in many ways
Of love in parting, I will speak,

NOTES

1. The Poet goes on to describe the characteristics of each of these kinds of *nāyikās* in subsequent verses.

The eightfold division of *nāyikās* is in the traditional manner of Hindi and Sanskrit writers. In *Anaṅga Raṅga* Kalyāṇa Malla, too, makes a similar classification, though there are minor differences. The division made here is on the basis of behaviour, and not on the basis of physical characteristics.

2. One of the many castes amongst Hindus. *Ahīrs* kept cattle, and the cowherds were of that race. At the present day also this class exists. They tend cattle, sell milk, some are farmers, and the poorer ones work as domestic servants.

3. In those days this was the popular method cleaning the soles of the feet which often became dirty as the women in the *zenānā* generally went barefooted because of the large number of ornaments they wore on their feet.

4. The Hindu *trimūrti* or triad, consisting of the gods Brahmā, Shiva and

Viṣṇu, the Creator, Destroyer and Preserver respectively. The three exist in one, and one in three. Brahmā is the embodiment of rajoguṇa—the quality of passion or desire, Shiva of tamoguṇa—the attribute of darkness, wrath, and destruction, and Viṣṇu of satoguṇa—the property of mercy and goodness by which the world is preserved. The representation of the *trimūrti* is one body with three heads—in the middle Brahmā, on the right Viṣṇu and on the left Shiva. Shiva and Viṣṇu are the more popular and widely worshipped.

5. A saint and descendant of Sāgara whose austerities made Shiva give permission to the sacred River Gaṅgā to come down to the earth for the purpose of bathing the ashes of Sagara's sons whom the rage of the sage Kapila had consumed. Bhagīratha called the River by the name of Sāgara, and took it to the nether world, leading it from earth to sea, so that its waters could purify his ancestor's ashes. Consequently the River Gaṅgā is also called Bhāgīrathī.

6. The injunctions of the *Vedas* have authority and are to be obeyed by all Hindus. Hence here the bosom companion says that whatever the *nāyaka*, Kṛiṣṇa, speaks, the *nāyikā* follows to the letter, as though it were a *Vedic* injunction. (See also note 17, Chapter I).

7. The waiting *nāyikā* is getting impatient because her lover has not arrived in time to meet her, and she conveys this impatience to her bosom companion, pointing out reasons which might be the cause for his not coming to meet her at the appointed time. The next verse, too, expresses the same situation.

8. Sandal wood—wood of the sandal (Sanskrit *chandana*) tree, This is an evergreen tree whose wood is hard and very close-grained and oily. the branches slender and drooping. Sandal-paste is still commonly used in India especially in summer as it has a cooling effect.

9. A woman's loveliness is frequently compared to the light of a lamp. In Satsaī, Poet Bihārī describes a beautiful woman moving through a dark grove in much the same manner :

'The groves dense are, and thick the hovering clouds,
The night, O! Kṛiṣṇa, is also binding dark :
Yet moving through the trees cannot be hid
That maiden bright as the flame of a burning lamp.'

So too, a Bengālī maiden, Bheluā, is described as 'shining like a lamp.' The daughter of Jalāluddīn is likened to a living flame, and the famous poet Chaṇḍīdāsa, compares Rādhā's face to stilled lightning.

10. Nandalāl—like Nand Kumār, Brajabhūṣaṇa, Gopāla, etc., is another name for Kṛiṣṇa. Lal means darling, dear boy, or son; and so Nandalāl means the dear son of Nanda, i. e. Kṛiṣṇa.

11. Wife of Kāmadeva (See note 9, Chapter 4).

12. The basil plant. A kind of aromatic herb. The leaves are tender and a little rough on the surface. The *tulasī* plant is considered sacred, and its leaves are used by Hindus as offering to gods. Most Hindu houses have a *tulasī* plant—it can be grown in flower pots. A decoction of the leaves of the plant in hot water, and sugar added, is considered good for colds, and the leaves of the plant are much used in the *Vaidic* system of medicine.

13. Lakshmī—(See note 10, Chapter 4).

14. These are by nature cool things, but due to the fire of separation, the *nāyikā* imagines they are burning her. Similar is the condition of Poet Ghanānanda's *nāyikā* :

'The odour of sweet scented things
Her breath does stifle, sandal-paste
Cools not.

The same idea occurs in a description of the separated *nāyikā* in Vidyāpati's poems. Her separation burns her so much that nothing can cool her, and in despair she exclaims: 'O ! who is there who would call saffron, musk, sandal-paste, or the moon, cool ?'

At another place relating her mournful condition of separation from her lover, his *nāyikā* says, 'The necklace round my neck seems to be a burden, and the god of love is also troubling me with desire. At this moment the moon too seems to me as hot as the sun...the sandal-paste with which my body is anointed is burning me fourfold.'

15. The *nāyikā* cannot make up her mind whether her lover has been unfaithful to her or not. His eyes are indeed red but she cannot decide if they are red from having wept for her, or because they have been reddened by the red henna dye which some other girl has put on her palms and in taking love to her it has stained his eyes. At one time his eyes seem to be red with rage, and at another time they appear so due to infatuation. With this uncertainty agitating her mind the *nāyikā* fires off a volley of questions at the *nāyaka* to clear up the matter.

16. The Hindu *karma* theory believes that the soul suffers the good or bad result of its actions done in previous births. At death the body dies, but the soul which is immortal takes birth in a new body, (the doctrine of transmigration), according to its tendencies which are conditioned by our past deeds. Having done so it becomes involved again in enjoyment or suffering according to its previous good or bad acts. When the results of such acts, (*Karma*), are exhausted and the soul becomes so enlightened that it ceases to bind itself with its actions, it achieves emancipation (moksha).

17. The *nāyikā's* bosom companion is upbraiding her for her obduracy. She tells the *nāyikā* that due to good fortune and pious acts done in former births she has been able to get such a good husband as Kṛiṣṇa. And now all because he returned home with a little delay and even though he has begged her pardon by falling on her feet she does not speak pleasantly to him and shows such obstinacy as is contained in a hard log of wood which even the accumulated fire of separation cannot burn. (The metaphor is mixed, for what the poet really means is that the *nāyikā*'s obstinacy is so great that she does not leave it even when her husband has come to her after such a long period of absence).

18. The *nāyaka* is late for his assignment with the *nāyikā*, and the bosom companion is telling him how she somehow kept the woman's mind engaged with talk and suppressed her anger and disappointment at her lover's neglect. 'Go away now', the bosom companion says to him. 'What is the use of

sitting here? If the maiden wakes up now the memory of her sorrow and chagrin will again come back to her, and you know well that once she starts crying she cannot be stopped.'

19. Hindi poets have dwelt much on the part played by go-betweens in bringing lovers together. It must be remembered that most of the Hindi love poets lived at the time of Muslim rule when women largely observed *purdāh*, and did not mix in society. Under such conditions it became necessary for someone to convey love messages between lovers and their beloved. This work was assigned to clever women who acted as go-betweens. Their task was not only to press the suits of lovers but also to bring them together at a mutually agreed place, and in some cases even to instruct the shy or inexperienced lovers in matters concerning lovemaking. Poet Vidyāpati devotes a number of verses to such instruction which the maid-servants of Rādhā give her or her lover, Kṛiṣṇa, in regard to amorous dalliance. Space does not permit a detailed account of such instructions, but the interested reader could profitably go through the *Poems of Vidyāpati* in which they are vividly narrated. In *Kāma Sūtra*, Vātsyāyana devotes an entire chapter to the go-between and her trade. He gives in detail the methods by which the go-between should first of all create a rift between the couple and then press the lover's suit by telling the woman of his over-powering passion for her—('this man born of a good family has gone mad on your account. He is tender, and so much distressed that he may die because of his love for you etc.). The go-between should bring presents from the lover and keep on observing the reaction of the woman. When she thinks the moment ripe she should bring the lovers together at some suitable place. Vātsyāyana thinks that female astrologers, female servants, female beggars, and female-artists, are most suited for this work. He classifies go-betweens into eight divisions according to the nature and extent of the task undertaken by them.

The writer of *Anaṅga Raṅga* lists fifteen types of women who can serve well as go-between. These are, a gardener's wife, a woman who is a personal friend, a dancing girl, a nurse, a widow, a female servant, a female labourer, an attendant woman, a sweet-tongued woman who goes around many families, a young girl, a woman who does not feel shy when talking of love, a female mendicant, a tailoress, a woman who sells milk or curd, an old experienced woman. The list is so exhaustive that lovers would not have the slightest difficulty in finding a go-between of their choice.

20. Sixteen adornments are the sixteen ways in which women adorned their bodies (See notes 38 to 45, Chapter 3).

21. Spanish jasmine, A small flowery tree about ten feet high with large smooth leaves. During the hot and rainy seasons it bears large corymbs of big white exquisitely fragrant flowers with the interior of their cups yellow.

22. *Abhisāra* means going to meet a paramour in a secret place for having sexual intercourse with him, and the *nāyikā* who goes out for this is called an *abhisārikā*. According to Kalyāṇa Malla the *abhisārikā* is a sexy type of woman who puts on a robe and goes out at night shamelessly to the house of a stranger in the hope of having carnal intercourse with him.

Keshavadāsa's conception is more exhaustive and accurate, as he has further divided the *abhisārikā nāyikā* into three types, according to the motive which impels her to go out. Kalyāṇa Malla is obviously thinking only of the *Kāmābhisārikā*. The *abhisārikā* has also been depicted by other Hindi poets of love. Vidyāpatī's *abhisārikā* is of two kinds—one who goes out to meet her lover on a dark night is a *Kṛiṣṇābhisārikā* (*Kṛiṣṇapaksha* means the dark half the lunar month), while the woman who goes to meet her lover in a moonlit night (which is not so often, due to fear of being seen) is a *Shuklābhisārikā* (*Shuklapaksha* means the bright half of the lunar month). Nothing can stop Poet Vidyāpati's *abhisārikā* from meeting her lover—not even if there were thousands of moons in sky. She says : 'Oh my bosom friend, I will go to meet my lover today. I will care not for the worthy people of my house, and I will not break my promise. I will anoint my body with sandal-paste. My eyes free from collyrium will yield clear light. Even though thousands of moons may be looking down from the sky, I will cover my body with white clothes and go slowly without any care. I will not hide, nor will I stop any one from seeing me.'

Poet Bihārī's *nāyikā* becomes one with the moon-light around her: 'This maiden because of the fairness of her limbs has completely mingled with the moonlight and cannot be seen at all. Her female companion goes behind her with the maiden's perfume as her only guide.'

23. The *abhisārikā nāyikā* has arrived at the appointed meeting place to meet her lover Kṛiṣṇa. They exchange pleasantries about the hurdles which the *nāyikā* had to overcome before she could reach the place (the darkness, thorns, slush, the roughness of the road, etc.) She tells him that she counted all this as nothing to the joy of meeting him.

24. An elephant's gait is considered graceful by Hindi poets. Vātsyāyana describes the gait of a Chitriṇi as having the majestic swing of an elephant. The gait of Princess Padmāvatī is compared to that of an elephant, while the Sanskrit writer Bāṇa tells us that in the district of Sthāṇvīshvara there were women like elephants in gait. Kālidāsa addresses a beautiful girl thus, 'O ! lovely woman with gait like a tusker's.' In the *Mahābhārata* we are told that Draupadī moved with the proud step of the elephant, and in the *Agnipurāṇa* a woman walking with the gait of a she-elephant is praised.

25. Both Persian and Sanskrit poets compare a woman's eyes to those of a doe or gazelle. Describing the eyes of the *Yaksha* bride Kālidāsa says they are as the gentle eyes of a timid fawn. In his *Shatakas*, Bhartṛihari speaks of his 'antelope-eyed mistress' and 'fawn-eyed darling'. The eyes of Sītā are described in the *Mahābhārata* as being like those of a young gazelle. Priyadarshikā's eyes are describesd as being like those of a gazelle bounding again and again. The eyes of Behārī's *nāyikā* surpassed those of a deer, and Bālachandrikā, the daughter of a prostitute, is said in the *Adventures of the Ten Princes*, to have eyes like those of a frightened deer. In another poem describing women playing with a ball they are described as being 'doe-eyed' and deer-eyed'

26. The moment of the *nāyaka's* meeting with the girl is near.

27. A village in the country of Braja, the native place of Kṛiṣṇa, and the land of the cowherd men and women.

28. One of the many names of Kṛiṣṇa.

29. The *nāyikā's* bosom companion is searching for Kṛiṣṇa and finds him hiding beside a cow. She asks him to help her to get together the calves that have strayed, reminding him that he himself has tended cows all his life, being a cowherd's son, and should not consider himself so proud as not to give a helping hand.

30. See note 10 of this chapter.

31. A stringed musical instrument.

32. See note 51, Chapter 3.

33. Though Hindus are largely monogamous, at that time it was the practice to have more than one wife—usually two. The second wife (*saut*) was a rival of the first, and Hindi poets have written much about the jealousy of the co-wife. In *Kāma Sūtra* Vātsyāyana counsels the first wife to give the second a position superior to her own, and look on her as a sister; but in practice the two were greatly jealous of each other, and it is thus they are depicted by the poets. Seeing the *nāyikā* blossom into youth the co-wives increase their love for the *nāyaka* lest he shower all his attention on her: 'Seeing the *nāyikā* grow from girlhood to maidenhood, the *nāyaka* became as lovable to the co-wives as one about to go to a foreign land'.

34. The Indian red-legged partridge who is supposed to be enamoured of the moon and to eat fire. Hindi poets frequently dwell on the attraction of the *chakor* for the moon and compare the passion of lovers to it.

35. So also Poet Vidyāpati's Rādhā runs through darkness and rain, not minding the snakes she steps on, in order to meet her lover, Kṛiṣṇa : She did not at all care for the clouds thundering in the sky; and even the crackle of lightning did not make her leave her path...She appears to dance on the heads of the running serpents...It seemed the clouds had gathered all around to kiss that belle.

36. The Poet does not describe all these types of *nāyikās*. Indeed they would be too numerous for anyone to describe.

37. The sidelong glance of a woman was much praised by Hindi poets. In *Satsaī*, Poet Bihārī vividly narrates the effect of such a glance :

'Who is not restless made
With a woman's sidelong glance ?
Ardent, so it does slay
Long after 'tis withdrawn.
As wound within the heart
Long after it has healed,
E'en when the pain departs
A twinge of pain does feel.

38. Hindu women take pride in long hair. The girls in Kālidāsa's *Ṛitusaṁhāra* had gorgeous hair dropping to the hips. Rādhā's flowing locks described in a Vaiṣṇava lyric came waving to her waist. The dishevelled hair of Maluā a Bengālī-women almost touched her feet (and, the Poet says, was worth a lakh of rupees). The hair of Adhuā Sundarī

daughter of king Dubrāj almost kissed the ground when she walked, while that of Morasu Okkālu a beauty of South India was so luxuriant that she used it as a rope to lead her pet calf with.

Women of Burma, Java, China, and Arabia too, appear to be fond of long hair. In a Burmese play, a water-seller girl is said to have hair so luxuriant that its knot was as big as an orange pip. Of a beauty of Java we are told that 'her hair when lowered, hung down to her feet waving in dark curls'. Describing the hair of Princess Rudabāh, Firdausi says:

'And o'er her silvery brightness richly flow
Dark musky ringlets clustering to her feet.'

The ringlets of Lailā were long and loosely flowing to the ground. Zuleikhā's hair descended to her feet. In a Chinese account the hair of a young princess reached to the ground, and more to spare. In *The Arabian Nights* a young man alights on a young girl lying on the bed with her abundant hair for her only covering.

39. Large eyes are praised by the Hindus. A woman's eyes should be big and long—so long as to stretch almost to the ears. The lovely ladies in Kādambarī's mansion had eyes stretching up to their ears. Bhartṛihari is all praises for women of splendid eyes, with arches curved almost to their ears. In a Burmese play Rāvaṇa addresses Sītā as, 'O ! thou large-eyed dame !' In the painting of Ajantā we find the eyes of women so depicted.

40. Both Kalyāṇa Malla and Vātsyāyana give a list of women with whom sexual congress is prohibited. The former distinguishes two classes—the first consisting of those women who are absolutely and under all circumstances to be excluded from such congress, and the second consisting of those who should not be enjoyed however much one may be tempted to do so. In the former class he mentions the wife of a *Brahmin*, of a priest, of a reader of the *Purāṇas*, the wife of a man of the warrior class, of a friend, and of a relation. In the latter class are, an unmarried virgin, a widow, a virtuous wife of another man, a friend's wife, that of a foe, a pupil or disciple, a defiled woman, a woman born in one's own family, a mad woman, a woman older than oneself, the wife of a *guru*, a relation of sister, a pregnant woman, a woman who is a stranger or a sinner, and a woman whose complexion is entirely yellow or black.

In *Kāma Sūtra*, Vātsyāyana mentions the following women who are not to be enjoyed: a leper, a lunatic, an outcaste, one who reveals secrets, who publicly expresses a desire for congress, a woman who is extremely white or black, or who smells badly; a near relation, a female friend, the wife of a relation or a friend, or of a learned *Brahmin* or king; and lastly a female ascetic.

Poet Keshavadāsa follows more or less the same pattern, except that with a foresight which these ancient writers seemed to lack, he also includes disfigured women who lack a limb or two.

CHAPTER VIII

Love and the Ten States

In this chapter Poet Keshavadāsa describes that love which is born when the lover and his beloved are separated from each other due to unavoidable circumstances. This he calls the *vipralambha* kind of love (*vipralambha* is a Hindi word meaning 'separation of lovers'). He classifies this love into four types—love at first sight, tenderness or compassion, arrogance, and the feelings which arise in a woman's heart when her lover or husband has to reside in a foreign land because of his work. Love at first sight springs in the hearts of newly-wed couples when they see each other's splendour, without seeing which they remain sorrowful.

The states of lovers' minds are ten in number. These arise when on seeing a beautiful person, or on hearing him or her sing bewitchingly, desire for meeting is born. These ten states are yearning, anxiety, narration of merits, remembrance, fury, raving, intoxication, disease, stupor, and death. Each of these states is described by the Poet and illustrations thereof given, following the usual division of 'hidden' and 'manifest'. When due to the meeting of eyes, speech, and the soul, desire arises for the union of the body also, that is the state of yearning. When a woman's mind is occupied with devices to meet her lover Kṛiṣṇa, and to bring him under her control, the state of anxiety is said to be born in her. The state of narration of merits is one where description of talents, and of the body's splendour, is made under the influence of desire. The state of remembrance is one in which the lover and his beloved, forgetting all else, care only for meeting each other. Fury is that condition in which pleasure-giving things turn painful. The state of raving or disjointed talk is produced when the minds of the lover and his beloved both 'go round and round as a bumble bee', and being pervaded with sorrow, the two speak in defence of each other. When the woman talks animatedly to her lover, sometimes getting up suddenly as if to leave, then filled with pleasure gazing fixedly at him, sometimes weeping and sometimes laughing; this is the state of intoxication. The state of disease, as defined by Keshavadāsa, is one in which the limbs of the body become devoid of radiance, breathlessness is experienced, and the eyes begin to water. When consciousness is lost, and joy and sorrow both appear to be the same, this is the state of stupor. Last of all, there is the state of death. This, for lovers, comes when stratagem and force both fail to achieve a meeting between them in any way whatsoever. Obviously when every device of the lovers to come together fails, their love comes to an abrupt end, for without meeting nothing can be accomplished. The failure of all attempts to affect such a union has therefore appropriately been called 'death' for lovers by the Poet. This condition has not been illustrated by examples (as in the other cases), by Keshavadāsa because he has taken as his model lover, Kṛiṣṇa, who being a god, is immortal, and so it is not possible to think of death in relation to him.

The Poet goes on to say that the *nāyikā's* mistresses and intimate friends assist her in furthering her love suit. At first her mistress conveys to the *nāyaka* by hints the feelings that lie in her heart. After that her bosom friend, who knows both the *nāyaka* and the *nāyikā* well, clearly tells him of her love which has long remained hidden.

Before going on to the concluding verse in which the reader is informed of the subject matter of the next chapter viz. the arrogance of woman, the Poet observes that honour, intimacy, and greed, are so powerful that they can cause restlessness even in the minds of sages, an observation which is indeed as true now as it was then.

Vipralambha love.

Says Keshavadāsa, love that does rise
When lovers separated are,
Is of the *vipralambha* type.

The kinds of *vipralambha* emotion

Four kinds of *Vipralambha* emotion
There are—love at first sight,

Arrogance, and compassion,
And in foreign lands to reside.

Love at first sight

Know that love at first sight to be
Which springs when couples newly-wed
The splendour of each other see,
And when parted, with grief are vexed.

The hidden love at first sight of the *nāyikā*

The nāyikā says to her bosom companion:

'Show flowers to me not, for they seem
Like darts, and garland keep away,
Which like a snake is; do not wave
The fan or whisk,[1] their scented breeze
Does madden me: no sandal deign
To rub, its coolth to fever turns!
Apply not saffron, for its burns!
Oft do I ask you to refrain,
Are you, oh! bosom friend, distraught,
That you oft do what I forbid?
Give me not betels, for they are,
Oh! friend, as poison now to me.'

The manifest love at first sight of the *nāyikā*

The nāyikā says to her bosom companion:

'Since Shrī Kṛiṣṇa came within my sight
Much different has my mind become,
If you tell this, all will deride
You; being a friend to you I come
To seek your counsel: how should I
Meet him? If not, how pass my days?
Though in my eyes love for him lies,
Yet in my heart I am afraid?

The hidden love at first sight of the *nāyaka*

The nāyaka says to his bosom friend:

'One day the daughter of Vṛiṣabhānu
Among her bosom companions sat,
Her mother midst them, when I chanced
That way to pass: Oh! friend, thereat
On me she glanced; tongue cannot tell
The manner of her covert gaze[2]
Which her love showed; all maidens dwell
On it since then, and vain words say:
My glance-shaped wheel all sides has turned,
And carefully has scanned all ways,
But yet nowhere has it discerned
Such splendour as shines on her face.'

The manifest love at first sight of the *nāyaka*

Shrī Kṛiṣṇa says to his bosom companion:

'The instant Vṛiṣabhānu's daughter cast
Her eyes in mine, and knit her brows,
And frightening me, my gaze did force
On her: and laughing, did somehow
My innocent eyes enslave—from then
E'en though cajoled, they do not glance
With favour e'er on anyone,
These eyes of mine! Yet they perchance
The love of all do swallow soon,
As *chakor* bird does embers eat[3]
When it deprived is of the moon!'

The ten states

When sight, or some bewitching song,
For meeting does one restless make,
Yet meet he cannot; then are born
Ten states, which Keshava now relates:

Yearning, concern, remembrance,
Telling of merits, fury blind,
Disease of age, intoxication,
Raving and stupor—these are nine:
The tenth state which springs up is death,
Which, others being born, comes of itself!

Yearning

When meet the speech, and soul, and eyes,
The body also should unite:
This men of steady wisdom call
The 'yearning' state, says Keshavadāsa.

The hidden yearning of the *nāyaka*

One bosom companion says to another about the nāyikā :

'Her presence of mind has vanished clean,
And body's splendour, which should rise
Each day, has gone; she speaks to hide
Her inner suffering, but it seems
Writ large upon her face, I fear;
Oh ! bosom friend, her appetite,
Her joy, her thirst, her sleep of night,
Are all forgotten; it appears
She wants a rendezvous to prove
Her love; 'tis as if something tied
Of hers had dropped :[4] I know not why
In sorrow does that lady move.'

The manifest yearning of the *nāyaka*

The nāyikā says to her bosom companion :

'As for your saying, desire will hold
Me, on my love if once I gaze,
And seeing him not my grief will grow

Twofold : believe me when I say,
Oh ! bosom friend, that if I might
But see him once, I will no more
Desire to meet him, I will hide
And see him, but myself not show :
Why so you try me to deceive,
Think you him now I'll really see?'

The hidden yearning of the *nāyikā*

The bosom companion says to the nāyikā :

'I touch your feet, for you I die,
Make her not as yourself you've done;
Seeing her for long, yet satisfied
You're not, and so must you return:
Consider, Keshava,[5] is it right ?
For now you trust not anyone,
You will repent your appetite,[6]
Let viands cool lest the mouth they burn !'

Another example of the manifest yearning of the *nāyaka*

One bosom companion to another within earshot of Kṛiṣṇa :

'Is there no well-wisher of his
Oh ! friend, who will to him convey
Which way the wind is blowing, 'tis
Not without reason that the jades
Of Gokul of him do oft speak :
Oh ! bosom friend ! see how intent
Is he to entrap—as a cheat
Who dropping gold, does see who bends
To take it, and him soon does catch !"
Hearing this Shrī Kṛiṣṇa who stood close
Said, "Who is the vile man who does that?"
To which the dear friends did retort :
"How you pretend ! whose message 'twas
Of which oh ! Shrī Kṛiṣṇa, you had spoke

Only the other day? And now
You feign, as if you do not know !'

Anxiety

'How Kṛiṣṇa to meet so that he may,
Dwell in the heart, under my sway.'
When in the mind hovers this thought,
Anxiety's state, all men it call.

The hidden anxiety of the *nāyikā*

When your own master you can't remain
Oh ! mind, how can you another tame ?

Another example of the hidden anxiety of the *nāyikā*

The bosom companion says to the nāyaka

'You, as soon as that belle did see,
A wager of chess she did plan
Within her mind : Love is indeed
Its King; and Shyness and Concern
The Knights : Parting's Diversion is
The Elephant—her Glances twain
Of pity are the Horses swift :
Desires the Men, skilled, of the game—
Thus with draughtsmen ranged she begins :
On both sides moves are made with zeal
Let us see who the board will win,
And to whose share will fall defeat.'

Yet another example of the hidden anxiety of the *nāyikā*

Thinking aloud, the nāyaka says:

'When will that happy day arrive
When my afflictions she will end
By her eye-brow's sweet merriment ?

And she says "I need not apply
Perfumes, for I am their abode !"
How full of love will that day be,
How fortunate, when she will go
Where'er I beckon, after me ?
Oh ! god, will it ever be that
In my heart she at length abides
With her camphor and musk-like eyes
As of a deer, so white and black?
And oh ! will that sweet moment dawn,
When with pupils of eyes which be
As though painted, she gazes on
The lamp, and laughs and talks with me ?'

The manifest anxiety of the *nāyaka*

The nāyaka Kṛiṣṇa says to the bosom companion of Rādhā

'To Rādhā's mother would someone
Speak soon of that maid's *svayaṁvara*;[7]
And Vṛiṣabhānu may with honour summon
The cowherd youths, who like gods are :
And then Rādhā, that lovely belle
May round my neck, to choose me, throw
Her garland; and friend, you as well,
Would they as dower on me bestow !'[8]

The telling of merits

Where splendour, which in limbs does lie,
And talents, worthy, are described
With longing intense—there exists
The state of telling of merits.

The hidden telling of merits of the *nāyikā*

Praising Kṛiṣṇa in her mind the nāyikā says :

'Shrī Kṛiṣṇa has repute, while Chandrarāja[9]
Remains with deep dishonour cursed :

As soon as *champā* leaf is touched
It withers, but 'tis filled with joy
On contact with Shrī Kṛiṣṇa, whose hands
Are tender and sweet smelling, while
The lotus has a thorny stem :
And big are Madan Gopāla's[10] eyes
While poor Kāmadeva can't see, being blind
So in all ways superior Kṛiṣṇa,
My dear beloved, do I find.'[11]

The manifest telling of merits of the *nāyikā*

The nāyikā says to her bosom companion :

'Tell me, O ! friend, are wagtail's eyes[12]
More captivating, or of Kṛiṣṇa ?
Is honey sweeter, or his lips ?
Do not his sparkling teeth outshine
Pomegranate ?[13] Is the moon sweet
Or sweeter is his moonlike face ?[14]
Is his form good, or of Kāmadeva ?
Is lotus tender, or the feet
Of my loved one ?'[15] Hearing these words,
At once replied her bosom friend,
'Your dear one's form, as you contend,
In truth is best, so I aver.'

The hidden telling of merits of the *nāyaka*

The nāyaka addressing his mind says :

'If I compare her beauteous face
To the moon, lip homage I do pay :
If her eyes as lotus I declare
The black bees will fly everywhere
Upon her, and annoyed her keep !
If to pomegranates her teeth
Compare I, and her firm round breasts
To quinces : lips to coral red—

Then 'tis not meet, for they are sold
Along with things both new and old
In th' open market, and suffer
A million troubles ! and if her
Eyes, I to ruddy geese compare,
And to a snake her braid of hair,
Like to an elephant her gait,
And to a lion's her narrow waist,
Voice to a cuckoo's, nose as seems
A parrot's[16] then all these are deemed
Foul and filthy, for this reason
The *nāyikā's* parts are, as I see them,
Unequalled : only with themselves
Can they compared be, with none else !'

The manifest telling of merits of the *nāyaka*

The nāyaka says to the nāyikā's bosom companion :

'Rādhā's splendour has pierced inside
My soul, now nought can it remove,
The layer of saffron-paste applied
On her, is as 'twas my love true.
In the shining blue of her splendid dress
It seems my body's colour shines,
The lotus which she stands and smells
'Tis as she smelt this heart of mine !'

Remembrance

When *nāyaka* and *nāyikā* do not fret
For anything, except the wish
In meet each other, and forget
All else—that state 'remembrance' is.

The hidden remembrance of the *nāyikā*

Describing the nāyikā's condition one bosom companion says to another:

'To speak she likes not, nor to play,
Nor cares to laugh or raise her eyes;

Her sorrow seems to mount all day,
No good she hears nor does surmise.
Her mind remains as if engrossed
In someone's pleasure, and she keeps
Searching; as if one should be taught,
And yet in ignorance be steeped!
Who will arrange the clothes to please,
Who will the lonely lyre resound ?
Her mind as though upon a wheel
Mounted, keeps going round and round'.

The manifest remembrance of the *nāyaka*

The bosom companion says to the nāyikā:

'When by my effort you will meet
Shrī Kṛiṣṇa; why then your soul renounce
With longing to him ? nought achieved
By silence is, why do you drown
Yourself in love ? Even if you take
Not betels, water why refuse ?
How will you love ? If one betrays
Your secret, then what will you do ?'

The nāyikā says:

'O! bosom friend, say what you will
I have no care at all for this.'

The bosom companion replies:

'Even if no care you have, my sweet,
Some shame you should retain at least!'

The hidden remembrance of the *nāyaka*

The bosom companion says to the nāyaka

'O! Ghanashyāma, all the camphor paste
Upon your limbs which you applied,
Your burning body black has made !

The bower with blossoms which invites
Is to you dull, you wander lost
And mumble as you go, what care
Your troubled mind, Oh! friend, does gnaw?
From all these signs I do declare,
Upon the strings of garland round
The neck of some maid debonair,
Your soul does swing, with longing bound,
Now up now down, now here now there.'

The manifest remembrance of Kṛiṣṇa

One bosom companion says to another:

'Clothes, home, and other things like these,
A poisonous look to him do bear,
And cosy beddings made to please
Like mosquitoes bite him, nor cares
He for moonlight or sandal-wood,
And camphor dreads as funeral pyre!
And nought he drinks, nor betel chews.
And merriment no more desires.[17]
Of which household of Gokul is
That woman who has made him so?
With her charm who has so bewitched
Shrī Kṛiṣṇa? Oh! friend, this would I know.'

Fury

Says Keshava, when what pleasure gives
Seems painful, that state fury is.

The hidden fury of the *nāyikā*

Addressing her mind the nāyikā says:

'This is not poison, but the moon
Which Rāhu[18] has not swallowed, friend,
Due to its evil; by chance soon
The holy sage, Agastya,[19] has drunk

This thing defiled, but still has not
Digested it ! God seems to act
Against all rules; for he has called
The moon as nectar's home, whereas
The serpent, Sheṣajī,[20] he has named
As holding poison,[21] of the sun
What should one say, who this, defamed
Sinner, has made with himself one ?'

The manifest fury of the *nāyikā*

The bosom companion says to the nāyaka.

'Who seeing you then had fled away,
Today would die if you don't come,
In poison drowned she is all day,
And in the night by moonlight burnt !
From bed to ground, from ground to bed
A million airs she takes; oh ! Kṛiṣṇa
Give her some ornaments, so that rest
Their sight may to her body bring !'

The hidden fury of the *nāyaka*

Relating the condition of the nāyaka, the bosom companion says to nāyikā :

'As do the clouds smile not at swans,
And swans love not the shape of clouds,[22]
As from her heart the lotus spurns
The moon, which likewise is avowed
Lotus to woo not:[23] to and fro
Between the garden and the pool
They wander—yet they do not go
Where lies both pool and *tamāla* tree[24]—
Those maidens, Oh ! friend, how are they
I know not, that alive they be
Even for a moment, when the state
Of their beloved one they see ?'

The manifest fury of the *nāyaka*

The bosom companion says to the nāyikā :

'Oh ! dear friend, oft he fills with tears
His eyes, when he my sorrow sees,
And when he spies the *tamāla* tree
In bloom, he trembles : here and there
He wanders, absent-mindedly,
And nothing speaks; sometimes he hies
Unto the garden, then beside
Your pool : If you desire to seek
Him, why do you go not ? I for one
Will not show him when thus he is :
Today, when nothing will him please.
Why does this longing to you come ?'

Raving

When the minds of the *nāyikā* and *nāyaka*
Go round and round as the black bee,
In mind and body sorrow spreads,
And in defence the tongue does speak
Of the beloved—then by all
The state of raving it is called.

The hidden raving of the *nāyikā*

(*In this stanza the words have been spoken by the nāyikā in her raving state, and consequently are incongruous and meaningless*).

Speaking of the state of the nāyikā, one bosom companion says to another :

'Thus mumbling she began to say :
"Nor play nor laughter, good nor bad,
Nor love, nor enmity does shake
My heart, naught is to give nor have,
No kinship and no parentage :
What should I tell ? Shrī Kṛiṣṇa does seek

With grief my pleasure to replace ?
How should I laugh, what should I speak ?"
So with tears which her eyes did flood,
That cowherd girl to me did say :
"Do you not know what grievous words,
Shrī Kṛiṣṇa has spoke to me to day ?"

The manifest raving of the *Nāyikā*

Speaking to her bosom companion the nāyikā says in an incoherent voice :

'I sported with my bosom friends
When lo from somewhere Shrī Kṛiṣṇa came.
Our eyes met—he showed insolence :
To the ground rooted I with shame
Was then ; my body burned with rage
And trembled : Oh ! I would have died
With anger—only one thing saved
Me[25]—that I could gaze with my eyes.'

The hidden raving of the *nāyaka*

One bosom companion says to another :

'In her blue dress her cheeks concealed,
Today inside soon she did haste
When she saw me—and filled with greed
To see the form of Kṛiṣṇa, she raves
To know him. You do I adjure
By curd and milk, and by my sire,
And by myself, to me declare
Who was she who stood by her door ?'

The manifest raving of the *nāyaka*

In this verse incongruous words are uttered, as one who raves would speak.

'As sunbeam Mohan[26] is : his fresh
Laughter as camphor, and his face

A lovely line of beauty decked :
The hair with flowers is interlaced,
As if Triveṇī[27] in which bathe
Desire-shaped sages ; eyes do stare
Entangled by love—restless they :
The artful eyebrows soon ensnare
Them who look on ! whose child is this
Whom Brahmā[28] as a goddess made ?
When you today she did visit,
What did that lovely maiden say ?'

Intoxication

When nāyaka and nāyikā first engage
In talk, and rise as though to leave,
And pleasure seeing, fixedly gaze
At times, and in one moment weep,
And in another laugh—that state
One of intoxication is.

The hidden intoxication of the *nāyikā*

Rādhā's bosom companion relating her condition to Kṛiṣṇa says :

'Lo ! Rādhā's wisdom is no more
When you are gone, oh ! Kṛiṣṇa, so deep
Has parting her affected so,
Her loosened tresses dangling keep
Unto her waist ; with vacant eyes
She gazes, and her body heaves :
Who shall cure her ? The splendour dies
From her fair face ; and though she breathes,
She faints and when again revived
With parting's fire still burning keeps ;
Her love profound, her greatly tries,
And bloodless as a ghost is she !'[29]

The manifest intoxication of the *nāyikā*

Relating Rādhā's state the bosom companion says :

'Her mind disjointed always is,
Her feet do stagger on the ground,
At every shadow startled she,
Says one thing, and another expounds !
All in a moment she does change,
Some eyes a spell have on her laid
I know not : has the wind her pained,
Or has her poor mind gone astray ?
What has been done her mood to mar,
Oh ! Kṛiṣṇa, that Rādhā of her veil
Is conscious not, nor of the jar
On head, nor of her dress today ?'

The hidden intoxication of the *nāyaka*

Describing the intoxicated state of Kṛiṣṇa the bosom companion says:

'Things plain and obscure he proclaims
Of this world and the other world,
Oft weeps, and oft laughing remains,
Dances and sings, as if he crushed
Shame's shadow even ![30] neither he
Ashamed is, nor is he concerned :
As soon as him the eyes do see
'Twas as a load fell off at once :
Whether a woman him affects,
Or he is by some passion cloyed,
I know not ; or it may be that
His wisdom someone has destroyed.'

The manifest intoxication of the *nāyaka*

Describing the state of intoxication of Kṛiṣṇa, one bosom companion says to another :

'With tears he fills his eyes, and looks
All round, and opens his mouth oft,

And restless runs; one moment broods,
Trembles the next : sometimes he laughs
And weeps; and then again he sings:
Come, my dear friend ! him will I show—
Perturbed by thus beholding him
I have made haste to let you know.'

Disease

Disease is, Keshava says, when limbs
Are shorn of brightness, and the breath
With labour comes : and eyes begin
To water, and great sorrow spreads.

The hidden disease of the *nāyikā*

Expressing her doubt about the nāyikā the bosom companion says :

'No more upon the pipe he plays,
And speaks not even; 'twere as if
His mind has somewhere flown away;
He listens not, nor yet does wish
To understand : has he been plagued
By spirits evil, I know not,
Or maybe love has in him waked
That he repeats your name so oft ?
No water drinks, nor betels takes—
Oh ! friend, you should to me disclose
Has Shrī Kṛiṣṇa cheated you, or say
'Tis you who have to him done so?'[31]

The manifest disease of the *nāyikā*

Speaking about the nāyaka and the nāyikā the bosom companions say amongst themselves :

'Eyes weep there thus to see her burn
With fever, here him to behold :
Her laboured breaths there cause concern,

Here treatment, his illness to cure.
The daughter of Vṛiṣabhānu there is
And here the son of Nanda does lie,
No one knows what strange malady 'tis,
That at the same time both so strikes !
To see them I am much afeared
O ! bosom friend ! so sick are they !
Go ! and at their bedside be near,
And find out for yourself, I pray !'

Stupor

When consciousness forgotten lies,
And joy and sorrow seem alike,
Then that condition, Keshavadāsa,
Says, is by all men 'stupor' called.

The hidden stupor of the *nāyikā*

Describing the condition of the nāyikā her bosom companion says to Shrī Kṛiṣṇa :

'By remedies warm she cool is made,
And by cool herbs she warm becomes,
And starts decaying ; in such state
If something amiss happens, then
What will I do ? E'en in my sight
Keeps drying this creeper of desire,[32]
What should I do, and to whom hie ?
Will she live on ? Will she expire ?'

The manifest stupor of the *nāyikā*

Relating the state of the nāyikā, her bosom companion says to Shrī Kṛiṣṇa :

'Her eyes met yours, the bosom friends
Did also meet, so well 'twas done,
Your minds met, and close were you then

As gold, which melting one becomes !
Oh ! Kṛiṣṇa, now come soon, lest that pass
Which is to be; for when she takes
Samādhi;[33] with you joined at last,
Who will be left to meet you, pray ?'

The hidden stupor of the *nāyaka*

Describing the nāyaka's state the bosom companion says:

'His body cold each moment grows,
All drugs and physic have been tried,
No grief or pleasure he does show,
Whate'er is done—nor does he strive
To listen or to comprehend;
Now say, from whom should I enquire ?
Who will believe me ? Has he done
Some *yoga* ?[34] Or burns he with the fire
Of separation from someone
He loved? What do the poor men know
About such maladies which come
On persons who much vexed are so?'

The manifest stupor of the *nāyaka*

Describing the condition of the nāyaka the bosom companion says :

'Naked and homeless, he exists
On air alone; senses restrained,
And mind controlled; absorbed he is
In rapt *samādhi*[35] till he gains
Success : Why don't you to him go
O ! goddess, while he so does stay ?
If boon you can't on him bestow,
At least your life's oblation make.'

Death

When e'en by force and by deceit,
A meeting, lovers can't achieve,

Says Keshavadāsa, whate'er be done,
Then of a sudden 'death' does come !
Says Keshavadāsa, I cannot, friend,
The state of death describe of him
Who no decay knows, and no end,
For he is the immortal Kṛiṣṇa.[36]

How love is made manifest

Says Keshavadāsa, at first is born
In a woman the desire for love,
Then taking hint, her friends ere long
Do make her craving manifest.

The power of honour, greed, and association

Honour, intimacy, greed,
Excessive when they are, they make,
Says Keshava, restless the mind feel
Of even he who is a sage.

Concluding verse

Says Keshavadāsa, I have described
Devotedly, the different states
Which are produced : and now the ways
Various, of arrogance, that arise
Will I pass on, friend, to relate,
Oh ! lucky one,[37] hear, and be wise !

NOTES

1. There being no electricity in Keshava's time, the way to get breeze and to keep off flies and mosquitoes was to wave to and fro a bamboo fan or a whisk made of straw or bird's feathers.

2. In India, where modesty and shyness in women are greatly valued, we frequently come across a maiden's covert gaze. So is Poet Bihārī's *nāyikā* who first glances covertly at her lover and shows him her limbs, but immediately after having done so begins to feel bashful and guilty:

'E'en though pretending not to see him,
Towards him she covertly glances,

And showed her lover all her limbs:
Then did she give a guilty start,
Shrinking with shame within herself,
And sat, abashed within her heart.'

3. The Indian red-legged partridge. According to popular belief this bird has a fascination for the moon, and is also said to be a fire-eater. Not finding the moon, the *chakor* has started swallowing embers of fire in its disappointment and anger.

4. Hindu women carry their keys, or something of value, tied to the end of their *saree*, which is the female dress in India. Here the Poet says that the *nāyikā* walks about brooding in sorrow as if something of value which she thus carried had dropped.

5. Here Keshava does not mean the Poet Keshavadāsa but Kṛiṣṇa, for whom this is yet another name. Keshavadāsa here means the slave of Kṛiṣṇa' (*Keshava* Kṛiṣṇa; *dāsa* slave)

6. The bosom companion advising the *nāyikā* says, 'You will be sorry for making haste in your lovemaking. You should go slow and take time; just as it is necessary for food to become cool before eating, lest being too hot it may burn the mouth.

7. In ancient times a girl of a princely family was married to the youth of her choice at a tournament, or display of skill in the use of arms or simply a gathering to which all the near-by warriors and princes were invited. If there was no wager or condition, then the girl just walked around the assembly with a garland of flowers and cast it round the neck of the youth of her choice. This was the way in which *Saṁyuktā* chose the bragand king, Prithvī Rāja, when she placed the garland round his image, and he and his men carried her away, much in the manner of Lochinvar. In a *svayamvara* in which the condition was that the successful suitor should break Shiva's-bow, Rāma broke the bow and married Sitā. Arjuna won his bride' Draupadī, in a *svayaṁvara* in which the condition was that the winner should be able to send five arrows in succession through a hole in a moving wheel and hit the target. Arjuna succeeded in doing so, and won her.

8. The amorous *nāyaka* is fascinated both by the *nāyikā* as well as by her bosom companion. So he would like to obtain both—the former as a bride and the latter as part of the bride's dower. In times past maid-servants accompanied a bride to her husband's home but the practice is now dying out.

9. Lord of the moon.

10. Another name for Kṛiṣṇa.

11. The *nāyikā* is praising Kṛiṣṇa in her mind. She compares him to the moon, saying that while Kṛiṣṇa is famed far and wide, the moon's lord has a bad reputation. It is not very clear why the lord of the moon is said to be of ill repute. It may be because the word *soma* (wine) was later associated with the moon, and wine drinking goes with bad reputation. Also it is popularly believed that the lord of the moon became so arrogant and licentious that he carried off Tārā, wife of the sage Bṛihaspati and refused to give

her up on the entreaties of her husband. This licentiousness would naturally make him a god of ill repute.

Again, the *nāyikā*, dwelling on the big and beautiful eyes of her lover, says that while the god of love is blind (in this respect Kāmadeva shares the attribute with Cupid, his counterpart) the eyes of Kṛiṣṇa are big and lovely.

12. Beautiful eyes were compared by Hindu writers to the eyes of the *chakor*, *chakava* or *khanjan* birds (*chakor*-red legged partridge, *chakava*-ruddy goose, and *khanjan*-wagtail). Describing the eyes of Padmāvatī, Poet Jāisī says: 'Like-*khanjan* birds in autumn were her eyes'. The eyes of another lady described by him were 'like *khanjan* birds sporting in the air.'

13. Sometimes teeth are compared to seeds of pomegranate. In a Moplā love-song a girl, Hasanu'l had teeth which were 'small and white like the seeds of pomegranate.'

14. The moon is a favourite, while describing a beautiful woman's face, of that of a man. In *Shṛiṅgāra Shataka* Bhartṛihari praises 'a face that shames the splendour of the moon'. In *Gīta Govinda* Rādhā's face is compared to the moon. The dacoit, Vāsū, describing the beauty of the maiden Maniktārā says, 'Verily your face is like the moon, How beautiful do you look with drops of sweat on your brow.' Mālatī's face is described as being moon-like 'the lovely image of the moon-faced maid.' Poet Bihārī describes the face of *nāyikā* thus: 'within her blue attire her lovely face looks like the moon reflected in the rippling water of a stream.'

15. Feet are frequently compared to lotus or lily flowers. Padmāvatī's rosy feet were like a lotus, and those of Rani Vasumatī were like 'the lotus umbrella of the god of love. In *Ṛitusaṁhāra* the maidens in autumn are described by Kālidāsa thus:

'the anklets in symphony sweet
Caress their lotus feet.'

Describing the feet of a beautiful woman an Oriental poet says:

'Her feet, like leaves of lotus in the lake
When with the passing breeze they gently shake.'

16. The description of the *nāyikā* in this verse is in the traditional manner. The metaphors are the usual ones used for the various parts of the body. So is the picturesque description of Padmāvatī (in Jāisī's *Padmāvatī*), as given to King Ratansena by the parrot:

'Rays were emanating from her red lips which looked like newly grown rosy leaves. Her face was fragrant like a blossoming lotus, and when she breathed it seemed as if flames of perfume emanated from her...Her shut eyes appeared like two black bees lying quietly within two closed blue lotuses'.

17. One bosom friend is relating to the other the sad condition of Kṛiṣṇa since the moment he has fallen in love with his beloved Rādhā. Familiar things, like clothes and home, appear distasteful to him, and cosy beddings which should bring thoughts pleasurable are obnoxious. All good things like moonlight, sandal-wood, camphor, betels, and so on, have lost all charm for him.

18. Rāhu is believed by orthodox Hindus to be the cause of eclipses. He is also considered to be one of the planets or meteors, and guardian of the south-west quarter. Mythologically Rāhu is a *daitya* (demon) who is supposed to swallow up the sun and moon causing eclipses. He was son of Viprachitta and Siṁhikā having four arms, his lower part ending in a tail. He was a great mischief-maker, and when the gods produced nectar by churning the ocean, he managed surreptitiously to steal some of it for himself. He was detected by the sun and the moon who reported him to Viṣṇu (the Preserver), who as punishment cut off his head and two of his arms, but as he had secured immortality, his body entered the stellar sphere in which he wrecks vengeance occasionally by swallowing the sun and the moon.

19. A *ṛiṣi* to whom several hymns in the *Rig Veda* are ascribed, and a celebrated sage. One account has him to be the son of Mitra and Varuṇa whose seed fell from them at the sight of Urvashī a celestial nymph. Agastya was said to have been born in a glass-jar as a fish of great lustre, and at birth he was not more than a span-long. According to a fable he commanded Vindhya mountains to prostrate themselves before him, so that they lost their original height. According to another story, he is supposed to have drunk up the ocean because it had offended him, and because he wished to help the gods in their wars with the *daityas* when the latter had hidden themselves in the waters. This incident gave him the name 'ocean-drinker.' The reference here is to this . The *nāyikā* compares her mind to something so defiled that it is not palatable even to the great ocean-drinker, Agastya, who could swallow the sea, and contain it.

Agastya is such a fascinating sage that a little more information about him may not be out of place. It is said that the sage saw his ancestors suspended by their heels in a pit, and was told he could rescue them only by begetting a son. So he formed a girl out of the most graceful parts of several animals, named Lopāmudrā (*Lopa*-destruction), and in due course married her. He is also said to have turned King Nahuṣa into a serpent when the latter kicked him, but afterwards restored him to his proper form.

In the *Rāmāyaṇa*, Agastya is said to have dwelt in a hermitage in the Vindhya Mountains, where he killed many demons. He received Rāma, Lakshmaṇa, and Sītā, when they were wandering in their exile, gave Rāma bow of Viṣṇu, and when he was restored to his kingdom, accompanied him to Ayodhyā.

20. Sheṣa or Sheṣanāga, is King of the serpent race (called *nāgas*), and of the infernal region—pātāla, He is a serpent with a thousand heads. While sleeping during the intervals of creation, he supports the world and upholds, the seven pātālas, or hells. Earthquakes are the result of his yawning. When the gods churned the ocean, they made use of Sheṣa as a great rope which they twisted round Mount Mandāra and used it as a churn. He is represented as clothed in purple and wearing a white necklace, holding in one hand a plough and in the other a pestle. He is also called Ananta, or endless, as a symbol of eternity. He is said to have been incarnated in Balarāma the brother of Kṛiṣṇa.

21. The meaning of the Poet seems to be as follows: 'God has, it appears, acted strangely in this matter, for to this mind of mine which is like poison, he has given the name *sudhākara* (or *sudhādhara*)which implies that it is full of nectar (*sudhā* nectar, and *kara*-possessing). *Sudhādhara* is also an epithet for the moon, and *sudhikara* means the mind (*sudhī*-remembrance or recollection, and *kara*-possessing; so that *sudhikara* means possessing remembrance, i.e. mind). Thus there is a pun on the word which means three different things at the same time—'mind' 'the moon,' and 'possessing nectar.'

On the contrary, Sheṣajī on whom the whole world rests, and who serves as couch and canopy for the Lord of the world, Viṣṇū—the Preserver, is called *Viṣadhara* i.e. full of poison. (*viṣa* poison). Thus strangely enough, the *nāyikā's* evil and poisonous mind is called moon-like, or full of nectar, and the serpent Sheṣa, who is the supporter of the world, is called one being full of poison. Such is the strange judgment of god.

22. Swans love sunlight and a clear sky, and so do not relish the appearance of clouds. On the other hand, clouds like to rain, and thus ease their burden, and so they do not like swans. The repulsion is mutual.

23. The lotus-petals open out in the day, and in the night they close up. So the Poet says, the lotus spurns the moon, and the moon has no liking for the lotus.

24. An evergreen tree with straight trunk and dropping branches, and leaves having shining veins.

25. The insolence of the *nāyaka* would have killed the *nāyikā* but, as she says, it was only because of her eyes that she was saved. She could gaze on her lover with them. and his sight gave her strength to bear his rudeness.

26. Shrī Kṛiṣṇa.

27. (See note 2, Chapter-4).

28. (See note 2, Chapter 3).

29. The *nāyikā*, Rādhā, is pale because of the sorrow of parting. Poet Ghanānanda also speaks of the paleness of his *nāyikā*, who is long parted from her lover :

'Weak and pale she lives estranged
From her beloved.'

30. Crushing shame's shadow implies that no shame at all has been left in the *nāyaka*.

31. The bosom companion is doubtful whether the disturbed condition of Kṛiṣṇa is due to some fault in him, or in the *nāyikā*. Maybe that Kṛiṣṇa is trying to make a fool of the *nāyikā* by outwardly pretending that he is upset so that she may be moved by compassion and relent , or it is also possible that the *nāyikā* has led him on, and then jilted him, and thus upset his calm.

32. The *nāyikā* who was fresh and desireful like a green creeper, now withers due to the sorrow of separation.

33. The meaning is, that when the nayikā sits in *samādhi* (meditation), and becomes united with the *nāyaka* then who will there be for him to meet! *Samādhi* is trance in which the mind and body cease to exist, and the soul is one with god. So the bosom companion says to the *nāyaka*,'when the *nāyikā* sits in a trance and loses consciousness of her body, and consequently of her

individuality, who will there be left for you to physically meet?'

34. *Yoga* is from the Sanskrit root *yuj*—'to join'. It is a discipline in Hindu religion which implies control of the mind and of the body. The latter is *haṭha yoga* and consists of a series of postures designed to help in mind and body control. Breath control and meditation are also part of the *yoga* system and the ultimate object is the union of the soul with god which results in ecstatic bliss. Here the bosom companion says, 'Has he undergone the *yoga* discipline, that he has become indifferent to pleasure and pain, heat and cold?

35. *Samādhi* means transcendental contemplation, or ecstasy. This is a super-normal state produced by meditation and concentration. The *yoga* system of the Hindu-philosopher and saint, Patañjali, enunciates eight stages leading to union of the soul with God.

These are:

(1) Self-control (*yama*)—consisting of right relations with living creatures, mercy, kindness, love, non-injury, truthfulness, chastity, non-covetousness and non-acceptance of gifts.

(2) Religious duty (*niyama*)—purity of thought and action, contentment, simplicity, love of god, and performance of religious duties.

(3) Postures (*āsana*) body-control by postures.

(4) Breath-control (*prāṇāyāma*)—exercise in inhalation and retention of breath.

(5) Sense-control (*pratyāhāra*)—mastery of the senses under control of will.

(6) Mind-control (*dhāraṇā*)—perfect control over mind by divesting of the shackles of the senses, desires, emotions etc.

(7) Meditation (*dhyāna*)—the fixing of the mind on some object of knowledge.

(8) Transcendental contemplation (*samādhi*)—which the verse mentions, is the last step in *yoga*, in which the soul enters into the cosmic consciousness, followed by spiritual illumination and mental advancement.

36. While the *Bhāgavata Purāṇa* describes the playful, frolicsome, and amorous aspects of Kṛiṣṇa, the *Mahābhārata* and the *Bhagavad Gītā* emphasise his transcendental aspect. Kṛiṣṇa is considered to be the eighth incarnation of Viṣṇu, and by some as a direct manifestation of Viṣṇu himself. Indeed his worshippers consider 'Kṛiṣṇa' to be another name for the Absolute or god.

37. The lucky one is obviously the reader. How the printed-book reaches every corner of the world, but before it was invented there existed only a few hand-written volumes, and a person who had the good fortune of being able to secure one was indeed a lucky man.

Chapter IX

Arrogance

In this chapter Keshavadāsa gives an account of the different types of arrogance which affect a women in love. In doing so he follows the traditional practice, for almost every Hindi poet of love wrote about arrogance which lovers showed to each other 'lest too light winning make the prize too light.' A woman's arrogance takes many shapes and forms in the hands of these poets. Keshava, who analyses and classifies everything, does the same with arrogance, which he defines as 'the excitement of loveliness which is caused by the power of perfect love.' Arrogance, according to him, is of three kinds—great, small, and middling. The great arrogance is born in the mind of the lover when the *nāyikā* says something which disregards or sets aside worldly conventions. The small arrogance arises when she sees with her own eyes the *nāyaka* glancing at another woman, or hears of it through her bosom companion. The middle arrogance is produced when the *nāyikā*, while talking to another women, gazes at her lover.

All the three kinds of arrogance are illustrated by vivid examples which fall into the usual categories—hidden, and manifest. Sometimes it is the arrogance of *nāyaka* which is described, but more often that of the *nāyikā*, for it is she who has to wear the thin armour of love which can protect her from all but the more determined lovers. How this armour of arrogance is finally pierced and the ways in which the lover sets about doing it, is described in the next chapter, in which the Poet writes about the devices by which the arrogance of a woman can be removed.

Arrogance, and its kinds[1]

When sway of love supreme, excites
The mind, loveliness does seem

More lovely, then does arrogance rise,
Says Keshavadāsa, so do I deem
That arrogance which lovers show
To one another, of three kinds,
So Keshava says, as all men know,
Great, small and middling, is defined.

The great arrogance

When the beloved boldly speaks,
Not minding what the world my say,
Then in her lover's mind born is
That arrogance which is known as 'great'.

The hidden great arrogance of the *nāyikā*

The son of Nanda did meet today
Rādhā, his days of parting past;
Her sullenness he drove away
With laughter, and with joy at last,
As love to her he made: when lo!
Beneath his doublet she did espy
Nail-marks[2] upon his chest, and so,
Dumbfounded did remain her eyes !

The manifest great arrogance of the *nāyikā*

One bosom companion says to another:

'When that cowherd maiden today
Did laugh and converse with Gopāla
Of talents, by chance he did take
The name of some girl, whom he called
His bosom friend! on this remained,
The betel she was about to put
In the *nāyaka's* mouth, within her hand,
And that in her mouth stayed unchewed!
So agitated, friend, was she
No sooner she that name did hear,
Her feelings could restrained not be,
And lo! her eyes were filled with tears!'

The hidden great arrogance of the *nāyaka*

Kṛiṣṇa's amorous pranks the heart do please,
As when the *nāyikā* found one day
By chance within his turban's crease
A love-letter from another maid!
'This piece of paper is', she said,
'A furnace to destroy our love!
I have been born by fate to tread
My path of pain, why do you thus
Seek out another ? Oh! what more
Shall I say ? 'Tis poison to me!'
Hearing this, Shrī Kṛiṣṇa laughed, and spoke
To tease her, 'But to me 'tis sweet!'[3]

The manifest great arrogance of the *nāyaka*

The nāyikā says to the bosom companion:

'One speaks to him, who is his own,
Just as his treasure he lays bare
To his near one; I have forsworn
To look on him, how can I tear
Eyes with a knife? Ghanaśyāma, this is,
On whom his many wives attend,
And in a while much camphor mix!'[4]
The bosom friend replied, 'Dear friend,
What words you speak! That you should say
Which should be said; one does not speak
O! friend, to him e'en in this way,
Whom buying in bondage he does keep!'

The small arrogance

When the *nāyikā* herself sees at last
The *nāyaka's* glance on another cast,
Or hears of it through her bosom friend,
'Small arrogance' know it is then.

The hidden small arrogance of the *nāyikā*

Wisdom and folly of the one
Dear to you, Kṛiṣṇa, are in my mind,
Whether 'tis arrogance or affront,
See for yourself; nought can you find
By guessing! her grief or joy none
Can you know; for she looks the same,
If laughs she, or angry becomes!
One moment cold she does remain,
And the next warm, changeful as are
The changing shadows by clouds cast.

The manifest small arrogance of the *nāyikā*

The bosom friend to the *nāyikā* spoke:
'Be not enraged without a cause,
For he is the one by you adored;'
The *nāyikā* said, 'who ever was
Beloved by going away?' 'I know,'
The bosom friend said, 'tis Nandalal!'
'Oh! cowherd girl, if thought you so,'
The *nāyikā* said, 'Why didn't you call
Yesterday? Dear friend, to create
Discord you come today, like the bud
Of the *kanail* flower which is different made
Inside and out!' Her friend said, 'Love,
How should I know 'tis the truth you say,
So that your words I may believe?'
The *nāyikā* said, 'what need is, pray,
Of belief, when I myself did see?'

Another example of the hidden small arrogance of the *nāyikā*

When the lover does not as his lady wants,
And she cares not for her lover's words,
There the smaller arrogance is born,
Thus have reputed poets heard.

Yet another example of the hidden small arrogance of *nāyikā*

The bosom companion says to the nāyikā :

'What you will do hence I know not
But now his words obeying you have
Much sorrow suffered ; you've forgot
Yourself so much in shame and love,
That loveless you have turned ! Shrī Kṛiṣṇa
Embraces you as you would crave,
But you do nothing new to him !
With relish you have never gazed
Intently at him : why at last
Is then your mind unsettled made,
Only today? When in the past
Him no encouragement you gave?'

Another example of the manifest small arrogance of *nāyikā*

Instructing the nāyaka, the bosom companion says :

'You do not speak to me today
As you have been speaking till now,
Have I some great omission made
Which you liked not? Oh ! dear Kṛṣṇa, how
If you do neither speak nor show
Can I know what lies in your mind?
You do not yet, beloved, know
That the porridge cooled should be, ere trying
To eat ! Oh ! Kuñja Bihārī,* this
Hunger of yours is a new type,
That you the half-cooked pulse should wish
To taste as soon as you arrive !'[6]

The middle arrogance

When the *nāyikā*, while engaged in talk
With another woman, yet does glance
On her lover, then, says Keshavadāsa,
Is joyful middle arrogance born.

The hidden middle arrogance of the *nāyikā*

'My Kṛiṣṇa, where did you pass the night ?'
'Pining for you, oh ! my delight !'
'Why nail-marks on your limbs appear ?'
'Thorns in the forest scratched them, dear !'
'Why thus your eyes burn, and red glow ?'
'Grief of your parting made them so !'
When thus did Kṛiṣṇa remove her doubt
With crafty words, her to console,
Reluctantly him she allowed
To clasp her his bosom close ![7]

The manifest middle arrogance of the *nāyikā*

When that woman with whom Kṛiṣṇa was conversing came to appease the nāyikā, the latter said :

'As him you caused to prattle loud
So now you've come to make me do,
As though my teacher ! I've avowed
To speak not what I wished, to you :
Who will prepare to die of shame[8]
Brazenly baring her thighs ? That Kṛiṣṇa
Cares least of all for his good name,
Should I be lower even than him ?'

The middle arrogance of the *nāyaka*

When the arrogant woman is not appeased
Though much her lover tries, and he
Gets tired of trying—then we find
The middle arrogance in his mind.

Another example of the *nāyikā's* hidden middle arrogance

Beseeching the nāyikā to abandon her arrogance her bosom companion says :

'Oh ! you of face which does outvie
The lovely lotus,[9] oft have I

Bid you your arrogance forsake,
But you do not : the mirror take
And see how in your eyes it shines !
Now sit you with an arrogant mind,
But soon I know your lips you'll drown
In love's juice ! you glance all around
Feigning to see much loveliness,
Yet cast your eyes not on the *nāyaka*,
You listen not, though oft we plead.
No one's to blame ; you don't agree
To your own pleasure ! 'Tis not good—
Leaving your arrogance you should
Yield unto him :[10] for when he leaves
You will beg me, him to appease !'

Another example of the *nāyikā's* manifest middle arrogance

The bosom companion says to the nāyikā :

'The arrogance of woman soon
By honour set at nought is—else
Can man's endeavour e'er remove
It ? That one arrogance can tell
Which by appeasing goes, my friend :
But when the limit it does cross
'Tis vanity, not arrogance.
When you, my friend, dishonoured are
Amongst the co-wives, will it, pray,
Be to your good ? Be with him pleased
While still he begs, for when enraged
He is, 'tis you who will appease !'

Concluding verse

Give ear unto me, oh ! wise friends,
Thus Kṛiṣṇa's and Rādhā's arrogance
I have described—now I will show
How arrogance can be made to go.

NOTES

1. Hindi poets have dwelt much on a woman's arrogance which makes her maintain a taciturn silence before her lover, and defeats his attempts to remove it. Arrogance can be born by the woman's consciousness of her own loveliness, as Poet Keshava says in this verse, or as a reaction to the *nāyaka's* clandestine affairs with other girls. This is especially true of Rādhā, because her lover, Kṛiṣṇa, was a confirmed amorist, and there was no end to his flirting with other women. So much so, that in the *Sūrasāgara*, Poet *Sūradāsa* mentions one of the reasons of Rādhā's arrogance as being that when she sees her own image reflected in the heart of her lover, Kṛiṣṇa, she begins to suspect that it is another woman seated there.

2. Padmāvatī, Poet Jāisī's heroine, gets nail-marks on her breasts from her lover after her night of love :

'The orange garden of your budding breasts
The bee has sucked, and lines of colour rise
Where nails have touched them.'

So too a lady in the *Chaurapañchāshikā*, a Sanskrit work :

'I recollect the moment when, mad with love , I sipped the nectar from her lips, and the nails of my fingers dug deep into her round breasts.'

Describing a maiden in a similar situation Mayūra mentions her bosom 'wounded by her lover's nails.'
Bihārī's *nāyikā* is so fond of the nail-marks made on her body by her lover that she keeps on removing their scales so that they may never heal, and so be a constant reminder of their lovemaking. So much for nail-marks made by regular lovers as a reminder of their love but sometimes they are eloquent witness of that which one tries to hide, as in this verse, in which everything goes on well, till Rādhā sees the tell-tale marks of her lover's faithlessness. So also are the nail-marks on the breasts of Bihārī's *nāyaka* which are more eloquent than all his explanations :

'Splendid shine the nailmarks on your bosom
Made newly by her, and drowsiness lies
Heavy on you: your eyes you cannot raise:
Then why, O ! beloved, do you vainly swear
That another woman you have not approached?'

See also note 35, Chapter 3.

3. The *nāyikā* has discovered by chance a love-letter of Kṛiṣṇa's beloved which he hid in his turban. She decries it, calling it a furnace in which wedded love will burn to ashes, and so on; but it has no effect on the happy-go-lucky Kṛiṣṇa, who answers with a laugh that whatever it may be, the words of love it contains are to him, sweet.

4. This would be for applying on Kṛiṣṇa's body. Camphor has a sweet smell and so it would act as perfume.

5. The *Kanail flower*—the Indian oleander. A shrub of indoor culture having leathery lance-shaped leaves and handsome deep rose-red, or white flowers. The Indian species has fragrant blossoms. The leaves, flowers, and bark of the shrub are poisonous. The inside of the flower is different in texture from the outside, and hence it has been used to illustrate that the bosom companion's exterior behaviour is different from her inside thoughts.

6. It seems the *nāyikā* has repulsed Kṛiṣṇa when he was too precipitate in love-making, and that has angered him. So she tells him not to be impetuous in his desire but act gently and patiently. The examples of the porridge and pulse are given to illustrate this. Obviously the *nāyaka* has not followed Vātsyāyana's sagacious advice to lovers: 'Women have a tender nature and want to be approached tenderly. When men who only know them slightly approach them forcibly, they sometimes acquire a hatred for sex and even for the men too.'

*Kuñja Bihārī— One of the several names by which Kṛiṣṇa is known.

7. The nail-marks on his body, and his reddened eyes, make the *nāyikā* suspect that the *nāyaka* Kṛiṣṇa has come to her after enjoying another woman. In this case he is successful in removing her doubt but only to some extent, for after having heard his explanations, though she allows him to embrace her, it is only with reluctance. Poet Vidyāpati's *nāyaka* is not so lucky, and seeing the proofs of his fault the *nāyikā* will not suffer him to make love to her. She says: 'Having seen your red eyes I have understood everything. They testify to your having woken up much at night. O Kṛiṣṇa, do not make excuses. Go back now to that woman with whom you have spent the night.

8. The *nāyikā* is telling the woman who has shamelessly flirted with Kṛiṣṇa 'Who will pretend or care to remain bashful after having bared her thighs, as you have done ?'

9. Hindi and Sanskrit poets often compared a lovely woman's face to a lotus. Mālatī's face is, 'bright as the golden bud, of the young lotus.' In *Ṛitusaṁhāra*, Kālidāsa compares the faces of the girls in autumn and winter to lotuses. Those of the autumn beauties are described thus :

'The full blown silver lotus has stolen
The charm of their radiant faces.'

In winter the women look themselves in the mirror :

'Behold the young girl, mirror in-hand
Making up her lotus face
In the sidelong morning sun.

The face of Padmāvatī is 'like lotus blossoming in the crystal lake', and in *Gīta Govinda*, Rādhā's face is compared to a crimson lotus.

10. In a similar situation Poet Vidyāpati's *nāyikā*, Rādhā, repents having showed arrogance: 'Oh ! my bosom friend now I sorrow over the arrogance I have shown...Kṛiṣṇa tried to appease me in many ways, and even shed tears. It was a bad day for me when I showed arrogance, and even now my soul does not part with my body....In the anger-shaped darkness I could not understand anything and taking a jewel for a clod of earth, I threw it away.'

CHAPTER X

Ways to Remove Arrogance

In order to consummate love it is necessary to remove any arrogance on the part of the lover or his beloved which may stand in between. Arrogance is a self-imposed barrier which prevents complete union and sows misunderstanding and dissension in the path of love. When, therefore, the woman, who though inwardly wanting amorous dalliance, yet impelled by modesty or self-respect, hardens her interior, it is for the lover to break the unwanted screen which has come up between the two, so that she comes flying into his eager arms. There are six devices which lovers employ in removing arrogance. These are, gentleness, the giving of gifts, the creation of difference, division or diversion, and humility. Gentleness means removing the woman's arrogance by fascinating her mind. The giving of gifts means, giving the woman some gift which pleases her, or uttering some sweet falsehood, as for example, exuberant praise and flattery, or paying a compliment which though false and exaggerated, wins her favour. The device of creating difference by strategy is one in which the bosom friends are won over so that they combine their efforts in removing arrogance and in bringing about a rapprochement between the lovers. The way of humility is, when impelled by intense love and longing, and beset by feelings of guilt, the lover and his beloved fall on each other's feet. This is the moment of complete surrender in which all faults are forgiven, and the torrent of love gushes forth as though from a spring. The device of diversion is that in which, in the place of words which are normally used, other words are spoken, as for example, calling clouds 'war drums' and 'messengers of death', or speaking of the flitting of a black bee from one honied flower to another as if it were the description of a lover enjoying various women ! Finally, when arrogance is removed by diverting the mind it is called the way of delusion of the mind, as for example, telling the *nāyikā* that the peacocks who are crying are passion's servants delivering their message to lustful women !

After having described the ways of removing arrogance, Keshavadāsa advises lovers on the need for caution in showing arrogance or removing it. The woman, he says, should not sulk too much because when her lover becomes dejected by her excessive fretting it might become the point of no return, and it would then be impossible to win him over. Arrogance should be a weapon reserved for a very special occasion. If it is used too often it would be harmful. Without fear there is no love and without love no fear. The two are interlinked. This factor too, deserves to be borne in mind by the person who shows arrogance. In the end, the things by which the minds of husband and wife are saddened are listed. These are, vanity, affliction, wealth, renunciation, harsh words, greed, unloving acts, and separation caused by residence in foreign lands.

Having dwelt on the ways of removing arrogance, Keshavadāsa goes on in the next chapter, to narrate about the estrangement of lovers.

Ways to remove arrogance.[1]

I will narrate all those six ways
Which I have heard, says Keshavadāsa,
By which the lover and loved one may
Their arrogance lovingly destroy.
Gentleness, and the giving of gifts,
Difference, diversion, humility,
Delusion—these are the ways six
By which does arrogance cease to be,
Chastisement does not in them fit
For it to loss of pleasure leads.

The way of gentleness

When the arrogance of someone
By the mind being charmed does vanish,
This, says Keshava, by all known
The sweet way of gentleness is.

The way of gentleness of the *nāyikā*

Give him no grief who cares for nought
But your well-being. Oh! woman vain!
For one whom e'en by error you thought
Your own, no anger entertain.
Live you together, beauteous one!
As you in truth are—bodies twain
But one in soul, it ill becomes
Between you if discord remains ![2]

The way of gentleness of the *nāyaka*

Now this perforce I have to say
Never before on me you glanced,
Why should one tread that rugged way
And hurt his feet with prickly thorns!
As the small tender pumpkin is
Which withers even if one points
A finger[3], I fear so will be
This love which you and me has joined.
Therefore, Oh! Kṛiṣṇa, whate'er you do
Consider this, to you I pray,
That in truth always I am you
And, dearest, you are me always!

The way of giving of gifts

When giving a gift on some excuse,
Says Keshava, arrogance is removed,
Or by a statement falsely made[4]
A woman's mind one captivates—
Then know, Oh! friend, that this way is
The sweet device of giving gifts.

The way of giving of gifts of the *nāyaka*

The bosom companion of the nāyikā bringing a garland of flowers on behalf of the nāyaka and entreating her to wear it, says:

'Shrī Brahmā[5] petals these bestowed
Tender and rosy, which appeared

Pleasing to Sūrya[6]; they have the glow
Of moon-like lips; when they did hear,
Of your breasts, as the Malaya mounts[7],
And saw your hair which serpent-like
Did those delicious breasts surround;
Then hope in them did soon arise
To be perfumed; as are indeed
All things upon those mountains—bend
Your neck, these flowers of *bandhujīva*
To wear, so that they may have scent ![8]

Another example of the way of giving of gifts

The bosom companion says to nāyikā:

'This string of elephant pearls[9] did live
In elephants insane, which did cause
Many a creature to be killed,
Both still and moving; since that hour
Brahmā did pierce them, and put round
Each pearl a string to chastise them!
A charming manner they have found
For their wrong-doing to make amends,
That they wish to amuse themselves
By lying on your delicious breasts!'

Yet another example of the way of giving gifts

One bosom companion says to another :

Today Rādhājī laughing came
And did a verse recite,[10] and said
'Oh ! Kṛiṣṇa ! its sense to me explain,
Tell me how couples newly-wed
The honey of each other's lips
Enjoy; tell me where should be made
Marks with the nail and teeth ? What is
The thing which has been called "embrace ?"

Upon my word ! hide nought from me !
Oh ! how, my friend, should I relate
Rādhā's cleverness, she appeased
Her spouse herself by what she spoke !

The way of creating difference

When the *nāyikā* wins to her side
Her bosom friends, and then removes
Arrogance—know then the device
Of causing difference she does use.[11]

The way of creating difference of the *nāyikā*

On behalf of the nāyaka the female attendant says to the nāyikā :

'The nurse, the maid, the bosom friend,
All in their manner being afraid
Do speak not; but oh ! dear one, lend
Your ears to what I'm forced to say,
To you I'm tied : speak softly,[12] girl !
I fear to be misunderstood,
As butter soft's his mind; your words,
Are harder than a log of wood !'

The way of creating difference of the *nāyaka*

The bosom companion says to Kṛiṣṇa :

'To her someone these words did say,
"Shrī Kṛiṣṇa is angry"; from that hour
She racks her mind to find a way
That friend and wealth may both be hers![13]
But all in vain ! on both sides burns
This fire, how can one put it out ?
To please you should your loved one come
Or, filled with arrogance, turn about ?'

The way of humility

When lovers clasp each other's feet[14]
With love intense, or passion swayed,
Or filled with feelings of much guilt,
Of humbleness this is the way.

The way of humility of the *nāyikā*

The nāyikā says to her bosom companion :

'Dear friend ! thus my companions say :
"When your lover came and clasped your feet
Then too you looked not on him straight !"
Thus rumours false about me, sweet,
They have spread: swear by me I pray,
And tell me others will not speak—
Were my words arrogant on that day
When thus Kṛiṣṇa came, me to appease ?'

Another example of the *nāyikā's* way of humility

The bosom friend to the *nāyikā* said,
'Why don't you speak even on being called?'
'You'll make me prattle unto death!'
She answered : 'Oh ! no, not at all,
You foolish girl !' Her friend did say :
'Whom maidens hold more dear than life,
He on your feet does fall, forsake
Your obstinacy, and arise,
And on your neck your lover lay—
Your lover who loves you all the while !
How long will you, oh ! maiden, gaze
Thus insolently at the sky ?'

Yet another example of the *nāyikā's* way of humility

The nāyikā's bosom companion says to her :

'Now sad you are, and mournful keep
All day; but when till midnight deigned

Your friends and kinsmen to beseech,
You heeded not: your maid explained,
Your bosom friends instructed you
In vain : O ! arrogant one ! tell me,
As you were told why didn't you do,
While your loved one lay at your feet ?'

The *nāyaka's* way of humility

The bosom companion says to the nāyaka:

'Can fish do aught of water shorn ?[15]
In sooth the water is its life,
Do that alone that girl which charms,
Without whom nought to you seems bright:
On my feet you fell, her to gain,
And now she falls upon your feet!
Why don't you raise her up and strain
Her to your bosom, oh! my sweet !
I for one will thus you advise:
"Shut not your door, when Beauty stands
Upon your threshold; 'tis not wise!"
Lift her and take her by the hand.'

The way of diversion

Where in the place of words that should
Of woman's arrogance make an end,
Others are said which arrogance remove,
It is the way of diversion.

The way of diversion of the *nāyikā*

The bosom companion says to the nāyikā:

'What you consider lightning, is
The gleam of weapons! These are not
Peacocks which cry, but poor captives
Of rival cohorts! Nor is fraught

With thundering clouds that roam the sky,
Methinks war drums are sounding there!
With shame the sun her face does hide:
To the dark moon-faced Kṛiṣṇa repair—
That Kṛiṣṇa who does the pleasures slay
Of all his foes! the clouds do ride
Wind horse, as Yama's[16] warriors may,
Searching the pale moon[17] far and wide!'

Another example of the *nāyikā's* way of diversion

The *nāyikā* to Shrī Kṛiṣṇa thus spoke:
'How much she on the *ketakī*[18]; fawns
All day and night! and more and more
Her mind and sight do dwell upon
The *kamalinī*[19]; nor can see
This blind man anything when drunk
With nectar of the *mādhavī* ![20]
Sometimes the eglantine amongst
He wanders, and sometimes he tends
The *champā*[21] flowers.' When Kṛiṣṇa this heard
Abashed he was; the bosom friend
Then said: 'For black bee were my words,
Why are you thus ashamed[22]? Foul seems
Your mind!Oh! love, this shameless bee[23]
Even by his mate accompanied dreams
The elegant mālatī[24] to meet!'

The way of delusion of the mind

When by delusion which does rise
Within the mind, arrogance goes,
Of mind's delusion the device
This, Poet Keshavadāsa does know.

The *nāyikā's* way of delusion of the mind

The bosom companion says to the nāyikā :

'These are not peacocks which make cry,
But Passion's servants[25] going around

Proclaiming, "In this passion's night
Each lustful woman who is found
To sulk, their anger will invite !"
These are not clouds which loud resound
But drums of pleasure : when 'tis light
Then you may fret, to silence bound,
My bosom friend ; on you I die !
But now when Kṛiṣṇa speaks, should you frown,
And answer not ? I ask you, why ?
Oh ! speak, and your love-tale expound !'

Another example of the *nāyikā's* way of delusion of the mind

The bosom companion says to the nāyikā :

'That mynah see—when she beholds
The ruddy goose, and his dear one
Secretly she her love makes more !
And the she-parrot faint becomes
With shame; therefore rise up and please
Her; in a trice their quarrel's made
More ! Even then he's not appeased,
Though she tries much him to assuage :
Oh ! amorous Kṛiṣṇa, 'tis strange that you
These tricks have taught to the parrot too !'

Arrogance as an art

Says Keshavadāsa, thus bosom friends
The arrogance of the lovers end,
And plan each moment diverse means
Their mutual love more to increase.
Fret not too much, beloved one !
Lest you your lover drown in woe
For when dejected he becomes,
His favour he may not bestow.
Arrogance should not oft be shown,
Says Keshavadāsa, but once alone,
So that respect on either side

May more by such endeavour rise.
Without fear there's no love; without
Love there's no fear; where'er exists
Fear, there is love too—this no doubt
The manner of all arrogance is.

The sorrows of lovers

By vanity, affliction, wealth,
Renunciation, or harsh speech,
Or in far lands alone to dwell
Or greed, or by unloving deed—
The minds of both husband and wife
By these things sorrowful do lie.

Concluding verse

Says Keshava, thus I have told you
The parting that does emanate
From arrogance; now I'll relate
Of separation pitiful.

NOTES

1. In *Kāma Sūtra*, Vātsyāyana mentions several ways in which a woman can be won over. Gentleness is one of these, and a tender approach is advocated, especially towards the inexperienced woman. The giving of presents is also emphasised. 'The man', says the writer, 'should get for the girl whatever gifts she may want to possess, and give them at different times personally whenever he has the opportunity to meet her.' The giving of presents is also advocated for maintaining the woman's love. If an affair is carried on with another woman and the man wishes to keep the affections of the first at the same time, the way is to give her gifts. Similarly the go-between who is carrying the message of the lover should show to the woman the presents, like perfumes, ornaments etc., which he has given her.

The third way is the creation of difference between the woman and her husband. About this Vātsyāyana says that the go-between should create discord between the husband and the wife so that the latter may be drawn to the lover. She should dilate on the weakness of the husband's passion, his jealousy, roguery, ingratitude, dullness, meanness and aversion to amorous dalliance.

The fourth way, diversion, also finds mention in the *Kāma Sūtra*. When the boy has begun to woo the girl of his choice, he is advised to amuse her with various games and diversions, such as collecting flowers, making garlands, playing games of dice, cards etc. The idea is that by doing so the lovers will come close to each other and get opportunities of advancing their love. The fifth way, indifference, perhaps means that the girl should not brazenly offer herself but put on a little gentle resistance. The *Kāma Sūtra* says that although the girl loves the man, she should not offer herself or make the first overtures, for thereby she loses her dignity and is liable to be scorned and rejected. When her lover tries to kiss her she should oppose him; when he begs for sexual intercourse she should allow him to touch her private parts with great difficulty, and should not willingly yield herself but make some show of resisting him.' The sixth way, humility, is enjoined by Vātsyāyana where he advises the new huband to kneel at his bride's feet if all entreaties fail, 'for it is a universal rule that however bashful or angry a woman may be she cannot disregard a man who falls on her feet.'

In agreement with Hindu erotic writers, Keshavadāsa excludes 'chastisement' as a way of removing the arrogance of a woman, though Tulasidāsa the author of the *Rāmāyaṇa*, and Keshava's contemporary, made the controversial observation that a boor, a low caste man, an animal, and a woman are fit to be chastised.

2. Obviously these words are spoken by the lover to his beloved.

3. It is a superstition that if one even points a finger at the small tender fruit of the pumpkin it will wither away. In the heated exchange which took place between Lakshmaṇa, and the sage Parashurāma, after the former's brother, Rāma, had broken Shiva's bow Lakshmaṇa at one place says, O ! sage, here there is no tender young fruit (meaning himself) which will wither on seeing even your little finger pointed towards it.'

4. Even speaking a lie seems to be allowed when the object is to win over a woman's love.

5. See note 2, Chapter 3.

6. The sun, or the sungod, and one of the three chief deities in the *Vedas*. Uṣas, the dawn, is his wife, and he moves through the sky in a chariot drawn by seven ruddy horses or mares. In the *Rāmāyaṇa* and the *Purāṇas*, however, he is mentioned to be the husband of Saṁjñā, daughter of Vishvakarmā. His effulgence was so powerful that his wife gave him *Chāyā* (=shade) for a handmaid and herself retired into the forest. Karṇa was his illegitimate son by Kuntī. Sūrya travels in a chariot drawn by seven horses, or a horse with seven heads surrounded with rays. His wives are Savarṇā, Svāti, and Mahāvīryā.

7. The hills of Malabar, the south part of the Western Ghats. According to legend all things on these mountains became perfumed by their touch.

8. The Poet fancies that the garland of *bandhujīva* flowers wishes to get scented by the touch of the *nāyikā's* neck just as things on the Malaya mountains get perfumed merely by their touch. *Bandhujīva* is a small flowering creeper.

9. The elephant-pearl (Hindi, *gaja motī*), is an elephant gem (pearl)

supposed to be found in the heads of mad elephants. The Poet fancies that Brahmā, the Creator, in order to keep them out of mischief pierced each of the pearls and turned them into a garland. Since then the pearls have made amends for their wrong-doing (in lying in the heads of mad elephants which kill many living creatures), by caressing the bosom of the beautiful *nāyikā*.

10. The verse recited by Rādhā would of course be an erotic one, probably describing the manner of lovemaking.

11. This is a round about way of removing arrogance, in which instead of speaking the words which would normally remove it, some other words are spoken. The result, however, is the same—viz. that arrogance is thereby destroyed.

12. The female attendant is asking the *nāyikā* to speak softly and not to utter words, which she says are so harsh that their hardness is greater even than that of a log of wood.

13. The meaning is somewhat abstruse. The *nāyikā* has heard that her lover, Krisna, is angry with her. She searches furiously in her mind for a device whereby she may please the angry *nāyaka* and at the same time maintain her pride—but both the things are not possible. Either she stays away and keeps her lover angry, or she goes to appease him, and in that case she surrenders her arrogance. The position is just like one in which a choice has to be made between friends and wealth. Either one can lend money to a friend who lacks it and asks for a loan, and thereby keep the friend but lose the money, or he can refuse to give the friend any loan and lose the friend but retain his money.

14. Falling on the feet is the extreme limit of humility and implies complete surrender. In India it is customary to touch the feet (fall on the feet, or take the dust of the feet) of elders, revered persons, and sages. It is almost a form of greeting. Amongst lovers, of course, there is no such formal custom, but as Vātsyāyana advocates in *Kāma Sūtra* falling on the feet is a final bid to win over the shy bride. When the new bride has accepted the embrace of her husband, the latter should put a betel in her mouth and if she does not take it he should persuade her to do so by conciliatory words, oaths, and entreaties. If she still does not accept the betel, he should fall upon her feet, for it is a general rule that no woman, however bashful or angry she may be, will ever remain stubborn once a lover humiliates himself to the extent of falling at her feet.

15. The metaphor of the fish is also used by Poet Ghanānanda, who compares the state of the eyes of the lover which behold not the beloved, to the restless condition of fish drained of water.

16. The Indian Pluto or Minos—god of Death, with whom the spirit of the departed dwells. He is progeny of the Sun by Saṁjñā (conscience) and father of Yudhiṣṭhira. The road to his abode is guarded by two insatiable dogs with four eyes and wide nostrils. When the soul of a dead man goes to the nether regions, the recorder, Chitragupta reads out an account of the dead man's deeds, and the soul gets its just sentence according to which it either ascends to the abode of the fathers, or goes down to a hell, or is reborn on the earth in some form. Yama is regent of the south quarter and so is

called Dakshiṇaspati. He is represented as being of a green colour, wearing red clothes, sitting upon a buffalo, and armed with a ponderous mace and a noose to secure his victims. His messengers, called Yamadūtas, bring in the souls of the dead. The door of his judgment hall is kept by his porter, Vaidhyata.

17. The dark clouds driven by the winds would destroy the moon's light by covering it. So the clouds are said to be riding horses of the wind, and are likened to warriors of the god of Death, bent on exterminating the moon.

18. *Ketakī*, also called *kevṛā*, is the screwpine, so called because of the curious screw-like arrangement of its long spine-edged leaves. It is a shrub blossoming in the rainy season in panicles of large pale sheath-like leaves enclosing small white flowers. The girls of Mahārāṣṭra love to wear the *kevṛā* leaf along with flowers in their braided hair.

19. A small lotus.

20. A creeper which blossoms in February, and resembles the horse-chestnut, with yellow and white scented flowers borne on short spikes.

21. Spanish jasmine. A small flowering tree about ten feet high with large smooth leaves. During the hot and rainy seasons it bears large corymbs of big white exquisitely fragrant flowers, with the interior of their cups yellow.

22. The *nāyikā's* words, decrying Kṛiṣṇa's amorous nature, make him ashamed. The words have a double meaning, and so when the *nāyikā* sees Kṛiṣṇa hang his head in shame, she hastily adds, 'I was thinking of the black bee, why are you feeling bashful! It seems your mind itself is foul, that you give my words a different interpretation.'

23. The attraction of the black bee for flowers is proverbial. The *nāyikā* means that the bee goes to woo the *mālatī* blossom, yet takes with him his mate, the female black bee. So shameless he is, thus to woo his beloved in the presence of his wife.

24. A creeper which flowers from July to September, with bay-like leaves. Its flowers are white, of middle size, star-formed with petals twisted and irregular. It is a climbing shrub which easily fastens to trees and goes up to a considerable height.

25. Vidyāpati's *nāyikā* says: 'Hearing the cries of the peacocks in the forests I begin to be grieved by the god of love. The fearless and spiteful birds being startled, speak suddenly, as if the god of love is discharging his gun.' These sounds seem depressing to her because they remind her of her far away lover, but to the bosom companion who speaks to the *nāyikā* in this verse, they signify love and joy, for the *nāyikā*'s lover is near at hand.

Chapter XI

The Separation of Lovers

The joys of lovers appealed to Keshavadāsa, and he was loath to write about their sorrows. He was, however, too much a stickler for convention, to dare omit writing about the separation of lovers, as indeed he himself admits:

> 'Though sorrow should not find a place
> Where ways of pleasure I expound,
> Yet of it, too, I must relate
> As I think—to my theme I'm bound.'

Keshavadāsa writes about separation half-heartedly, and his utterances about parted lovers lack the depth and spontaneity of other Hindi love poets like Ghanānanda and Bihārī.

Sorrowful separation arises when all devices of pleasure fail. Not finding their joy, the lovers remain unhappy and morose. Another kind of separation is when the lover is forced to reside in some foreign land in order to attend to some business of his, leaving his poor lady alone to pass her days and nights in seclusion and grief. When the *nāyaka* is away, sleep eludes the *nāyikā* like a newly-wed bride who, filled with bashfulness, departs from her husband's bed at midnight, not heeding his prayers.

The agony of separated lovers is described. The *nāyikā* roams restlessly through the forests and groves at night, speechlessly gazing at the moon, and tormented by the joyful cries of the peacocks. Similarly the *nāyaka* has become so affected with parting that he has started living in mountain caves, frail and demented, behaving almost like a mad man.

On the whole, Keshava's descriptions of the separated lovers lack conviction, and they might not have been written at all if he was not so particular about following the accepted canons of the Hindi love poetry of his times.

Sorrowful separation

Where all devices of pleasure are gone,
Says Keshava, there is pathos born.
Though sorrow should not find a place
Where ways of pleasure I expound,
Yet of it, too, I must relate
As I think—to my theme I'm bound.

The *nāyikā's* hidden sorrowful separation

Addressing her mind the nāyikā says:

'I sent my thought-shaped bosom friend
To fetch him, but she tarried there,
Now who remains for me to send?
My generous eye-shaped messengers
In the day met him, but they failed
My body's longing to describe:
So now at last I will prevail,
Whate'er be, on my soul to fly:
For all devices are undone
To meet my lover; nor I can
For shame speak. How can anyone
Sans speech my sorrow understand?'[1]

The *nāyikā's* manifest sorrowful separation

Describing the state of her separation a bosom companion says to the nāyikā.

'My doe-like eyes do gaze and gaze
Till tired they are, on the woods green,
Whose beauty hearts does captivate
But still Shrī Kṛiṣṇa cannot be seen.
Upon Braja, round which forests lie,
The clouds do rain, and Kṛiṣṇa is gone
Far, far, away, oh! how can I
This sorrow bear? If I gaze on

Him, lotus-eyed, with my eyes shaped
As the heart's lotus, they'll no doubt
With tears be filled—thus mournful made.
What more can I say? These dark clouds
Laden with rain, as a weight are
Upon me, how shall I live, pray,
When my Ghanashyāma does dwell afar
Through these relentless *Sāvan*[2] days?

The *nāyaka's* hidden sorrowful separation

The nāyaka Kṛiṣṇa addressing his mind says :

'As hearing of her soon did fly
My heart, and on her praises soared,
And when hearts met then met the eyes
With wantonness; and drunk with hope
Of seeing her beauty, cheeks forgot
Themselves in palms, where they did rest,
And on eyes meeting wisdom dropped
Guile, and conceit, when it beheld
Her body's splendour—even so
My soul bent on Rādhā to meet
By might or wile prepares to go
Each instant, and this body leave.'

Another example of the manifest sorrowful separation of the *nāyaka*

The bosom companion says to the nāyikā :

'Shrī Kṛiṣṇa, who is compassion's core,
Into an ocean you have turned,
Youth is the stream in it that pours,
Your past love wonderful, my friend
The water is : desires that sway
Are ships upon it and fears are
Its whirlpools : argument, the waves
Upon it; and the grievous darts

Of separation are indeed
The fishes big that swim that sea.'[3]

Residence in a foreign land

Says Keshavadāsa, when the lover remains
In foreign lands, his work to attend,
Such parting, poets and wise men name,
'Separation while in a foreign land.'[4]

The *nāyikā's* hidden separation due to residence in a foreign land

Addressing her mind the nāyikā says :

'My Nandakumāra[5] left me forlorn
Oh ! mind, now when will you be gone ?'

The *nāyikā's* manifest separation as a result of residence in a foreign land.

The bosom companion says to nāyikā :

'Who is the woman without a lover ?
Who is the woman whose lover goes not
To a foreign land, nor parts from her ?
The bird, with an effort, is trapped and caught,
Does the trapper run to catch her say ?'

The same bosom companion addressing another one says :

'If to my words she pays no heed
And lays her life down, come away,
Leave her to do as she does please,
Go not to one who does not own
You as a friend; this woman's wish
Is that her lover should come back home
Today, or else she would perish !
Tell me, I ask you, my dear friend !
Can this be done ? Can it ever be
That water be found to be near at hand
To put out a fire instantly ?'[6]

Deceptive separation of the *nāyikā*

Speaking to her mind the nāyikā says

'The peacock's and the cuckoo's cries
Do fill my lonely heart with ache,
So that my understanding dies,
The cool and scented breeze does take
My calmness, which as wool does fly !
In the moonlit night somehow I saved
Myself, when loud I did make cry ;
'Long live the sage ! long live the sage !'[17]
The memory of that night persists,
How should I then alive remain ?
This poisonous lotus, friend, which is
Cause of my ruin has flowered again !'

Another example of the *nāyikā's* separation as a result of residence in a foreign land

Addressing his heart the nāyaka says :

'By speaking sweet and priceless words
She did the limbs to joy enslave
When that alluring girl made love,
Whose eye's rare nectar did assuage
The greedy heart's thirst, so it stayed
Alive, and her feet when caressed
All sorrows were at once allayed !
And thence arose such happiness
Which knows no bounds ! Oh ! tell me this,
When you left that beloved maid
O ! heart why in a million bits,
Oh ! fie on you ! you did not break ?'

Another example of the *nāyikā's* manifest separation as a result of residence in a foreign land

One bosom companion says to another :

'Somehow he went his beloved to meet,
But ere two paces he had gone

A million messages did speak !
Then taking courage he moved on
His feet, but lo ! fell backward they !
And rooted stood he, as if charmed
By some spell, and he could not say
E'en "come !" for fear of prattling tongues
Nor did he dare go back that way—
All in a moment he began
To speed, as though ten *kos* a day
He'd cover, friend, so fast he ran !'[8]

The *nāyikā's* deceptive separation

'Much like an old hag she does throw
A starry mantle over her,
And glancing all around she goes
Her lotus-shaped hands—as if they were
Shrunk as a leper's ! so too turned
As leper's white her body,[9] that
On meeting her my heart does burn :
All seven pleasures[10] she has snatched
From me, what should I do ? How save
Myself from her ? That night, ill-famed
Like hobgoblin with fiery face,
To vex me now does come again !'

Sleepless separation of the *nāyikā*

The nāyikā says

'When he comes, Sleep o'er my eyes creeps
And wandering stays as though 'twere bought:
She sleeps not, nor does let me sleep
E'er since me in friendship he sought :
'Tis in sooth my forgetfulness,
What can I say? Can a co-wife[11]
A friend be ? For their interest
All men to sleep in this world try.

My lover Kṛiṣṇa, has gone away
Unto a foreign land, afar,
Since he left, friend, in truth I say
With him did sleep also depart !'

Another example of the *nāyikā's* sleepless separation

The nāyikā says :

'This Sleep is like a new-wed maid
Who only comes close to the heart
By scheming in a million ways,
Her startled eyes all round do dart:
E'en though asleep she keeps awake !
Knowing that her lover dwells afar
In foreign lands, this Sleep does stay
Mistrustful, nor her own state marks !
This Slumber, like a bride afraid,
At midnight from my bed departs,
She listens not but goes her way,
Leaving me lonely in the dark !'[12]

The *nāyikā's* prayer to the *nāyaka* in separation

Rādhā's bosom companion writes in a letter to Kṛiṣṇa :

Rādhā, the daughter of Vṛiṣabhānu
As forest nymph does wander forth
In groves and forests; and at one
Place stays not : like Kamalānujā[13]
The lotus fears she; like Kālī[14]
Smells not the sweet *ketaki*[15] flowers,
And inflamed is like Sītājī[16]
Her eyes when do instantly fall
On demon with a lovely face :
When Cupid-shaped Duryodhana[17] deigns
His mouth to open, then she takes
Oft, like Draupadī[18] your sweet name.'

The restless separation of the *nāyikā*

The bosom companion says to the nāyaka

'As female black bee Rādhā roams
Forests and groves ; like female swan
Loves tender lotus roots alone,
Like sparrow hawk "pi ! pi !" she chants.[19]
And gazing at the moon she is
Speechless as ruddy goose would be,
From forest where the lion does live
As hind afeared does swiftly flee,
So does from saffron woods she fly
As female snake her hole within,
Does rush, so hearing peacock's cry
Does she run forth, I say, oh ! Kṛiṣṇa
Your Rādhā's body does not stay
At rest when you are far away !'

The restless separation of the *nāyaka*

The bosom companion says to Rādhā :

'Shrī Kṛiṣṇa lives in the mountain caves
As a lion; and as when seeing the king
Of beasts, with fright the elephant shakes,
So trembles he when perfumed things,
As saffron, sees he ; as a *chakor*
Sees not the sun, he gazes not
At food ; and still is saddened more
As a ruddy goose who the moon saw.
As hearing a peacock's cry the snake
To his hole hastens, so Shrī Kṛiṣṇa
The cry of that bird agitates !
He withers with the thunder's din
As *javāsā*[20] does with sudden fright :
Circling as black bee he remains,
As *yogī* waking in the night,
And as *chātak* repeats your name.[21]

Concluding verse

Says Keshavadāsa, thus I have told
Of residence in foreign lands,
As I believed, now I'll unfold
The ways which dear friends understand,
By which ends that which intervenes
Between the love of Rāḍhā and Kṛiṣṇa.

NOTES

1. The *nāyikā* first sends her thought to her lover (thought-shaped bosom friend), but the thought remains with him. Her glances which she sends to him in the day, too, fail to convey her love. Now all her endeavours being defeated, she determines to send her soul itself to plead her love, i. e. she is prepared to die for her lover. She would speak to him, but is restrained by her shyness. How can her grief be explained when bashfulness prevents her even from speaking?

2. The fifth month of the Hindu calendar, corresponding to August. It is one of the two months in which the monsoonic rainfall is the heaviest in India. Poet Ghanānanda compares the tears that gush from an estranged woman's eyes to the showers of *Sāvan*. The Hindi poets write much of the grief of the woman who remains far away from her lover. In the *Sāvan* month it rains excessively, and it is not possible to get out of doors. This increases the loneliness and the tedium of separation. In a verse of Ghanānanda a parted *nāyikā* upbraids the dark clouds for torturing her when her lover is away:

'Fearful and bad, you thunder make
And fret me till my lover returns,
For you know well that when he comes,
No longer you, poor me can plague.'

Vidyāpati's *nāyikā*, who has been separated long from her lover, complains, 'Oh! my bosom friend, there is no end to my sorrows. The cloud is fully laden with rain, it is the month of *Bhādoṁ* (after *Sāvan*), and my house is lonely without my beloved. Again, 'the month of *Sāvan* is coming. The light drizzle of rain pleases the mind, and the water-laden cloud looms splendidly above. The god of love is about to discharge his arrow; then say how can the separated woman keep on living.' At another place he says, 'The month of *Sāvan* has come. It is raining heavily. The way cannot be seen because of darkness, and all around streaks of lightning flash in the sky, because of which it has become difficult for the separated women even to live.'

3. Here the lover, Kṛiṣṇa, is compared to an ocean The state of youth, or puberty, is the stream which pours into this ocean. The past love of Kṛiṣṇa is like the water in the ocean. Desires are the ships which move on it, fears the whirlpools, disputations the high waves, and the darts of separation the big fishes in the ocean that move hither and thither.

4. This is a favourite theme of Hindi poets, especially of the *Rītikāl* period, in which foreign travels had started. Of course by 'foreign' was meant a city or state different from that in which the lovers lived (not necessarily overseas travel). Many people had work in Mughal courts, or the courts of Hindu chieftains, and so such voyages were not unusual. Both Vidyāpati and Bihārī describe vividly the pitiable condition of the *nāyikās* when their lovers have to go away to foreign lands The condition of Bihārī's *nāyikā* is one of near hysteria:

> 'One moment trembling she is, thrilled the next.
> With love for him: one moment drenched in sweat.'

Vidyāpati's *nāyikā* tries her best to restrain her lover from going abroad, but when she is not successful she sends messengers after him charging them to 'explain him that it is not proper to leave one in whom youth has just blossomed.' The girl had slept with her beloved on the same bed but, 'I do not know when he departed, leaving me sleeping alone, and now the bed, which is empty, pains my heart greatly.' In the fearful month of *Bhādoṁ* (September) when the toads croak and the peacocks cry, young lustful girls are filled with fear and hide themselves in the laps of their lovers, while other women sleep clasped close to them, but the separated *nāyikā* has to remain alone. Again, in another verse, the *nāyikā* bemoans that her lover should have left her under the impression that she was a mere child. But meanwhile she has grown and is ready for love : 'Oh! my bosom friend, having watered the creeper of hope with my tears I nurtured it. Now that creeper has given fruit and I am young; and my growing breasts cannot be contained in my dress. Oh! my friend, he saw my tiny unripe breasts at the time of his departure, seeing which he was disappointed, but day by day my breasts kept growing and my lover knows not. The husbands of all other women remembered love and came back, only my husband is so hard-hearted that love arises not in his mind.'

Vātsyāyana has some sober advice for the woman whose husband goes on a journey. During his absence she should look well over the household affairs, keep things in repair, increase the income and exercise thrift, observe fasts and feasts, sleep near the elder women of the house, and when her husband returns receive him in her ordinary clothes so that he may be convinced of her parsimony, and greet him with gifts. The longing, the passion, and the grief of separation which the Hindi poets write of, Vātsyāyana does not mention.

5. A name for Kṛiṣṇa (*kumāra* son; so Nanda Kumāra son of Nanda i.e. Kṛiṣṇa).

6. The bosom friend is fed up with the attitude of the *nāyikā*. How can her

lover come back instantly from where he has gone? . . It is not possible—just as one cannot hope to obtain water immediately to put out a fire. It should be remembered that there were no pipes or hydrants in Keshava's days. In case of fire, water would have to be hand lifted from wells or tanks by buckets. Even today, except in a few big towns, in India fire brigades do not exist.

7. The parted *nāyikā* is afflicted by all joyous things, like the cry of the peacocks and the cuckoos, the scented breeze, the lotus flowers, and the moonlight. All these seem to set an edge to the grief of her separation. When the moonlit night came she could no longer stand it, and her sorrow at not having her lover to share it with her was so great that she could preserve her life only by repeating the holy name of her *guru*, or patron saint !

8. The lover, Kṛiṣṇa, is being edged on by one of the bosom companions to go to meet his beloved. At first he goes a step or two, and then, much to the annoyance of the messenger, begins to give all sorts of messages instead of proceeding himself. When he does proceed, his steps begin to fall backward instead of forward and sometimes he stands rooted to the ground for fear of what men might say. He cannot return the way he has come, and in his embarrassment begins to speed up so fast as if he would cover twenty miles in a day (A *kos* is two miles).

9. The lines are about night, and its effect on the separated *nāyaka*. Separation is felt all the more in the lonely night. The comparison to lepers is presumably to bring out the unpleasing aspect of the night of separation. It may also be because the dim moonlight is of the colour of a leper's body.

10. The meaning is rather vague. Vātsyāyana mentions five diversions viz (1) holding of festivals, (2) social gatherings of both sexes, (3) drinking parties, (4) picnics, (5) other diversions, and says that these should be indulged in occasionally by a citizen. As the pleasures are mentioned as seven, however, the reference could not be to this. More likely it is to the seven pleasures of lovemaking mentioned by Hindu erotic writers, viz. (1) embrace (2) kiss, (3) marking with the nails, (4) marking with the teeth, (5) stroking, (6) normal sexual intercourse, and (7) the reversed role.

11. A rival wife. Vātsyāyana advocates harmony between the first wife and the co-wife, and advises the former to look upon her as a sister, but in actual fact there was much rivalry between them, which indeed was natural, seeing that they were competitors for their husband's love.

12. These lines are addressed by the *nāyikā* to sleep, which comes only after trying many devices, just as the husband has to make many attempts before he can embrace his newly-wed bride. As it takes much scheming and persuasion to make a newly-wed bride come close to the bosom of her husband so it is after much effort that sleep comes to the parted *nāyikā*. She (sleep) departs from the sleepless *nāyikā* as a new bride would at the middle of the night from her husband's bed not listening to his entreaties for more lovemaking.

13. Sister of Lakshmī, the goddess of wealth. The reference to her fearing the lotus is not clear. Maybe it refers to the goddess Annapūrṇā or Apnapūrṇā (Latin *Anna Perenna*—the bestower of fruitful seasons) who is

described as of a ruddy complexion, wearing a multi-coloured robe, and having a crescent on her forehead. She gives subsistence, and is bent by the weight of her full breasts. All good is united in her. *Apna* (Sanskrit root *ap*) points to nourishment by water, while pūrṇa comes apparently from the same stem with the latin *pario*, to produce. Since the word *apna* implies nourishment by water, it may mean that the goddess feared the lotus as it was a rival in obtaining nourishment through water.

14. The goddess Durgā, the terrible form of Umā or Devī. She is represented with a black skin, a hideous and terrible countenance dripping with blood, encircled with snakes, and hung round with skulls and human heads. Being of such terrible mien, Kālī would hardly be the one to be interested in sweet *ketakī* flowers which are frail and sweetly scented.

15. See note 18, Chapter 10. A shrub yielding small white scented flowers.

16. The wife of Rāma. She was abducted by Rāvaṇa, the demon king of Laṅkā (Ceylon)and kept. in his palace garden where she was surrounded by demons. The meaning here seems to be that when she would see the face of some beautiful demon the remembrance of her husband, Rāma, would turn fresh and her heart again become inflamed with his love.

17. Duryodhana means literally 'hard to conquer', He was the eldest son of King Dhṛitarāṣtra, and leader of the Kaurava princes in their battle against the Pāṇḍavas in the great Mahābhārata war. Duryodhana hatched a number of schemes and plots against the Pāṇḍavas, and finally prevailed on his father to invite them to Hastināpur, in a gambling match, in which, with the help of his confederate Shakuni he won from Yudhiṣṭhira everything he possessed—his entire kingdom, and even his wife Draupadī. Duryodhana, exulting in his triumph, sent for Draupadī to act as a servant, and sweep the room. When she refused to come, his brother Duḥshāsana dragged her by the hair while Duryodhana insulted her by inviting her to sit upon his lap. When she was dragged and insulted, Draupadī called on Kṛiṣṇa to save her. The incident is related in the Mahābhārata. When after the gambling match, the pāṇḍavas and Draupadī were won over, Karṇa said that even the clothes they wore were now not their own and should be removed. Hearing this Duḥshāsana made ready to seize Draupadī's clothes. When she found in this sad plight she called on Kṛiṣṇa to protect her, and lo! as soon as her garments were pulled-off, fresh garments appeared for ever and ever without end ! Duḥshāsana pulled and pulled, but finally he got tired and sat down without being able to accomplish his foul work.

18. Daughter of Drupada king of Pāñchāla, and wife of the five Pāṇḍu princes all of whom married her at the same time, for they had made a vow to share all things in common. She was of dark complexion but very beautiful : 'as radiant and graceful as if she had descended from the city of gods.' We have a description of her in the Mahābhārata where Yudhiṣṭhira having lost everything in the dice game to Shakuni, finally stipulated to play with her as stake : 'Yudhiṣṭhira said,—"With Draupadī as stake, who is neither short nor tall, neither sparse nor corpulent, and who is possessed of blue locks, I will now play with thee! Possessed of eyes like the leaves of the autumn lotus and fragrant also as the autumn lotus, equal in beauty

unto Lakshmī, who delighteth in autumn lotuses, and unto Shrī herself in symmetry and every grace. Her face too, when coverd with sweat, looketh as the lotus or the jasmine. Of slender waist like the wasp, of long flowing locks, of red lips, and body without down, is the Princess of Pāñchāla. O! King, making the slender-waisted Draupadī, who is even such, as my stake, I will play with thee! O! son of Suvaha."

19. The constantly repetitive cries of birds and insects have a tentalising effect on the separated *nāyikā*. Speaking of a similar situation Vidyāpati says : The sparrow-hawk who calls out "pi pi" pains the heart of the parted *nāyikā* even more.' At another place the bosom friends of the *nāyikā* shout at the cuckoo and drive it away, for hearing its cry 'pi kahāṁ!" (Where is my love ! Where is my love)! the poor estranged *nāyikā* begins to faint.

Poet Ghanānanda's *nāyikā*, however, is assisted by the sparrow hawk's cry in her trial of separation, and its plaintive cry contains promise of reunion:

'The sparrow hawk cries out "pi, pi"
Vowing love for her.'

20. A prickly plant used in medicine. According to popular belief it is so tender that it withers even when dark clouds thunder loudly.

21. This verse is almost the same as the one in Keshava's *Rāmachandrikā* in which he describes the state of separation of Shrī Rāma in the forest, after Sitā's abduction. Shrī Hanūmānji (the monkey god) finding occasion relates the state of separation of Shrī Rāma. He says 'Like the lion, Rāma lives in big caves, and on beholding beds of saffron flowers he becomes as afraid as a wild elephant on seeing a lion. The light of the day is as distasteful to him as to an owl, and seeing the moon he is even more agitated than a *chakava* bird. On Hearing the voice of peacocks he hides himself in caverns as a snake would, and hearing the thunder of dark clouds he withers like the *jawāsā* plant. He wanders about restlessly in the forest as a black bee. In the night he keeps awake like a *yogī* and cannot sleep a wink, and thinking you to be his family goddess he keeps repeating your name.'

CHAPTER XII

Love's Messenger

For a woman who was confined to the inner apartments a female companion, or a confidante was invaluable inconveying messages to her lover, and in bringing back his messages to her. The importance of such an intermediary in love was acknowledged by Ovid who offers the following advice to the expectant lover : 'But first you must get to know the girl's maid : she will make things easier for you—provided that she is completely in her mistress's confidence, and can be trusted with the secret of your intrigue."*

The woman who thus acted as a go-between would naturally be one who was absolutely intimate with a girl in love, so that she could freely talk about her attachment and tell her everything which lay hid in her heart. The messenger would also have to be a woman with free ingress into different homes and families without exciting suspicion, and completely loyal and trustworthy. She would help the girl either because of her nearness and friendship or for money. Of the messengers of the former category viz., friends, Keshavadāsa mentions a woman neighbour, a dancer, a female recluse, and a faithful nurse. Most of the go-betweens, however, fall within the latter class, viz. those who did the work for gain. These are, a maid-servant, a barber's wife, a gardener's wife, a female bangle seller or betel seller, a goldsmith girl, a girl of mixed caste, or the clever wife of a worker in ornaments with silk and gold threads. These women were most probably professional go-betweens of the kind mentioned by Indian erotic writers like Vātsyāyana, employed by ordinary women. Those of the elite, like the daughters of princes, chieftains, and nobles, would depend more on their famale friends and women companions, a large number of whom surrounded them.

In this chapter Keshavadāsa merely narrates the messages of love which are conveyed by the go-betweens, the confidantes,

*** Ovid, The technique of love, Trans. Paul Turner (Panther : London 1968) P. 37**

and the lovers, conveying the good points of the one to the other. Of the actual acts done by them to bring the lovers together, he goes on to write in the next chapter.

The kinds of messengers[1]

A servant maid, or faithful nurse,
Says Keshavadāsa, or barber's spouse,
A dancer, or a woman neighbour,
A gardener's wife who roams about :
A female bangle or betel seller,
A goldsmith girl, or of mixed caste,
Woman recluse, or the wife clever
Of one who in ornaments works
With silk and gold threads—these I deem
The *nāyaka* and the *nāyikā's* bosom friends,
And when of mutual love they dream
The two use them to serve their ends.

The nurse's message to the *nāyikā*

The nurse says to the nāyikā :

'Why day and night do you sit so
With Mohan as if chess to play ?
Your mother if this comes to know,
Will keep you in your home all day.
Oh ! friends, when I counsel you thus,
Your brows you knit and look enraged :
Who in this world is not beloved,
And who is not with beauty graced ?
But you alone, I know not why
With vanity stretch to the sky !'

The nurse's message to the *nāyaka*

The nurse says to the nāyaka

'Today, dear boy ! converse with her
Tomorrow I will bring to you

Another lovely cowherd girl
Who will a passionate princess prove !
Younger will she be, with big eyes,
And tresses long, like Pārvatī[2]
Majestic, fair-skinned, artless, like
Sister-in-law of Shaṅkarajī :[3]
A girl whose limbs were as if cast
Within a mould, and scented limbs,
With nectar filled, who seems as dropped
From heaven; or from sea arisen.'

The maid-servant's words about the *nāyaka*

The maid says to the nāyikā :

'The dark dense cloud cannot attain
The splendour of my Ghanashyāma[4] bright,
His radiance which does ever change,
Seeing which the mind is much surprised.
In Him all scented things remain,
Laugh and make merry so that flies
All your affliction—nothing deign
The dawn's glow to his beauty I :
Before him honey's sweetness wanes
And nectar is naught in his sight !
What pleasure can you hope to gain
By gazing shyly with your eyes
Towards him, if you give him not
My love, a place within your heart ?'

The maid-servant's words to the Nāyaka about the *nāyikā*

Seeing the fault of the nāyaka the maid-servant says to him :

'Such words as you bid me to speak
I cannot to that girl convey,
Who is much bashful; when she meets
Me, she complains ! "Oh : friend mine, say
Why comes he not to me, but goes

To see my maid, alone ? the kind
Of women O'er whom he has hold
By grovelling at their feet, as mine
Slave's slaves are !'' You remain indeed
Nandajī's son, on whom he so fawns
But how can I forget that she
Too is the daughter of Vṛiṣabhānu !'[5]

The words of the barber's wife about the *nāyaka*

The barber's wife says to the nāyikā :

'The city he has yet left not,
And still to speak to him you run
By waking night and day if aught
Should happen to another's son,[6]
What will you do ? If you can't live
Alone, and only when he's nigh
Find joy, then as your mirror is
Keep him always before your eyes !'

The words of the barber's wife about the *nāyikā*

The barber's wife says to the nāyaka :

'Much pleasure gave she when she gazed
So charmingly with her big eyes,
High ideals she has, and good taste,
Somehow to meet her you should try
Much bashfulness lies in her heart,
To bosom friends respects she pays,
To elder women speaks with awe,
Thus worthy she herself has made.'

The words of the female dancer about the *nāyikā*

The female dancer says to the nāyikā :

'I went to show, but you did hold
My neck ! why so you wish today

To see him ? By and by I'll show
Shrī Kṛiṣṇa to you; but dear friend, say
Why thus indifferent you remain
Before him, when sad you become
On seeing him not? It is so strange,
This mood of yours ! In the night one
Is your condition; but at day,
Another : Oh ! my bosom friend !
Tell me what should be done, I pray !'

The words of the female dancer to the *nāyaka*

The female dancer says to the nāyaka :

'Whenever that *nāyikā* tries to hide
Herself, she glimmers as moonlight,
How should I hide her ? When she moves,
With her move black bees : and so too
Her bosom friends, who always try
To be with her : they follow like
The female black bee does her mate :
So how can you, friend, meet her, say,
As you're resolved ? How should I bring
You to her ? Dost a bird me think ?
The splendour of her body was
Painful before, and my friend, now
The fragrance of that lady's limbs,
Like poison wholly to me seems !'

The woman neighbour's words about the *nāyaka*

The woman neighbour says to the nāyikā :

'When he fell humbly on your feet
You let him touch your bed, engaged
Yourself thus, in lovemaking sweet,
And his love sought to estimate.
When he made you take oaths you turned
Your face to him, as now you be !

And feigning innocence you have come
Early this morn to pester me
To take you to him ! In the night
When him you offer betels, friend;
Then to your lover, tell me why,
You in the day are insolent?'

The woman neighbour's words to the *nāyikā*

The woman neighbour says to the nāyaka :

'Laughing some words I spoke in fun,
And she too jestingly did speak—
'Twas your gain : she did not become
Yours, just because your eyes did meet !
Such meeting is not meeting friend,
The *chātak*[7] may shout, and die too,
Or quiet remain, but the clouds send
The *svāti* raindrop when 'tis due[8]
How can that maid today be brought
To meet you here, though you may yearn,
When her own courtyard she sees not[9]
E'en when with passion's fire burns !'

The words of the gardener's wife about the *nāyikā*

The gardener's wife says to the nāyıkā :

'How will the glow your youth has known
Be hid by clothes and ornaments,
When by your body's light alone
To bright day is the dark night turned ?
How 'twill be if your perfume joins
That of your husband, when black bees[10]
By your own scent drawn, swarm around ?
So think I when your face I see :
Oh ! moon-faced ! with greed you're possessed,
Shrī Kṛiṣṇa to see; how will you then

Walk with the burden of your breasts,[11]
Your hair's weight if your waist does bend ?'

The words of the gardener's wife about the *nāyaka*

The gardener's wife says to the nāyaka :

'Oh ! Ghanaśyāma,[12] do not bar my way
Let me go home; just now you will,
A moment hence, behold that maid
Clasped to your bosom—she who is
As lightning ! Common if she was,
Without much ado she'd have come
But of gait graceful, is she not
Vṛiṣabhānu's daughter ? See, the sun
Is setting now, on you I die !
Repair you to the forest—she
Is coming fully decked, and night
Comes too ! This passion's hold to flee
Do you in this cool arbour roam,
And she afeared of the black bee
Has taken shelter in her home ?'

The words of the female betel-leaf seller about the *nāyikā*

The female betel-leaf seller says to the nāyikā :

'Soft even as wax, friend, is your heart,
Tender as lotus stem it stays,
The sound of your melodious voice
At once the mind does captivate.
As pomegranate seeds your teeth,
And like young sprouts your red lips are,
With joy fill they whom your eyes meet !
For your goodness I have regard,
O ! friend ! Yet with fear question I,
From tongue as butter soft, and mouth
Which is as lotus dainty, why
Words hard as a log of wood come out ?'

The words of the female betel-leaf seller about the *nāyaka*

The female betel-leaf seller says to the nāyaka

'Oh ! lower your eyes, for they behave
Improperly, as all men know,
And you conceive, too, in a way :
Your fickle nature first would throw
A spell upon the heart, and steal
It : and then would its help desire !
In some heart you would entrance seek
In someone's breasts entangled are !
How can she live, if you in love
Thus are attached? Would it be so
The hearts and minds of belles of Braja
Secretly you'd sell to Kāmadeva !'

The words of the female artist to the *nāyikā*

The female artist says to the nāyikā :

'To call him back you're eager, though
The city's limit he has not left,
It seems you are in Kṛiṣṇa's control
More than he in yours : if bereft
Of him your eyes do quiver so
In pain, as fish of water drained,
Why for a moment let him go ?
Keep holding him as picture framed !'

The words of the female artist to the *nāyaka*

The female artist says to the nāyaka

'You're like a stubborn stallion, strong,
who restive is, when to peg tied;
No other place know, right or wrong
By coaxing move not, but when strikes
A whip unseen! Within your mind
O! Kṛiṣṇa, a million times revolve

What I tell you, and be advised
By your well-wishers: You go forth
Charmed by her body, but this know—
Love is not love which does reside
In outward form, but hid does flow,
From heart to heart, from eye to eye.'

The words of the female bangle seller to the *nāyikā*:

The female bangle seller says to the nāyikā;

'If your soul and her's have not met,
What happiness will you derive
By meeting thus? Meet him yourself,
Or ask some woman to describe
Such meeting's joy. If he now strays
Into your eyebrows, how long then
Will you there bind him, tell me pray?
I die on you! Shrī Kṛiṣṇa, O! friend,
With garland of flowers you should tie,
If you away turn from him thus,
Your passion's fury will not die!
Beat it to death with lotuses!
How long will you so laugh always,
And with your eyes your love explain?
Now with your tongue that message say
Which in your heart so long has lain!

The words of the female bangle seller to the *nāyaka*

The female bangle seller says to the nāyaka

'Why give her sorrow—she who means
Much to you—for whom sad you keep,
Oh! Kṛiṣṇa! without whom nothing seems
Good to you? Do what her will please.
Blest are you that she loves you so,
What will you get by making fun
Of her? If anger in her grows,

Or else offended she becomes,
You should make haste her to appease,
And beg forgiveness of her: think!
If a glass of milk hot should be
Would you not cool it, ere you drink?'

The words of the goldsmith's wife about the *nāyikā*

The goldsmith's wife says to the nāyikā:

'Restless your eyes are, and your gaze
Sidelong, does charm; oh! tell me why
When first to love you shelter gave,
Away you turn now? Sweet! your eyes
Are sharp, and big, and lovely; they
Are pleasing to the mind, and full
Of love, and greatly piercing, pray
What wonder, if Shrī Kṛiṣṇa they should
Have in an instant made their slave!
Your lovely eyes, friend, are the home
Of splendour, excitement, and shame!
On whom they fall, his calm does go,
And troubled does his heart remain!'

The words of the goldsmith's wife about the *nāyaka*

The goldsmith's wife says to the nāyaka

'Now when she laughs she slowly bows,
And by her glances steals the soul,
Her heart with love inflamed is now,
And in her mind clearly unfolds
The mystery of love strange, so she
Knows it, and does to others tell!
Till midnight she did wake with me,
So long you've waited, oh! Giridhara[13],
Be patient now, the time is near:
Who is more blest than you? for much
Since yesterday she lends her ears
When I do talk to her of love!

The words of the woman of mixed caste about the *nāyikā*

The woman of mixed caste says to the nāyikā:

'My Kṛiṣṇa, friend, is of mind serene
And tender, but your eyes, my sweet!
Though pure, ardent and restless seem,
As dirty young blue lotus leaf.
And straight his nature is, but used
To crooked deeds your eyes, and bold,
Savage, and cunning! and when you
Catch them, they will not be controlled!
They take more airs than you, my friend!
Why don't you stop them ? This I've said
So often to you ? Yet e'en then
My Kṛiṣṇa your flirting eyes caress!'

The words of the woman of mixed caste about the *nāyaka*

The woman of mixed caste says to the nāyaka

'Howe'er yourself you satisfy
By making love to lustful maids
By millions; without Rādhā's eyes
Beholding, 'twill no joy create.
If powdered chalk you do apply
Instead of camphor to your face,
No coolness nor perfume will rise
From it, and 'twill not give you grace.
Thus only will your greed survive
Oh ! darling of Braja ! thus you may
Be discontent; for can thirst die
By licking of dew only, pray ?'

The words of the female recluse about the *nāyikā*

The female recluse says to the nāyikā :

'Oh ! bosom friend when someone falls
In love with you what will I do ?

Will that love then leave you at all,
E'en though you try? Your hunger too
And thirst, will of a sudden fly,
And song and dance forgotten be !
Your mind all work will leave aside,
Nought good around you will you see :
And nights and days will sleepless turn,
And fire such in your heart be lit
As in the heat the more will burn !
And when already cool it is
A thousand times more cool you make !
Therefore I humbly beg of you
With my end-cloth spread, for your sake,
Your insolence you should eschew.'

The words of the female recluse about the *nāyaka*

The female recluse says to the nāyaka

'In your heart frigid she remains
Not; nor you in her fervent heart
E'en for a while, then why exchange
Yours for hers ? Still no care at all
She has for you, though ever dwells
On her your mind, so that departs
Your hunger, and all joys as well !
Oh ! handsome boy ! with saffron were
You always beautifying her face,
And did not leave off so to do
A moment, even by mistake !
Oh ! how was it that even you,
O ! Kṛṣṇa, within the sway did come
Of the eyes of a rustic maid ?'

The words of the worker of ornaments in silk and gold threads about the *nāyikā*

The worker of ornaments in silk and gold threads who has come to fetch the nāyikā says to her :

'Is it for this that I did cause
O ! mistress, that fop, Kṛiṣṇa, to meet

You ? having won him with sweet talk
Past prying eyes, and each to each
Brought you together ? First your eyes
Did meet, and now he pines to speak :
Make haste that I my mission might
Accomplish, and depart.' When she
These words did hear, that *nāyikā* who
Did fretting sit, said : 'When defiled
Mind was with speech alone what you
Will gain now if our minds unite ?'

The words of the worker of ornaments in silks and gold threads about the *nāyaka*

The worker of ornaments in silk and gold threads says to the nāyikā:

'None can be like that fawn-eyed[14] maid
Whom to befriend you did come near,
Dissemble not, and your hand stay
From brass, though it like gold appears !
Though *Sarasvatī* should instruct,
Herself, crows can't like cuckoo's sing !
Can he who likes the mango much
Be satisfied with tamarind ?'[15]

Concluding verse

Says Keshavadāsa, I have described
Attributes like talks, and the like
Of bosom friends; now I'll go on
To speak of acts which they perform.

NOTES

1. *Sakhī* literally means a near friend or confidante. The intimate friend (bosom friend) of a young girl helped her in her love affairs. In this role he was a sort of go-between, though not in the bad sense of a procuress. In old India where women lived a comparatively secluded life and could not publicly meet their friends and lovers, the services of a trusted female friend were invaluable. She carried messages from the girl to her lover, helped

her to meet him, and made the course of their love smooth. Kalyāṇa Malla gives a list of such women who were adept as messengers of love. These are a gardener's wife, a personal friend, a widow, a nurse, a dancing girl, a woman engaged in manual or technical work, a maid-servant, a social woman who moved from house to house, a woman with whom one could be free, a young girl under sixteen (because one would hardly suspect her), a tailoress, a woman ascetic, a cowherd girl who sold mik and curd, and an old woman.

In *Kāma Sūtra*, Vātsyāyana groups the different varieties of friends as follows: a childhood companion, a fellow student, one bound by an obligation, one of the same disposition and fond of similar things, those whose secrets and faults are mutually known to each other , a child of one's nurse, those brought up together and those, who are hereditary friends. Also Chārāyaṇa says that citizens form friendships with washermen, barbers, cowherds, florists, druggists, betel-leaf sellers, tavern-keepers, beggars and the like, and with the wives of these people.

Vātsyāyana also commends especially a female astrologer, a female beggar, and a female artist, for gaining another woman's confidence, and says, 'the man who is clever and wise, who has the assistance of a friend, and who knows the intention of others, as also the proper time and place for doing things, can gain over with ease a woman very difficult to obtain.'

2. Wife of Shiva. and daughter of Himavat (the Himālaya mountain). Also known as Umā, Gaurī, and so on. She was famed for her faithfulness and beauty.

3. Shaṅkara is Shiva, the Destroyer, and one of the gods in the Hindu triad. He married Umā (Pārvatī) who was one of the daughters of Daksha. Since Daksa had as many as forty or fifty daughters it is difficult to say which one is meant here. Most probably it is Satī, who also married Shiva before Pārvatī. She is said to have killed herself because of a quarrel between her father, Daksha, and her husband Shiva. She is also famed for her faithfulness and beauty.

4. One of the many names of Kṛiṣṇa, others being Nandalāl, Giridhara, Gopāla, etc.

5. The *nāyaka*, Kṛiṣṇa, asks his maid servant to convey something vulgar to Rādhā. The maid-servant protests, and tells him,'That girl Rādhā is very bashful, how can I convey such unrefined words to her. Only the other day she was complaining to me, "Your master, Kṛiṣṇa, does not come to me but goes instead to my maid. Indeed the kind of women he favours and whom he beseeches even by falling on their feet, are so low that they are not fit to be even the slaves of my slave. It may be that you are the dear son of Nanda, but how can I ever forget that Rādhā, being daughter of the influential Vṛiṣabhānu, is no less than you are?'

6. This may mean (1) 'If the *nāyaka* has to keep awake day and night—in the day because of his work, and in the night worrying about you (the woebegone *nāyikā* whom he has left behind)—and god forbid, falls ill or dies, then what will you do?' or (2) If you (the *nāyikā*) worry so much yourself and if something should thereby happen to you, what a great misfortune would be to your departed lover'. The more likely interpretation is the former one

7. The Indian cuckoo which drinks only rain-water and pines specially for the *svāti* raindro p.

8. *Svāti* is the name given to the fifteenth lunar mansion in the path of the moon. It is for the rain drop, which falls at this particular time only that the *chātak* pines. But he may shout himself hoarse, or even die, the raindrop of *Svāti* will fall only at the fixed time. So too, the girl's love can be obtained by the *nāyaka* only when it is ripe, not before.

9. The woman neighbour says: 'The maiden is so shy that she cannot even cross her own courtyard for fear of being found out, even though passion's flames devour her; then how did you expect me to bring her all the way here to you?'

10. In one of Bihārī's verses also, black bees are attracted to the *nāyikā's* perfumed body.

'The black bees round her gathered, by the scent
Sweet of her body drawn.'

In Bāṇa's *Harṣacharita* black bees settle on Mālatī's face:
'A thick swarm of bees settling eagerly upon her eyes beautiful as a pair of blue lotuses, half hid her face which thus appeared as if it was covered with a dark blue silk veil.'

11. Praising the heaviness of women's breasts, Bhartṛihari says, 'Breasts should be so full that they make a woman bend with their weight'. When the courtesan Urvashī moved, we are told, 'Her breasts scented with heavenly salve dark-nippled, rubbed with heaven's sandal-wood, and shining from her necklace, were shaken up and down, and so heavy were they that through the upborne-burden of them, and the sharp movements of them, she was bowed down at every step.'

12. Kṛiṣṇa (See note 4 of this Chapter).

13. See note 4 of this Chapter.

14 Women's eyes were compared to those of a fawn or a ntelope both by Sanskrit and Persian writers. Describing the eyes of the Yaksha bride, Kālidāsa says they were as the gentle eyes of a timid fawn. Bhartṛihari speaks of his fawn-eyed-darling.

15. The mango is king of the fruits with a delicious sweet taste. The tamarind is a common fruit, sour and acid, and of unpleasant taste. So one who has taken a liking for the sweet mango can never be satisfied with sour tamarind.

Chapter XIII

The Act of Bosom Friends

This chapter completes what the other had left unsaid. We have been told about the messages which go-betweens convey from the lover to his beloved, and vice versa in the last chapter, and in this one Keshavadāsa tells us what they do to bring the lovers together. The most appropriate go-between is the near and trustworthy friend of the woman, whom Hindi poets call sakhī (bosom companion), and the devices described in this chapter are the ones employed by her. The acts done by the bosom companion to further the cause of lovers are to instruct, entreat, adorn, stoop and chide. By these means she persuades the lover and his beloved to be inclined towards each other, and brings the affair to a successful conclusion. In doing so the bosom friend has to encounter many obstacles, most of them of the lovers' own making, as for example, bashfulness, ignorance, obduracy, arrogance, deceit, and frigidity, on the part of the woman, and hesitancy, lack of zeal, and infidelity on the part of the lover. These impediments the bosom companion removes by the means mentioned above. She instructs the woman when she finds her ignorant in the ways of love, causes her to leave shyness, overcomes her arrogance and harshness by sweet words, inflames her with passion when she finds her frigid, and reproves her when she encounters deceit. In like manner she encourages the lover by urging him on when he is hesitant and lacking in zeal, and by censuring him when she finds him to be false to his beloved. In the course of the performance of these intimate duties sometimes the bosom friend herself gets involved with the *nāyaka* and then the position becomes complicated and instead of pressing her friend's love-suit she begins to plead her own. Despite this, however, she is more sincere than the other go-betweens whom we had encountered in the previous chapters, viz. the maid-servant, the nurse, the wives of the gardener and the barber, and the betel-leaf seller, and when the others deceive the *nāyikā* by trying to win over the *nāyaka* for themselves she alone remains faithful. Without the bosom friend many a girl would stay deprived of the pleasures of love, and many a lover remains thwarted in his amorous advance. The incentive of the bosom companion is his friendship and a desire to oblige, and not financial gain, as for other go-betweens. It is perhaps for this reason that she proves herself to be a better and more reliable intermediary than the others.

After having narrated the ways used by bosom companions in uniting lovers, Keshavadāsa goes on, in the next chapter, to describe the various emotions and their qualities.

The acts done by bosom friends[1]

To instruct, entreat, unite, adorn,
To stoop, and chide—these are the acts
Which bosom friends for lovers perform.

Instruction to the *nāyikā*

Giving instruction to the nāyikā, her bosom companion says :

'If love you to your lover show
Your co-wife[2] will with sorrow burn,
And if you firmly stick to "no",
To your own body pain will come !
This "no" may please you for a while,
Your lover will you ever please,
Oh ! bosom friend, no good there lies
In "no" ; but good lies, friend, indeed
In loving your beloved : may
I die on you, if you will thus
Not love him, and "no" always say
How long will you maintain your love ?'

Instruction to the *nāyaka*

Instructing the nāyaka the bosom companion says :

'Having smeared her limbs with sandal-paste,
And bathed her with saffroned water

With perfumed things having her arrayed,
For making love have you brought her ?
Put sandal-marks on her, and laid
Flower garland her neck to adorn,
And beautified her in all ways
All to no end ? Her eyes how come
You have dark with collyrium made ?
Why betel-leaves you have begun
To give with camphor scented, say ?
Oh ! Kṛiṣṇa ! your mind in merriment
Remains absorbed, why don't you lay
Yourself upon her feet, that won
With fawning she's whose mouth always
Imbued with fragrance, sweet becomes ?'

Entreating the *nāyikā*

The bosom companion says to Rādhā:

'How long will I, oh! bosom friend,
Thus tolerate your arrogance
And quiet remain? How can this task
Be done, if friend, I meet him not ?
A million schemes though you may plan
The joy to meet him ne'er you can
Obtain till then: in the mirror see
Your limbs, in what a state they be!
How long will you in secret meet
Your lover thus, tell me, my sweet?'

Entreating the *nāyaka*

Entreating Kṛiṣṇa the bosom companion says:

'Brahmā[3] as lotus flowers has made
Her eyes; her jewelled teeth to wit,
Are as seeds of pomegranate,
And as the *bimba* fruit[4] her red lips.
Her laughter rich, he did create

As nectar; as Triveṇī[5] flows
He did that woman's tresses braid—
That maiden with a voice mellow
As cuckoo's—as a hair her waist!
Her breasts delicious he did form
As twin fruit of the wishing tree[6]!
And poor Brahmā did then become
Enamoured of her! ne'er did see
You, oh! Gopāla, my bosom friend's
Whole body; as the hue of gold
Is that fair woman, and a scent
Pleasing and sweet from her does flow.'

Appeasement of the *nāyikā*

The bosom companion says to Rādhā:

'You please him, and yourself please you,
And from the casement your glance cast[7]
On him, and show him your face too,
And when you're called you silent are,
Which I like not: O! I have amused
Many as you, now needlessly
Me you amuse, O! woman deceitful!
Saying "no" to me, and "yes" to your Kṛiṣṇa!'

Appeasement of the *nāyaka*

Entreating Kṛiṣṇa the bosom companion says:

'With flowers and ornaments you decked
Her, and, oh! Kṛiṣṇa, thus did increase
Her good fortune and happiness;
Advanced your suit, and loved her deep
Within your heart, and clasped her feet!
Sweet smelling things to her applied,
And forcing on her betel-leaves,
Kept her awake many a night!
Oh! Kṛiṣṇa, I pray you, now arise!

Why sit you yet, when you should go?
Stealing another's heart, now why
Do you still your displeasure show?[8]

Another example of the appeasement of the *nāyikā*

The bosom companion says to Rādhā:

'When I about his faults do speak,
His virtues you start to describe,
Your love adroitly you conceal
As in a moment lightning hides
Amidst dark clouds; Oh! how can you
In her house stay on dreadful nights
Of *Bhādoṁ*,[9] when within the woods
Your lover keeps? You make me rise
When I sit, and then you create
A scene; dear friend, I wonder why
You do not trust me so, to say
What buried in your mind does lie.'

Meeting of Kṛiṣṇa

The bosom companion says to Kṛiṣṇa

'Of counselling her friends wearied were,
Dark clouds of frightening her were tired,
The lightning weary to lay bare
The midnight path; love wearied was
To stoop before her: Passion so
Of striking her; the Three Winds[10] stayed
Weary of blowing her to and fro!
Unfeeling god! why did you make
Her mind such that her body's fire
She will seek no wise to allay?
I have oft tried, and now I tire,
But my advice she will not take.
The cuckoo tired of singing is,
The *chātak*[11] too is wearied out:

But all in vain, for nothing will
Make that cold maiden turn about.'

The *nāyikā's* adornment

The bosom companion says:

'I cleaned her feet with pumice stone,[12]
And with red dye I did them deck,
And then her lovely eyes adorned
With collyrium: around her neck
A garland placed; ornaments on
Her body: now the glass she holds
Wherein her beauty she does gaze:
Who will now, as the *nāyaka* throw
A sidelong glance on her, and take
Her gently in his lap; and out
Of deep affection, fondly place
A betel in her quivering mouth?'

The *nāyaka's* adornment

The bosom companion says to Kṛiṣṇa:

'A lovely turban you have worn,
And jacket: and around your waist
A pleasing scarf; with scent adorned
Yourself, and on your breasts displayed
A garland fair; and your mouth, Kṛiṣṇa,
By betel pleasing you have made!
But oh! Gopāla! dull are, I think,
All your adornments, till that belle
Rādhā, your loved one, of sweet face,
The *ṭikā*[13] mark on your forehead
By her own fair hands does not place!'

The *nāyikā's* stooping

The bosom companion says to Rādhā:

'Again and again the mind I turned
Of Kṛiṣṇa towards you; and when he
Did favour show, it seemed returned
The hour of your good fortune, sweet!
And that same lover whose feet you once
Did often clasp, fell on your feet!
So I have for your sake begun
His feet to touch too. What did speak
The proud new brides[14] I brushed aside,
And sang your praises: that you'd feel
Obliged I knew full well, but why
Should I now that vain lad entreat,
When, as before he made you sigh,
Now, oh! so cruelly, he makes me![15]

The *nāyaka's* stooping

The bosom companion says to the nayikā:

'How can that god influenced be
Who bracken with beauty together did bind,
And on the ugly *tendū* tree[16]
The *Kāmalatā* creeper[17] entwined?
Who on the serpent's head did place
A shining jewel?[18] Oh! such a god
Possesses that abiding state
Which cannot, friend, be e'er destroyed!
First in the mirror see your face
Then say what the truth is; I for one
Of all wed maids will offering make
On Rādhā, daughter of Vriṣabhānu.'

The bosom companion's complaint against the *nāyikā*

The bosom companion says to the nāyikā:

'How great your beauty you esteem
And your birth, that in anger steeped

Your mind e'er is! nor do you deem
Your equal anyone; but keep
Encircling in the sky upon
Pride's chariot! thus do not behave,
With insolence; subdue this storm
Of vanity, and captivate
Him with your glance, for his heart, prized
As diamond, he with pleasure yields—
And oh! you girl, antelope-eyed,
With tender words unto him speak!'

The bosom friend's complaint against the *nāyaka*

The bosom companion says to Kṛiṣṇa;

'To take an oath you are not tied,
Nor of a go-between have fear
But from the corner of your eyes
The betel juice wipe off, my dear!
Somewhat there lingers in my mind
The memory of those days when you
Did butter steal;[19] if now you find
Me to be innocent, it would prove
My folly, what else can I say?
Oh! Kṛiṣṇa! ashamed you did not feel
To go unasked thus to her place!
Your falsehood is so great indeed
That her you have offended, though
The dust you from her feet did take
Has yet till now not blown away!'

The desperate *Nāyikā*

Rādhā says to her bosom companion :

The maid-servant is as midnight
Elusive, the nurse as blaze dwells,
With grief's fire are the slaves alight!
Pierced with the nāyaka's love themselves
Are the gardener's and barber's wives,

And betel-leaf seller—oh! my friend
You only are my hope! unite[20]
Me with Shri Kṛiṣṇa, or I will end
My life, and you' ll see me no more!
My heart's secret to you I've told.'

Concluding verse

So of such kinds all beings say,
Is the enjoyment of the love of Kṛiṣṇa
Which men of the four castes[21] and stages[22]
With pleasure do recount and listen.
Of Rādhā and Rādhāramaṇa[23]
Adornments I have thus described,
I go on now tell of some
Sentiments, and their qualities.

NOTES

1. Vātsyāyana classifies go-betweens-or messengers of love into different types according to the different kinds of work they are called upon to perform. According to him they fall into eight types—(a) who performs the entire job, (b) who does only part of it, (c) who bears letters only, (d) who acts on her own account and gets involved with the lover herself, (e) who acts for an innocent young woman, (f) a wife who serves as go-between, (g) a mute go-between and (h) who carries a message of double meaning.

2. A rival wife. Apparently polygamy was allowed and was prevalent in those days. At the moment the trend is towards monogamy, and according to a prevailing government regulation no government servant can have more than one wife living. (See also note 11, Chapter 11).

3. The first member of the Hindu triad, the Creator, (See note 2 Chapter3).

4. *Bimba* is a perennial climber with tendrils and fibrous roots, producing white flowers during the rainy season. The fruit is elongated and hard like a small gourd, and turns scarlet when ripe, hence the comparison to a woman's lips.

Hindi and Sanskrit writers often compare a woman's lips to the ripe *bimba* fruit. In Mayūra'a *Shriṅgāra Aṣṭaka* there is the following description of a lovely damsel:

'Who is this beauty, her face shining like the full moon
Advancing along the path in the full bloom of youth,
Drunk with love-and sleep her eyes rolling, her lips full
and red, like ripe *bimba* fruit.

In *The Adventure of the Ten Princes* of Daṇḍin, Rānī Vasumatī has lips like *bimba* fruit : 'The new leaves of the tree which torture travellers away from home with the memory of the lips of their beloveds, went into the making of her lips red as the *bimba* fruit.' Describing Rādhā's lips in *Gīta Govinda*, Poet Jayadeva says:

'Your lips like a *bimba* fruit, but infatuates further
And your bosom so chaste, how it ravages playing with my life.
These are with her the pleasures of being intimate;
The charms vibrant and moist of her eyes and the scent of her lotus mouth
The ambiguous sweet nectar-dripping of her words and the sweetness of her *bimba* lips.'

(Trans. Keyt)

In the *Bhāgavata Purāṇa*, when the *gopīs* (cowherd girls) are unable to find Kṛiṣṇa, 'their faces, with lips red and luscious like *bimba* fruits were downcast'.

In *Kathā Sarit Sāgara*, Upakoṣṭā's lover says: 'Then my heart was cleft by the stroke of love's arrow, and I could not sleep that night through my desire to kiss her *bimba* lips.'

Finally, Draupadī who was considered to be a paragon of beauty, had lips red as the *bimba* fruit.

5. The place where the Rivers Gaṅgā and Yamunā meet (See note 2, Chapter 4).

6. The *Kalpa vṛikṣa*— A mythical tree which has the merit of fulfilling all desires.

7. In Keshava's time women were still not free to mix in society, and kept mostly to the *zenānā*, or inner-quarters meant for them. These sometimes had windows which overlooked the men's quarters and the lovelorn maiden could occasionally come upto basement-window and steal a hurried glance at her beloved. So does Bihārī's *nāyikā* look on her lover throwing on him a quick glance:

'Timidly her face veiling,
That moon-faced lady swiftly peeped
Through the casement-window, and then withdrew
Suddenly, like a tongue of lived flame.'

8. Obviously the lovers have had a quarrel, and Kṛiṣṇa is reviling his beloved Rādhā. The bosom companion entreats him to go away and stop displeasing one whom he loved so fondly.

9. The sixth month of the Hindu year corresponding to August/September. It is the month of heaviest rainfall, hence the nights are dreadful with dense clouds, streaks of lightning and rain.

10. These are the three winds, *shītala* (cool), *manda* (gentle), and *sugandha* (perfumed).

11. A kind of Indian cuckoo.

12. Pumice-stone was used for scrubbing dirty feet clean. It is still used by some Indian women for this purpose.

13. An auspicious mark placed on the forehead both by Hindu men and

women. For women it serves as an adornment, and the mark is red or vermillion, of small size, round, or vertically elongated. Men wear different kinds of *ṭikā* marks, mainly sacerdotal, varying with the cult to which they belong. *Shaivites*, or the followers of Shiva, wear the mark horizontally placed across the forehead, while the followers of Viṣṇu, *Vaiṣṇavites*, have it placed vertically in the centre of the forehead. These marks are usually of sandal-wood paste.

14. The co-wives or the rival wives. Vātsyāyana lays down meticulous codes of conduct for the wife towards her co-wives. When a new bride comes she should look on her as a younger sister and give her a position superior to her own. She should give her good advice and cherish her and not mind the favours her husband may lavish on her. The younger wife should regard the elder one as a mother and should not approach her husband without her permission. While giving this advice to maintain harmony, however, Vātsyāyana also gives detailed instructions on how the elder wife should instigate the others to join her in a concerted move to oust the favourite wife and to remove her from her husband's favour. In practice the co-wives did not get along well and they were always jealous of each other.

15. The go-between in this case is of the kind acting on her own account..., mentioned by Vātsyāyana in *Kāma Sūtra*. She is described as follows:

'A woman who goes herself to a man, and tells him of her having enjoyed sexual union with him in a dream, and expresses her anger at his wife having rebuked him for calling her by the name of her rival instead of by her own name, and gives him something bearing the marks of her teeth and nails, and informs him that she knew she was formerly desired by him, and asks him privately whether she or his wife is the better looking, such a person is called a woman who is a go-between for herself. Now such a woman should be met and interviewed by the man in private and secretly.

The above name is also given to a woman who having made an agreement with some other woman to act as her go-between, gains over the man to herself by the means of making him personally acquainted with herself, and thus causes the other woman to fail. The same applies to a man who, acting as a go-between for another and having no previous connection with the woman, gains her over for himself, and thus causes the failure of the other man.

16. A tree of average size like ebony, not particularly good or symmetrical, hence rough and ugly to look at.

17. An ornamental climbing plant which has shapely and good looking leaves. It generally climbs on a tree like the *tendū*.

18. According to popular superstition the king cobra's head bears a bright jewel which shines out in the night.

19. Kriṣṇa loved butter, milk, and curd, very much; so much indeed that he did not mind stealing it, sometimes forcibly, from a cowherd maiden. He earned quite a bad name in *Gokul* for it, and because of this was often called *mākhanchora*. i. e. 'thief of butter'. (mākhan—butter; chor—thief)

20. All her helpers and friends have deceived Rādhā. The elusive maidservant cannot be seen, just as one cannot see midnight, (being fast asleep).

The nurse of Rādhā is a conflagration of love herself, what heed can she give her mistress. The bodies of the slaves are full of sorrows. The gardener's wife, and that of the barber and the betel-leaf seller, instead of conveying Rādhā's love to the *nāyaka* have become infatuated with him themselves. Rādhā's bosom friend alone is faithful to her, and it is her whom she begs to somehow unite her with her lover Kṛiṣṇa.

21. There are four classes amongst Hindus as mentioned in Manu's code.

(i) *Brahmin*— the learned or priestly class whose duty it is to study the *Vedas*, and to perform sacrifices and religious ceremonies.

(ii) *Kshatriya*—the kingly or warrior class.

(iii) *Vaishya*—those engaged in trade and agriculture.

(iv) *Shūdra*—the servant class.

In the *Bhagavad Gītā* the Lord says: 'The four orders of society (i e. the *Brahmin*, *Kshatriya*, *Vaishya* and *Shūdra*) were created by me, classifying them according to their proclivities and assigning suitable duties to them; but I the author of this Creation am immortal and a non-doer.

22. The *Upanishads* divide the entire life of a man into four stages or *āshramas*. These are (1) student life, or *brahmacharya*, in which the youth leaves his home and lives with a preceptor till his education is over, (ii) the life of the householder or *gṛihastha*, in which the student having completed his education, marries, has children and lives a family life, (iii) the life of retirement from the world and preparation for the other one, the *vānaprastha* stage. This begins when, in old age, being absolved of family duties the man prepares for final enlightenment and release from worldly life. This is the stage of austere discipline and penance, a life of tranquillity and desirelessness, and (iv) the stage of *sannyāsa*, or renouncement, in which the man becomes a sort of wandering mendicant or ascetic, not bound by worldly rules of conduct.

23. Rādhāramaṇa is a name for Kṛiṣṇa. Ramaṇa means a 'husband' or 'lover'. So Rādhāramaṇa means the husband or lover of Rādhā, i.e. Kṛiṣṇa.

Chapter XIV

Laughter, and Other Sentiments

In this chapter Keshavadāsa describes the nature of laughter and its various types. Where delight is produced by means of the eyes and speech there laughter is born. There are four kinds of laughter—feeble, sweet, violent, and loud. Feeble laughter arises when the eyes, lips, cheeks, and teeth blossom out somewhat. This is the mildest kind of laughter which is almost a smile. The lips open only a little and disclose the glimmer of bright teeth, the cheeks sparkle with joy, the eyes are bewitching and restless, and the eyebrows are a little aslant. Such mild laughter comes to the nāyikā's lips when she is exchanging pleasantries with her lover in a chance encounter, or is filled with bashfulness while listening to a love tale. Where on hearing some melodious sound the mind and body is captivated by tender and winning coquetry, this is called sweet laughter. This also arises during the course of courtship when the nāyaka entreats the nāyikā in order to obtain her willingness. Violent laughter arises when on laughing fearlessly the odour of the mouth causes pleasure, and broken words issue from the lips. This type of laughter is for lovers who are free with each other and clasp each other's hand joyfully again and again; who being overwrought with love mumble incomplete words in the excitement of their passion. Loud laughter is produced when relations who are gathered at the home of a newly-wed couple begin suddenly to laugh without having any consideration of decorum. Of this the Poet gives two vivid examples, one of the laughter of cowherd girls when Rādhā fails to recognize her lover who is disguised as a woman and clasps him to her bosom, and the other when they see Kṛiṣṇa's embarrassment at being deceived into thinking that an empty pot carried by a milkmaid contained butter and trying to steal it.

Other sentiments are described by Keshavadāsa, though not in such great detail. Tenderness is produced by separation from the loved one, violence from rage, valour from zeal, dread from great fear, loathsomeness from abhorrenc, wonder from surprise, and evenness following dejection from all worldly things. Conforming to a convention in Hindi poetry various colours are ascribed to different sentiments. Tenderness has the hue of a young pigeon, violence is red, valour white, dread black, loathsomeness blue, and wonder is yellow.

These sentiments are illustrated by the behaviour and moods of the nāyaka and the nāyikās in various situations. Keshavadāsa classifies his illustrations into the two divisions of 'hidden' and 'manifest' which indeed are followed right through the book. Having described sentiments he goes on, in the next chapter, to tell of the four rules or conditions which govern all Hindi poetry.

The sentiment of laughter, and its kinds

Where by the means of eye and speech
Delight produced is, there the wise
And clever-minded do indeed
The birth of laughter recognize.
Says Keshavadāsa, poets and wise men
Four kinds of laughter have described,
First feeble, than sweet merriment,
Third violent, and fourth laughter loud.

Feeble laughter

When eyes, and cheeks, and teeth, and lips,
Do blossom out somewhat, then 'tis
By diverse men of wisdom called
Feeble laughter, says Keshavadāsa.

Rādhā's feeble laughter

'For the past month or so she smiles
As soon as words of love she hears,
That girl who loves you all the while

Does sit purposely to give ear
To such love-talk; and much delight
I know she finds in love-filled words
Which king Nala's messenger[1] recites
In that love-tale so I have heard.
That yearning of your heart's delight[2]
I reckon will now be fulfilled,
It seems to me that now the light
Of your good fortune has been lit.'

The feeble laughter of the *nāyikā*

The bosom campanion says to the nāyikā :

'While putting betels in your mouth
Against your youthful lips did brush
His eager finger who knows how ?
Then you too glanced towards him thus
As though you would swallow his eyes,
And laughing spoke to him some words
By which it seemed that he did lie
Completely in your love submerged.
Seeing this, my friend, I could discern
That at long last you had appeased
The fire that in the heart did burn
Of your young lover, him to please'.

The feeble laughter of Kṛiṣṇa

The bosom companion says to Kṛiṣṇa :

'The splendour of your teeth does show
Beneath your lips; you make me quite
Insensible by love's downpour !
The shadow of your restless eyes
Does sparkle in your lovely cheeks :
By mind, act, speech, her you enslave,
Your eyebrows her emotions speak.

Dear boy ! why do you silent stay ?
Your laughter manifest and sweet
May bring some heart within its sway !
Lo! now your laughter soft indeed
The heart of someone steals away !'

Sweet laughter

Says Keshava when upon the ears
Some sweet melodious sound does fall
Which mind and body holds in thrall
That 'laughter sweet', do poets declare.

The sweet laughter of Rādhā

Oh ! Shrī Kṛiṣṇa in your eyes I see
It seems a dancing space inscribed :
The pupils of your eyes indeed
The dancers are; and black and white
Their waist-garments :[3] a million types
Of sizzling dances there abound !
The male dancer is your own eye,
And drums of soft laughter resound
In it; and laughter flash I ween
The light that in a lamp is seen !

The sweet laughter of Kṛiṣṇa

The bosom companion says to the nāyikā :

'Oh ! bosom friend mine Kṛiṣṇa today
Spoke long to you words with love filled,
A scarf around your neck he placed,
A necklace on your breasts, and did
Entreat you of a sort; amazed
Was I and much surprised to see
Such ardent love him oft display ;
And why upon your head did he
His hand so place ? Why did he laugh ?
And in your end-cloth[4] tie a knot ?'

Violent laughter

Where upon laughing fearlessly
The odour of the mouth does please,
And from lips, broken words issue,
There violent laughter is produced.

Rādhā's violent laughter

Oh ! you of sly and restless eyes,
The mind of my Kṛiṣṇa you astound
With laughter soft; as flashing lies
The studded ornament that crowns
Your head, so does the tilaka[5] please,
Oh ! girl, which gleams on your forehead
So sparkles too, your splendid teeth,
And the red stone in your necklace :
So shines the lustre of your cheeks
And the soft smoothness of your chin,
The glittering pearl that wavering keeps
As to and fro moves your nose-pin ![6]

Kṛiṣṇa's violent laughter

One bosom companion says to another :

'Shrī Kṛiṣṇa and Rādhā dalliance make
Rising and falling; gratified
With one another, they embrace;
Anon the two do in strange wise
From one another separate
Being with emotion overwrought
They speak words sweet and meaningless
Which pleasing are, but yet cannot
Be understood; friend I have marked
Beside the Yamunā[7] river stand
Shrī Kṛiṣṇa and Rādhā—seen them laugh
And wild with pleasure, clap their hands !'

Loud laughter

Says Keshavadāsa where caring not
For a married couple, relations all
Begin to laugh, that I surmise
Is 'laughter loud' to poets wise.

The loud laughter of the cowherd girls

Said someone there's a cowherd lass
From Mahāvana[8] who sings as sweet
As Saraswatī;[9] her loveliness
Does match the wife of Kāma, Rati.[10]
Then Rādhā said, 'call her inside,'
And when that cowherd girl was brought
In agitation she did rise
To do her honour, and did clasp
That maiden who was Kṛiṣṇa disguised !
Seeing this the cowherd girls around,
O'ercome with mirth, did hold their sides,
And peals of laughter did resound.

The loud laughter of Kṛiṣṇa

Hear what happened to Kṛiṣṇa today
Oh; bosom friend : 'A cowherd girl
An earthen jar on her head placed,
Did venture forth; with milk and curd
That jar was spattered, and she passed
On the way, Kṛiṣṇa, who forward stepped
With hope to taste what in it was,
And lifted it from off her head,
But empty, lo ! that jar he found;
And Kṛiṣṇa, dear friend, was much abashed;
Seeing this, their end-cloth throwing around
Their heads, the maidens laughed and laughed.

The sentiment of tenderness

By separation from one loved
Is tender sentiment produced,
And like a pigeon young, is said
To be that dear emotion's hue.[11]

The tenderness of the nāyaka

More lustrous than the sun who is,
More tender than the moon serene,
More bounteous e'en than Shaṅkarajī,[12]
Lovely as Rāma[13], more strong than Indra;[14]
With charm the heart who captivates,
Firm as the ocean whom I wist,
And greatly skilled, as Shrī Gaṇesha;[15]
How does he pass his days amidst
Such simpletons? Oh ! tell me what
To unwise Nanda, friend, shall I say
And Yashodā[16]—who having got
Such a son, herdsman have him made?

Rādhā's tenderness

She who is filled with smell as sweet
As is a perfumed *champā*[17] bud,
A creeper of beauty who is
And by the minds of lovers loved;
Whose speech is as of god's divine,
As Indrajī's spouse[18] who joy spreads wide
In all the world whose body shines
As Kāmadeva's,[19] who's as lightning bright,
Or as Lakshmī[20] who incarnates,
Who is obtained by much merit;
Fools are these cowherds so to make
Such a lovely girl as Rādhā, sell milk;

The sentiment of violence

Says Keshavadāsa, the sentiment
Of violence does from rage arise,

In which the body hot becomes
And with itself remains at strife !
This sentiment's colour is said
By all who speak of it, as red.

The violence of the *nāyikā*

The lion has likened his thin waist
Oh ! Rādhā, unto yours, but you
Its slenderness have snatched away !
So the eyes of the deer, so too
Fish's unrest, and elephant's gait !
The mottled parrot, and cuckoo,
And lotus lovely, and wagtail,
Ashamed have to the forest moved !
The *champā* flower and the saffron,
The swan, the tender lotus root,
Wood-apple, and pomegranate,
Are all undone : and gold, poor fool !
His body burns ! less grows the moon;
The *bandhujīva*[21] its scent has lost,
And Kṛiṣṇa your slave has turned; on whom
Oh ! Rādhā, you are angry now ?[22]

Kṛiṣṇa's violence

The bosom companion says to Kṛiṣṇa :
'Strife you did slay, and kill and drown
Parting, who was of you afraid;
Of all the love and good fortune
You rifled, and to Rādhā gave;
Guile you did prune, destroyed knowing,
And in love's combat even churned
The mind of Kāmadeva : say, Oh ! Kṛiṣṇa
On whom your anger now has turned ?'

The heroic sentiment

Says Keshavadāsa from zeal is born
The sentiment heroic, whose

Colour white is described by all
To be—so doth convention choose.

The *nāyikā's* heroism

The bosom companion says to Rādhā :

'Taking with you the elephant
Of motion, and the fiery steed
Of body's gleam, of dalliance
The chariot, and the soldiers fleet
Of feeling; having overawed
Shame, name, anxiety and the like;
Taking the sword of laughter soft,
The warriors of your breasts, the pikes
Of nail-marks, and armour of love
Donning, with courage as your mate :
You should overcome Madan Gopāla
In love's sweet encounter today.'[23]

Kṛiṣṇa's heroism

The bosom companion says to Kṛiṣṇa :

'Will you kill her as you did slay
Aghāsura ? Or to pieces hack
Her as Bakāsura ? Or as Kesha
And Keshī[24] throw her down ? Or snatch
Her soul as Pūtanā's ?[25] Or will you
Drive her as you did Kālīnāga[26]
From out the stream ? Or her denude
Of all ecstasy! oh ! Ghanashyāma,
As arrows do the clouds ? Always
You've won, why to her lose ?
With passion maddened are Braja-maids,[27]
Their longing when will you remove ?'

The sentiment of dread

Says Keshavadāsa the sentiment
Fearful, is always of dark shape,

And much dread in the minds of men
Its sight and hearing does create.

The dread of Rādhā

The sky was laden with dark clouds,
Over the earth all round they poured,
Helped by the wind they rumbled loud,
And threateningly the thunder roared,
Nor for a minute did it die :
And when that lustful woman saw
The lightning flash from every side,
Unto her lover's neck so fast
She clung, as flames which pounced upon
Arjuna,[28] who in Indra's woods sojourned.

Kṛiṣṇa's dread

The words unpleasant which are said
In anger, e'en more bitter turn
Than poison—only he can tell
The strength of bile who eats currants ![29]
The woman who in your mind remained
Till now, at last you have today
Grieved; and indeed you're very plain
To teach me ! when she simple stayed
She naively spoke : but rage now mars
Her, and her eyebrows as the bows
Of passion she knits ; from afar
I see them thus, how, can I go ?

The loathsome sentiment

Says Keshavadāsa the sentiment
Loathsome abhorrent is, and blue
Its shape, which seeing and hearing, makes
The mind and body sorrowful.

The loathsomeness of Rādhā

The bosom companion says to Rādhā :

'Your mother's flesh to you is sweet
Because you swear, "her flesh I'll eat !"
Your father's blood does satisfy
You not, for, "I drink it !" you cry :
So also is your heart pained not
Your brothers' throat to cut, because
You swear "I will their throats sever !"
Such false oaths take you whenever
We meet. Whose child are you, accursed?
Of friend, or spirit ? or demoness ?
O ! swear by Kṛiṣṇa, and tell me true
Yourself, of what strange birth are you ?'[30]

The loathsomeness of Kṛiṣṇa

The nāyikā says to the nāyaka :

'Where hundreds of woodworms infest
The broken framework of the thatch,
And smoky 'tis all round—where dwell
Spiders and snakes, and scorpions black :
In that place full of evil smell,
You do for a bed go a begging,
And at midnight you are restless
For women dark, with dirty limbs !
Are you with disgust not filled so,
Oh ! Ghanashyāma, always to remain
In stifling rooms where wood is stored,
And in the narrow winding lanes ?'

The sentiment of wonder

On hearing or on seeing which,
Amazement and surprise are born,
Says Keshavadāsa, know you that is

Of wonder sure the sentiment :
The hue of which, by all who know,
Is said to be colour yellow.

The wonder of the *nāyikā*

Oh ! Rādhā, daughter of Vṛiṣabhānu
With wonder filled you move all day
To sell your curd, and those who come
To buy it are themselves purchased !
Your radiance as a woman's shines
Though yet you be of tender age,
Your voice is low, and sharp your mind,
And tender is your heart, and chaste,
But hard your budding youthful breasts !
Though you are woman, yet you bind
Shrī Kṛiṣṇa in bondage, and restless
Your eyes are, but calm is your mind.
The tales of your lust are a stain
Upon your virtue, and so I deem
Immoral does your mind remain.

Another example of the nāyikā's wonder

To parrots and starlings who are tamed
The belles of Braja discourse do make
On the sex art ; fair are these dames
And innocent—of tender age :
And all of them rush out to view
Shrī Kṛiṣṇa from forth their hiding place
As goddesses unseen ; I swear on you,
Each maid stretched her bow eyebrow-shaped,
And with arrows of looks sidelong,
Mischievous, each assault did make
Kṛiṣṇa's mind invisible upon !
So strange it was, the war they waged,
And from the front they did not aim,
But slyly from where they were hid,

And sure they were so of their game
That not one glance its target missed !

Kṛiṣṇa's wonder

Of curd and butter he is a thief,
Of honey and milk—but in a trice
The soul of everyone he steals !
I know not why saints and the like
Should speak of him as Brahmā great,
And seeing this wondrous mystery
The god's wives in their minds debate
That how can such a one as he,
Who when he sees the charming gait,
Of cowherd women wandering free
Is in a moment captive made !
To wrong-doers such destruction deal ?[31]

The sentiment of evenness

Says Keshavadāsa, when from all sides
The mind dejected is, and rests
At one point; this call poets wise
The sentiment of evenness.

The evenness of the nāyaka

The bosom companion says to Kṛiṣṇa

'She looks not at the lotuses
Nor yet the splendid moon does see,
That lustful woman concentrates
Her mind on tales that passion breathe :
None in the three worlds can excel
Her loveliness ; and naught appeals
To her, since on you her eye fell !
Therefore, oh ! Kṛiṣṇa ! I pray take heed
When she is bent her life to lay
If you she sees not : Why don't you

Meet her somewhere, so that she may
At length her cherised lover view ?'

The evenness of Kṛiṣṇa

From the day when he boldly drew
The essence from your dainty lips
All the world's sweets, and nectar too,
He has left : dates he no longer eats,
Nor butter likes he, nor raisins
Honey and sugar-cane he hates,
Pomegranates do please not him !
Of this have I come for your sake
To tell, e'en though such things to speak
Were for an elder one not meet.[32]

Another example of the evenness of Kṛiṣṇa

Says Keshavadāsa, in this world wide
Demons and men, and other beings
Of land and water, ever fight
A war with time : and gods even
Divine and ageless, also die,
And are born on the earth again.
Therefore in truth immortal lies
He only who such knowledge gains
As from birth's rounds[33] he free becomes :
That noise which in your ears resounds
Is not of words, but Shaṅkara's drum ![34]
So brothers mine, do not be bound
Upon this mortal wheel, and run !
By good fortune who can escape,
Let him : know here for those that come
The whirlpool of awe ever gapes.

Concluding verse

Says Keshava, thus should be portrayed
Other sentiments, but I fear

Too bulky will this book be made,
So I have not described them here :
All sentiments under two main heads
Do fall—hidden and manifest.[35]
'Tis for this reason I've defined
Nine sentiments only, and I will speak
Now of four conditions which bind
The writing of all poetry.

NOTES

1. The messenger conveys the love of Damayantī, his beloved, to King Nala. The story of Nala and Damayantī is an Indian love tale related in the Mahābhārata (translated into English by Deane Milman, and into Latin by Bapp). It is like that of Romeo and Juliet, Lailā and Majnū etc. Nala was king of Niṣadha and Damayantī the only daughter of Bhīma king of Vidarbha. They had not seen each other, but merely by hearing of each other's nature and qualities they began to love one another to distraction. They were married at a *svayaṁvara* after Damayantī had selected Nala against some odds. They led a happy married life and had two children, but due to the enmity of rival, Nala was induced to play against his younger brother at dice in which he lost everything—even his clothes, as Yudhiṣṭhira did to Shakuni. Thereupon Nala wandered along with Damayantī in the forest, and later on due to poverty had to desert even her. Damayantī returned to her father, where, after a number of adventures, Nala, too, was driven, and at length was united with her, after which he won back all that he had lost from his brother in another game of dice.

2. The yearning of the heart's delight, means the desire of Kṛiṣṇa to get Rādhā. The bosom friend says to him, 'You will soon be united with Rādhā, your beloved. The fact that she has begun to be attracted to tales of love, such as *Nala and Damayantī* shows that love has awakened in her.'

3. Waist-garments, mean the garments worn by men and women (*dhotī* for men, and saree for women). These are tucked tight around the waist while dancing so that they may not obstruct the dance movements.

4. The corner or end of the saree in which the Indian house-wife ties her keys or any other valued thing. The actions performed by the *nāyaka* in this verse are all indicative of his love for the *nāyikā*.

5. The auspicious, ornamental, red or vermilion mark which women apply on their foreheads.

6. Hindu women, especially those who are married, wear a large nose-pin to which a pearl or precious stone is attached. The fashion is going out of date, and now the women of some communities wear it only on their wedding day.

7. A tributary of river Gaṅgā which meets it in Prayāga, (modern Allāhābād). The banks of the Yamunā were the scene of many of Kṛiṣṇa's exploits, including the famous *rāsalīlā* dance with Rādhā and the gopīs (cowherd girls).

8. One of the provinces of Mathurā in Kṛiṣṇa's times which contained large patches of forest land.

9. The lovely goddess of learning and the fine arts.

10. The Hindu god of love. Rati is his beautiful wife.

11. The colour of the emotion of tenderness is like that of a young pigeon. Hindi poets were fond of ascribing colours to various emotions—for example rage was given the colour red, heroism white, loathsomeness blue, and so on.

12. Shiva, the Destroyer, one of the three gods in the Hindu triad—the fierce god, 'dark, black, destroying, terrible.' He is commonly represented as seated in profound thought, with a third eye in the middle of his forehead, contained in, or surmounted by the moon's crescent, his matted locks gahered up into a coil like a horn which bears upon it a symbol of the river Gaṅgā which he caught as it fell from heaven. He wears a tiger or deer skin, and is seated on his bull Nandī. In the *Vedas*, Shiva is lauded as the lord of songs and of sacrifices, who heals and remedies, who is brilliant as the sun, the best and most bountiful of gods, who grants prosperity and welfare to horses, and sheep, men, women and cows; the lord of nourishment, who drives away diseases, dispenses remedies, and removes sin. It is this aspect of Shaṅkara that this verse emphasises.

13. The eldest son of Dasharatha, King of Ayodhyā, of the solar race, and an incarnation of the god Viṣṇu. His story is told in the *Rāmāyaṇa*, one of the most holy books for Hindus. Rāma broke the bow of Shiva and married Sītā, daughter of Janaka, King of Videha. Due to the plotting of one of the maid servants of the court, Rāma had to go into exile soon after his marriage, along with Sītā and his brother Lakshmaṇa. There Sītā was abducted by Rāvaṇa, the demon king of Laṅkā, which led to war between the two, in which Rāma and his forces won. Sītā was restored, and Rāma became King of Ayodhyā. Rāma was very beautiful, though dark-complexioned. The Rāmāyaṇa gives the following description of him when he came to wed Sītā.

'The dark body of Rāma is inherently lovely and its splendour puts millions of gods of love to shame. His lotus feet tinted with red dye look very beautiful, and near them the mindshaped black bees of the sages are constantly hovering. His charming *dhotī* of pure yellow robs the early morning sun and the lightning of their light...he wears enchanting ornaments on his broad breast...his eyes are lovely as the lotus; in his ears dangle charming ear-rings, and his face is the very treasure-house of beauty. He has lovely eyebrows and captivating nostrils... All his limbs are so beautiful that they steal the soul.'

14. The god of the firmament, described of being of a ruddy or golden brown colour, and having arms of enormous length. His forms are endless, and he can assume any shape at will. He rides in a bright golden car, drawn by two tawny horses with flowing manes and tails. His weapon is the thunder-bolt which he carries in his right hand. He also uses arrows, a great

hook, and a net in which he entangles his foes. He takes enormous quantities of the *Soma* juice and getting drunk with it goes forth to fight his foes, helped by troops of Maruts. He sends forth lightning and thunder, governs the weather, and dispenses rain.

15. Son of Shiva and Pārvatī, God of wisdom, and remover of obstacles. Hence he is invariably propitiated at the beginning of any important undertaking. (See note 1, Chapter 1).

16. The foster parents of Kṛiṣṇa.

17. Spanish jasmine, a small flowering shrub yielding big white exquisitely fragrant flowers with the interior of their cups yellow.

18. Indrajī's spouse is Indrāṇī, wife of Indra, also called Shachī and Aindrī. She is said to be the most fortunate of females, for her husband shall never die of old age. The *Taittirīya Brāhmaṇa* states that Indra chose her for his wife from a number of competing goddesses because she was the most voluptuous of them all.

19. The god of love, the Hindu Cupid (See note 2, Chapter 1).

20. Goddess of fortune, and wife of Viṣṇu (See note 4, Chapter 4).

21. A small flowering creeper.

22. The verse describes the beauty of Rādhā in superlative terms. All the things to which the various parts of her body could be compared to are undone, so much are they surpassed.

23. The imagery is from the implements and actions of war. The bosom companion instructs Rādhā to overcome her lover, Kṛiṣṇa, in love's battle, armed by motion as of an elephant, dalliance (as of a chariot), felling (the swift soldiers), laughter (the sword), her devastating breasts (warriors) nail-marks made in lovemaking (pikes), love (armour), and courage (mate). She should by the help of these, remove (overawe) shame, anxiety, social opprobrium etc. and proceed to conquer her lover in love's fray.

24. Aghāsura, Bakāsura, Kesha and Keshī were demons whom Kṛiṣṇa killed.

25. When Kaṁsa heard sage Nārada's prophecy that he would be killed by the eighth child of Devakī, the daughter of his uncle, he was greatly upset, and much more so when the eighth child (a daughter), of Devakī was exchanged with Kṛiṣṇa, and she confirmed the prophecy when Kaṁsa tried to kill her. So he ordered a general massacre of all children born near about that time. This horrible task was given to Pūtanā. After she had accomplished it, Kaṁsa found out that Devakī's son, Kṛiṣṇa, still lived, so he spurred on the unwilling Pūtanā to kill him. Pūtanā smeared arsenic on the nipples of her breasts and gave them to the infant Kṛiṣṇa, but instead of the child being poisoned, he sucked out her very life and left her dead.

26. The incident is related in the *Bhāgavata Purāṇa*. The snake Kālī nāga, or Kāliyā lived in the poisonous pool whose water was so deadly that cattle which drank of it immediately died. The fierce snake lived in the middle of the pool. Kṛiṣṇa once waded into it with a rope and fearlessly cast a noose round the serpent, tying the other and round his waist. Thus he pulled the snake out of the poisonous pool and got the better of it. The taming of the snake Kāliyā is the subject matter of a famous painting.

27. The women of the Braja country lying beside the river Yamunā, which was the scene of Kṛiṣṇa's early exploits.

28. Son of Indra, and a brave warrior. He was taught the use of arms by Droṇa whose favourite pupil he was. He won Draupadī at a *svayaṁvara*. He also married Chitrāṅgadā, daughter of the King of Manipur, and Subhadrā, sister of Kṛiṣṇa, and had connections with Ulūpī, a Nāga princess. He fought against the Kaurava princes, assisted by Kṛiṣṇa who became his charioteer, and who gave him the teaching contained in the *Bhagavad Gītā* on this occasion. Arjuna was a great fighter and he fought against a number of Rājās including his own son, Babhruvāhana, his father, Indra, the Dravidians and on one occasion even with the great Lord Shiva himself disguised as a mountaineer, though he begged pardon when the god's true nature was revealed to him.

29. This conforms to the concept of *Vaidic* (Indian) medicine, according to which eating of currants increases the flow of bile.

30. The Poet is trying to illustrate the sentiment of loathsomeness and hence picks on the most abhorrent and disgusting images, like the *nāyikā's* saying she will eat her mother's flesh and drink her father's blood, and so on. The thoughts are symbolic of the emotion which the Poet is attempting to create in the reader.

31. The verse expresses the dual aspects of Kṛiṣṇa—the one amorous, and the other transcendental. In the one he steals butter, milk, and curd, plays childlike pranks, flirts and dances with cowherd girls, especially with Rādhā, the chief of them. At the same time he is the incarnation of Viṣṇu, the supreme Lord. The Hindus do not find any discrepancy in these two aspects of Kṛiṣṇa and accept both. The amorous exploits of the cowherd girls are said to allegorically signify the affinity of the souls to god, and the dance of Kṛiṣṇa with the maidens of Braja is the union of the soul with the Supreme Being.

The idea has been admirably expressed by the Hindi religious poet Rasakhān :

'He of whom Shaṅkara, Gaṇesha and other gods ever sing, who is endless unblemished, unknowable, perfect, and the source of all the *Vedas*, whose name sages like Nārada and Vyāsa repeat with rapture, but even then knowing him—not in his entirety—such a one the cowherd girls dance and flirt with.'

And again

'I wandered about seeking him in the entire universe, reciting the *Purāṇas* and giving ear unto the *Vedas*, which only increased fourfold my desire for seeing him. I never heard of him nor saw his form or knew of his nature. I got tired of searching for him, and no one told me where to find him, when lo! I saw him afar off in a forest hermitage pressing lovingly Rādhā's feet'.

32. The words in the verse are spoken by some old woman to Rādhā. So she ends by saying, 'I have told you all this (the condition of Kṛiṣṇa since the day he kissed Rādhā), even though it is not proper for one who is your elder to speak to you so familiarly about love.' In India there was, and still is, a distance between the elder and younger person (like between

father and son). Even a grown-up son will not smoke or drink in the presence of his father, and will hesitate to do so in the presence of an elderly man.

33. The Hindus firmly believe in the doctrine of re-birth—that souls come back again and again in the world, being born indifferent bodies in accordance with their past deeds on earth. The experience of eternal truth, however, can bring about the soul's emancipation, and then it does not take re-birth, but is united with the Absolute.

34. Shaṅkara, or Shiva, is the Destroyer, so his drum would mean the call of death.

35. Keshavadāsa's division of all things and emotions into 'hidden' and 'manifest' is peculiar to him, and we do not encounter it with this persistency in any other Hindi poet.

Chapter XV

The Kinds of Poetry

This chapter, and the one following it, are somewhat different from the general trend of the book because they describe the art of poetry instead of the art of love. This subject has been dealt with in greater detail in the poet's 'Kavipriyā'. Keshavadāsa was a believer in conventions and rules so far as the writing of poetry was concerned and he conformed strictly to them. He tried to lay down the canons of good poetry for those who came after him, and would not suffer any departure from them. In this chapter he classifies poetry into four types—the Kaushikī, in which merriment, love, and tenderness combine in happy proportion, and which is written in simple yet forceful words; the Bhāratī, which combines the sentiments of wonder, heroism and joy, and which appeals to them ind and delights the soul; the Ārabhaṭī in which dread, loathing and the violent sentiments come together, which is full of alliterations and words of double meaning; and lastly the Sāttvikī where wonder, valour, and evenness merge in equal measure, and the sense is so clear that the reader can understand it as soon as he reads the words. Examples are given to illustrate each kind of poetry.

It is difficult to give the parallel types of English poetry, for the rules and conventions of the two are different, but perhaps the ballad and lyric approximate to the Kaushikī, the ode to the Sāttvikī, and heroic poetry to the Bhāratī. The Ārabhaṭī has no parallel in English poetry, but we get glimpses of it in some poems, as for example, the shooting of the albatros, in 'The Ancient Mariner,' and the dreadful consequences which arose from it and 'The Dream of Eugene Aram.'

After having described the four types of poetry Keshavadāsa goes on to enumerate in the next chapter, what he considers to be its defects.

Kinds of poetry

Says Keshavadāsa all poetry
Is of four kinds, as poets do know,
Kaushikī, Bhāratī, Ārabhaṭī,
And Sāttvikī, which is the fourth.

The Kaushikī kind of poetry

Says Keshavadāsa where merriment,
And love, and tenderness combine,
Of simple words and happy sense,
That's poetry of Kaushikī kind.

Example of poetry of Kaushikī kind

Some women to meet him essay,
Through go-betweens,[1] and some enjoy
In their minds the bliss of sport; some take
Many a vow in sacred spots,
So that they may some converse make
With him, and hear his winning speech :
Some who as goddesses are, always
Do run to see him, and appease
All day the gods with gifts, I fear
Oh ! bosom friend, that he's so dark,
What can I do ? No sooner hears
She, my Kṛiṣṇa's name, this woman laughs.

The Bhāratī kind of poetry

Says Keshavadāsa that verse in which
The sentiment heroic is,
And wonder too, and merriment;
Appealing to the mind whose sense—
That soul delighting poetry
Is of the kind called 'Bhāratī.'

Example of poetry of the Bhāratī kind

The ear-rings of gold which she wears
Are verily the chariot's wheels,
The pendants which are glittering there
The banner which does greatly please :
Head ornament the charioteer,
The saffron lines on forehead laid
As though spokes are, and the nose-pearl
Is as it were the hub well made.[2]
Her one glance does Shrī Kṛiṣṇa purchase !
Big eyes she has; and a gem shines
On her forehead, as if Kāmadeva
On fishes' chariot[3] were reclined !

The Ārabhaṭī kind of poetry

Says Keshavadāsa that verse in which
The violent sentiment, and dread,
And loathing are, in which there is
Alliteration, and words have
Meanings diverse : such poetry
Should be considered 'Ārabhaṭī.

Example of poetry of the Ārabhaṭī kind

Dense and dreadful clouds, rain-filled,
Whose splendour is of black and white,
Do thunder on the first and fifth
Of Sāvan's lunar days : the sky
They roam, these hideous messengers
Massive as elephants; all around
The lightning strikes ! Braja women are
With awe filled by the fearful sound.
Now that Shrī Kṛiṣṇa is far away
Grim horror stalks all people thus,
It seems as though all night and day
Death dances on the land of Braja.[5]

Poetry of the *Sāttvikī* kind

Where wonder, valour, evenness,
All the three sentiments do merge
In equal measure, and the sense
Is understood as soon as heard,
That is considered by all men
To be the pure Sāttvikī verse.

Example of poetry of the *Sāttvikī* kind

The bosom companion says to another nāyikā:

'Oh! foolish girl burn and destroy
Your million cravings and desires,
Oh! kindle not within your heart
A blaze that burns like Holi's fire!
The love of Rādhā and Shrī Kṛiṣṇa
Consider of the highest kind,
Kāmadeva's[6] and Rati's love even
Inferior to their's is I find,
Bhavānījī[7] too cannot sow
Discord between them : not to speak
Of other's; Sarasvatī's[8] glow
Before them too does little seem :
Though simple she considered is,
One are their souls, and thoughts, and minds,
Though separate are their bodies, still
Through ardent eyes the two are joined !'

Concluding verse

Says Keshavadāsa thus I've portrayed
The sentiments of poetry, nine,
Now of their four faults I'll relate
But unto these give not your mind.[9]

NOTES

1. Messengers employed by lovers to advance their love-suit.

2. The imagery used in the verse is of the various parts of the chariot, which was used as a conveyance in those days by warriors and the well-to-do people.

3. The banner of Kāmadeva, (the Hindu love god) is the Makara, or fish on a red-background. Most probably the chariot on which he sits bears the insignia of his banner and has the fish painted on it, so it is called the chariot of fish.

4. The fifth month of the Hindu calendar corresponding to August—one of the months of the heaviest rainfall in India.

5. The sense of horror is vividly brought out in this verse by the dark and dreadful clouds, lightning, and fearful sounds, culminating in the grim picture of Death stalking the Braja country.

6. The Hindu god of love. Rati is his wife.

7. A name for the wife of Shiva, daughter of Himavat, (Himālayas). In her milder form she is Umā—light. She is also Gaurī, the yellow or brilliant, Pārvatī the mountaineer, Jaganmātā, the mother of the world, and Bhavānī. In her terrible form she is Durgā, the inaccessible, Kālī, the black goddess, Chaṇḍī and Chṇḍikā, the fierce, and Bhairavī, the terrible.

8. The goddess of speech and learning.

9. Since these are defects of poetry which all good Poets should avoid, Keshavadāsa says serious consideration should not be given to them.

Chapter XVI

The Defects of Poetry

In this chapter Keshavadāsa enumerates the faults of poetry which debase and corrupt it, having cautioned the reader in the last chapter not to give too much attention to them, for they are to be known only to be avoided. These faults are conflict, dryness, nauseousness, contrariness, and lack of wisdom. The conflicting sentiment in poetry arises where along with loathing, awe and violence, tenderness and love are described side by side. Dryness or insipidity arises when, while speaking well outwardly, the lovers remain insincere at heart. The disgusting or nauseating sentiment is produced when some poet narrates about sexual pleasures with relish in the midst of grief. In moments of pain and sorrow appetite for sex vanishes, and the poet who places the two together certainly proves to be disgusting in his attitude and his poetry is bound to repel. Contrariness is where good and bad, are indiscriminately mixed together by the poet, while impropriety is produced where he thoughtlessly describes those very things which are vague and hard to understand. In brief, Keshavadāsa's conception of bad poetry, is poetry which lacks clarity, consistency and purity. These qualities are in fact hall marks of all good writing, and it is easy to understand why Keshava considered poetry where they were absent, to be of an inferior type. As usual, illustrations of the various types of defect are given. Keshavadāsa goes on to mention those sentiments which are mutually opposing. There are tenderness and merriment, love and loathing, valour and awe. Finally he concludes the chapter by mentioning what he thinks is the merit of his book and his aim in writing it. He says: 'As amorists appear to be unhappy day after day without their beloveds, in the same manner poets of the spoken language seem to be inferior without Rasikapriyā. By reading it knowledge of love increases, information is gathered about various sentiments and practices, and both joy and salvation are attained.'

Lack of goodness

Conflict, dryness, and nauseousness,
Contrariness, and the unwise,
Says Keshavadāsa, these lack goodness,
So these the poets don't describe.

Conflicting sentiment

Where contrary sentiments, like love
And loathing, and awe, are described,
And violence too, and tenderness,
Are by poets mentioned side by side—
There the conflicting sentiment
Is by all men known to arise.

Example of a verse with conflicting sentiment

When laughing I converse, then all
Do laugh ; when shorn of shame I see,
With loathing are they filled, and fall
Away from me ; if words I speak
I am reproached, and if I long
For something, passion in me wakes—
So your advice to love him not
I kept in mind, oh ! friend, always,
Knowing that love will my heart not win,
And for a moment if my gaze
I chance to throw upon Shrī Kṛiṣṇa
To censure me men will not stay.

The sentiment of insipidity

Where outwardly the lovers speak
With loving words, but in hearts hid
There lies deceit and duplicity,
That is the sentiment insipid.

Example of insipidity in verse

Whose mind in cunning is so steeped
On seeing this world, her do you tell
Love's riddle ; oh ! so sad it is,
And laughable ! ne'er have I heard
A co-wife could be thought a friend,
As with my eyes today I see !
So woman vain ! I understand
With your heart you love not, but with speech !

The sentiment of disgust

Says Keshavadāsa where a poet tells
Of pleasures of sex in the midst of grief,
With relish ; there is known to dwell
The sentiment which disgusting is.

Example of the disgusting sentiment in verse

The bosom companion says to the nāyaka :

'To bathe, to give alms unto all,
To eat, drink, and with song console,
All this the nāyikā has forgot :
Her wisdom has fled, and her soul
Hard as a stool's top has been made !
Oh ! lover fond, consider not
No sooner she on you will gaze
All pleasures she will leave unsought !
Thus anxious, dull your letter proved
Sweet words her please not—she who turns
From love, how will she laugh and look
When in her heart grief's furnace burns ?'[1]

The sentiment of contrariness

Says Keshava where good and bad mix,
'Tis sentiment of opposites.

Example of the sentiment of contrariness in verse

When Shrī Kṛiṣṇa said, 'Give me some milk,'
The cowherd girl thus made reply,
'I will not give it on credit,
If you should need it, friend, then buy,
And you will get !' Then he exclaimed,
'I'm used to free milk, why should I ?'
The cowherd maid said, 'tis the same
If I give or give not, for nigh
My home is where I soon will be !'
Shrī Kṛiṣṇa then said, 'why do you fight ?'
'When was there love' twixt you and me ?
I love to fight !' the maid replied :
Shrī Kṛiṣṇa then said, 'will fighting make
Your milk sell ?' 'And the girl said, 'if
It does not sell, I'll myself take
The milk, but you I'll never give !'[2]

The sentiment of impropriety

Where thoughtlessly those very things
Emagined are, and by poets described,
Which far from understanding lie,
That sentiment unseemly is.

Example of impropriety in verse[3]

A dagger of deception bright,
A casket of romantic love,
And beneficial to all life
As holy Gaṅgā water, pure,
The treasure selfishness does hold,
The source of good to others—like
The story of love's god in gold
Entangled—and outspreading wide
As stream of nectar ; giving joy
To wise man : shaming Gaurā[4] quite,

And Girā[5]—which the hermits foil,
And creatures of the world, unwise—
A voice such as these, know my queen,
Is poisonous ; thus do I well ween.

The opposing sentiments

Know tenderness, and merriment,
Love, loathing, valour, awe, to be,
Says Keshavadāsa, such sentiments
As are opposing mutually.
So do I say : from the hateful
Is fear born, from love merriment:
From valour is the wonderful,
From horror follows compassion.
Says Keshavadāsa, so I with care,
Have various sentiments described,
And lack of sentiment, and where
I've erred, may poets set it right.[6]

The significance of Rasikapriyā

As lovers miserable appear
Without their loved ones, even so
Poets of the language are, I fear,
The Rasikapriyā—who do not know.
More knows he of love, who has read
The Rasikapriyā, and knowledge gains
Of sentiments, and practices,
And joy and salvation attains.[7]

NOTES

1. The *nāyaka* has relinquished all his works and amusements. The bosom companion tells him not to despair. The hard-heartedness of the *nāyikā* is momentary. She expects much more from the *nāyaka* than a mere letter, the cold words of which fail to move her. But when the furnace of the grief of separation burns in her heart and awakens desire of union with the *nāyaka*. she will leave all other pleasures, and laugh and look on him with love.

2. There is a swift exchange of repartees between the amorous and mischievous Kṛiṣṇa and the cowherd girl who flirtatiously denies to give him milk for the asking. Even in her fond denial love lies hidden.

3. The verse is an example of the sentiment of impropriety which has been defined in the previous verse to mean that in which description defies understanding. Hence we should not look for much meaning in the verse, yet the 'poisonous voice' is quite emotionally described, and each word is well chosen to create the right atmosphere.

4. Another name of Devī or Pārvatī wife of Shiva.

5. A name of Sarasvatī, goddess of speech and learning.

6. The humility shown by the Poet in this verse contrasts forcefully with vanity shown in the succeeding two.

7. The *Rasikapriyā* of Keshavadāsa is to a great extent a dissertation on various aspects of love, lovemaking, the union of lovers, and the ways in which such union can be effected.